Shelter

Ría de Ribadeo: sheltered, some swell, marina and facilities.

Ría de Viveiro and Barqueiro: picturesque anchorages, marina at Viveiro, few facilities.

Ensenada de Santa Marta: picturesque anchorages, bar entry to Ortigueira.

Cedeira: picturesque, sheltered anchorage.

Golfo de Ártabro: all weather, good marina and facilities, usual first port of call from Biscay cruises.

Coruña to Corme: long journey, only emergency shelter.

Ría de Corme y Laxe: shelter from N, E, S at quiet anchorages, some protection W.

Ría de Camariñas: all weather shelter at marina, selection of anchorages for all winds.

Ría de Corcubión/Finisterre: shelter W, N, E at quiet anchorages.

Ría de Muros: shelter N E S, open ría, marina and facilities at Portosín, picturesque anchorages.

Ría de Arousa: all weather, largest ría, cruising ground protected by Isla Sálvora, good marinas and facilities at Pobra do Caramiñal and Vilagarcía.

Ría de Pontevedra: all weather, sheltered by Islas Ons (National Park), picturesque anchorages, large marina and facilities at Sanxenxo.

Ría de Aldán (Ría de Pontevedra): shelter E S W, unexploited, pleasant anchorages, no facilities.

Ría de Vigo: all weather, sheltered by Islas Cíes (National Park), good harbours and facilities at Baiona and Vigo.

A Guarda: exposed small harbour, river anchorage, few facilities

Fuel

Marinas of Ribadeo, Sada, Coruña, Camariñas, Portosín, Ribeira, Caramiñal, Vilagarcía, San Vicente, Cangas, Sanxenxo, Vigo, Baiona.

Smaller harbours can arrange delivery from local petrol stations.

Lifts

At least 30 tons at Ribadeo, Viveiro, Sada, Marina Seca (Coruña), Portosín, Riberia, Caramiñal, Vilagarcía, Sanxenxo, Vigo, Baiona.

Chandleries & repairs

Extensive chandleries at Vigo and A Coruña. *Ferreterías* (ironmongers) in all larger towns.

Mechanic workshops at Ribadeo, Sada, Marina Seca (Coruña), Portosín, Caramiñal, Vilagarcía, Sanxenxo, Vigo. Local mechanics, electricians, divers arranged through marinas.

RÍAS ALTAS
Ribadeo
Viveiro
Ortigueira
Cedeira

GOLFO ÁRTABRO
Ferrol
Ares
Sada
A Coruña

COSTA DA MORTE
Corme
Camariñas
Finisterre

RÍA DE MUROS
Muros
Noia
Portosín

RÍA DE AROUSA
Ribeira
Pobra do Caramiñal
Rianxo
Vilagarcía
Cambados

RÍA DE PONTEVEDRA
Portonovo
Sanxenxo
Combarro
Aguete
Isla Ons

RÍA DE VIGO
Cangas
San Simón
Vigo
Baiona
Islas Cíes

PASSAGE AREAS
Rías Altas
Ártabro / Costa da Morte
Rías Baixas

CRUISING GALICIA

Carlos Rojas and Robert Bailey

Imray Laurie Norie & Wilson

Published by
Imray Laurie Norie & Wilson Ltd
Wych House, St Ives
Cambridgeshire PE27 5BT England
Tel +44 (0)1480 462114
Fax +44 (0)1480 496109
Email ilnw@imray.com
www.imray.com
2008

All rights reserved. No part of this publication may be reproduced, transmitted or used in any form by any means - graphic, electronics or mechanical, including photocopying, recording, taping or information storage and retrieval systems or otherwise - without the prior permission of the publishers.

1st edition 2008

© Carlos Rojas and Robert Bailey 2008
Carlos Rojas and Robert Bailey have asserted their right to be identified as the authors of this work in accordance with the Copyright, Designs and Patents Act 1988.

© Plans Imray Laurie Norie & Wilson Ltd 2008
© Town plans Imray Laurie Norie & Wilson Ltd and Carlos Rojas 2008
© Roadmaps and credited photographs Turgalicia, A Xunta de Galicia
© Aerial photographs Patrick Roach and Imray Laurie Norie & Wilson Ltd 2008
© Photographs Susan Kemp-Wheeler, Carlos Rojas and Robert Bailey

ISBN 978 184623 0417

British Library Cataloguing in Publication Data.
A catalogue record for this book is available from the British Library.

PLANS

The plans in this guide are not to be used for navigation. They are designed to support the text and should at all times be used with navigational charts.

CAUTION

While every care has been taken to ensure accuracy, neither the Publishers nor the Authors will hold themselves responsible for errors, omissions or alterations in this publication. They will at all times be grateful to receive information which tends to the improvement of the work. Please forward any suggestions or corrections to cruising.galicia@mac.com or to the publishers at the above address.

CORRECTIONAL SUPPLEMENTS

This book will be amended at intervals by the issue of correctional supplements which will be published on our website www.imray.com and may be downloaded free of charge. Printed copies are also available from the publishers at the above address.

Printed in Singapore

Contents

Introduction 3
How to use this book 6
Symbols 6

What you need to know as a yachtsman 8
Introduction 8
Crossing the Bay of Biscay 8
Coming from Portugal 12
Coming from northern Spain 12
Cruising Galicia 13
Berthing & anchoring 15
Suggested summer itineraries 16
Radio services 17
Formalities 17
Crew 17
Technical and navigational information used in this book 18

What you need to know as a tourist 19
Transport 19
Public services 19
Sources of information 20
Money and security 21
Customs and behaviour 21
Environment 21
Communications 22

Rías Altas 24
Sailing in the Rías Altas 26

Rías Altas 28
Introduction 28
⚓ Ribadeo 32
⚓ From Rinlo to Punta do Castro 40
    ⚓ *Ensenada de Cegoñas* 40
    ⚓ *Playa de San Miguel* 41
⚓ Foz 42
    ⚓ *Río Ouro* 43
    ⚓ *Punta de Fazouro* 43
⚓ Burela 44
⚓ San Cibrao 46
    ⚓ *Playa Rueta* 47
    ⚓ *Los Farallones* 47
    ⚓ *Puerto Alúmina Española* 47
    ⚓ *Playa de Portocelo* 48
⚓ Ría de Viveiro 50

⚓ Ría do Barqueiro 54
    ⚓ *Vicedo* 54
    ⚓ *Barqueiro* 54
⚓ Ensenada de Santa Marta 58
    ⚓ *Ortigueira* 58
    ⚓ *Espasante* 60
    ⚓ *Cariño* 60
⚓ Ría de Cedeira 62
Cedeira to Cabo Prior 66
    ⚓ *Playa da Frouxeira* 66
    ⚓ *Playa de San Xurxo* 66

Golfo Ártabro and Costa da Morte 68
Sailing in Golfo Ártabro and Costa da Morte 70

Golfo Ártabro 74
Introduction 76
Approach and key facilities 78
⚓ Ría de Ferrol 82
    ⚓ *Playa de San Felipe* 82
    ⚓ *Ensenada do Baño* 82
    ⚓ *Dársena Curuxeiras - Ferrol* 82
    ⚓ *Puerto Deportivo da Graña* 83
⚓ Rías de Betanzos & Ares 84
    ⚓ *Ares* 84
    ⚓ *Sada* 84
⚓ A Coruña 88
    ⚓ *Dársena de la Marina* 88
    ⚓ *Marina Coruña (planned 2008/09)* 89
    ⚓ *Marina Seca (Oza)* 89
    ⚓ *Club Marítimo de Oza* 89
    ⚓ *Real Club Náutico* 89

Costa da Morte 96
Introduction 98
Coruña to Sisargas 100
    ⚓ *Malpica* 100
⚓ Islas Sisargas 101
    ⚓ *Puerto de Barizo* 101
Ría de Corme y Laxe 103
    Approach & entrance 103
    ⚓ *Corme* 104
    ⚓ *Laxe* 104
Ría de Camariñas 106
    Approach & entrance 106
    ⚓ *Camariñas* 108

CONTENTS

⚓ *Muxía*	*112*
Approach & entrance	*114*
⚓ *Finisterre*	*116*
⚓ *Sardiñeiro*	*116*
⚓ *Corcubión and Cée*	*120*
⚓ *Ensenada de Ézaro*	*121*
⚓ *Carnota*	*123*
⚓ *Porto Cubelo*	*123*

Rías Baixas — 125
Introduction	126
Sailing in the Rías Baixas	130

Ría de Muros — 134
Introduction	136
Approach and key facilities	138
Monte Louro	142
⚓ *Playa de Louro*	*142*
⚓ *Ensenada de San Francisco*	*142*
⚓ Muros	144
⚓ Esteiro	148
⚓ Freixo	149
Noia	152
⚓ Portosín	154
⚓ Porto do Son	156
From Porto do Son to Corrubedo	157

Ría de Arousa — 160
Introduction	162
Approach and key facilities	164
⚓ Ensenada de Corrubedo	168
⚓ Aguiño	170
⚓ *Isla Vionta, Isla Sálvora, Cabo Falcoeiro*	*171*
⚓ Ribeira	174
⚓ *Playa Corosa*	*175*
⚓ *Ensenada de Palmeira*	*175*
⚓ Pobra do Caramiñal	178
⚓ Ensenada de Cabo Santa Cruz	184
⚓ Rianxo	186
⚓ Vilagarcía de Arousa	190
⚓ Vilanova de Arousa	194
⚓ Isla de Arousa	196
⚓ *Ensenada de San Xulián South*	*196*
⚓ Cambados	198
⚓ La Toxa	200
⚓ O Grove	200
⚓ Meloxo	200
⚓ San Vicente de Mar	205

Ría de Pontevedra — 207
Introduction	208
Approach and key facilities	210
⚓ Portonovo	214
⚓ Sanxenxo	218
⚓ Combarro	220
⚓ Pontevedra	224
⚓ Aguete	226
⚓ *Playa do Mogor*	*227*
⚓ Bueu & Beluso	228
⚓ *Isla De San Clemente*	*229*
⚓ Ría de Aldán	230
⚓ Isla Ons	233

Ría de Vigo — 234
Introduction	236
Approach and key facilities	238
⚓ Barra and Limens	242
⚓ Cangas	244
⚓ Ensenada de Moaña	248
⚓ Domaio	250
⚓ Ensenada de San Simón	251
⚓ Vigo	254
⚓ *Puerto Punta Lagoa*	*260*
⚓ *Real Club Náutico de Vigo*	*262*
⚓ *Marina Davila Sport*	*264*
⚓ *Liceo Marítimo de Bouzas*	*264*
⚓ *Isla de Toralla*	*266*
⚓ Baiona	268
⚓ Islas Cíes	273
⚓ A Guarda	275
⚓ *Camposancos/El Pasaje and Río Miño*	*276*

Background to Galicia — 279

Santiago de Compostela — 288

Appendix — 292
Weather – sources & times	292
HF Radio Facsimile Broadcasts	296
Internet weather	296
Language cross-reference	297
Wind speed conversions	299
Useful Internet sites	299
Charts	300
Useful addresses	302
Recommended Books	302
Music	302
Comments on Cruising Galicia	302

Foreword

It is recognised that any book on pilotage has to fulfil different roles at different points in time. At the planning stage there is time to sit and consider alternatives, plan refits and discuss experiences with others. Here general information is required, to consider alternatives and to be inspired to go to a particular area.

During a passage the navigator is often found re-evaluating a passage plan in a bunk. Now information on distances, hazards, general geography, tide times, ports of refuge and facilities are needed easily to hand. Then there is the final approach where there is little time and the information presented must be succinct, clear and simple. Once moored there is again time to plan trips ashore to re-provision and enjoy the local culture. The content of this book attempts to recognise and provide for these different, conflicting roles and clearly differentiate between them, while the layout of the sections has been designed for maximum ease of use.

For each area described in this book the 'initial shelter' is specifically identified. This is followed by a detailed pilotage plan which takes the navigator from safe water out at sea to that shelter with little or no use of a GPS position. Under normal daylight conditions with the boat in full working order the majority of the pilotage plans described in this book are perhaps overly detailed. It is likely that they will only be used in their entirety when the weather is not favourable or the boat, including navigational instrumentation, is not fully operational.

Experience has shown that the navigators are frequently found debating the alternatives for a plan with themselves. This book offers a reasoned opinion for both passage and pilotage plans. The intention is as much to provide the navigator with something to argue with as to offer a ready made solution.

The reader will also notice that the shore side information is very comprehensive with details of things to do and see and how to get around. With the introduction of GPS and more reliable forecasting the emphasis on many cruises these days is as much on the 'arrival' as it is on the 'getting there'. Often, however, the guide books disappoint, with little information on a coastal region for sailors who also have needs and tourist interests. This book seeks to address this imbalance as well as deliberately setting out to view the history of the shore from the context of the sea, which, for Galicia, is fundamental to understanding and enjoying it.

We hope you are inspired by this book into visiting a cruising area whose past, present and future is completely moulded by the waters that we sail on.

About the authors

Carlos Rojas has sailed yachts since the beginning of this century, a short but intensive period during which he has crossed the Atlantic, cruised in the Pacific, made several passages across Biscay, sailed to Ireland and to France. His professional involvement in technology companies as an engineer, manager and director has given him an insight into design and usability that he has tried to apply to this project.

His passion for travel has taken him to many remote corners of the world. He is always keen to learn about new cultures, landscapes, history and food.

Carlos has lived most of his life in Britain but he is originally from Spain, a country that he knows well. Galicia is one of his favourite areas.

Robert Bailey was brought up in a sailing family at a time when landfalls were routinely made just before dawn to help that first navigational fix and weather forecasts looked only 12 hours ahead. The enthusiasm of the children took the family further afield from their Solent base than the parents had ever expected. Over a period of 35 years, and with the aid of a Nicholson 32 and Rustler 36, much of the coastline of the north western approaches to Europe, from the Faroe Islands in the north to the Morbihan in the south, were avidly explored.

In 2001 he adopted a more flexible approach to his career as an aerospace engineer and this allowed him to take up cruising instruction. Further experiences rapidly followed, amongst them voyages back from the Baltic, deliberate ventures out into uninviting weather around the English Channel and skippering Fastnet race boats. Now a Yachtmaster Instructor, these experiences, as well as his background in aerospace, have led him to question why and how new technology is impacting the navigational judgments that sailors make close to shore under pressure, the supplementary information that is required and how it is presented. His contribution to this book is, in no small degree, a reaction to that examination.

Acknowledgements

We started work on this book with complete naïvety as to the magnitude of the undertaking. All our design and management experience, even coupled with a considerable passion for sailing and travel, would not have been equal to the challenge were it not for the help of many people.

Willie Wilson of Imray has been hugely encouraging, as well as patient with our ideas as they developed. His confidence in the project has been a great foundation for our enthusiasm. The team at Imray have taken our draft in their stride and provided very detailed and invaluable comments.

At home many friends and family have supported our dedication to this work, making useful comments or simply accepting graciously all the occasions when it has taken us away from other priorities.

Our friends John Banks, Dave Stoppard, Bill Bates and Phil Markham generously gave their time for passages across Biscay. Fishing was not an enormous success but a lot of things got fixed!

Ashore Carlos' Spanish family and friends provided invaluable help, company and knowledge. Mr Rojas senior kindly wrote the pieces on granite and aluminium.

We are grateful to Cándido Pazos at Turgalicia for his help. We have used materials from this department of A Xunta and we share their enthusiasm for Galicia.

A most special thank you to Susan Kemp-Wheeler who accompanied us on all the passages, took watches and dealt with victualling. We ate well and she listened patiently to our ongoing ideas and frustrations. Susan also took many of the photographs we have used including that on the front cover.

Finally, we want to say thank you to those who have helped us whilst in Galicia. Amongst them the crew of *Ciona II* from Manchester who provided a tow after we fouled our propeller one night and, later, members of the diving club at A Coruña who thought nothing of jumping into the water to cut the offending net clear. Both would only accept *gracias* for it. The marineros at A Coruña, Pobra, Ribadeo, Marina Seca and Aguete were especially informative and went out of their way to be of help. Roxomar from Arousa invited us to his *batea* and presented us with 5kg of mussels which were delicious. Armando and Mariluz at the Cathedral of Santiago gave us a special insight into the workings of the Botafumeiro.

We hope you the reader enjoy this book and we will appreciate any comments or suggestions you send to us.

Carlos Rojas and Robert Bailey
Hamble, Hampshire
2008

Acknowledgements from Carlos Rojas

I am very grateful to Richard Hicks, whose generosity and friendship introduced me to yacht sailing and to the sturdy Vancouver 38P, *La Farandole*, that has been our office as well as our boat. The distraction of sailing conversations in the midst of business frenzy and many hours in the middle of the Atlantic were a good precursor to my adventures on the water since.

Thank you also to Robert, my co-author, who was the first sailing instructor Susan and I had one dreary winter weekend in the Solent. We had no idea then that a joint project such as this might evolve.

Susan has been an enormous source of wisdom, patience and cups of tea while I have been buried among page layouts. Thank you.

Acknowledgements from Robert Bailey

I wish to thank my wife, Amanda, for her patience and understanding whilst my attention was shared between book writing and wedding preparations. Both Carlos and Susan have also made significant sacrifices during the preparation of this book and I would like to thank them both as well for turning a casual conversation in Baltimore Harbour into a reality.

Galicia
Ría cruising and passages

CRUISING GALICIA

Galicia
Introduction

Galicia is the northwest region of Spain, distinct from the rest of the country because of its green rolling landscape and very strong local culture. Sea facing and cut off geographically by substantial mountain ranges, Galicia has always been the remote part of the Iberian Peninsula, welcoming but difficult to reach. Modern development has done away with past transport issues on the land, but the coast continues to offer challenges to and rewards for the sailor, beautiful to cruise but occasionally daunting.

The Galician coast is shaped by large estuaries called Rías, each with a personal character that can be easily appreciated but is best enjoyed cruising leisurely. The **Rías Altas**, from Ribadeo to Cabo Prior, are the more remote, wilder part of both coast and land. These Rías are smaller than in the south and offer picturesque and quiet settings. Rías of Ribadeo, Viveiro, Barqueiro and Cedeira are easy to reach and will reward the sailor with pretty anchorages. Ensenada de Santa Marta, with Ortigueira beyond a sand bar, is unique and very much a favourite. Small fishing harbours and inlets, such as San Cibrao or Portocelo, are subject to swell or difficult to enter but will provide a great sense of achievement. Throughout this part of Galicia the small towns along the coast are a delight. Laid back and relaxed they run at a different pace when compared with the south. From the coast it is also feasible to undertake day trips to some of the major sights of Galicia. These include historic towns, like Mondoñedo or World Heritage Lugo, and an extensive array of pre-historic and cultural sites.

Further west, **Golfo Ártabro** groups together the cruising rías of Ferrol, Betanzos, Ares and Coruña. Despite the proximity of these large towns there is ample space to find remote anchorages and enjoy beautiful scenery. A Coruña and Betanzos are two of the most interesting places to visit, both with traditional galleried buildings in the old town districts. A Coruña is one of the best sailing destinations anywhere, with an extensive array of services to the yachstman at marinas located almost in the city centre.

From Coruña to Finisterre, the **Costa da Morte** owes its name to ship tragedies over several centuries. Modern technology and accurate weather

forecasts put paid to many of the risks that earlier sailors faced, but planning is essential to cover this stretch of the coast, particularly on a northerly course against the prevailing wind and the difficult headlands of Finisterre and Sisargas. Rías de Corcubión/Finisterre, Camariñas and Corme offer shelter and reward the sailor with wild, untouched scenery.

Rías Baixas is the name given to the Rías south of Cabo Finisterre (Fisterra), an area that shares much of the coastal character of northern Galicia but offers unique conditions because of a more favourable weather and larger size of bays. The Rías Baixas contain four of the five largest rías in

INTRODUCTION

Galicia. The Rías of Muros, Arousa, Pontevedra and Vigo each have their own distinct character on land or at sea, while smaller estuaries, such as Aldán, provide opportunities for out of the way exploration.

The quieter **Ría de Muros**, unprotected by an island at the entrance, has a wilder, more remote feel while at the same time being host to the pretty towns of Noia and Muros. **Ría de Arousa** is one of the biggest natural harbours in Spain, home to much of the fishing fleet and a significant proportion of Spanish sea farms, of which the floating mussel beds (*bateas*) are the ever-present evidence. Arousa is also a sheltered cruising area with many anchorages to suit different conditions and serve as bases for exploration. **Isla Sálvora** at the entrance gives a taste of the protected Atlantic Island National Park (***Parque das Illas Atlánticas***). The Ría has a colourful past that includes being the port of entry for both apostle Santiago and the many seaborne pilgrims from northern Europe that followed.

Within **Ría de Pontevedra**, Marín is home to much of the Spanish frozen fish industry but other towns contain gems of Galician architecture including Combarro with its *hórreos* (stone grain stores on toadstool bases) and Pontevedra, whose old town is a granite patchwork of narrow streets and covered walkways. Sanxenxo is not to everybody's taste but it is one of the larger tourist spots that takes advantage of the warmer weather. **Isla Ons** at the entrance to the Ría, part of Island Park, is a wonderful place to anchor. **Ría de Vigo** is the last before the border with Portugal at Río Miño. Vigo is a large industrial city but there are more sedate refined coastal resorts towards Baiona. **Islas Cíes**, also part of the Island Park, are easily accessible and a delight for anchoring if conditions are appropriate.

The Galician Regional Government (*A Xunta*), through Portos de Galicia, has encouraged the development of the sailing industry on a scale that is quite remarkable. In ten years, by 2007, they have reached 9,000 berths and the plan is to build another 10,000 in the next ten years. Local demand for berths is buoyant, many marinas already having waiting lists, but Portos de Galicia requires of the company holding a concession that at least 10% of the berths are reserved for transiting boats, assuring space for visitors. Pontoons and hard standing at new or expanding **marinas** are being added all the time, increasing constantly the capacity available for short stays or for long term storage. While some of the facilities ashore are not the best, there is ingenuity to solve any problem and a willingness to help that you will appreciate and indeed may not find in other parts of Europe. Befriend the *marineros*, they are genuinely on your side.

No trip to Galicia should exclude a visit to **Santiago de Compostela**, the centre of Christian pilgrimage for over 1,000 years and easy to access by train or bus from the coastal ports. The medieval old town is almost entirely built in granite and the old streets, covered walkways, buzzing restaurants and bars will captivate you, even if you are not taken by the spiritual pursuit of the pilgrims. The **coastal towns** of Ribadeo, Ortigueira, Viveiro, Cedeira, Coruña, Muros, Noia, Combarro, Pobra do Caramiñal, Cambados, Pontevedra and Baiona are all worth a visit. If you have the time to travel further, **inland destinations** like Mondoñedo, Lugo, Tui or Ribadabia are within easy reach and will be very satisfying trips. A visit to prehistoric dolmens and petroglyphs, the remains of pre-roman fortified towns (*castros*), Roman buildings and medieval constructions are all possible.

Anchor along Rías Altas, Betanzos, Camariñas, at Ría de Corcubión, Islas Cíes, Ons and Sálvora, behind Isla Tambo, the northern side of Arousa and at Ría de Aldán for some of the best settings in the area. **Berth** at Coruña, Portosín, Pobra do Caramiñal and Baiona for good facilities and pleasant surroundings.

You will find Galicia has a strong regional identity. Most obviously the local language is not Castillian Spanish, although the two are very similar. The cultural background has strong Celtic connections which are celebrated in numerous festivals during which the Galician bagpipe is centre stage. The food in Galicia is famed for its freshness and quality. Try *pulpo* (octopus) and talk to some of the mussel boatmen to exchange stories. Buy fish and shellfish straight from the sea, local fruit and *pimientos de Padrón* (small green peppers) at the local *plazas* (markets) and you will not be disappointed. Finally, Galician people are renowned for their helpful manner and, although tin and gold are long gone, everything that attracted Phoenician, Viking, Norman, Arab, French and British sailors before you is still here to be enjoyed.

INTRODUCTION

Pontevedra

Lugo

Small harbours

Quiet anchoring

Santiago de Compostela

Vibrant culture

CRUISING GALICIA

INTRODUCTION

How to use this book

This book covers the Galicia region of Spain. The coast is known for its estuaries called 'Rías', deep tide and river flooded inlets which offer shelter and extensive cruising opportunities.

The book is organised from northeast to southwest, following ports and destinations as they fall in order along the coast. After the **introduction** which provides generic information, the book is divided into **three main passage areas**, very distinct with respect to sailing conditions and local character. These areas are each given an introduction to aid passage planning. **Rías Altas** represents the northern coast of Galicia, with smaller, less sheltered and more remote rías - a beautiful wilderness. **Golfo Ártabro**, home of Coruña, and **Costa da Morte** are combined into another area. This is a notorious stretch, which can challenge the sailor with difficult conditions and few ports of refuge, particularly rounding Sisargas and Finisterre. Further south, the **Rías Baixas** benefit from warmer weather. They offer a very extensive cruising area within each of the four colourful and contrasting Rías found there.

The introduction to each passage area provides one chart with navigational marks and offlying dangers and a second with harbour features. This provides a quick and simple impression of the key information necessary for planning, together with explanatory text describing initial shelter, passages, major facilities and destinations.

The book describes **five cruising areas**, arranged around the five large Rías that form natural, local cruising grounds for the sailor: **Golfo Ártrabro, Ría de Muros, Ría de Arousa, Ría de Pontevedra** and **Ría de Vigo**. Each section is introduced with charts and text that provide information about the approach, harbours and local interest. Diagrams provide data about the area that allows the sailor to quickly grasp the key information.

Finally **local destinations** are detailed within sub-sections that describe the approach, berth, local facilities, provisioning and interest.

Detailed **local charts** show the specific navigation marks and coastal features for the destination. **Port boxes** provide the essential details about the harbour, shelter and facilities. These also include a chartlet that serves as a quick reminder of location relative to the surrounding area.

For **shoreside information**, Town boxes include **maps** and provide a short summary of transport, chandlers, restaurants, markets and health facilities. Local places of interest and things to do are described in the text. Occasionally **interest boxes** give details of a connected story, event, site or recipe.

An **Appendix** provides detailed information on a number of specific subjects such as weather and local contacts.

The **front** and **back covers** of the book show an overall chart and land map that can be used as a quick reference to locations, and coloured tabs for quick entry into the book sections.

Symbols

⚓	Marina (visitors welcome)	🛒	Market/supermarket
⚓	Marina (private)	⇌	Train station
⚓	Wall mooring or isolated pontoon	✈	Airport
⚓	Anchorage	🚌	Bus station
⚓	Anchorage - red section exposed	🚗	Car hire
~	Swell	ⓘ	Tourist office
	Chandler	✕	Restaurant/bar
	Fuel	☏	Telephone
	Travel lift	📷	Sight
	Repairs		

6 CRUISING GALICIA

INTRODUCTION

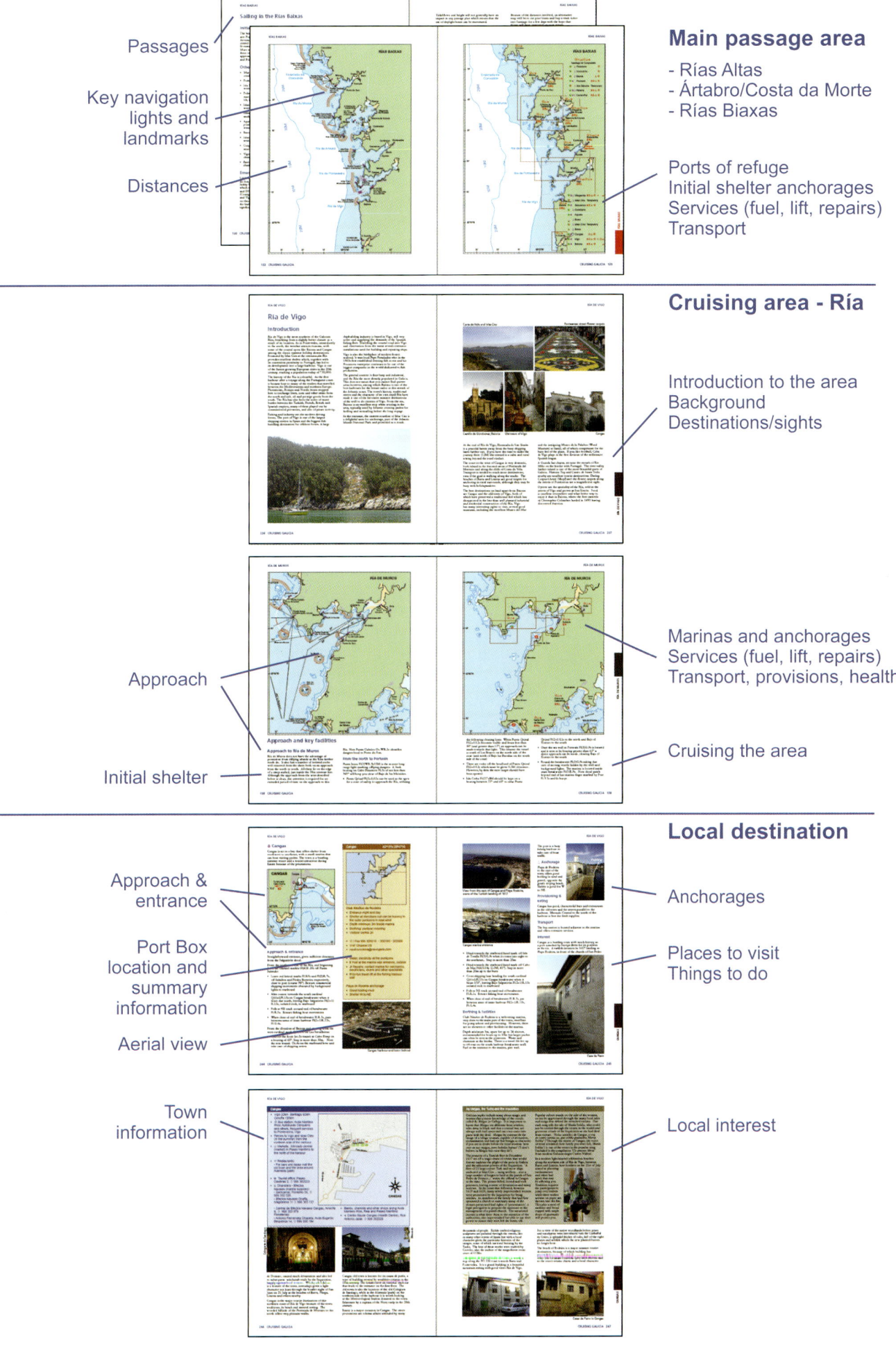

Main passage area
- Rías Altas
- Ártabro/Costa da Morte
- Rías Biaxas

Ports of refuge
Initial shelter anchorages
Services (fuel, lift, repairs)
Transport

Cruising area - Ría

Introduction to the area
Background
Destinations/sights

Marinas and anchorages
Services (fuel, lift, repairs)
Transport, provisions, health

Cruising the area

Local destination

Anchorages

Places to visit
Things to do

Local interest

Passages
Key navigation lights and landmarks
Distances
Approach
Initial shelter
Approach & entrance
Port Box location and summary information
Aerial view
Town information

CRUISING GALICIA 7

INTRODUCTION

What you need to know as a yachtsman

Introduction

Galicia is an attractive destination, offering extensive cruising grounds and providing opportunities to the sailor for pleasant sailing as well as more challenging passages. Planning is more important than for channel cruises, due to the distances involved and the exposure to the ocean swell and different weather conditions than you may be otherwise used to. In addition, the continental shelf edge is much closer to the coast than in waters further north in Europe.

North of Cabo Finisterre ports of refuge are further apart and remote than to the south of it. The area is also subject to the influence of low pressures passing towards North Europe.

South of the Cabo Finisterre the weather is warmer, albeit more prone to lingering fog, but with shelter more readily available and varied in character.

The approach of the Azores high closer to Spain's central low pressure in the summer can produce force 5-6, sometimes stronger, from the north / northeast for several days at a time. This can have a significant impact upon any plan, particularly one based upon a circular route.

Spanish offshore hazards are not marked as clearly or as comprehensively as in European countries further north, possibly because of the sheer quantity of rocks and the weather they would have to endure. Onshore, lighthouses can often be on top of cliffs and hills, good for long distance detection but difficult to see in poor visibility or low cloud.

The local charts from the Spanish Hydrographic Office are extensive and very detailed. They are also the source of information for any other chart you may obtain from another supplier. The original copies are the most accurate but are manufactured on large, not easy to use sheets of card paper. If electronic charts are being relied upon for 'rock hopping' then it is important to check that they have all the detailed chart data available. The rate of development in this area means that even up-to-date charts are quickly out of date with sea walls being built, new buoys being introduced, etc.

Crossing the Bay of Biscay

The discussion below is based on a boat capable of travelling (either by sail or power) at an average speed of 5 knots between Plymouth and A Coruña or Gijón.

When to cross

Historically for the months between May and September you are unlikely to encounter a gale on passage across the Bay of Biscay. If one does occur, it should be forecast in advance. For March, April and October it may be best to set aside 2 consecutive weeks for the voyage, with the choice of which to use being made on the basis that if a gale is forecast in the first week, it is unlikely to occur in the second and vice versa. Any gales will generally be from the W or SW. Outside these months the chances of getting a 'gale-free' voyage are not good.

On the whole you are twice as likely to meet visibility of less than 2 nautical miles in the Channel than in the Bay at any particular time of the year.

The probability of meeting wave heights greater than 12ft increases the further west you go and on the whole is no different between the English Channel, the Bay and the Coast of Spain at any particular time of the year. Large waves of this type are unlikely to be met between the months of May and September. The worst month, in line with the prevalence of gales, is February when there is a significant chance of meeting these. It should be noted, however, that this takes no account of the local conditions generated by the rapidly shoaling continental shelf, which can both increase the wave height and make the seas steeper in nature.

Boat & equipment required

Any boat crossing the Bay of Biscay should of course be well maintained and equipped. Highly recommended reading are the special regulations provided by RORC (www.rorc.org) for their Fastnet (Category 1) Race. Preparation is key and will take time to carry out.

In addition it is worth having the following both for the crossing and the cruise:

- Generous fuel range (450M)
- Reliable engine
- Good ground tackle
- Navtex
- VHF with DSC (which should help reduce any misinterpretation of position information)
- Registered EPIRB
- Internet or HF radio facsimile capability for synoptic charts
- Good set of spares for engine and navigation lights
- Radar and reflector (an 'active' reflector system should be seriously considered)

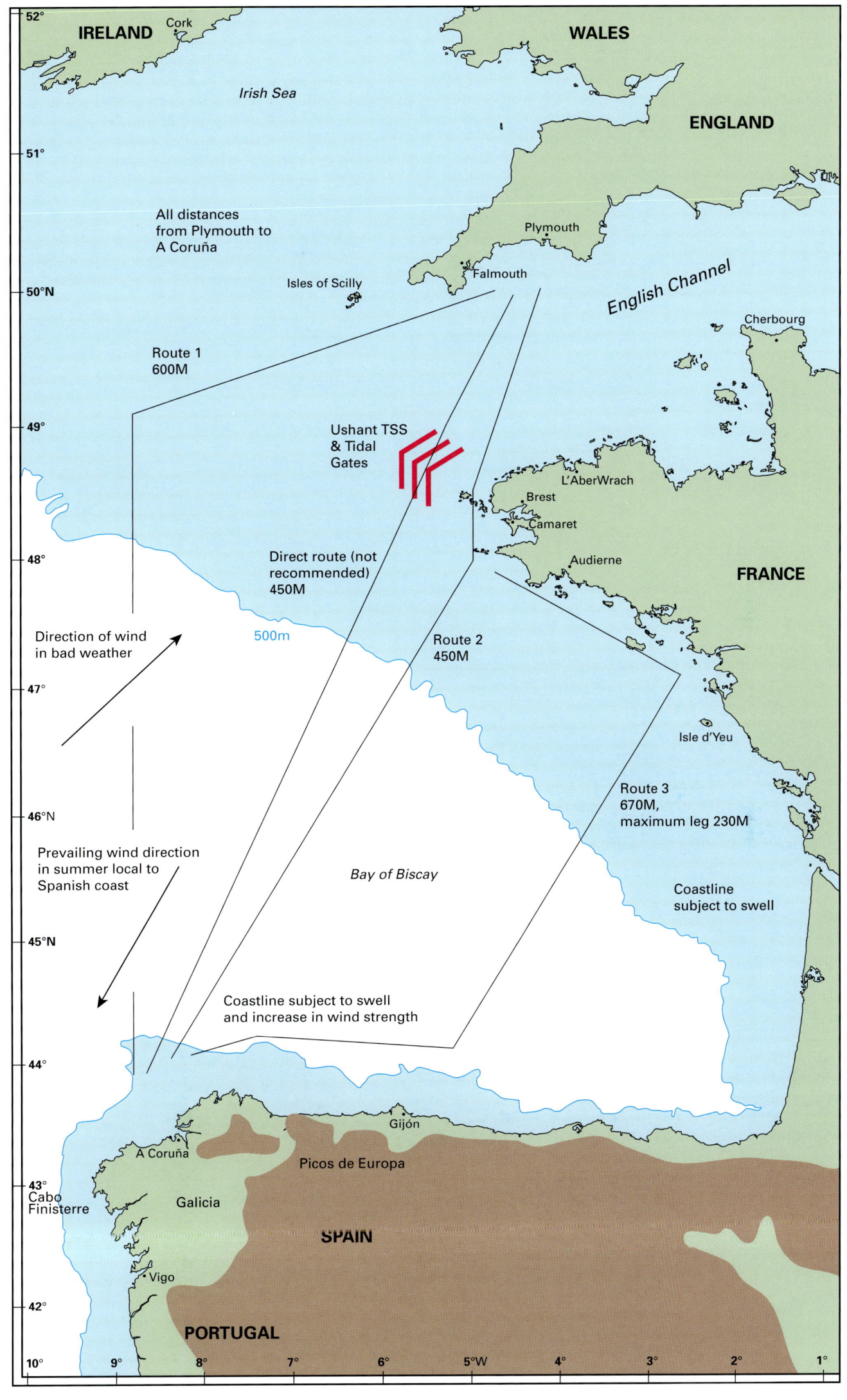

INTRODUCTION

- Handheld GPS as backup
- Satisfactory medical kit with ample supply of crew medication
- Adequate insurance
- Rope cutter
- Wet suit, snorkelling equipment, serrated knife
- Electrical and mechanical tool box
- Digital camera with screen to simplify any translation ashore with chandleries or marinas
- Extra fenders, long warps, ladder and fender boards for quayside berths
- Leather scraps for mooring rope chafe prevention alongside in swell
- Hose pipe with a variety of end fittings
- Equipment for connection to electricity supply. 16A connections are standard but it is worth having 16A/32A adapters for use on the occasional berth
- Dictaphone or other recording device for weather forecasts.

North to south

It takes between 4 and 6 days to reach Galicia from the south coast of England, depending on conditions and boat cruising speed. The possible routes are mostly dependent upon the weather and possibly your fuel capacity. Assuming a start from Plymouth there are three broad alternatives.

Traditional route - Route 1

This takes you outside the TSS off Ushant and out to beyond 10° west where the slope down from the continental shelf to the abyssal plane is less steep than further south and will therefore produce less severe sea conditions. From there you turn south.

The advantages of this route:

- Gives you plenty of room to leeward
- Minimises the period off the NW Spanish coast (which is susceptible to locally higher winds)
- Allows you to choose when and where to approach the Spanish coast.

On the negative side it adds over 100M (1 day) to the trip.

Cutting the corner - Route 2

A direct route is about 460M but takes you directly through the TSS off Ushant and leaves you in the path of traffic between it and the TSS off Cape Finistère.

With a favourable long range forecast and little to no wind (minimising any wind over tide effects), it is quite possible instead to aim to pass close to Ushant, enabling a refuelling stop at L'Aberwrach, Cameret or Audierne in Brittany. With L'Aberwrach it is just possible to pick up fuel at the tidal berth (assuming it's within office hours) and satisfactorily clear the tidal gates around Ushant and Pointe du Raz in one tide.

Audierne is 320M (3 days) from A Coruña and leaves all the tidal gates off the French coast behind you. All three stops take you well away from the shipping passing between Ushant and Finistère.

This option will allow mobile phone contact to be made with the shore contact, enabling a confirmation or change to the passage plan.

Along the shore - Route 3

Alternatively, from Audierne, it is possible to travel down the coast as far as Isle d'Yeu before heading

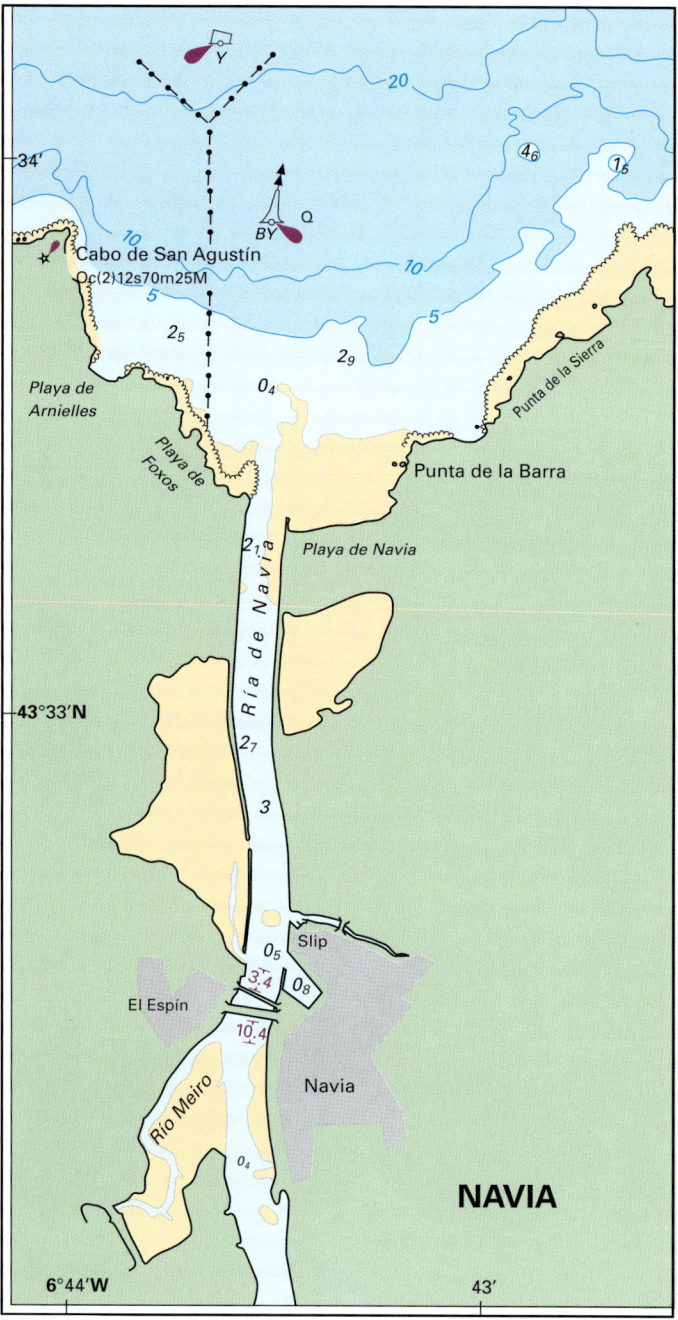

for Gijón 230M (2 days) away. The disadvantage is that it maximises the time spent close to the Spanish north coast trying to get to the cruising ground. This can make the trip more subject to wind and swell than crossing the Bay directly. Note that if swell conditions exist on the French coast they are likely to exist on the Spanish coast and a change of strategy may be in order. As before this option does obviously enable updates to be made with the shore contact.

South to north

The same alternatives apply as north to south except for one important aspect. For Routes 2 and 3 the period of time between choosing to leave Spain and being close to the French coast (and the dramatic change in sea depths) is close to the end of the 5 day forecasting period, where its original prediction could have been proven inaccurate. Being further north also brings you closer to the influence of low pressure systems from the Atlantic. As the trip progresses the skipper must stay in touch with the forecast conditions. If there is any sign of deterioration in the forecast then a decision must be made whether to stand inshore for shelter or stand off for sea room. The worst position to be in is neither one nor the other, caught on the steeply shelving continental shelf with deteriorating conditions, an unpleasant coast to leeward and shipping around you.

This would tend to suggest that Route 1 detailed above is a more secure route north-bound than the other two. It has the additional advantage that it places the boat further away from the aggressive tides off Ushant, where the timing uncertainty after 3 days at sea can result in facing a shut gate for six hours or one that makes the sea conditions unpleasant. The negative side of choosing Route 1 is one additional day of passage.

Shore contact

Before setting off a list of crew, any medical conditions and next of kin details should be obtained and held by a reliable shore contact. This person should ideally have experience of both the boat and crew. Details of the passage plan will also be needed and should include:

- Proposed course
- ETA (and the extent that engine and fuel will be used to maintain this ETA)
- Points where mobile phone contact will be attempted
- Proposed ports of refuge.

The Coastguard should hold an up-to-date CG66 with EPIRB registration number and be informed on departure and arrival. Bear in mind that no action will be taken by the Coastguard unless alerted by the shore contact, hence the importance

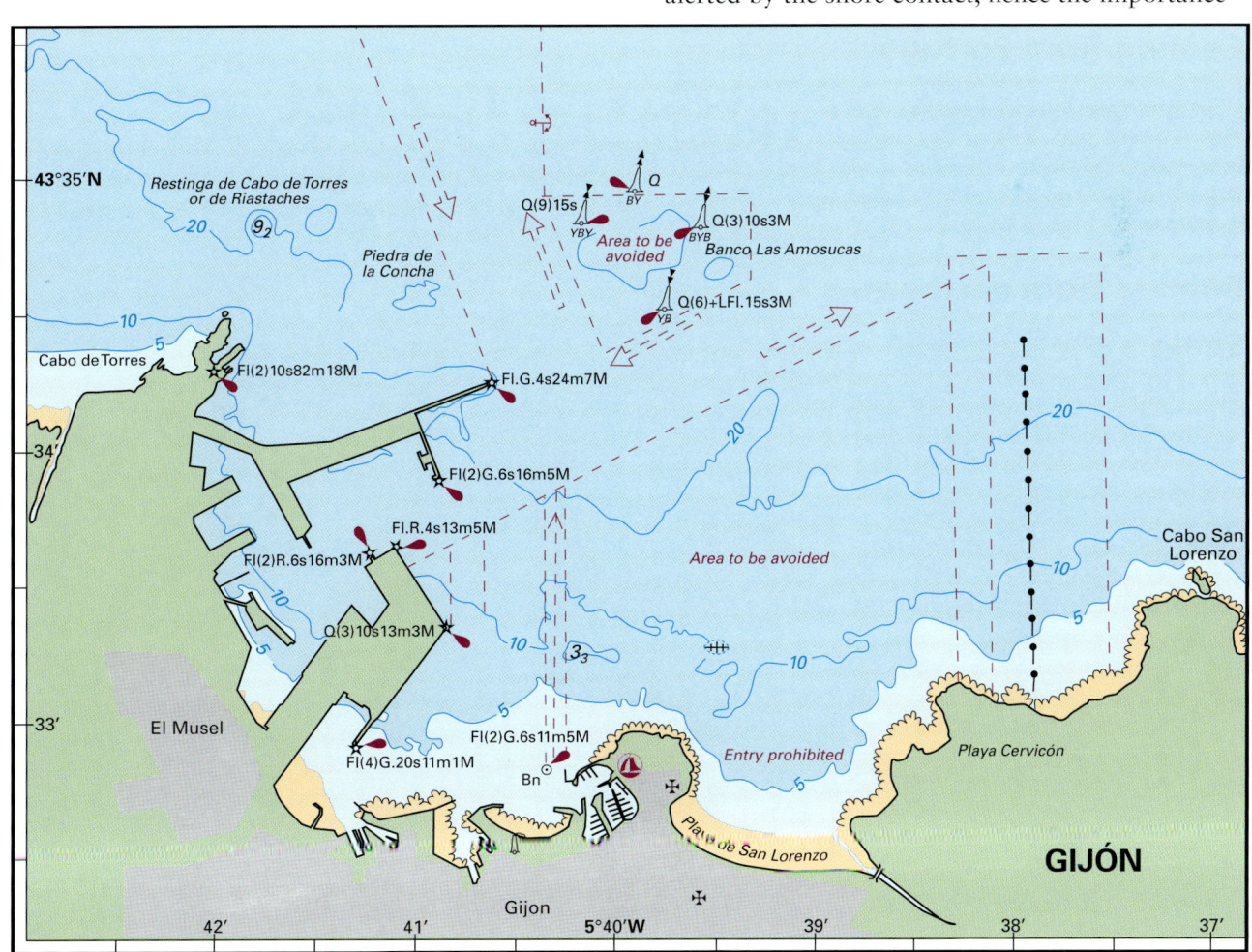

INTRODUCTION

of that person. Instructions on what to do under various scenarios should be left with the shore contact. A couple of examples are given below:

- The boat is late, but there hasn't been any wind. This could be due to engine / fuel trouble or a fouled propeller. The action will be to inform the Coastguard, but not necessarily to recommend mounting a search, particularly if an EPIRB is on the boat. Instead ask that if boats traversing the area be informed and requested to keep their eyes open

- Late arrival with unexpected high wind conditions – it could be that the boat has stood offshore to clear the continental shelf and provide adequate sea room. Inform the Coastguard on the basis of the experience and fitness of crew and the severity of conditions.

Without doubt an EPIRB will help move the responsibility for asking for external help back from the shore contact to the boat, where it should be.

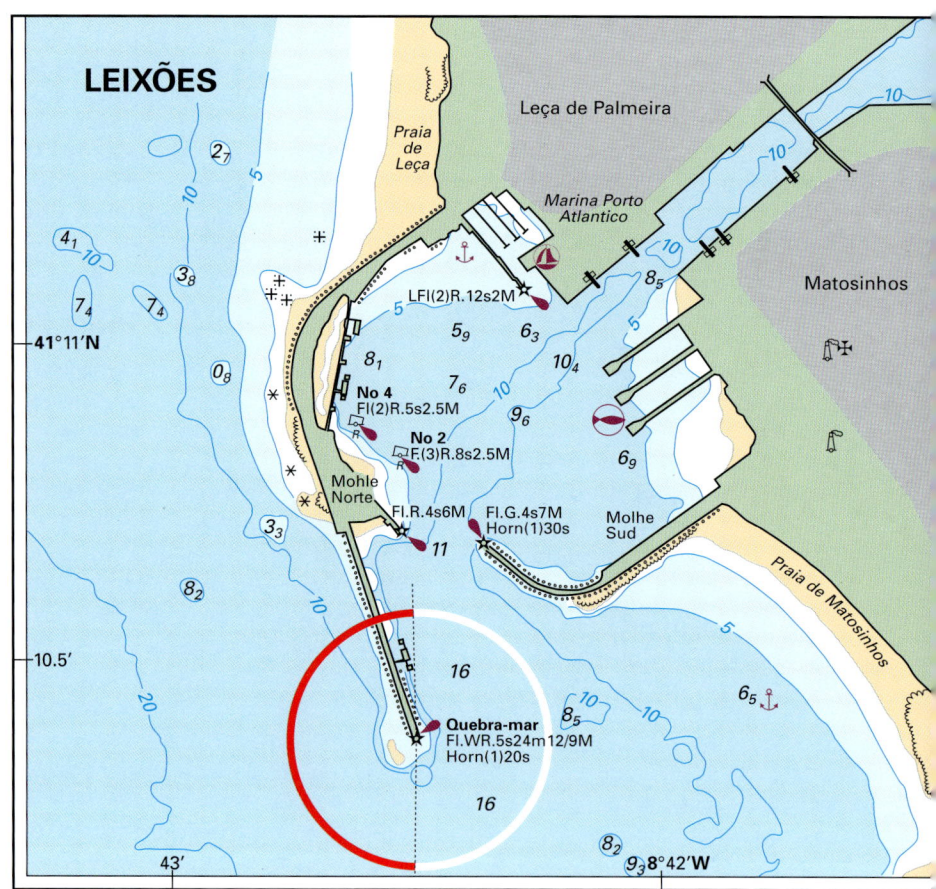

Coming from Portugal

Viana do Castelo is the northern most all-weather harbour in Portugal, 35M south of Baiona and will be the obvious jumping off point from Portugal into Galicia.

Coming from northern Spain

Avilés is the most westerly all-weather harbour in Asturias, 50M to the east of Ribadeo. Gijón is on the other side of the major headland of Cabo Peñas as well as being 15M further east. Either will be the obvious jumping off points from the northern Spanish coast into Galicia.

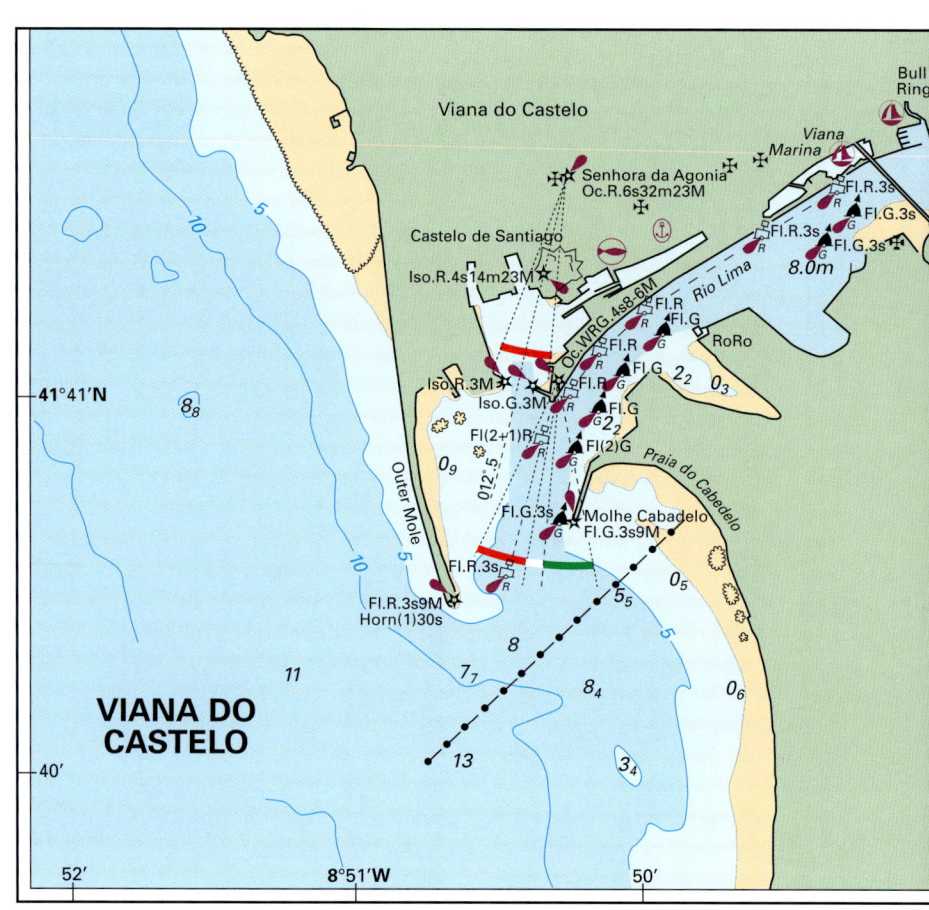

Cruising Galicia

The information provided in this section is intended to support the creation of passage plans. Where local conditions are significantly different they are detailed in the relevant section of the book.

Getting help close to the Spanish coast

The **Coastguards** in Spain speak English and respond both to telephone and VHF calls. The extensive radar system will allow them to monitor your location close to the coast, in addition to the information exchanged with you. Their equipment is modern and ready, capable of attending to the needs of the very large fishing fleet in Galicia. The lifeboats are, however, contracted from private firms, so anything involving rescue of property (i.e. your boat) will involve a charge, generally calculated as a cost per hour. Life rescue is of course free and immediately put to action in cases of emergency.

Helicopters are based at Gijón and A Coruña. A reconnaissance plane is based at Santiago airport. The rescue boats are at Luarca (east of Ribadeo), Burela, Cariño, Coruña, Camariñas, Porto do Son, Ribeira, and Cangas. The control centres for the northwest of Spain are at Gijón, Coruña, Finisterre and Vigo. The area is covered by two rescue ships at sea.

Chandleries & repairs

All the harbour authorities will have contacts with mechanics, electricians and good knowledge of local chandleries or *ferreterías* (ironmongers), so it should always be possible to arrange advice or repairs as well as obtain spares.

For complex equipment spares A Coruña and Vigo have the most extensively stocked chandleries. Sailing, electronic or other specialist equipment may need to be couriered from your home base, and this is often best arranged with a competent chandlery which will be used to such arrangements. In this day of digital cameras there is a lot to be said for taking a photograph of the required object if you can't get it out of the boat.

There are plenty of divers, both commercial and amateur. To arrange their services it is best to talk with marina staff, who will have contact methods.

English is not widely spoken in Galicia, but communication with marina staff ashore is not a problem, even if somewhat unorthodox on both sides. If you are confident in Spanish phone and radio calls will be much easier. You need not be particularly concerned about Galician, it is very close to Spanish.

Tides & Currents

The weak tide at sea theoretically runs west (on the north coast) or south (on the west coast) on the ebb and opposite on the flood. On top of this there will obviously be the flood and ebb in and out of Rías. The latter are generally less than 0.5 knots, but where they are more significant they are detailed in the text associated with the Ría.

Offshore these reduce further and can be overridden by significant surface current. The latter is largely dependent upon the wind in the Bay of Biscay. In summer this can result in a flow west along the north coast of Spain and then south around the corner towards A Coruña. This is due to consistent northeasterlies close to the Spanish coast. This can be accentuated by westerlies further north, driving water into the southeast corner of the Bay of Biscay, from whence it has to escape. In winter a northeasterly flow could occur with westerlies generated by low pressure systems running along the north coast of Spain. Under normal circumstances any current is less than 0.5 knots, but may run as high as 2 knots close to headlands on the north coast when the winds are strong and persistent.

To establish what you actually have will depend upon noting and interpreting observations from fishing buoys over time and correlating to a high water time. The best strategy for using the tide will obviously depend upon what you want to achieve, whether to use the tide to speed up a passage or to reduce the waves met off the headlands. Standing offshore will certainly make a difference if in doubt.

Tidal heights

Tidal heights in *Reeds Nautical Almanac* north of Finisterre are based on Point de Grave, a disconcerting 400M away on the French coast. South of Finisterre they are based on Lisbon, 200M to the south. Experience has shown that the secondary port calculations for height are suitably accurate under normal circumstances. High barometric pressure, local silting in the estuaries and strong winds from a consistent direction could all adversely affect the clearances given in the text. The timing of high and low water is more uncertain, but, as the tidal curve adheres to the classical shape, the last hour of tide will only bring in one twelfth of the range. Significant rainfall in a river's catchment area will create a stand at high water.

Note that care should be taken when looking at Spanish ports for tidal height information in *Reeds Almanac* that are listed as secondary to Lisbon. Portugal keeps UT, whereas Spain is UT +1. The correction has been incorporated within the secondary port tables. Thus when doing a secondary port calculation, start with UT; apply the time differences as listed under the Spanish port in which you are interested; and the answer will be in UT +1, to which in summer you need only apply the DST correction (+1).

INTRODUCTION

Weather

On the north coast in typical summer weather, with a Spanish low and Azores high in position, you should expect to see an easterly to northeasterly wind. On the west coast you should expect to see a northerly wind. As the land heats up the pressure over it will fall. This will cause an increase in wind strength by the afternoon.

When the Spanish low and Azores high are 'squeezed' together, by low pressure systems passing to the north, a *'nordés'* wind can be a significant factor. This is prevalent between April and August, sometimes with wind strengths of more than 20-25 knots for periods of up to a week. This can severely affect a cruising strategy based upon a circular route.

In winter the area is dominated by low pressure systems from the Atlantic, giving the same poor weather as the English Channel, but against a much less compromising coastline. It has the additional hazard of the sudden drop from the continental shelf to the abyssal plane being so close to the coast that it causes dangerous sea conditions.

The quiet months for gales are May to September with on average 1-2 gales a month, increasing outside this period to a peak of possibly 8 a month in December.

Land breezes, where cold, dense, heavy, air drains down hills and valleys to the sea, occur where these features are present and the weather is suitably settled and the sky clear. The effect will be a temporary change in wind direction overnight which should be accounted for when anchoring the evening before.

Fog can occur from May to October with the most significant occurrences close to the coast being in June to August. It can last for days at a time, but may be local to a particular Ría. The presence of fronts causing rain further north in Europe will result in moist maritime air being brought ashore and 'mizzle' or cloudy conditions locally, often with the hill tops (and lighthouses) shrouded in mist. Land fog can sometimes be a problem and should be treated with respect until it clears mid to late morning.

If caught out in poor visibility, using radar and switching between the 3 and 12 mile ranges will pick up the small fishing boats and large ships respectively at maximum range. Standing inshore or onto shoal ground will avoid large ships.

The Appendix gives sources of information for weather forecasts as they occur through the day. Independent of this, many marinas also provide useful information, usually from web sites. The Maritime Safety Information (MSI), obtainable through Navtex, provides information for the areas offshore. For Spain this is often very different from what will actually happen along the coast. The Spanish Coastguard reports in English provide this information, but only for the next 48 hours.

Access to synoptic charts will enable an assessment up to 5 days ahead. This is particularly useful for predicting the possible onset of a *'nordés'* wind and the consequences upon a plan based upon a circular route. The Appendix details the options for getting these.

Swell

Swell generated by significant weather systems, sometimes deep in the Atlantic, can build up and stay for days. If at sea, the best strategy will be to stand offshore. If in harbour then extra warps should be used and a watch on chafe mounted. Entrances that are susceptible to becoming impassable in significant swell are highlighted in the test. The swell and consequent movement of fuel in the tank can also lessen effective range under engine, as well as stirring up sediment that can block a filter. Spanish Coastguard weather reports in English provide information on swell height, independently from the assessment of wave conditions.

Traffic Separation Schemes (TSS)

Between 20M northwest of Cabo Villano and 20M west of Cabo Finisterre there is a TSS, with plenty of room in the Inshore Traffic Zone (ITZ) for the safe passage of yachts. The two approach channels into Ría Vigo have been formalised into TSS with a precautionary area established where they meet within the Ría.

Firing Range, Submarine Exercise Area

Firing exercises are carried out in the waters lying between 6 and 24M north of Islas Sisargas. A submarine exercise area is located in an area beyond 12M northwest of Cabo Ortegal and 12M northwest of Cabo Villano.

Local magnetic anomaly

There is a local magnetic anomaly reported within an area 13M offshore between Camariñas and Cabo Finesterre.

Rock hopping

Without the quantity of marks of more northern countries, rock hopping can certainly be more interesting in this part of the world. This is reinforced by there sometimes being a discrepancy between data on electronic and paper charts. If at all possible seek local advice and use Spanish Hydrographic Office charts. Proceed with due caution and take the simple but effective measure of making sure people are sitting down.

Fishing activity

Fishing boats are present in significant numbers, with their size and type of activity dependent on how far offshore they are found. Some examples are given below:

- Fishing boats in groups searching for and tracking shoals of fish with sonar
- Leisure fishermen in small, fast boats
- Fishing boats towing or guarding nets in small channels
- Pairs of fishing boats with nets between them (indicated by a flashing light)
- Boats in large groups using searchlights to attract fish at night
- Tuna boats motoring fast in straight lines, often in company abeam
- Boats creating a circle with their net to catch sardines or mackerel.

A good lookout should be kept and the Watch made aware of the action to take after a sighting. Early and effective action, particularly going downwind, will normally be the best plan, but can sometimes seem to be deliberately nullified by a target's subsequent action.

If planning a crossing of the Bay of Biscay, the simple expedient of arriving or departing on a Saturday evening or Sunday (commercial fishermen do not work on Sunday in Spain) may well eliminate many of the potential 'targets'.

The major fishing harbours have consolidated their position over the years at the expense of the smaller ones. This has meant that often the light blue crane of Portos de Galicia is the only evidence of a harbour's fishing past. Conversely the major fishing harbours are becoming less able to cope with the odd errant sailing boat. These will often fill up completely in August, during the fiestas, as fishing boats return from offshore trips. Fishermen are generally helpful towards yachtsmen.

Expect fishing pots close in (in anything up to 150m). These can be all shapes, sizes and degree of visibility and can sometimes have pick-up buoys and floating lines trailing. Nets strung between buoys have not been sighted along this section of the coast.

There is a quantity of debris floating in and around the NW coast of Spain. Most of this takes the form of discarded or lost fishing equipment (nets etc). A good lookout should be kept and the Watch made aware of the action to take after a sighting or, in the worst case, after a collision to reduce damage and prevent a worsening of the situation.

Fish farms

Bateas (shellfish farming platforms principally for mussels) are present in large quantities within many Rías. These are moored in regimented and regulated grids. This theoretically means that in low visibility it should be possible to take a bearing along the edge of a couple to get an idea where the next will be. Radar returns have been shown to be effective but potentially confusing. Abnormally high returns could indicate the presence of workboats. All *bateas* are moored from the centre which means that there are no offlying lines to worry about. It should be noted, however, that sometimes the shore-side row of the grid can be within areas of offlying rocks, so do not make the assumption that because you are sailing between *bateas* you are in deep water. Areas containing *bateas* are often guarded by lit yellow marks.

Other types of fishfarm can also be found in the waters, including circular arrangements used for experiments (eg Ría de Barqueiro). These are sited within designated areas, occasionally marked by lights.

Bateas and other forms of fish farm are located in areas designated as *'viveros'* on charts.

Shipping

On the north coast there are small ships berthing at Ribadeo and very large ones berthing at Puerto Alúmina. On the west coast, shipping from Rías de Coruña, Ferrol and Betanzos, Pontevedra (Marín), Arousa and Vigo (Vigo) should be expected.

Fuel and refuelling

Gasóleo A is used for pleasure boats and B for fishing boats. The member nations who had a special derogation on tax on fuel for pleasure boating (including the UK) are loosing that privilege and the other nations are tightening up both on inspections and prosecutions. Keep receipts if coming from UK on untaxed fuel.

Refuelling can be troublesome due to the lack of facilities, their location and the quality of the berthing. The detailed text offers advice on the favoured places. Ultimately the only alternative could be a garage and cans, which many marinas can arrange (including tanker deliveries to the harbour).

Some fuelling points operate 24hour self-service (Marina Seca Oza, Vigo), useful but difficult if something does not work in the credit card system.

Note that swell and subsequent movement of fuel in a nearly empty tank can lessen the effective range under engine, as well as stirring up sediment that can block a filter.

Berthing & anchoring

There are some marinas that have Mediterranean style moorings. These can be tricky on a windy day in the type of boat that often makes the trip across the Bay of Biscay. Where this style of berth is present then it is indicated in the text. The staff at the marinas ('Marineros') expect to be called, not just to allocate a berth, but also to help you moor up. If your command of Spanish is not good for transmission over the VHF then go for an easy berth and ask for help.

Marina shoreside facilities can be disappointing in quantity and quality, and are very behind the times when compared with the extensive amount of new pontoon building. There is, however, often a washing machine/dryer.

The marinas of Sada, Dársena Deportiva Coruña, Vilagarcía, Sanxenxo, Punta Lagoa, Davila Sport Vigo and Baiona operate together (www.marinasdegalicia.com) and offer a 'passport' which gives you discounts on berthing and lifts.

The only restrictions on anchorage in Galicia are naval areas (Marín) and underwater shellfish farms.

The use of a tripping line is advisable if entering an anchorage in the dark because buoys and associated ground tackle could remain unsighted. Areas marked as fishing areas but seemingly unused could have ground tackle present. The text also details the other places where a tripping line should be used. Beware also of the token, abandoned, semi-submerged, fishing boat which can be difficult to spot in the dark.

Beach swimming areas are enclosed by buoys in summer. These can reduce the degree of protection offered from that suggested by the chart as boats anchor further offshore.

Growth of marinas

The rate of expansion of berths for leisure boats is enormous. Portos de Galicia has overseen an increase to 8,000 by 2007 and plans to add another 10,000 in the next ten years. This is part of a plan to expand sailing tourism in the area, taking advantage of the attractive natural cruising grounds that the Rías provide. The plans include expansion or construction of new marinas at Cedeira, Coruña (at breakwater), Camariñas, Muxía, Finisterre, Cee-Corcubión and Muros.

Marinas are privately managed, under the terms of a licence (*concesión*) granted by Portos de Galicia through public tenders. Funding of the pontoons is mixed, ranging from fully public to privately owned.

Yacht Clubs

Yacht clubs in Spain vary widely in character. At one extreme there is the club with 'yacht' in the name as a accident of history, where wet boots or dripping waterproofs looking for a peg to dry on, would certainly not be met with approval. At the other extreme are those clubs dedicated to fishing. Squeezed between the two are a significant number of clubs that welcome sailing non-members. Fortunately an accurate assessment can usually be made from the outside of the building. Not surprisingly a degree of politeness during any initial approach will usually reap dividends.

Holding tanks & heads

- No discharge in port is permitted
- Up to 4 miles from shore for discharge with treatments (but no solids or discoloration of the water) is permitted
- From 4-12 miles discharge is acceptable if crumbled and disinfected
- More than 12 miles offshore any discharge permitted.

Laying up

The following places are recommended for laying up:

Rías Altas: Ribadeo and Viveiro - more limited on shore support than Coruña and Sada.

Golfo Ártrabro: Coruña (Marina Seca) and Sada - secure close to A Coruña airport.

Ría de Arousa: Vilagarcía de Arousa and Pobra do Caramiñal - secure, good transport to Santiago.

Ría de Pontevedra: Sanxenxo.

Ría de Vigo: Vigo (Davila Sport) and Baiona - secure and close to Vigo airport.

Water

A hose pipe with a variety of end fittings is needed. Spanish water is very clean and is drinkable from marinas, but bottled water is universally available.

Electricity

Galician marinas have modern electrical systems with power breakers and clean earth. Most connections are 16A. It is worth carrying a 16A/32A adapter for occasional use.

Cooking Fuel

Camping gaz is available from *ferreterías* (ironmongers) and *efectos marinos* (chandlers) outlets. Ask at the marina office for the nearest location.

Provisions

Provisioning in Galicia is straightforward, there are many shops, markets and supermarkets. The best option is always the local *mercado* or *plaza* (market) where you can find fresh fruit, veg, meat and fish. At the indoor markets and supermarket counters there is a queueing system, even though it may not be apparent: ask people waiting who is the last person (*'quien es el último?'*).

Supermarket chains Gadis, Froiz and Eroski are widespread and very well supplied. Many of them will deliver your shopping (*'entrega a domicilio'*) at no extra cost, which is extremely helpful.

Suggested summer itineraries

2 weeks in the Rias Altas working from Ribadeo to Coruna will offer a chance to savour this fantastic cruising ground to the full. By ensuring the first week is during a period of neap tides then Foz, San Cibrao, Ría do Barqueiro will be open to exploration. Before you leave Ribadeo make sure you have a full tank of fuel. Finishing at Coruna

will allow easy crew changes, provisioning and refuelling.

Exploring the Rías Baixas using a circular route which leaves and returns to Coruña will require 3 weeks because the trip is likely to be upwind on the return and may well be delayed due to the onset of the *nordés*. This length of time will also allow exploration of Santiago. Indeed the canny skipper will withhold any shore exploration just in case the *nordés* sets in, thus maximising the use of favourable conditions. Santiago is easily accessible at any point on the route with the extremely efficient train service.

Given favourable weather, Baiona can be reached in 2 days with an overnight stop inside Finisterre breaking the journey. The return can then be broken up into periods of 2-3 days in each Ría. With each Ría being distinct in nature, it can be left for the crew to decide where to make progress north and where to linger. Constant attention to the synoptic charts should give fair warning of changing conditions and allow suitable plans to be made.

Radio services

Safety

The Maritime Safety Co-Ordination Centre (MRCC) at Madrid co-ordinates via 3 MRCC's at Bilbao, Gijón and Finisterre. These are supplemented by Maritime Safety Sub-Centres (MRSC's) at Coruña and Vigo.

All centres monitor VHF channel 16, MF 2182kHz and DSC Channel 70. They also broadcast Maritime Safety Information, including weather (see Appendix).

Coast Radio Stations (CRS) do not now monitor Channel 16, so contact has to be made on their Working Channels (see Appendix).

Weather

Maritime Safety Information (MSI) is broadcast by the following coast radio stations:

- Cabo Peñas
- Navia
- Cabo Ortegal
- Coruña
- Finisterre
- Vigo
- A Guarda

Times and channels are in the Appendix.

Port Radio Stations

Generally VHF09. These are detailed in the relevant Port Boxes.

Formalities

The following documents (originals and copies) will be required on board:

- Passports
- Certificate of registry, or Small Ships Registry documents
- RYA certificate of competence
- Insurance (a Spanish translation is recommended, available from your insurance company)
- Evidence that VAT has been paid on the boat (such as a VAT receipt or a Bill of Sale on older boats)
- Ships radio licence and radio operators licence.

If there are people on board requiring entry clearance into Spain (non EU citizens) or there are goods on board that are dutiable in Spain or arriving from outside the EU then fly Q and enter where there is a customs presence (usually the major marinas).

If the boat is being exported VAT-free from the UK then seek advice from the UK Customs and Excise before departure. If entering in a boat registered outside the EU on which VAT has not been paid then seek advice from the UK Customs and Excise before departure.

Crew

You will find no other mention in this book of this most important part of any passage plan being by its very nature infinitely variable. To draw attention to it, a few words are listed below. Weighing up and balancing these represent the ultimate challenge to any skipper:

- Experience, reliability
- Health, fitness
- Sea sickness
- Foredeck work
- Accommodation
- Desires
- Expectations
- Compatibility
- Crew changes and additions
- Sailing, motoring, site seeing, resting
- Provisioning and feeding
- Preparation, training
- Personal clothing and gear.

INTRODUCTION

Technical and navigational information used in this book

Place names

Names in this book are taken from the Spanish charts of the area. The Spanish Hydrographic Office (IHM) is gradually changing names to those used locally as a result of a process of political devolution to the regions. In Galicia these names are in the original Galician language. There are many inconsistencies across existing derived charts and publications, which will persist for some time until the updates have been replicated throughout. The inconvenience is not serious as the place name spellings are very similar.

Time

Spain keeps Standard Euro time (UT+1) that advances one hour in summer.

Chart datum

All depths given in this book are those above or below chart datum. This is the depth at which the sea level will not drop under normal circumstances, and is hence conservative for navigation. For British Admiralty, Imray and Spanish IHM, it is the Lowest Astronomical Tide (LAT). Abnormal circumstances where this assumption may not be true are described in the text. For this coastline swell is the major contributor to abnormal circumstances.

Heights

British Admiralty charts are switching from a system of using Mean High Water Springs (MHWS) to a datum of Highest Astronomical Tide (HAT). The latter is the opposite of the LAT and as such is again conservative for navigation, unlike the MHWS. Spanish and French charts are also evolving and there may be the odd inconsistency in light heights between this book and the charts.

Horizontal chart datum

Positions derived from a GPS have to be referenced to some datum. This is set by the user, but will usually default to the World Geodetic System 1984 (WGS 84). It is important to check this by using the menu system of the unit. Equally important is to check that this is the same datum as that used on the chart (either electronic or paper) being used to plot the position. Some older metric charts (Spanish and those French and English charts derived from them) are expressed in other datums. This can mean that, unless a correction is made (which is detailed on the chart) or the GPS is changed to that datum, the position plotted will be incorrect.

Bearings

All bearing given are in degrees True. Use the charts to establish exact magnetic variation, but in 2005 it was approximately 4 degrees west.

Lights

The majority of the lights shown on the harbour and anchorage plans and within the text have abbreviated characteristics (not showing distance and height for easier reading). The exception to this is where particular attention is drawn to lights for navigation when transiting offshore.

Buoyage

The system used is IALA region A.

Charts

Available charts are listed in the Appendix. Note that where reference to a particular charts is made in the text an electronic copy on a chart plotter is an acceptable alternative.

Passage, harbour and anchorage plans

The latitude and longitude given in the port boxes is solely to locate the chart, not the harbour or anchorage, and cannot (and should not) be used for navigation. The plans themselves are drawn for illustrative purposes only and should again not be used directly for navigation.

Blue demarcations are used to indicate shallows to avoid in rough weather. Red demarcations indicate unmarked isolated areas generally more than 0.5M offshore which are a danger in all circumstances.

Pilotage plans

The pilotage plans in this book are consistent with the following 'rules':

- Attempt to be as simple and brief as possible
- Assume 'typical' summer sailing conditions (detailed in this introduction)
- Assume it is the navigators first sight of the destination and gives an indication of the severity of the plan under these conditions
- Detail the conditions under which the plan would become significantly more severe and why (such as weather, traffic, etc.)
- Distinguish, if necessary, between hazards in the final approach and those in the initial approach
- Use lights as the primary source of pilotage. (Where possible this is supplemented by photographs with prominent features highlighted to ease day-time pilotage)
- Use either a Latitude or Longitude to transit along where no lights exist and the shelter is considered important enough that it may be approached in the dark
- If the shelter has been recommended as 'initial' shelter the range and location of the nearest significant light (generally greater than 13M range) is given.

What you need to know as a tourist

Transport

Airports
A Coruña and Santiago de Compostela domestic/intenational. Vigo domestic.

Train lines
G1: A Coruña-Cerceda-Santiago-Padrón-Catoira-Vilagarcía-Pontevedra-Vigo. High speed line.

G2: Santiago-Lalín-Carballiño-Ourense-Puebla de Sanabria-Zamora.

G3: Vigo-Tui-Ribadavia-Ourense-Monforte de Lemos.

G4: Ferrol-Pontedeume-Betanzos-A Coruña-Teixeiro-Lugo-Sarria-Monforte de Lemos.

R29: Lugo-Ponferrada-León.

Narrow gauge railway: Ferrol, Ortigueira, Viveiro, Foz, Ribadeo, Navia, Avilés, Oviedo.

Bus stations
Extensive network links all towns. Main stations at the major cities, stops at the small towns. See schedules of private companies such as Arriva, Castromil and others.

Taxis
Taxis are numerous and equipped with regulated metering equipment. For long journeys taxis work on the basis of roughly 1 Euro per km.

Car hire
All the major companies operate in Galicia, albeit from the larger towns and airports. The easiest way to book a car is to call the national reservation line. If you do not speak Spanish ask the marina office or the Tourist Office to call on your behalf.

The reservations numbers of the larger companies are:

- Hertz ☏ 902 402 405
- Avis ☏ 902 135 531
- Europcar ☏ 902 504 880
- National/Atesa - no central reservation number.

Offices at Santiago, Coruña and Vigo airports and railway stations as well as at least one of them in the city centres of Lugo, Ferrol, Coruña, Santiago, Pontevedra and Vigo.

A number of smaller companies operate in the smaller towns. Autos Galicia has an office in Viveiro at the bus station.

National Atesa have offices in Vilagarcía de Arousa.

As always with car hire companies do take care with the details: excesses on the insurance can be very high and procedures for recording damage before you drive away are not always the best.

Public services

Health
The Galician heath service is called Sergas (Servizo Galezo de Saúde). Every town has at least a clinic with access to a doctor. All the major towns have a hospital, some of which may be private but are co-ordinated with the general health services.

Services from Sergas are available free for the time being to European citizens, but you must have with you a European Health Insurance Card (the replacement of the old E111 form in the UK).

See Town Boxes in this book for the specific location and number of the health centre near you.

Chemists
Chemists are very easy to find in Spain, there are many located near the centres or shopping streets. Service goes beyond sales of products and can often include advice on minor problems. They expect to answer questions so do ask them.

The range of drugs available without prescription is much wider than in other countries including the UK. Do consult before taking products that may not be appropriate.

The chemists in each town are co-ordinated so that at least one is always open 24 hours a day. The chemist on duty is named 'Farmacia de guardia'. A list of chemists and the rota is given in the main newspapers.

Emergencies
The main emergency number is 112. This gives access to police, fire and ambulance.

See the Appendix for Embassy and Consulate contact information.

INTRODUCTION

Sources of information

Galicia is well organised to assist tourists. A Tourist Office in almost every town you are likely to visit will provide information about local interest and things to do, as well as help you make phone calls for accommodation and transport.

The website of Turgalicia (www.turgalicia.es in Spanish, Galician, English, French, German and Italian) is almost a reference manual for any piece of information you may need.

The main newspapers publish useful pages about the weather (best for sailors is Correo Gallego), chemists, public services and transport schedules for airlines, trains and buses.

Faro de Vigo

Correo Gallego
(included within El Mundo national newspaper)

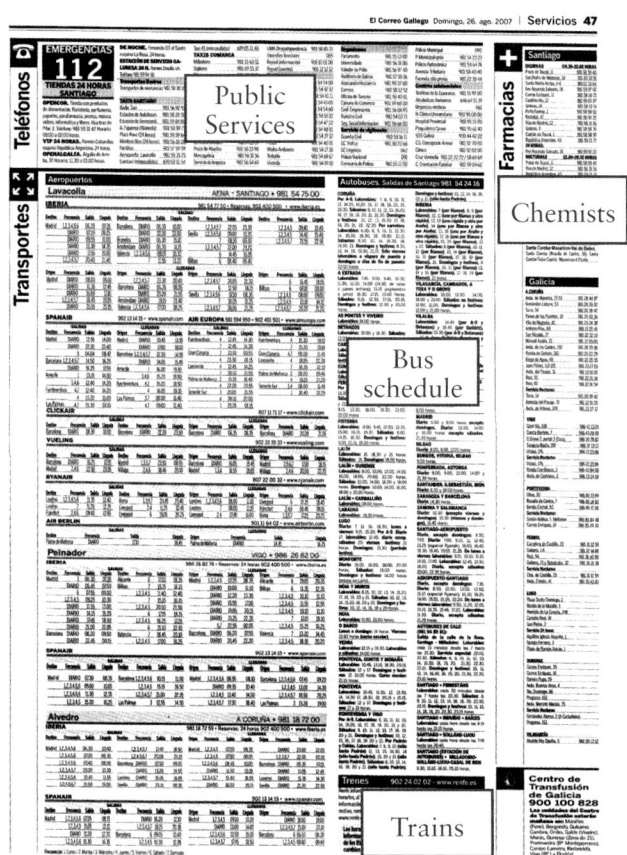

Correo Gallego - Weather

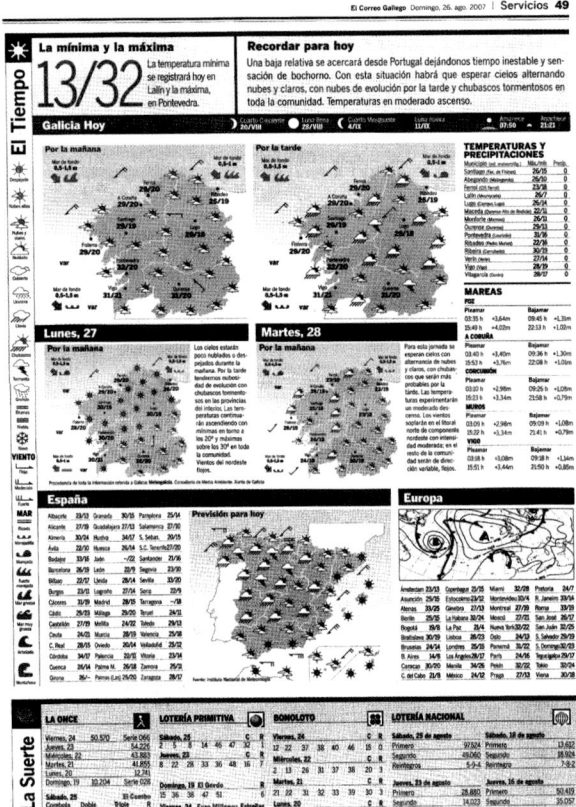

Voz de Galicia - Weather
(aimed at beaches)

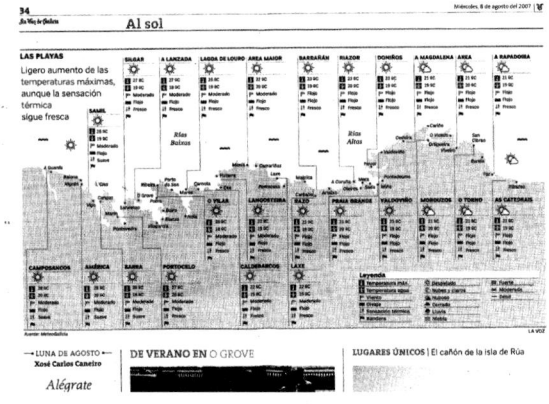

Money and security

Money

Spain's currency is the Euro.

Bank branches and cash dispensing machines are very numerous, so obtaining cash is very easy.

Security

Galicia is very safe and friendly, much more so than the larger cities in Spain and probably the one you live in back home. This is not to say that there is no crime but it is something you can prevent easily by taking basic precautions.

Take care at large events where pickpockets may be operating. It is always best to keep valuables within zipped pockets or at least put some difficulty in the way of nimble fingers.

Passports and ID cards

You are required to carry some form of identification with you at all times in Spain. It is likely that you will be asked for it in shops when making a payment with a credit card, but any of your passport, driving licence or ID card will suffice.

Spain is part of the Schengen border agreement so, unless you are coming from countries like the UK, you will not be required to pass through customs at borders or airports. Arrival by yacht in theory is subject to the same rules but, since passports are not stamped, the formality is somewhat academic.

Customs and behaviour

Opening hours

Galician shops generally open during traditional Spanish hours, 1000 to 1400 and 1600 to 2000. Large outlets tend to stay open till later.

Only large retail outlets open on Sundays.

Bars are open all day, there are no alcohol sale time restrictions. Restaurants open for lunch and dinner, the latter most likely not before 1930.

Wining and dining

Galicia, like the rest of Spain, functions socially all hours of the day and night but particularly late in the evening. If you go to a restaurant much before 2100 you will probably be on your own.

Bars are best for a snack, called *pincho* (small taster), *tapa* (snack) or *ración* (portion) depending on the quantity.

Food is always excellent and prices very moderate. Galicia is particularly good for *pulpo* (octopus), *empanada* (savoury pastry pie), *calamares*, *lacón* (topside bacon), *cocido* (boiled meats). Fish or shellfish of any kind will always be fresh. Meat is tender given the green spaces in which cattle live.

For wine try Albariño or Ribeiro whites and any Ribeira Sacra red.

Smoking

Smoking is banned in public buildings. Bars and restaurants are required to state whether they allow smoking within the premises, part of a planned transition to a total ban at some point in the future.

Smoking is very common, much more so than in northern European countries.

Noise

Noise is a problem in Spain and Galicia is no exception. The volume in bars and restaurants is very high but this is nothing compared with the all night fiestas that are organised by every village and town during the summer. If you have not joined the party the answer may be the ultimate defence: ear plugs.

Language

Galician (Gallego) and Spanish are the languages used in Galicia. They are very close so you will not have undue problems understanding Galician if you have any knowledge of Spanish. True Galician is only really spoken in the villages, what people use in the towns and official channels is a half way transition from Spanish, with a smattering of endings and some grammar that makes it sound like Galician.

Be prepared, however, for different spellings for the same place names. Ports and shore features have almost all been turned over in the Spanish Hydrographic Office charts to their original Galician names. In museums it is likely that text will be in true Galician, ironically often with English as the second language.

None of this is a real problem, and you will enjoy the kinder intonation of people's accent, much easier on the ear than the harsh sounds of Madrid or Barcelona.

Environment

Galicia is very sparsely populated when compared with central Europe. There are large areas of wilderness, which you can have to yourself given a bit of effort. Small town life and pace, albeit disappearing slowly, is much more apparent, and endearing, than in the bustling large Spanish conurbations.

There are some large sprawling cities and sections of Arousa, Vigo and Coruña feel like an industrial complex. The building of holiday flats in popular beach resorts has been indiscriminate and invasive but the construction boom is coming to an end.

The countryside is hilly with large mountains to the east. The land is very extensively forested, largely with managed woods of pine and eucalyptus, but there are many ancient forests of native oak that

INTRODUCTION

Markets in Galicia, fresh food paradise

have been protected. In the summer forest fires can be a significant problem if it has been particularly dry Each year this leads to arguments about who is responsible and what action should be taken, ultimately a question of money to clear bracken and other low level vegetation. Some fires are started deliberately but dry conditions and the wind are what makes the task of the fire service much more difficult.

Farmed land was traditionally arranged in small plots. *Minifundio* is the word that describes the system, where land is sub-divided to passed to subsequent generations. Poor families would also rent small plots of land for their subsistence living.

The land is very fertile and plenty of rain keeps it green for pasture. Galician meat is among the best in the world. Cultivation is traditionally corn and potatoes, with a large amount of market garden produce. Vines are extensively planted, used for light and fruity white wines like Albariño and Ribeiro in more northern areas, and the wonderful Ribeira Sacra (red) in the south.

At sea there is a wealth of fish and shellfish due to the proximity of the continental shelf edge and the welcoming, from the point of view of sea creatures, rocky coastline. The sea food chain includes the larger species, including dolphins and whales as well as huge shoals of tuna. Sea birds can be seen in abundance all the way along the coast and up to 100M off.

Communications

Telephone

Land telephony in Spain is provided by Telefónica, one of the largest telcos in the world. Prices are reasonable but you may be able to get a card for calls home for much cheaper rates, from a newspaper shop or Estanco outlet.

There are numerous mobile phone companies, all of which will provide pay as you go cards which will be much cheaper for calls than using your own mobile number in roaming mode. You will need a handset that is not locked to a particular provider.

Post

There are post offices in every town, providing all standard postal services including registered delivery and packages.

Stamps are also sold at outlets call Estancos, the old tabac dispensing shops that have outlived modern open competition changes to trade.

Courier services are also extensive, including the international companies like UPS and DHL and national companies like Seur. Check with the marina for the best local provider.

Internet

Internet access can be obtained at the many Internet Cafés in almost every town. Check with the marina or the local tourist office. Many marinas will also allow you to access the Internet from their office computers. Connection speeds are good as broadband is universal.

Accessing the Internet through your mobile phone is very easy and fast, the 3G network has very good coverage. The only issue is cost: the mobile phone providers have good packages but they will demand a Spanish bank from which to Direct Debit. Unfortunately the idea of pay as you go data access has not entered the mainstream thinking of their marketing departments. Your mobile will make connection very well under roaming but the charges will be very high - this can be made practical by limiting your data downloads, for example using GRIB files.

INTRODUCTION

CRUISING GALICIA 23

Rías Altas
The remote Galicia

RÍAS ALTAS

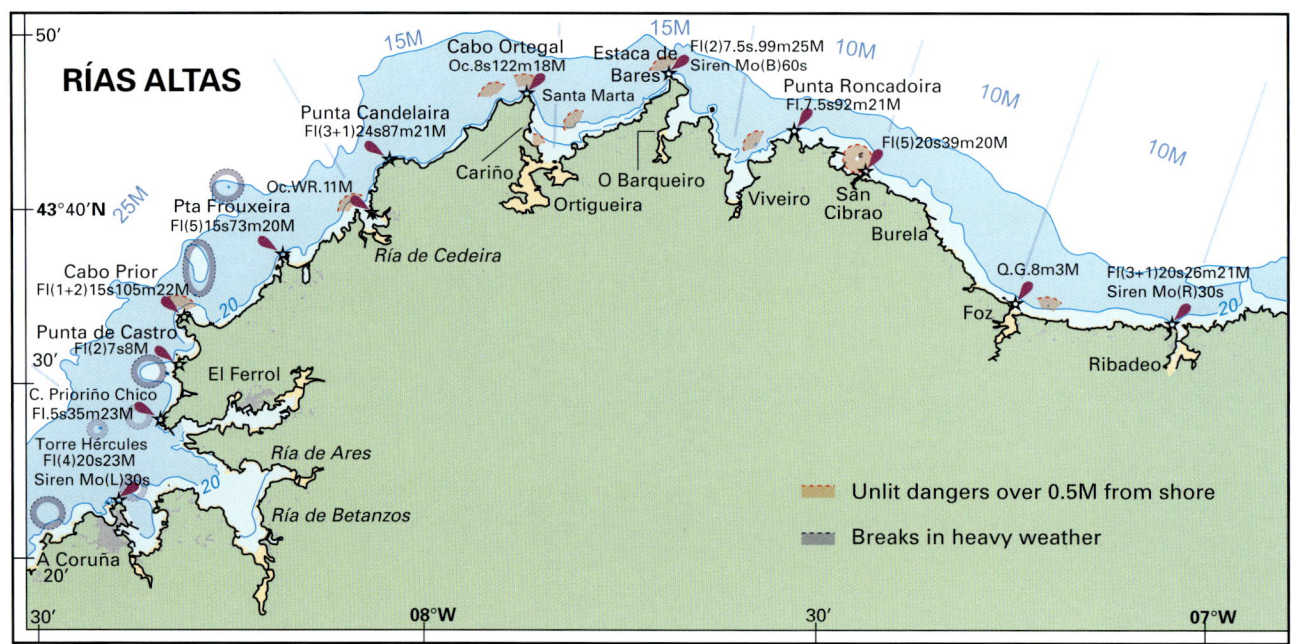

Sailing in the Rías Altas

Initial shelter

The best harbours along Rías Altas are Ribadeo (east), Viveiro (centre) and Cedeira (west). All of them have lit, straightforward entrances offering reasonable shelter inside.

Ribadeo and Viveiro have the only marinas (2007) along this coast apart from Ortigueira. A marina is planned for Cedeira (2008/09).

Other ports and facilities

Foz has an entrance over a sand bar and the harbour is shallow, though with good shelter and access to the local town.

San Cibrao is full of small craft moorings but it may be possible to lie alongside the fishing harbour wall.

Santa Marta de Ortigueira is a large estuary, with a channel over sandbanks that leads to the small marina at Ortigueira. The entrance is over a sand bar and the location of sand banks changes. Entrance or exit in any swell is not recommended.

There are several small harbours, inlets and beaches suitable for anchorage or alongside a harbour wall. Most are exposed so calm conditions may be required.

Emergencies

Lifeboats are present at Ribadeo, Burela, Cariño and A Coruña. Coast radio stations are based at Navia to the east, Cabo Ortegal in the centre and A Coruña to the west of the area. Timings of weather broadcasts are given in the Appendix.

In an emergency or storm conditions, Puerto Alúmina Española (just north of San Cibrao) or Burela can also be used. Both, along with A Coruña, have significant medical facilities and straightforward, well lit approaches.

Provisioning

The Rías Altas are much less densely populated than the rest of Galicia, with small towns along the coast not offering the same degree of services as further south. Nevertheless, there are good *mercados* and supermarkets in Ribadeo, Foz, Viveiro, Ortigueira and Cedeira. The smaller villages have shops that will have enough to see to basic victualling.

Bars and restaurants are not in short supply anywhere but the larger the town the better the offering.

Repairs and chandleries

There are no big chandlers and yacht services along this stretch of the coast like at Coruña and Vigo further south. However, there are plenty of skilled people at any of the harbours that are home to fishing fleets. Although not dedicated to yachts they are able to provide services or assist with repairs.

There are mechanic workshops at Ribadeo and Cedeira and extensive services at Viveiro.

All the towns along the coast have *ferreterías*, general ironmongers that hold basic bits and pieces.

The large chandlers at Coruña and Vigo will organise delivery of parts to the harbour you are based at if that is required.

Transport

The major towns of Ribadeo, Foz, Viveiro, Ortigueira and Cedeira are all served by bus routes

RÍAS ALTAS

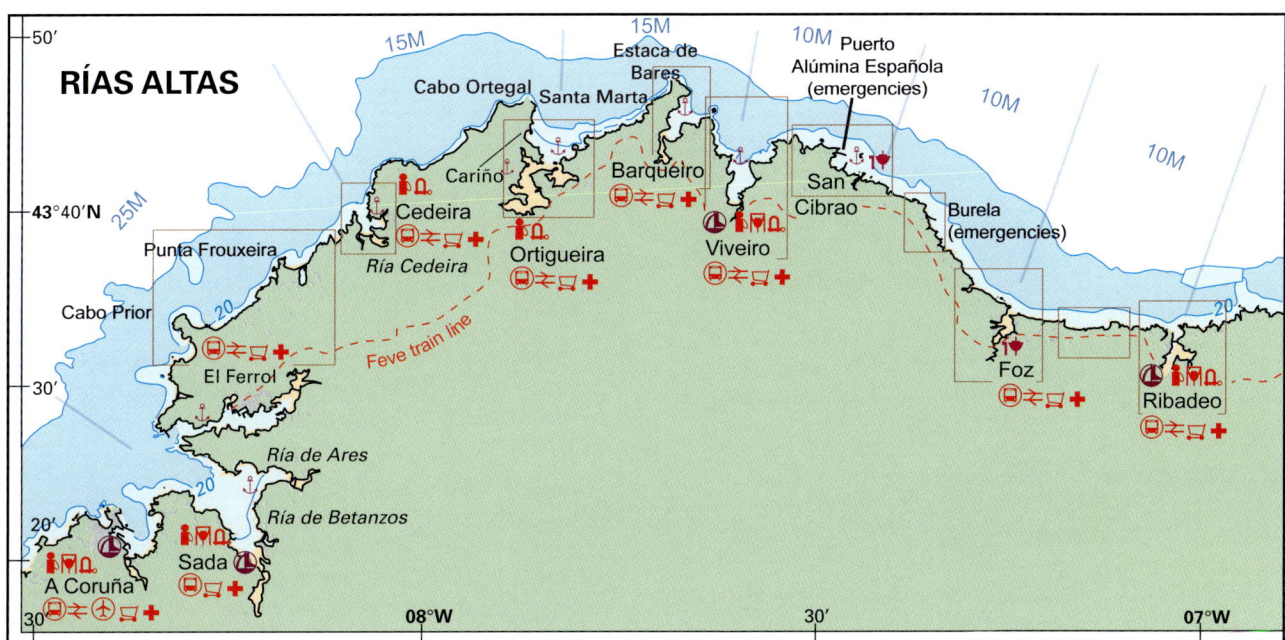

that link to Coruña and Ferrol as well as Lugo inland.

The FEVE train has stops at Ferrol, Ortigueira, Barqueiro, Viveiro, Burela, San Cibrao, Foz, Ribadeo, Castropol and Navia, as well as numerous villages along the way. It's slow but it gets you there, ideal for short sightseeing hops and with spectacular views along the way. Services are twice a day, more in the busier sectors.

FEVE stations from Gijón to Ferrol: Gijón, Avilés, Pravia main stations, then Las Campas, **Castropol**, Vilavedelle, Vegadeo, **Ribadeo**, Rinlo, Os Castros, Esteiro, Reinante, Barreiros, **Foz**, Marzan, Fazouro, Nois, Cangas de Foz, **Burela**, Madeiro, **San Cibrao**, Bidueiros, Lago, Xove, Xuances, **Viveiro**, Covas, Folgueiro, Mosende, **Vicedo**, O Barqueiro, Loiba, Espasante, **Ortigueira**, Senra, San Clodio, Ponte Mera, Santa María, Cuqueira, Cerdido, Entrambarrias, Labacengos, Moeche, Apalla, Lamas, San Sadurniño, Pedroso, Sedes, Ferrerías, Xuvia, O Ponto, Piñeiros, Alto Do Castiñeiro, Santa Icía, Virxe do Mar, San Xoan, Ferrol.

Passages

The total distance from Ribadeo to A Coruña is 85M. If transiting the area this can be broken up into three equal hops of 30M using Viveiro and Cedeira. If time allows, however, you will have many opportunities to find your own anchorage or wall where you can have the place to yourself.

See the main introduction for a description of tides and general weather.

Swell generated by significant weather systems, sometimes deep in the Atlantic, can build up and stay for days. The best strategy will be to stand offshore into more than 50m-100m. It will also restrict entrances, both entering and leaving. Arrival or departure at high water, providing another valuable 3 to 4m, should be considered in the timing of a passage.

The chart of the Rías Altas shows the significant lights that can be used for passage navigation at night and the unlit hazards more than 0.5M from the coast.

Tidal flows will not generally have an impact on any passage plan, but **tidal height** will, due to considerations of swell or clearance on the keel. This is true of the following harbours:

- Foz – entrance subject to swell and an overnight stay may only be possible on neaps
- San Cibrao - overnight stay may only be possible on neaps
- Viveiro – entrance subject to swell
- Vicedo (Ría do Barqueiro) – entrance subject to swell
- Barqueiro – entrance subject to swell and an overnight stay may only be possible on neaps
- Ortigueira - entrance subject to swell and an overnight stay on quay may only be possible on neaps. Note that deeper anchorage can be found in the river.

If setting off for one of these, then due consideration should be made to alternatives if swell precludes an entry.

Navigation in good visibility will be straightforward, with plenty of headlands and towns to confirm a GPS position. There are **few isolated dangers**, so, if caught out in poor visibility, without the aid of radar, most of the coast (except areas indicated on the chart) can be approached safely to within 0.5M for a fix. **Traffic**, mainly constrained to fishing boats, is not numerous but can be fast and a suitable lookout should be kept. Small coasters use Ribadeo and ships (with pilot boats) use Puerto Alúmina.

Refuelling is limited and best done at Ribadeo or Coruña.

Rías Altas

Introduction

The coast that stretches from Ribadeo to Cabo Prior is known as Rías Altas, a very remote and undeveloped part of Galicia. A succession of picturesque rías provide shelter to the sailor, each much smaller that those further south. They require some resourcefulness but reward the visitor with breathtaking wilderness and a sense of adventure.

Ría de Ribadeo straddles the eastern border between Galicia and Asturias, a relatively narrow estuary that is guarded by Ribadeo and Castroprol. The two small towns are full of character and have stories to tell, some linked with the Spanish American colonies, some with the old mining industry.

Inland from Ribadeo, the medieval city of **Mondoñedo** is a gem of Galician architecture, with a cathedral to show the pedigree of this ancient seat of power. Various villages nearby have monuments worth a visit, such as the church of San Martín dating from the Christian *reconquista* 700 year struggle against the Moors.

Further south, **Lugo** is an outstanding city surrounded by the World Heritage 2,000 year old Roman wall. Walk the 2.5km path along the wall and explore the traditional Galician streets of the old town.

Between Ribadeo and Foz, still wild but beginning to be developed, a long stretch of beach faces the sea. Standing out are the stone towers and arches of **Playa das Catedrais**. These show the effects of erosion which has carved them into shapes that resemble cathedral buttresses. Walk through them at low tide.

Viveiro is another harbour town that combines its connection to the sea with a historical past, Three medieval gates remain from the original wall that encircled the town.

Ortigueira is nestled at one of the bends of the channel that is shaped and reshaped by sandbanks. The small, noble village is home each summer to the international Festival, where the Atlantic facing regions of Europe gather to celebrate the Celtic theme.

The giant cliffs between Estaca de Bares and Cedeira are the sea facing side of a mountainous pristine environment, home to wild horses and the pilgrimage destination of **San Andrés de Teixido**.

Cedeira is one of the nicest places to stay in a boat in the whole of Galicia, picturesque and welcoming as well as offering good shelter. A marina is planned, so get there before people and boat volume increase.

The Rías Altas will give you a taste of 'old' Galicia, its natural beauty, delicious food and easy going friendly people. Independent transport ashore is probably needed and the FEVE narrow gauge railway is recommended as a good means to travel through the beautiful scenery at a leisurely pace.

RÍAS ALTAS

Mondoñedo

Cedeira

Ortigueira

Castropol

San Andrés de Teixido

Ribadeo

CRUISING GALICIA 29

RÍAS ALTAS

RÍAS ALTAS

⚓ Ribadeo

A pleasant estuary with a marina at the foot of an attractive town and a couple of quieter anchorages. Opportunities for a run ashore or excursions in the dinghy. Ribadeo is a historic town on the border between Galicia and Asturias.

Approach & entrance

Straightforward entrance with no isolated dangers and lit leading lights. Depth should be watched and shallows avoided in the presence of significant swell. The bridge is prominent in daylight. Note Isla Plancha (Fl(3+1)20s21M) lies just to the W of the entrance.

- Sail south to a position midway between the headlands using a 170° transit of the bridge centre and Castropol church (lit)
- Turn onto first set of leading lights (140°, Front Iso. R, rear Oc. R 4s)
- Turn onto second set of leading lights when Piedras Las Carraias Q.G.1s is on the stern (205°, front VQ. R, rear Oc. R 2s)
- Make for right hand arch of bridge (between Fl(4)R.11s and Fl(2)G.7s). (Note air height 30m)
- Turn parallel to the marina breakwater before entering marina.

Cross tide on the ebb (up to 3 knots) should be watched when entering or leaving the marina. Breakwater obscures possible vessel movements.

Berthing & facilities

Club Náutico de Ribadeo is a comfortable marina with plenty of space for visitors and acceptable manoeuvring room. Arrange a berth in advance using VHF or head for one of the outer hammerheads at the end of the pontoons opposite the entrance.

The visitor pontoons can be subject to swell. Discussion is in progress about extending the southern breakwater.

There is water and electricity at the pontoons. Showers and laundry facilities are excellent in the new (2006) marina building. The travel lift at 32-ton is adequate for even large yachts and makes this a possible winter dry dock location.

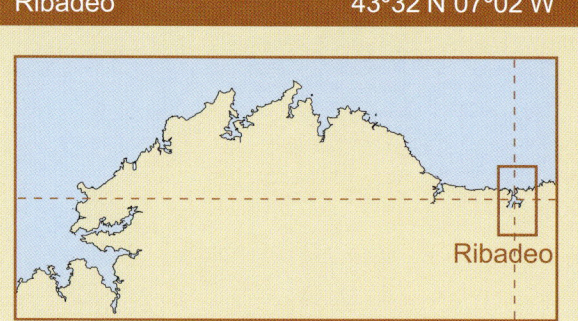

Ribadeo   43°32'N 07°02'W

Club Náutico de Ribadeo
- Straightforward day and night entrance
- Good shelter in marina
- Entrance difficult in strong onshore winds

- 20 visitors' berths, up to 20m length
- 4m minimum depth

- ☏ 982 120428   Fax 982 131144
- VHF Channel 09
- vela@clubnauticoribadeo.com
- www.clubnauticoribadeo.com

- Water, electricity at the pontoons
- Fuel by the Travel Lift (manoeuvring difficult) - dedicated fuelling berth planned
- 32-ton travel lift
- Mechanic, electrician through marina
- Good showers, laundry in new club building (2006)
- Bar and good restaurant in the marina area
- Sailing and diving club

Fuel is available from a tank by the travel lift (manoeuvring difficult). A dedicated fuelling pontoon is planned on the northern breakwater (2008/09).

Ribadeo is a small town without dedicated yacht chandlers or workshops, but there is plenty of local skill due to shipbuilding and other marine industrial activity. Eo Náutico in the fishing harbour can undertake engine and hull repairs. For other services arrange with the marina.

Ribadeo Marina

RÍAS ALTAS

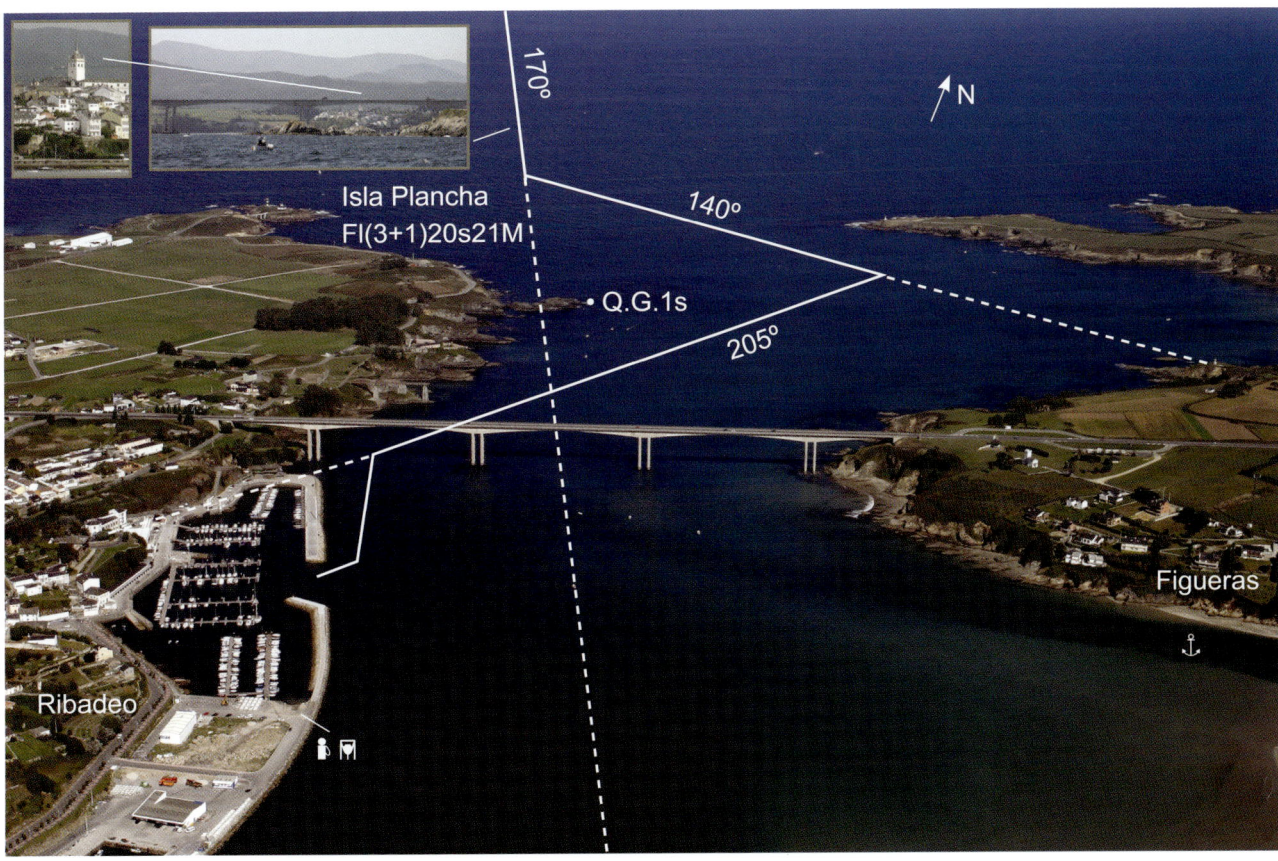

⚓ Anchorages

Banks in the centre of the river and the channels around them move and suitable care should be taken when navigating using charts.

⚓ Figueras

Anchor in 2m opposite beach in sand.

⚓ Castropol

Summer pontoon in front of sailing club (1m). Alternatively anchor off in main channel (4.6m sand and mud) downstream of buoys. It is possible to attach to the quay in 1.1m to 2.1m (the seaward end being deeper).

Restaurant and showers next to the sailing club on the quay.

Provisioning & eating

Shops in Ribadeo are located around Plaza de España, a short walk (uphill) from the marina. There is a large supermarket to the north of the town but as always the best supplies are in the Mercado de Abastos (market, Rúa Reinante). The Gadis supermarket is conveniently close to the marina.

CRUISING GALICIA 33

RÍAS ALTAS

Ribadeo

- Lugo 90km, Santiago 180km, Coruña 155km, Gijón 150km
- 🚌 Bus station: Avda Rosalía de Castro
- 🚆 FEVE station: Rúa de la Estación
- Car hire: nearest at Lugo and Viveiro

- 🛒 Plaza de Abastos (market) at - Rúa Reinante/Avda Asturias
- 🛒 Supermarket:
  - Gadis, Rosalía de Castro beyond Bus Station
- 🛒 Hypermarket:
  - Eroski, outskirts of town on the N-634/A8
- 🍴 Restaurants:
  - Plaza de España streets bars and tapas
  - Marina: restaurants north and south end (popular O Marinero opposite tourist boat quay)
- ℹ️ Tourist office: Plaza de España
  ☎ 982 12868

- ⚓ Chandlers:
  - Eo Náutico (fishing harbour) - workshop and some chandlery
  - Ferreterías (ironmongers) Rúa Asturias, Rúa Galicia
- ✚ Centro Saude Ribadeo, Rúa Reinante
  ☎ 982 130143

There are plenty of restaurants and bars in the centre of town around Plaza de España, all serving tapas/raciones in bar style.

Around the marina there are several places to eat. The restaurant overlooking the boats at the north end is one of the best in Ribadeo. O Marinero on the street going up to the centre near the tourist boat quay is very popular serving a full range of Galician dishes - you need to take a number from the machine at the entrance to reserve your place in the queue.

Castropol has a few shops in the main village on the hill top. There is also a bar at the harbour quay.

Transport

The bus station is only a five minute walk away and offers connection to many destinations. This makes possible day trips to Mondoñedo and Lugo.

34 CRUISING GALICIA

The FEVE railway station on the west side of town (15min walk) gives access to the infrequent but delightful train service that meanders along the coast from Oviedo to Coruña (see introduction to Rías Altas for additional information). A good day trip is from Ribadeo to Rinlo and Playa das Catedrais, giving you a few hours before the journey back.

Interest

Ribadeo is a historic town known as the gateway to Galicia because of its key position on the mouth of Río Eo. It is located on the border between Galicia and Asturias and manages a blend of the styles of both regions.

Ribadeo's wealth originates from the Spanish American colonies. Entrepreneur Raimundo Ibáñez set the scene for the development of Ribadeo by establishing a port that traded linen with the Baltic and cod with North America, and served as a base for shipbuilding and whaling. Among the heritage from this period of glory, the 18th century **Torre de los Moreno** in Plaza de España is being restored. It will become a museum dedicated to the *Indianos*, as the american adventurers were called.

During the 20th century Ribadeo became a mining port where ships were loaded with coal and iron ore from upstream at Vilaoudriz. The remains of the depot and elevated loading platform have been restored and form part of a park with magnificent views of the Ría. If you carry on north, a pleasant walk along a quiet road takes you all the way to **Isla Plancha**, the site of the Lighthouse, pretty and in a very dramatic setting.

Nearby, to the south of the town, Monte de Santa Cruz (186m) is the setting for the **Fiesta de la Santa Cruz** which also includes a celebration of the **Gaita Gallega** (bagpipes). The festival takes place the first Sunday of August and the bagpipe bands set off from Plaza de España.

RÍAS ALTAS

Castropol church

Gaita festival at Ribadeo

The journey up river is a delightful **small boat trip** to **Vegadeo**, set all the way against a rural backdrop with added interest provided by sandbanks and the occasional *casa indiana*.

Across the water from Ribadeo, **Castropol** is a very pretty small town with much character built on a hill with good views in all directions. You can anchor near the sailing club below or attach to the pontoons provided in the summer.

From Ribadeo several day trips are well worth the effort, by taxi, bus or the FEVE train along the coast. **Lugo** is one of the best preserved Galician cities, surrounded by a 2,000 year old Roman wall listed as a World Heritage site.

Mondoñedo is one of the old Galician kingdom cities, a mini Santiago with traditional stone streets, a central square with *soportales* and a historic cathedral. It is worth following the trail of the main Mondoñedo parishes, particularly the old medieval village and church of San Martín de Mondoñedo.

Along the coast to the west, the little harbour of Rinlo is very picturesque and a centre for good fish and shellfish restaurants (getting there by car or train is much easier than by yacht). Further along the spectacular Playa das Catedrais is well worth a journey for the stone arches revealed at low tide and resembling cathedral buttresses.

Castropol

Mondoñedo

Mondoñedo is one of the seven capital cities of the old Kingdom of Galicia. Together with Lugo, Santiago, A Coruña, Ourense, Betanzos and Tui, it still today rotates as the representative of the Kingdom in the traditional offering to Santiago on the 25th of July, a tradition over three hundred years old. Steeped in history, the position of Mondoñedo as capital of a province and seat of a Bishop attracted wealth and power, visible in the many monumental constructions within it.

The town is one of the highlights of any visit to this part of the world, its Cathedral and galleried houses, *soportales* (covered walkways) and stone paved streets among the most traditional of Galician style. Visit the Cathedral, started in the 13th century, and wander along the rúas before setting down at a café in Plaza España to taste Tarta de Modoñedo from the famous 'Rei das Tartas' coffee shop.

The romanesque church of San Martín de Mondoñedo near Foz and the monumental complex of Lourenza form part of the dioceses of Mondoñedo, both magnificent examples of the early Christian architecture of Spain.

Mondoñedo cathedral, murals and main square

Lugo

Lugo is the oldest city in Galicia, founded by the Romans in the year 15BC. The city was one of the key centres of the Roman administration, of strategic importance and location. This led to the construction of a 2.5km wall which remains as the only complete Roman wall still standing, and which has been declared as a World Heritage Site by UNESCO. The upper part of the original 85 towers has disappeared but the tower bases are still part of this impressive construction. The wall is well maintained and can be walked all the way around, accessed through several staircases sited inside the enclosure (see map 5, 8, 10, 12, 15).

Lugo's wealth of historic remains lies both above and below ground. The monuments built in the medieval age stand on top of a treasure trove of Roman streets, city infrastructure, villas and art which is only uncovered rarely, for example when a building has collapsed. Very few such Roman remains can be seen, but you can get a good feel for what lies under modern Lugo at the museum Casa de los Mosaicos Batitales in Rúa Castro (27). 14km away from the city, the murals of Santa Eulalia de Bóveda are an astonishingly well preserved and beautiful late monument, perhaps sacred baths dedicated to water which played such an important part in the beliefs of the Roman culture.

Galician traditional architecture is very much what you see as you walk around. The streets are beautifully appointed and lively, on a par with Santiago or Coruña. Many churches, religious buildings and palaces await your visit together with the cathedral (18). Iglesia de San Pedro houses the Provincial Museum (19). The Plaza (20) is the place to sit and watch life go by, perhaps from one of the park benches or having *café con leche* at one of the cafeterías.

Lugo is a perfect trip from Ribadeo, using a bus that takes you through beautiful scenery to the city in about one hour. It can be done in one day but Lugo is best enjoyed staying at least one night. The tourist office in front of the bus station is very helpful and will provide information as well as find accommodation. Car hire companies (Autos Galicia, Avis, Atesa and others) operate from Lugo.

Lugo's Roman wall

Plaza

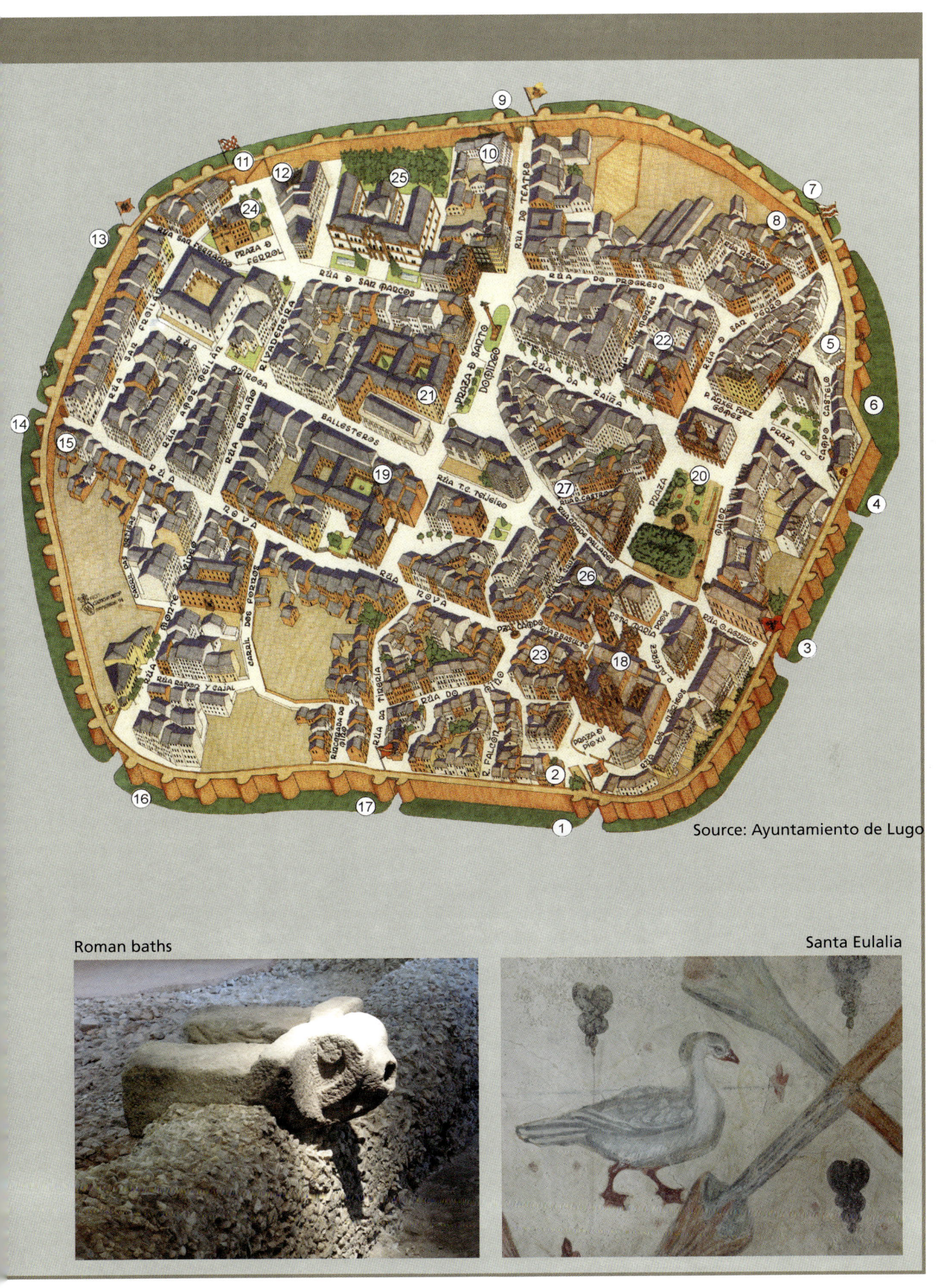

Source: Ayuntamiento de Lugo

Roman baths

Santa Eulalia

RÍAS ALTAS

⚓ From Rinlo to Punta do Castro

Rinlo is a very confined fishing harbour. Do not attempt except in totally calm conditions. Limited berthing alongside quay (0m). FEVE railway station and bus links provide easy access from Ribadeo to this picturesque village with good fish restaurants.

Approach & entrance

There is little detail on charted depths at Rinlo.

Approach from the N heading for Rinlo church. A concrete pier (Q. G.) and white building to the west identifies the entrance. Beware fishing pots on approach.

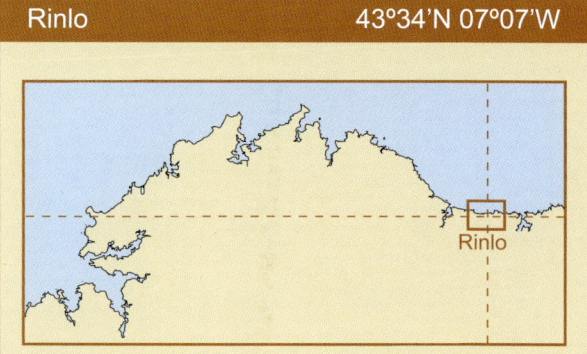

Rinlo   43°34'N 07°07'W

Rinlo

- Very difficult confined entrance, fishing floats on approach
- Do not attempt except at high water in totally calm conditions
- Berthing in fishing harbour (dries at low water), exposed to swell
- Tap on quay
- Anchorages west of Rinlo
- Open to swell, isolated rocks near the shore
- Some protection from east at Cegoñas, from west at Playa San Miguel

Rinlo harbour

Berthing & facilities

Moor alongside pier but do not leave vessel unattended. Minimal protection.

FEVE railway station on S side of village (15min walk).

⚓ Ensenada de Cegoñas

0.5M W of Rinlo is this open bay protected from east.

Approach on a course of a bearing of 190° on radio mast leaving Punta Corveira and offlying rocks 200m to port and submerged reef to starboard.

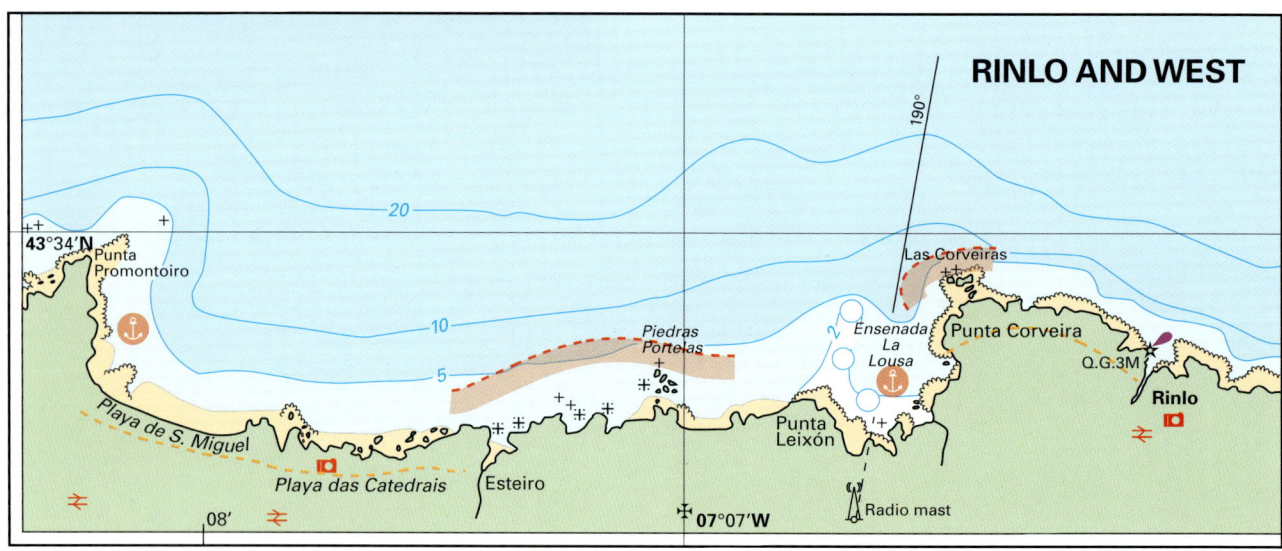

RINLO AND WEST

RÍAS ALTAS

Acceptable shelter may be found close to SE corner in 3-4 m of sand. Anchorage susceptible to swell. Changing wind direction could make it untenable.

⚓ Playa de San Miguel

3M W of Rinlo is Punta Promontoiro which offers protection from the west when anchoring off Playa de San Miguel. Anchor in sand. Anchorage susceptible to swell.

Interest

Rinlo is a picturesque fishing village, known for its selection of fish restaurants. It is probably best to reach it by land (train, bus or taxi from Ribadeo) rather than attempt an entrance from sea. If you are anchored at Ensenada de Cegoñas there is a pleasant 10 minute walk along the shore.

To the west the long stretch of beaches before and after Punta Promontoiro are increasingly popular destinations. The area centred on **Playa das Catedrais** sports a boarded walk which offers very good views of the dramatic rock formations below. Erosion has created spectacular formations which uncover at low tide, at the eastern end, resembling cathedral buttresses, from which the beach has gained its name. The area is still relatively quiet but development of chalets is underway, a new escape for stressed urbanites from Madrid. Visit at low tide for an amazing walk on the beach.

Playa das Catedrais

CRUISING GALICIA   41

RÍAS ALTAS

1 Foz

Small town at the mouth of a shallow river. Should only be attempted in calm conditions in daytime and at high water. Access to FEVE railway. Few sailing boats venture in due to the sandbanks so a yacht is likely to be alone in this harbour.

Foz first basin

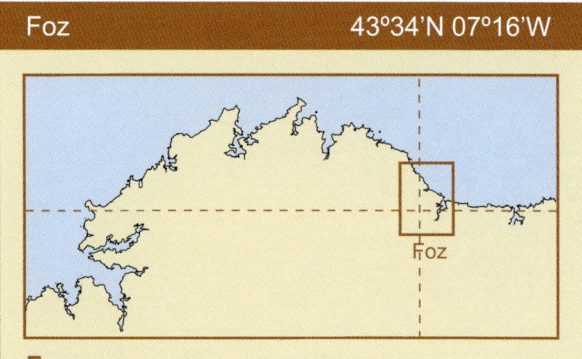

Foz

- Restricted and shallow entrance
- Approach just before high water with little swell
- Berthing alongside quay or other vessels; 2nd basin offers greater depth but less space (fishing boats)
- Water tap on quay
- Fuel only through arrangement with a garage

Approach & entrance

The entrance to Foz needs to be timed so that it is undertaken at high water and in calm conditions, to clear the sand bar (1m 2007, just NE of training wall) at the entrance. Charted spot depths are few and the sand moves, so suitable care should be taken. Swell will make an entrance or exit impractical. The town beyond the beach is prominent.

- Approach running parallel to the training wall Q.G (230°)
- Turn into first basin. Take care with cross tide at the entrance.

Berthing & facilities

Both first and second basin may only be suitable on a neap tide. For the first basin moor alongside the clean harbour wall immediately to port (1m in sand).

The second basin is used by fishing boats. There may be room at the entrance immediately to port beyond the refuelling berth. There are two recessed ladders and measured depth of 1.3m (2007) at the entrance.

Foz is a harbour in decline, the sand banks along the river too costly to maintain dredged and ready for a fishing fleet. The fishing boats have gradually moved to easier and larger ports along the coast.

Foz fishing harbour

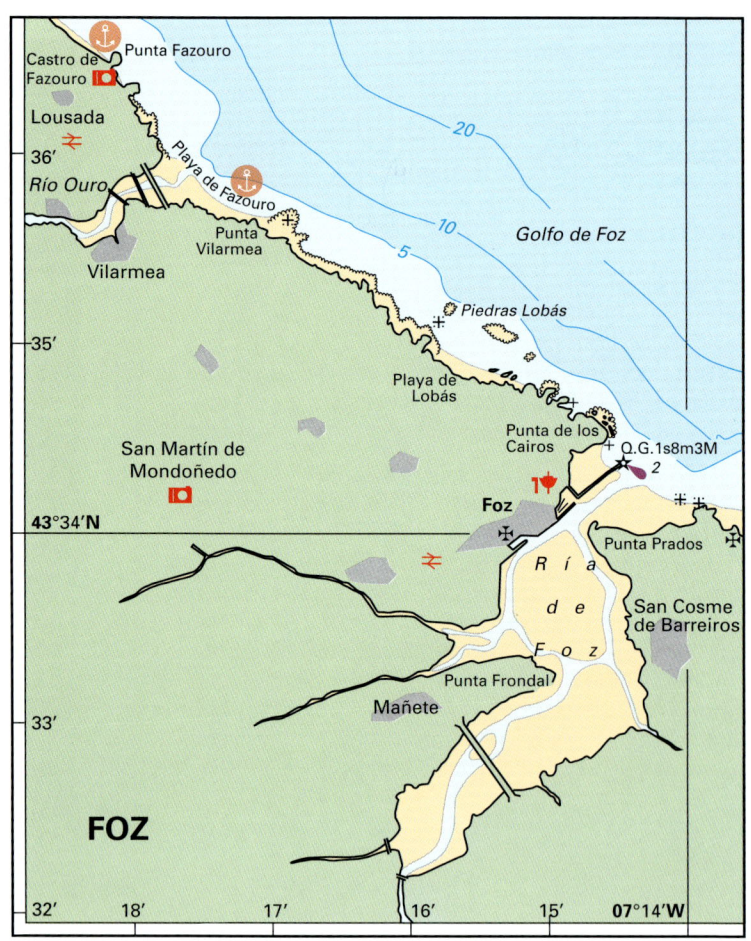

42 CRUISING GALICIA

The first basin on entrance is dedicated to leisure boats, but there are no facilities and no plans to invest the large sums it would require to upgrade and maintain it as a marina for larger yachts, a blessing for local boat owners who pay the lowest fees in Galicia.

⚓ Foz

Anchoring in the river clear of the main channels may be an option for a shoal draft boat. Care should be taken to avoid the strong ebb if possible.

⚓ Río Ouro

2.5M to the W of Foz lies the river of Ouro with a beach and a trained river offering the possibility of an excursion in a dinghy. Little shelter other than from the south.

⚓ Punta de Fazouro

The beach to the west of the Punta may offer an anchorage in calm conditions. This gives access to the Castro located on the headland.

Provisioning & eating

Shops in Foz concentrate along Avda da Mariña just beyond the church up from the harbour. There is a supermarket and a rather good fish market.

Restaurants and bars are located either along Avda da Mariña or along the shore from the first basin towards the beach holiday area.

Castro de Fazouro

Foz

- Lugo 95km, Santiago 165km, Coruña 140km
- ⇌ FEVE train station: south, near exit into town from N-642 road
- 🚌 Bus station: Avda Rúa Mariña
- 🛒 Markets:
  - Fish market and Gadis supermarket at Rúa da Mariña (up the hill from the harbour)
- 🍴 Restaurants:
  - By the first basin, along Rúa da Mariña and at the beach promenade
- ℹ Tourist office: Rúa de Lugo 1, ☎ 982 132426

San Martín de Mondoñedo

Interest

Interest in Foz for the leisure sailor is likely to be the fact that so few other yachts enter the harbour due to the sandbanks, but the town is lively and it has become a bit of a beach resort. The old streets are pretty around the 17th century church and the plaza up the hill. The town Fiesta is the 2nd week of August, a loud and boisterous affair.

8km west of Foz, **Castro de Fazouro** is another example of a pre-roman settlement, built on a prominent headland for good defence and easy access to the resources of the sea. To get there you can either anchor by in calm conditions or use land transport and walk along coastal tracks.

The church of **San Martín de Mondoñedo** (10km inland) on the other side of the N-642 road is an early cathedral from the 11th century built by the first Bishop of Mondoñedo in robust romanesque style. The church has a unique carved stone altar and is one of the major tourist destinations in the area. You will need road transport to reach it.

RÍAS ALTAS

⚓ Burela

Major fishing port which offers an all-weather entrance and shelter in the event of an emergency but has no dedicated facilities for yachts. Access to FEVE railway.

Approach & entrance

Straightforward lit entrance to the harbour in day or night with one well lit isolated danger to the north (Piedra Burela Q(3)10s). The north breakwater Fl(2)RG can be used as the apex for a cone of safety, utilising the following clearing lines:

- Safe approach can be made when Fl(2)RG bears between 200° and 300°. Depth should remain above 10m until within 500m of light. Note the green sector of the light offers no navigational security
- Leave northern breakwater to Stb (Fl(2)RG and Fl(3)G)
- NB: Cabo San Cibrao Fl(5)20s20M lies 5M NW.

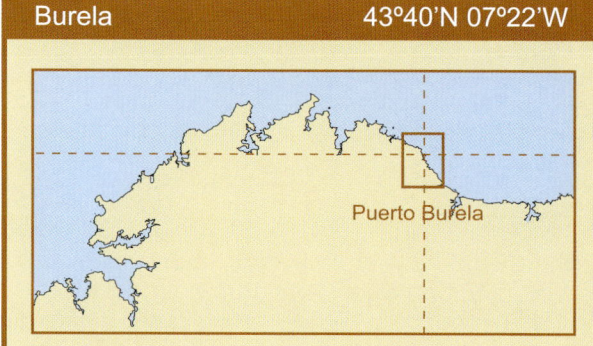

Burela   43°40'N 07°22'W

Puerto Burela
- Straightforward day & night entrance for emergencies only
- VHF 12 Burela Cofradia
- Fuel only if arranged with a garage
- Taps and electricity on quay
- Fishing boat repair facilities
- Dinghy sailing club at the harbour wall

Burela harbour north view

Burela harbour south view

Do not attempt the small harbour north of the main port (shallow and dangers on entrance).

Berthing & facilities

Berthing is alongside but it is very limited as this is a busy commercial fishing harbour. Use either the quay or small boat pontoons in the NE corner in 2m or more. The only option may be to moor against a fishing boat, such as the tuna boat museum.

Space may also be available temporarily in the inner harbour (first basin to port) alongside the quay or in one of the bow/stern-to pontoon moorings.

Burela
- Lugo 100km, Santiago 160km, Coruña 135km
- ⛟ FEVE train station: centre of town near harbour
- 🚌 Bus station: Rúa Leandro Cucurni, north of town
- ✚ Centro de Saúde: Rúa Eijo Garay-Suafonte (between N-642 road and Avda Arcadio Pardiñas, west of harbour) ☎ 982 580585

Tuna museum boat at Burela

Sargadelos pottery

44   CRUISING GALICIA

RÍAS ALTAS

BURELA

There are no facilities for leisure yachts at the harbour. The rescue boat (*salvamento marítimo*) for the area is based at this port.

⚓ Anchorage

Anchoring inside or outside the outer harbour at Puerto Burela is possible close to the SW shore.

Playa Marousa is a very small inlet that may be a possible anchorage in calm conditions only. This is a popular beach in the summer.

Interest

Burela is a busy commercial town centred on its fishing fleet and local shipbuilding company. It is convenient for victualling and any medical emergency. The FEVE railway station is in the centre of the town, very close to the harbour.

The old tuna boat Reina del Carmen has been turned into a museum, where you can learn about *bonito* fishing in this part of the world. Tuna is celebrated the first weekend of August.

The town of Burela celebrates its patrons (San Xoan Bautista and Virxe do Carme) in the first week of June with a series of lively events and a spectacular **flower carpet** laid along the central streets during Saturday. The whole town takes part in the construction of this colourful work of art.

3km north of Burela, at Cervo, the **ceramic factor**y of Sargadelos still produces the distinct blue and white style of this type of

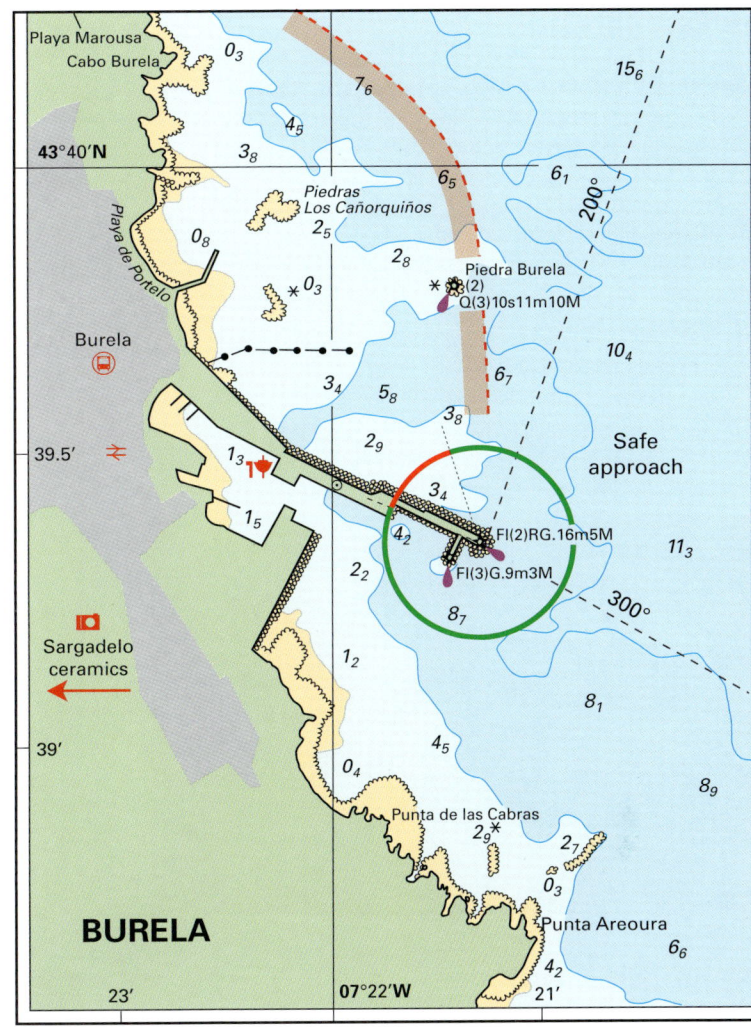

Galicia pottery. The company runs tours of the factory in the summer and the shop is stocked to tempt you.

Burela harbour

CRUISING GALICIA 45

RÍAS ALTAS

1 San Cibrao

The small harbour of San Cibrao (also known as San Ciprián) has a possible berthing spot against the quay with some shelter from swell (fishing boats have moved to more favourable ports). It is difficult at night because of unlit small boat moorings. Los Farallones are two offlying islands with a pretty lunch-time anchorage. The main port used by Alúmina Española is only to be used in an emergency.

The area is dominated by the large aluminium plant, at which most of the inhabitants of San Cibrao and Lieiro work. Despite the large industrial presence, San Cibrao has character and the area is very scenic.

San Cibrao

- Possible day and night entrance, although restricted by moored, unlit, boats
- Alongside berth subject to fishing movements (space likely)
- Harbour does not completely protect from swell
- Taps on quay and breakwater
- Fuel only arranged with a petrol station

San Cibrao harbour

A Maruxaina, the San Cibrao mermaid

Note: Lighthouse on Cabo San Cibrao Fl(5)20s has a 20M range.

Approach & entrance

Possible day and night entrance in settled conditions using sectored light. Entrance congested by moored, unlit, boats which make a night entrance difficult. There are also fishing pots on the approach.

- Approach from a position SE of Los Farallones (unlit) using S cardinal buoy Q(6)+LFl.15s to avoid offlying rocks
- Enter white sector (Dir. Q WR) on a course of 194°-198°
- Turn between Isla Anxuela (Fl.G.3s) and San Cibrao (Fl(2).R.7s) breakwaters. (Note this will put you into the red sector of the Dir. Light). Strong onshore winds and swell will make entrance and berthing difficult.

Berthing & facilities

Berth alongside the inside of the San Cibrao breakwater or quay (in 1.5m). It is very likely that space can be found along the quay as the fishing fleet has moved to larger ports.

Shelter in the harbour was improved through the construction of a wall on top of Isla Axuela at the entrance. A 1-1.5m swell can be dissipated by the defences, allowing a quiet night.

Small boats on long lines to the quay

Fishing harbour quay at San Cibrao

46 CRUISING GALICIA

RÍAS ALTAS

SAN CIBRAO

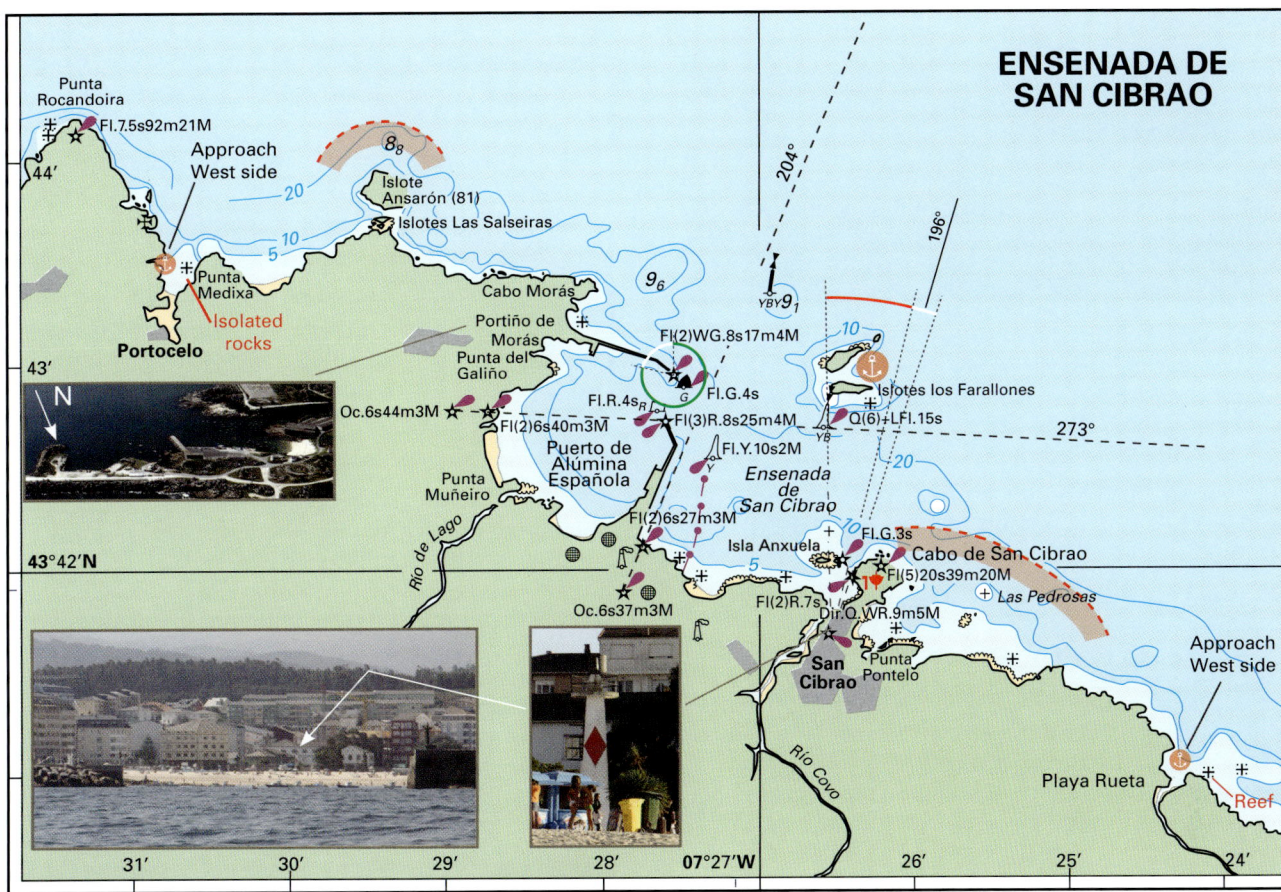

⚓ Playa Rueta

The small cove at Playa Rueta is a possible anchorage in sand for settled conditions. It is a very picturesque setting but exposed to swell. Submerged reef to the east of the small bay. Little detail available on charted depths.

- Approach closer to Puenta Rueta (to the W) than to Punta Castro (to the E) on a course of 195°
- Beware reef extending NE from Punta Castro.

⚓ Los Farallones

Space to the east between the pair of offlying island offers a settled weather anchorage in 1-2m (sand).

⚓ Puerto Alúmina Española

Emergency only at Portiño de Morás in the NE corner. This is a major commercial port for aluminium works which offers an all-weather entrance and shelter in the event of an emergency but has no dedicated facilities for yachts.

Straightforward entrance with leading lights with Los Farallones to E lit by cardinal on S side. Berthing alongside is limited to a fishing quay, or anchor off. Breakwaters obscure possible shipping movements. Pilot boats operate out of port.

Note: Cabo San Cibrao Fl(5)20s20M lies 1M east of Puerto Alúmina.

CRUISING GALICIA 47

RÍAS ALTAS

Portocelo

- Approach from the N of Los Farallones islands using transit lights (204°) Oc.6s (rear) and Fl(2)6s (front) located to the W of the entrance, if necessary. Note S cardinal Q(6)+LFl.15s marking Los Farallones 0.75M from entrance
- Steer between N Fl.WG 8s and S Fl(3)R.8s breakwaters
- Make for the NE corner of harbour (Portiño).

⚓ Playa de Portocelo

Very pretty mouth of a river with a beach offering some shelter from all directions except the north. Has shallows extending from shore on both sides on way in and offlying rocks on east side in small bay. Anchor in sand in 2-4m outside the small harbour.

- Approach from the north taking care of shallows extending from W shore just N of Isla de Cal and from E shore NW of Punta Medixa
- Proceed to a position clear of the isolated rocks (which cover at high water) and before the weed is reached in the narrow neck of the entrance to the inner harbour
- The entrance to the quay is very confined with steep sides. Limited depth information. It may be possible to lie alongside the outer side of the quay in 1.5m. Fishing boats use this quay.

Interest

San Cibrao is a small town which has kept a traditional feel with typical Galician houses in the small old centre. Ría de Lieiro, enclosed by the isthmus to Cabo de San Cibrao and the Anxuela island, provides a pretty beach setting to the village.

The local mermaid, A Maruxaina, is reputedly always ready to alert fishermen about bad weather. A statue stands at the beach promenade and she is celebrated during the very loud Fiesta the second weekend in August. Bands parade late into the night through the streets and ample quantity of *queimada* (alcohol 'brulée' to put it one way) is drunk.

The interesting **Museo do Mar** is located in an old building on the main street towards the harbour. It hosts a large collection of maritime objects, well arranged and interesting, including details about whaling which used to be a local industry. The old photographs in several extensive arrangements on the walls are a fascinating record of past fishing, industrial and local culture.

> **San Cibrao**
> - Lugo 100km, Santiago 160km, Coruña 135km
> - 🛒 Supermarket opposite mermaid statue, promenade by main beach of ría
> - 🚂 FEVE train station: 5 minutes from harbour, on the edge of the village
> - ✚ Chemist at beach promenade
> - ✚ Centro de Saúde San Cibrao, Avda da Mariña, Cervo ☎ 982 594519
>   Nearest major hospital Burela

San Cibrao old town centre

Museo del Mar

Turgalicia

Aluminium at San Cibrao

If you sail in this area you will not miss the sight of the plant of Alúmina Española, one of the large Spanish aluminium production plants owned by multinational Alcoa. It is not the prettiest sight but it is the employer of the majority of the local population and you may be interested in understanding what goes on underneath the towers.

Aluminium is the most abundant metal on the Earth's crust, always forming part of innumerable compounds but never found in pure form. It is a light metal of multiple application, used increasing on a mass basis from the end of 19th century when industrial processes were developed. Your boat is likely to have many structural components made of aluminium, taking advantage of its light weight.

One of the common ores used is an earth rich in aluminium oxide, first discovered in the town of Baux (France), know as bauxite. The bauxite mines with the richest ores are in the Caribbean, Australia and Africa. Aluminium is obtained through a double process. In the first place, bauxite is ground and mixed with chalk and caustic soda, treated at high pressure and temperatures. This first part of the process generates a white powder called 'alumina', which is aluminium oxide of great purity.

In the second part of the process the alumina is converted to pure aluminium through electrolysis. The alumina is dissolved in a bath of cryolite (aluminium, sodium and fluoride compound) fused at a temperature of more than 1000°C. This process is conducted in containers coated with carbon. As electric current passes through the electrodes the aluminium deposits in the cathode,

from where it is extracted continuously until the alumina is exhausted.

The factory at San Cibrao performs both processes. Bauxite arrives in large cargo boats from the producing countries. The aluminium obtained is shipped in ingots for subsequent processing by other businesses.

RÍAS ALTAS

⚓ Ría de Viveiro

Major fishing port to seaward with a separate marina harbour very close to the town centre. Viveiro mixes a busy commercial feel with the charm of an old medieval town.

Viveiro marina

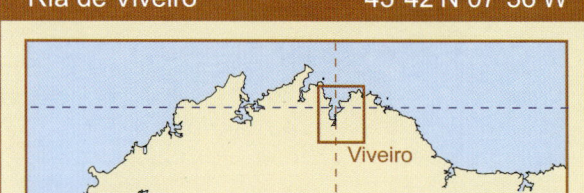

Porto Deportivo de Viveiro
- Straightforward day and night entrance, can be affected by swell
- Good shelter in marina
- Hard standing for dry over-wintering
- Visitors' berths 11, up to 18m length (often full as boats return from day cruises)
- Berthing: pontoon mooring
- Depth minimum 3m inside marina
- Possible spaces at the wall
- ☏ Office 982 570610 Fax 982 561014 (Casino building)
- ☏ Marinero 657 152214 (hut north end)
- VHF Channel 09
- viveiro@hotmail.com
- ⛽ Fuel by arrangement
- 🔧 Repairs: contact marina for mechanics, electricians, divers and other specialists
- ⛴ 32-ton travel lift

- Showers in Casino building
- Dinghy Sailing and Diving Club

Anchorages
- Numerous in the Ría, shelter from W S E winds but exposed to sea swell

Approach & entrance

Straightforward lit entrance with no isolated dangers. Depth should be watched and shallows avoided (indicated on chartlet) in the presence of significant swell. Cross tide on the ebb should be watched when entering or leaving the marina. Breakwaters obscure possible vessel movements. Note Punta Estaca de Bares Fl(2)7.5s.25M is 8M to the north east of the entrance and Punta Roncadoira Fl.7.5s.21M is 5M to the northwest.

- Punta del Faro Fl.R.5s can be used as the apex for a cone of safety with clearing line of more than 155° from the west and less than 200° from the east
- Once visible, alter course onto 195° for the Celeiro breakwater Fl(2)R.7s
- Turn for Fl(2)G.7s on end of west training wall if heading for the marina (or turn into fishing harbour at Celeiro)
- Proceed up to marina (3m dredged) entrance marked by Fl(3)G.9s.

Berthing & facilities

Follow directions from *marinero* or berth at one of the pontoon hammerheads and walk to office (Casino building behind fence) or hut. The marina is very spacious for manoeuvres. There are 11 visitor spaces at the entrance but beware these can be full as boats return from their day's cruising in the Ría. Viveiro is the only marina between Ribadeo and Coruña so it is popular despite its less than perfect facilities.

Diesel and petrol available by arrangement.

Viveiro marina entrance

RÍAS ALTAS

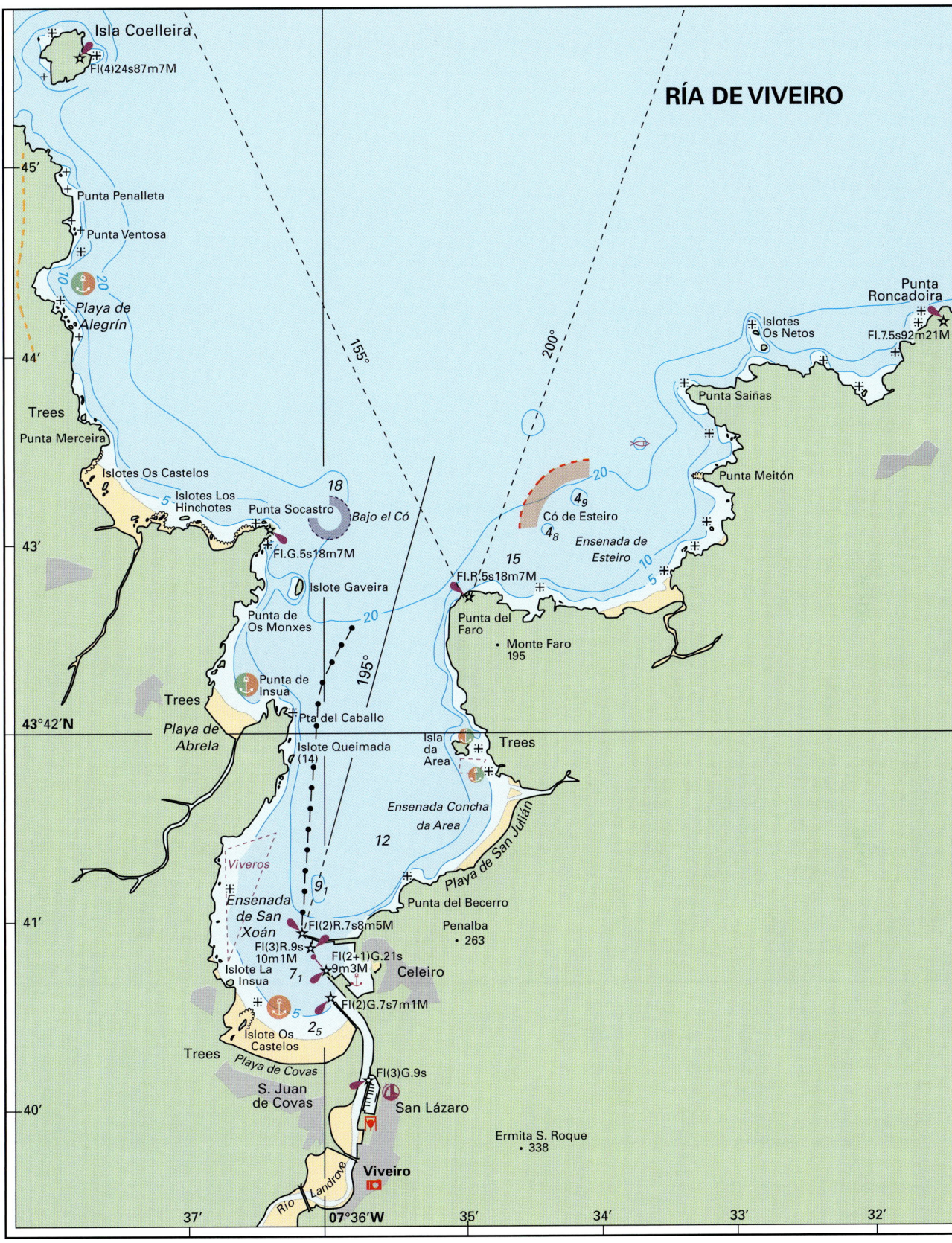

⚓ Anchorages

There are numerous anchorages in the Ría, most opposite sandy beaches. There is shelter from southerly winds but they are exposed to the ocean swell so they are best used in calm conditions. The most attractive are as follows:

- **Between I. de Area and shore,** east of Ría in 2m sand. Anchor either NE or SE of the island. Note fish farm as indicated was not present in 2007 but bottom may be foul

- **Celeiro fishing harbour,** near the small boat pontoons in 3m mud. Emergency use only as this is as very busy harbour

CRUISING GALICIA

RÍAS ALTAS

Viveiro

- Lugo 110km, Santiago 160km, Coruña 120km
- Bus Station: Avda Galicia northern end of old town, next to hypermarket, frequent services to Lugo, Coruña, Santiago and local
- FEVE train station: east side of old town, 5 minutes from marina
- Car hire: Autos Galicia at the Bus Station
- Ferries to Vigo and Islas Cíes (in the summer) from the northern side of the harbour.
- Markets:
  - *Mercado de abastos* (market) at the corner of Avda Galicia and Avda Cervantes
  - Supermarket Haley between marina and old tow at start of Rúa Ramón Canosa
- Restaurants:
  - Bars and restaurants in the old town around Plaza Mayor, A Praciña and the main street parallel to Avda Galicia
- Tourist office: Rúa Ramón Canosa, 982 560879
- Chandlers:
  - Efectos Navales de Celeiro (at Celeiro fishing harbour), serving the fishing boats but likely to have some parts for yachts 982 551 783
  - Ferretería Luis (ironmongers & general), Plaza de Lugo
- Banks, chemists and shops along Avda Galicia and streets parallel in the old town
- Centro Saúde Viveiro, Rúa Ramón Canosa (opposite marina), 982 561201

- **Playa de Covas**, to the west of Celeiro fishing 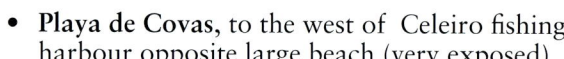 harbour opposite large beach (very exposed)
- **Playa de Abrela**, NW area of the Ría, some shelter from W, otherwise very exposed
- **Playa de Alegrín**, further NW from Playa de Abrela, good shelter from W but open to swell.

Provisioning & eating

Viveiro has a good *mercado* where you can buy fresh fruit, vegetables, fish and meat, located between Avda Galicia and the old town. Further towards the marina at Avda Galicia, the Haley supermarket is large and well stocked.

Restaurants and bars serving food are located in the old town, in the streets around Plaza Mayor. Viveiro does not have the bustle of either Santiago or Coruña but the atmosphere is good and the *tapas* and *pinchos* excellent.

Transport

Viveiro is well linked by bus to all major destinations in Galicia. The bus station is between the bridge and the marina, next to the supermarket.

The FEVE train station is very close to the old town. A delightful narrow gauge train runs between Oviedo and Ferrol all along the coast. Services are infrequent, see introduction to Rías Altas for further information.

Interest

Ría de Viveiro has some of the best landscapes along this part of the coast. You can enjoy it best of course from a well picked quiet anchorage, but it is not difficult to get to the wilderness. One of the best walks in the vicinity takes you to the **Punta Sucastro** ría entrance green beacon through an eucalyptus and pine forest track.

The streets of the **old town** are traditionally Galician, cobbled with large granite slabs and the houses decked with white galleried balconies. Around the centre three of the **medieval gates** still stand, all fitted with a small sanctuary within the inner arch. The best is opposite the bridge down from Plaza Mayor.

Surrounding the old centre a large modern town has grown as fishing and industrial activity has expanded. The town gets full at weekends as one of the major tourist destinations of the northern coast. Parking is limited and controlled by meters that you don't see elsewhere in Rías Altas.

The church/convent of San Francisco (Avda Cervantes) and the church of Santa María, with the convent behind, are imposing monuments and they are part of the **Easter Processions,** which are among the best in Galicia.

Fiesta del Carmen is one of the town's big events, on the second weekend of August (which can feel very noisy at the marina itself). The patron celebrations between 14 and 18 August (Virgin and San Roque) include an interesting International Folklore Festival and a craft fair.

Nearby, *A Rapa das Bestas de Candaoso* (Santo André de Boimente) is one of the best of these **wild horse** events traditional of Galicia. It takes place the first Sunday of July.

Rapa das Bestas

Mercado

Praciña

Plaza Mayor

West gate

RÍAS ALTAS

⚓ Ría do Barqueiro

Broad Ría with clean lit approach. It is possible to lie alongside the quays of Vicedo and Barqueiro harbours but they are not dedicated to yachts. There are numerous beach anchorages (exposed to NE) in pretty surrounds. Estaca de Bares is the most significant headland of the Rías Altas coast line and Isla Coelleira is also prominent.

Approach

Approach in the white sector of Punta de la Barra light Fl.WRG.3s.

Beware various unlit fishing farms in the ría.

Initial shelter

Vicedo is the simplest option in bad weather although the harbour is occupied by fishing boats and a clam research centre. The area to the south of the harbour is sheltered from the N but is obstructed with moorings. An alternative, if needing temporary shelter from the N to make preparations for mooring, would be off the beach at Puerto de Bares on on the west side of the ría, although again there are small craft moorings.

⚓ Vicedo

Straightforward lit approach but in less than 4m so should not be attempted in significant swell. Breakwaters obscure possible vessel movements.

- Turn out of the white sector of Punta de La Barra light (Fl.WRG.3s) once the port Fl(4)R.11s and starboard Fl(4)G.11s lights on the breakwater have separated
- Once inside turn to starboard, there is room to manoeuvre
- Moor alongside west or south walls in 1.9m amongst fishing boats if there is space.

There is a water tap on the quay.

⚓ Barqueiro

Restricted, shallow (1m), unlit, approach along river channel with strong tidal current making timing and sympathetic weather important. Berth alongside quay outside. Very little manoeuvring room inside.

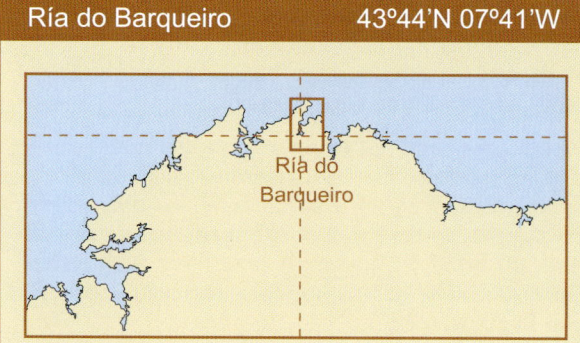

Ría do Barqueiro   43°44'N 07°41'W

Vicedo
- Straightforward day and night entrance; beware fish farms
- Good shelter alongside quay
- Entrance made difficult or impossible in strong onshore winds and swell
- Water tap
- Crane, Slip

- Pass close to Punta de la Barra light (Fl. WRG.3s) at HW -0100. Channel is steep to on W side (1m) which should be followed closely. Breakwater marked by mast and crane on S breakwater

Barqueiro harbour

- Cross tide on the ebb should be watched when entering or leaving the harbour. Breakwater obscures possible vessel movements
- Moor alongside N outer quay in 1.7m or on the west side of the south arm in 1.2m. Many small craft moorings.

⚓ Anchorages

Several anchorages in very pleasant surroundings but exposed to swell. Plans should be made in advance for a possible retreat if conditions change.

- Playa de Xilloi: open to the north. Anchor on gradually shoaling bottom (sand)

Vicedo harbour

RÍAS ALTAS

RÍA DO BARQUEIRO

- South of Vicedo: clear of moorings in extensive shoal area (1-2m), sand
- North of Vicedo: 2-3m sand, 2 bays either side of lighthouse. Beaches with tree-lined shores
- Playa Castro Vilela: in the SW corner clear of fish farms (none present 2007)
- Bares: anchor clear of moorings. There may be space between the buoys and the mole. A tripping line is recommended.

CRUISING GALICIA

RÍAS ALTAS

Playa de Xilloi

Barqueiro harbour outer quay

Provisioning & eating

The village of Vicedo has a number of bars and local shops. There is a tourist information point that opens in July and August.

Barqueiro is a picturesque destination, with bars serving food by the harbour.

Bares is very small but it has a restaurant by the harbour. There is water from a tap at the quay and there are a couple of shops.

The whole of Estaca de Bares is a natural park, remote and wild. Down at the water the beach of Bares is very pretty, enclosed by dunes and pine woods.

Transport

There are FEVE train stations at both Vicedo and Barqueiro.

Interest

Río Sor which feeds into Ría do Barqueiro is picturesque, hemmed between sandbanks and forested shores. If conditions are calm it is a rewarding small boat trip.

Barqueiro is a small fishing harbour placed at a bend of the river and backing onto the hills of Estaca de Bares. It is a pretty destination which receives tourists.

Fish farm in Ría do Barqueiro

Ría do Barqueiro

RÍAS ALTAS

Cocido

Galicia has hearty food in the interior, from the areas where fish is not the main staple. Lugo is a good place for *cocido*. Further south Lalín in Pontevedra celebrates this dish during Carnival.

The basic ingredient is meat, accompanied by pulses and greens. Choose your own mix or follow the list below.

Ingredients

1 piece of panceta (thick fatty pork meat)
1kg *lacón* (thick bacon), soaked overnight in water to remove the salt
0.5kg pork chops
0.5kg beef
4 chorizos
0.5kg chick peas, cooked separately or from a tin
One large bunch/bag of *grelos* (turnip tops); use greens if *grelos* are not available
8 large potatoes
Olive oil

Preparation

Place the meat except the chorizos in a large pan of boiling water. Cook at a slow heat for 1½ hours. Remove the meat. The liquid can then be used to make soup independently.

Use some of the liquid from the stew to cook the potatoes, *grelos* and chorizos, for around 15 minutes until the potatoes are soft.

Drain the meats and vegetables, add the chick peas and serve hot. Drizzle with olive oil at the last moment.

RÍAS ALTAS

⚓ Ensenada de Santa Marta

Wide bay with limited lit approach. Two isolated unlit dangers along the E shore (Piedras Meas, 0.7M off Punta da Bandexa and Piedras Lixeiras off Espasante). Three harbours and numerous beach anchorages (the latter generally exposed to north). The scenery on the way to Ortigueira is stunning, a good reward for crossing the sand bar.

Approach

From the east, ensure that a wide (1M) berth is kept off the E coast to miss Piedras Meas (0.7M off Punta da Bandexa) and shallows to the south. A bearing of less than 240° Cariño breakwater Fl(3)G.9s achieves this.

From the west and north the shore is clear and steep to, apart from Islas Marbeiras (unlit), 0.1M off the shore and 0.5M SE of Cabo Ortegal (Oc.8s18M).

Note: the west cardinal off Espasante shown on charts has been removed (2007). There is now a Norh cardinal at 43°43'.4N 07°50'.0W.

Initial shelter

Cariño is the simplest option in bad weather and the most protected (apart from the E and SE). There is enough room inside the breakwater to drop sails and organise an approach to a berth or anchor.

⚓ Ortigueira

Situated in an important wildlife area, the tricky approach and shallow bar to this historic town is worth tackling.

Approach & entrance

Tricky approach in daylight only with due caution taken of significant swell and strong onshore winds. Initial approach should be made not earlier than HW-0200. The first part of the channel is unbuoyed because of the shifting channel, making charts redundant and continuous monitoring of depth paramount.

- From a position north of the west end of Isla de San Vicente head due south leaving the island close (50m) to port
- Continue south until the depth shoals towards the beach
- Turn and head for Punta Postiña
- From Punta Postiña head directly for Punta Sismundi
- Follow shoreline around towards to Punta Redonda
- Follow the buoyed channel
- The quay is identified by its crane. The marina is beyond, marked by lit beacons (Fl.(4)R.11s and Fl (4)G.11s).

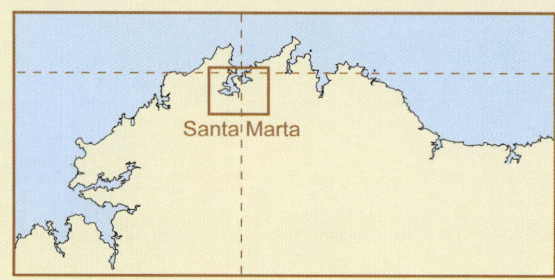

Ensenada de Santa Marta 43°44'N 07°51'W

Club Náutico de Ortigueira
- Tricky approach in daylight and only possible without significant swell or strong onshore winds
- Timing (HW-0200) important
- Shelter in marina from all directions
- Visitors berths: limited
- Berthing: pontoon mooring
- Depth: 1.3m at quay, 0.3m inside marina
- ☎ / Fax 981 422482 mobile 630 183901 mobile Marinero 629 840276
- VHF Channel 09
- ⛽ Fuel by arrangement (lorry delivers)
- 🔧 Repairs: contact marina for mechanics, electricians, divers and other specialists

Cariño
- Straightforward day and night entrance
- Shelter from all directions except S and SE
- Entrance made difficult in strong onshore winds and swell
- Berth alongside pontoon (2.5m deep end) behind small boat moorings or anchor off
- Pontoon might be extended 2008/09

Espasante
- Straightforward day and night entrance
- Shelter from all directions except W and NE
- Anchor clear of small boat moorings

Ortigueira

RÍAS ALTAS

Berthing & facilities

Moor alongside at the seaward end of the quay in 1.3m or continue to the marina (0.3m soft mud).

Water and electricity on pontoons. Fuel delivered by tanker, arranged through the marina. Very modern shore facilities, with a good shower and a restaurant. Sailing club at SE corner of marina.

Provisioning & eating

Ortigueira has good bars and restaurants in the streets next to the marina and promenade area. The main shops and two supermarkets are in the main road, up the hill from the harbour area.

⚓ Anchorages

- Punta Sismundi, Punta Redonda. In channel in 6-7m (sand and mud). Note very strong tide (up to 5knots) on ebb. Avoid small craft moorings.

- River channel west of Ortigueira in 3m. No wind shelter.

CRUISING GALICIA

RÍAS ALTAS

⚓ Espasante

Anchorage sheltered from the east with access to a beach. Lit night approach possible.

- From the centre of the bay pass west and south of the N cardinal Q.Fl. if it is present, or:
- From the 240° line to Cariño head south along longitude 07°50'W until the Espasante breakwater Fl.R.5s is due east
- Anchor south of the two arms of the breakwaters (Fl.R.5s and Fl.G.5s) in 2- 5m, sand clear of boats on buoys.

Note: 1.5m alongside west breakwater. No facilities ashore.

Espasante

⚓ Cariño

Fishing and commercial port sheltered from all directions except the W and SW. Straightforward, unlit, approach. Entry dependent upon swell. Berth either alongside pontoon (2.5m) beyond mooring buoys or anchor off.

Approach & entrance

Straightforward approach but due caution should be taken in significant swell. Breakwaters obscure possible vessel movements.

- From the centre of the Bay make directly for the end of the breakwater Fl(3)G.9s once it is visible.
- The pontoon is inside numerous small craft moorings so should not be attempted in adverse conditions of visibility.

Berthing & facilities

Moor alongside seaward side of the pontoon in 2.5m. This shoals towards either end. There is discussion about an extension to this pontoon. Anchorage towards the beach in sand offers good shelter from N and W winds.

Provisioning & eating

Cariño has a number of shops and bars towards the centre by the church and along Avda Constitución, and it is the larger of the towns in the bay.

Ensenada de Santa Marta

- Lugo 120km, Santiago 160km, Coruña 135km

Cariño:
- Shops and supermarket in Rúa de la Constitución (parallel to Paseo Marítimo)
- Bus station
- Mechanic workshop at south end of Avda Constitución (fishing harbour can arrange)
- Centro Saúde Cariño, Paseo Marítimo (opposite beach) ☎ 981 420410

Ortigueira:
- Shops and two supermarkets (Gadis) in main road, up the hill from harbour area
- Bus station next to FEVE station, main road
- FEVE train station: main road 10 minute walk from harbour area
- Centro Saúde Ortigueira, Rúa Mourón ☎ 981401051 - 981401076

Espasante:
- Limited shops
- FEVE train station 15 minute walk from harbour and at Ortigueira

Cariño

RÍAS ALTAS

Ortigueira

Interest

The bay into which Río Mera drains is one of the prettiest natural environments in Galicia, hardly developed and set off by wooded hillsides and sandbanks. It is not the easiest to reach by boat but the effort to get there is amply rewarded.

Ortigueira is a small town that is well maintained with a pretty centre. In the early part of July the international *Festival Celta de Ortigueira* welcomes 40,000 visitors from the Atlantic facing regions of Europe including Ireland, Cornwall, Wales, Scotland, Brittany, Asturias and Galicia. The festival celebrates the Celtic connection and bagpipes are in abundance.

The scenery around Ortigueira is stunning and can be explored through small boat trips to the many spots along the channel banks. By foot there is a well marked path along the shore north of the town, very well maintained and with good views.

From Cabo Ortegal to the west 10 miles of breathtaking **cliffs** line the coast. The highest, Vixia de Herberia, is 600m high. At the top it is very common to come across the wild horses that live there. To visit this area you need a car.

Nestled below the cliffs the monastery of **San Andrés de Teixido** is a major tourist and pilgrim destination. It is said that if you do not visit the pretty church here while alive you will be turned into a lizard living in the vicinity when dead. Whether motivated by belief in the legend or by the challenge, it is just about possible on a calm day to anchor below the gigantic cliffs between Rabaliceira to the east and San Andrés de Teixido to the west and visit the monastery. A walk starts by the pebble beach east of Islas Gabeiras, a good 6km with steep ascent and descent.

Ría de Ortigueira

ENSENADA DE SANTA MARTA

CRUISING GALICIA

⚓ Ría de Cedeira

Fishing harbour inside wide bay with lit approach. One isolated lit danger in centre of the bay (Piedras de Media Mar Fl.(2)5s). Cedeira is a very pretty town in a small Ría that contrasts with the dramatic cliffs to the north and the exposed coast to the south before Coruña.

Approach & entrance

Straightforward lit approach with isolated dangers. Note nearest lighthouse, 3M to the northeast of the entrance, is Punta Candelaria Fl(3+1)24s21M,

- Off lying rocks on west headland (Punta Chirlatera, 43°40'N 08°05'.6W, unlit) extend 0.7M to the NW. At night the white sector of the light on Punta del Sarridal (Oc.WR.6s) clears these, but can bring you close to the east shore (isolated rocks off Punta Folgoso and Punta do Carreiro). Stay on a bearing of 155° to Punta del Sarridal to avoid this

- Pass close (100m but not less than 10m depth) to Punta del Sarridal (Oc.WR.6s), passing into its Red sector on a course of 180° leaving Piedras de Media Mar Fl(2) well to starboard

- Stay in more than 10m depth until Punta Promontorio light is visible and bears less than 140°

- Aim for Punta Promontorio Oc.(4)10s until Port hand light on breakwater Fl(2)R.7s abeam. (Note isolated danger, Pedras de Media Mar Fl(2)5s left to starboard)

- Head for breakwater, giving suitable room for possible vessel movements.

Cedeira

- Straightforward day and night entrance with one isolated danger (Piedras De Media Mar Fl(2)5s)
- Shelter from all directions but subject to swell
- Anchor off old quay beyond fishing harbour, stay clear of small boat moorings
- Old quay (between breakwater and town):
  - Possible to lie alongside
  - Ten minute walk to town for provisions
  - 100-ton travel lift
  - 🔧 Mechanic workshop
  - Sailing and diving club
  - Red Cross (water tap & weather)

- Plans for large marina at the old quay, construction 2007/08

Berthing & facilities

Anchor in 2-4 m (sand, weed) clear of the moorings between the end of the outer fishing harbour quay and the old quay by the sailing club and the fuel pump (Gasóleo B only).

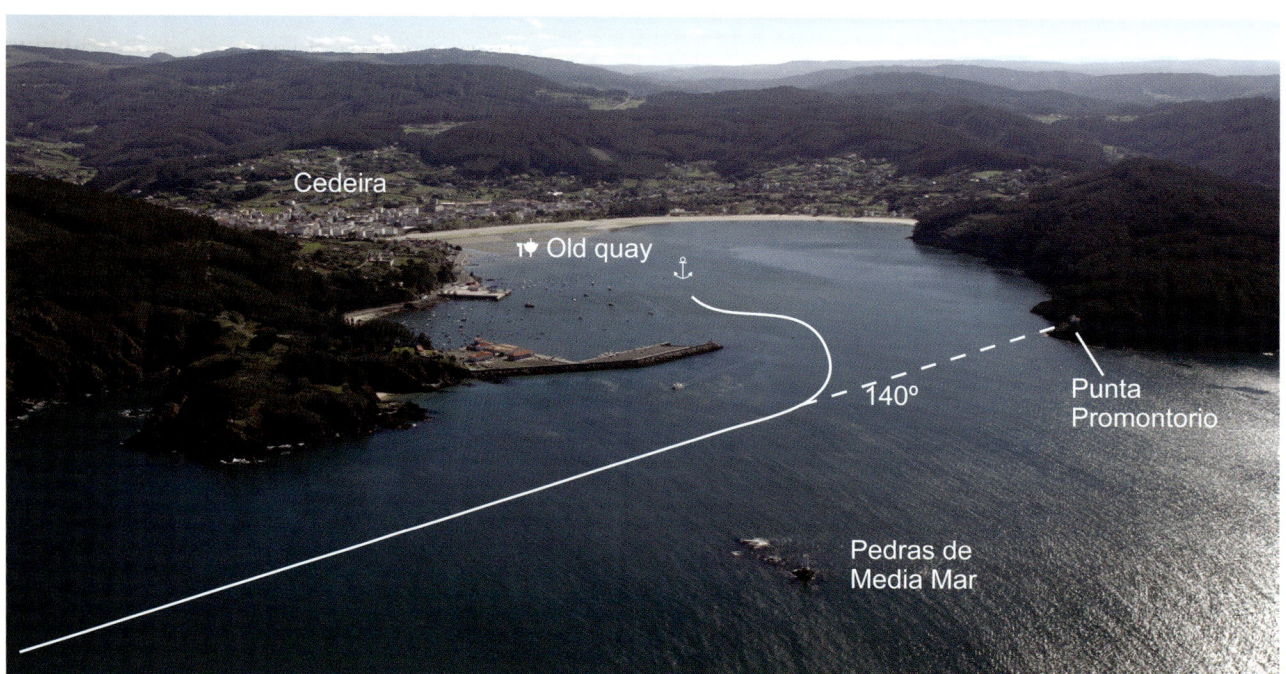

RÍAS ALTAS

It is possible to land alongside the old quay, the spot used by fishing boats for re-fuelling. Depth is 1.5-2m.

The old quay is a convenient dinghy landing spot for trips into town. At the quay, the Red Cross post shows weather information and provides a water tap. A sailing and diving club is next to it. Behind, Talleres García Otero is a workshop that can deal with engine issues and repairs.

There may be space in the fishing harbour but, while not large, this is a busy port with modern facilities built by Portos de Galicia (2005). A fleet of offshore boats operates in the North Sea and Ireland, and smaller coastal trawlers are also based at Cedeira.

⚓ Playa de Vilarrube

This is a very pretty location for a quiet anchorage in sand opposite the gradually shelving beach. It is exposed to north winds and swell.

Provisioning & eating

Shops, supermarkets and an extensive selection of bars and restaurants are 0.5M from the old quay.

The bars opposite the promenade on the way from the harbour into town are frequented by the fishermen, often engrossed in lively domino matches.

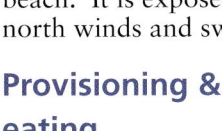

RÍA DE CEDEIRA

Playa de Villarrube

Cedeira bay and old quay

CRUISING GALICIA 63

RÍAS ALTAS

Cedeira

- Santiago 120km, Coruña 60km, Ferrol 30km
- Bus stop Avda de Castelao
- Markets:
  - Plaza del Mercado (old town) occasional market, good small shops nearby
- Supermarkets:
  - Gadis. Avda de Castelao 3
  - Eroski, Avda de Castelao
- Tourist Information at Plaza Roja
  981 482187

- Ferretería:
  - O Triqui, at the central roundabout
- Mechanic workshop at the Old Quay: Talleres García Otero.
- Banks, chemist at the central roundabout, Avda de Castelao and Avenida dos Suevos
- Centro Saúde Cedeira, Avda Zumalacárregui 981 480015 / 492120

Plaza 'Roja' is where the majority of bars serving tapas are located. Avda Castelao is the main street for supermarkets, chemists, banks and a good *ferretería*.

Interest

Cedeira is a very pleasant small town, located in one of the smaller Rías Altas. The surrounding area is among the most picturesque in this part of Galicia. Río Condomiñas, which splits the town in two before entering the Ría, passes through a gorgeous valley which is sheltered by wooded sea facing hills. A good area for bike rides.

The **old town** in Cedeira is very well maintained and it attracts summer tourism. Walk the west side of the river channel and visit the old streets near the Santa María do Mar church and the market square.

The second week of August is holiday time in Cedeira, culminating in large, and noisy, celebrations at the weekend.

From the fishing harbour, a short walk up a path takes to the **Fuerte de la Concepción,** a castle built to defend the harbour after an English raid in 1747. It has been restored and houses a small maritime museum.

Fuerte de la Concepción

Market square

Banks of Río Condomiñas

RÍAS ALTAS

Cedeira to Cabo Prior

Open, exposed coastline with some shelter from west at Playa da Frouxeira and north at Playa de San Xurxo.

⚓ Playa da Frouxeira

6M to the west of Cedeira. Clear approach. Anchor off the west end of the beach in 5m to gain shelter from the west. Walks ashore and beach.

Note to the west of Punta lies Cala Portonova which is sheltered from the north and east.

⚓ Playa de San Xurxo

3M south of Cabo Prior. Anchor just south of Punta Blanca (4m sand) to get maximum relief from swell.

Interest

This a wild, pretty area, best explored on land. If conditions are very calm the beaches are a very picturesque setting for a lunch time anchorage.

At Cabo Prior walk out to the disused gun batteries and the lighthouse along wild, open tracks. At Playa da Frouxeira there are tracks and paths among the dunes and towards the lighthouse.

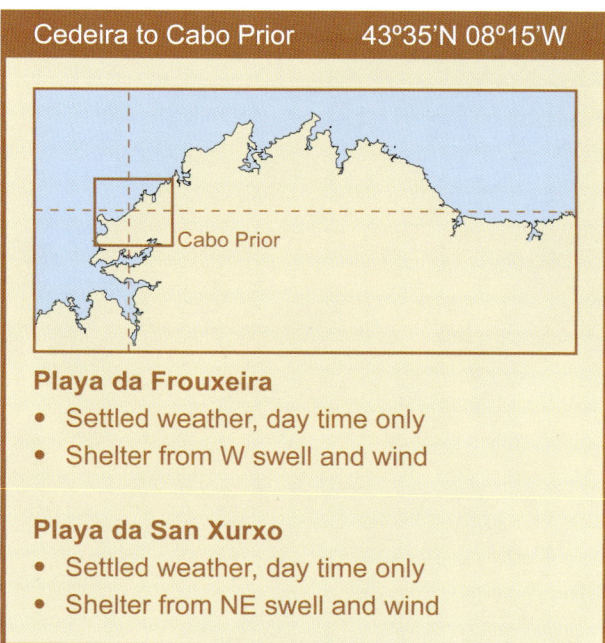

Cedeira to Cabo Prior   43°35'N 08°15'W

Playa da Frouxeira
- Settled weather, day time only
- Shelter from W swell and wind

Playa da San Xurxo
- Settled weather, day time only
- Shelter from NE swell and wind

Playa de San Xurxo from Punta Blanca

66 CRUISING GALICIA

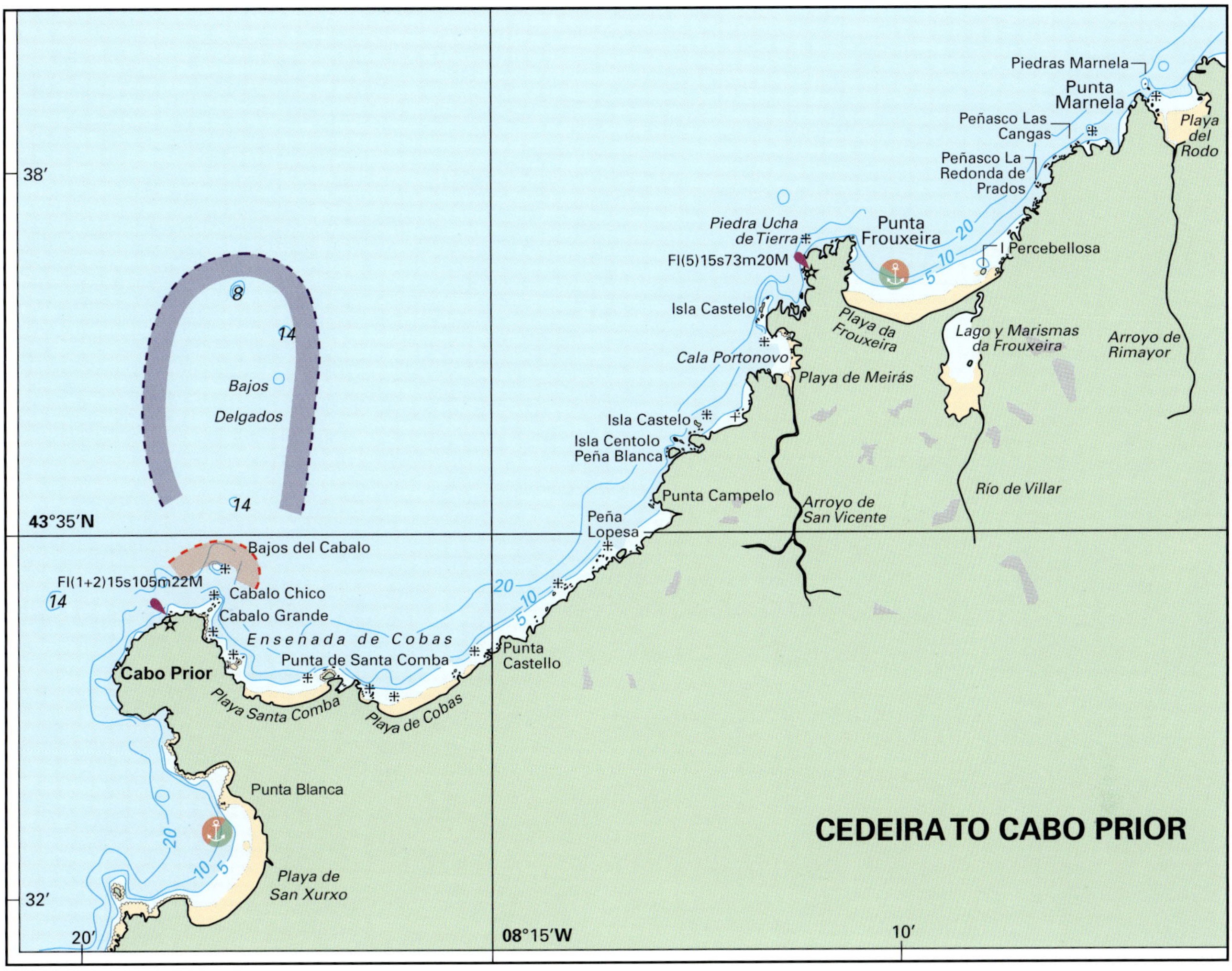

RÍAS ALTAS

CEDEIRA TO CABO PRIOR

Playa de Frouxeira looking northeast

CRUISING GALICIA 67

Golfo Ártabro and Costa da Morte

GOLFO ÁRTABRO / COSTA DA MORTE

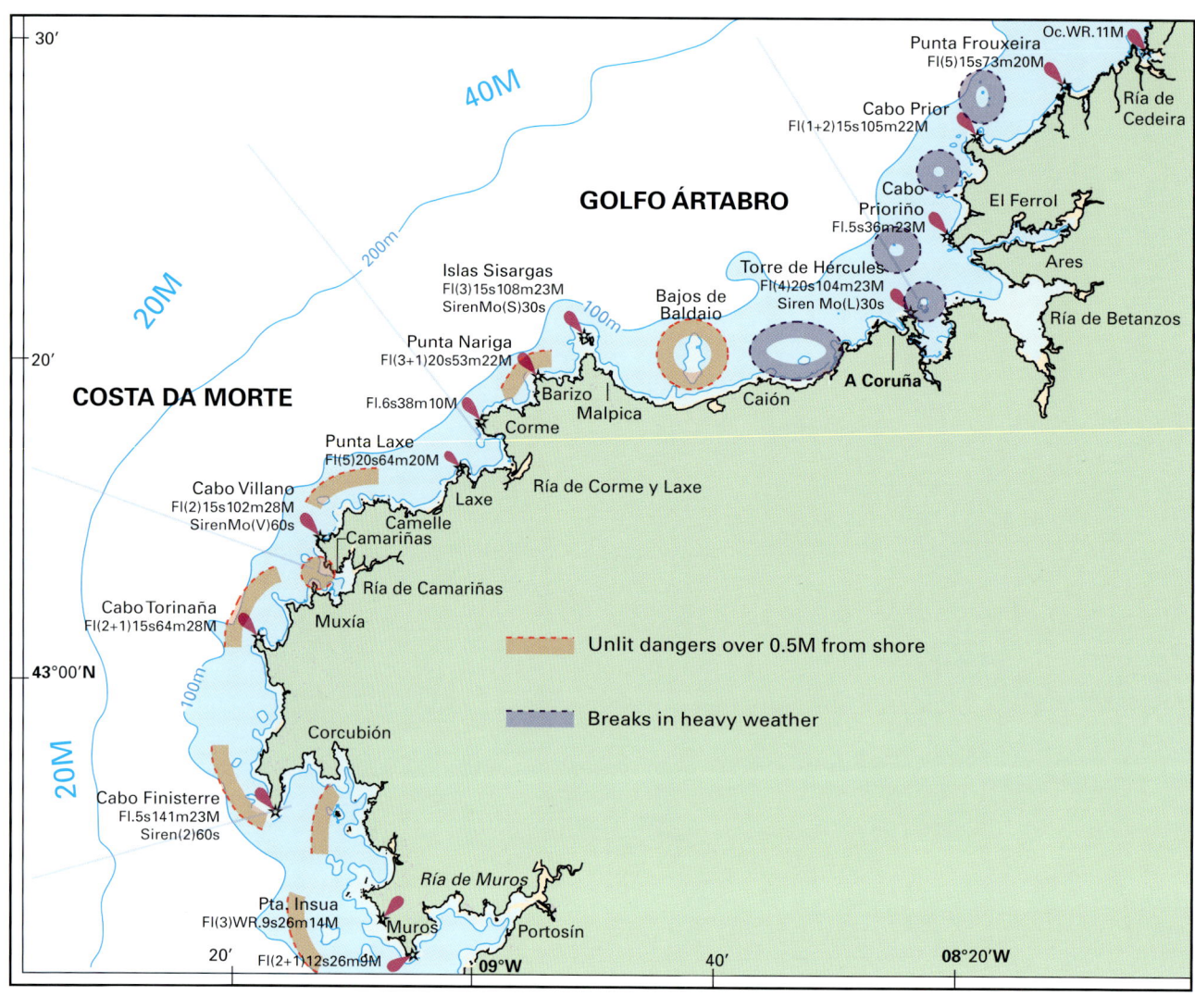

Sailing in Golfo Ártabro and Costa da Morte

Initial shelter

The best harbours for initial shelter in this area are: A Coruña (north), Corme y Laxe and Camariñas (centre) and inside Cabo Finisterre (south). A Coruña, Corme y Laxe and Camariñas have lit entrances offering good shelter inside. Corme y Laxe and Camariñas have a final approach that requires some care due to numerous offlying dangers. Only Coruña, Sada and Camariñas have marinas with pontoons. There are plans for additional marinas to be built at Muxía.

In bad weather Finisterre has a potentially arduous initial (albeit lit) approach around Cabo Finisterre itself. The choice of anchorage would then depend upon the circumstances, particularly wind direction, facilities required and visibility (not all of the final approaches are lit). All this makes Portosín in Ría Muros a sensible alternative to Finisterre.

These factors, combined with the distance involved (90M from A Coruña to Portosín in Ría Muros), show why this stretch of the coast requires careful planning.

The only additional harbour in this area that provides shelter in difficult weather to yachts is Malpica, the fishing port east of Islas Sisargas. Berthing is likely to be against a fishing boat and subject to swell.

Other ports and facilities

- Ferrol: all weather anchorage in the port entrance channel, fuel available at the town quay. Access to rail and bus transport
- Ría de Betanzos: large marina with all facilites and fuel at Sada. Several anchorages providing shelter from all conditions. Swell can be significant as the Ría is open to the sea
- Coruña: protected anchorage behind breakwater. Marina at Dársena commonly used by transiting European yachts. Marina Coruña planned to

GOLFO ÁRTABRO / COSTA DA MORTE

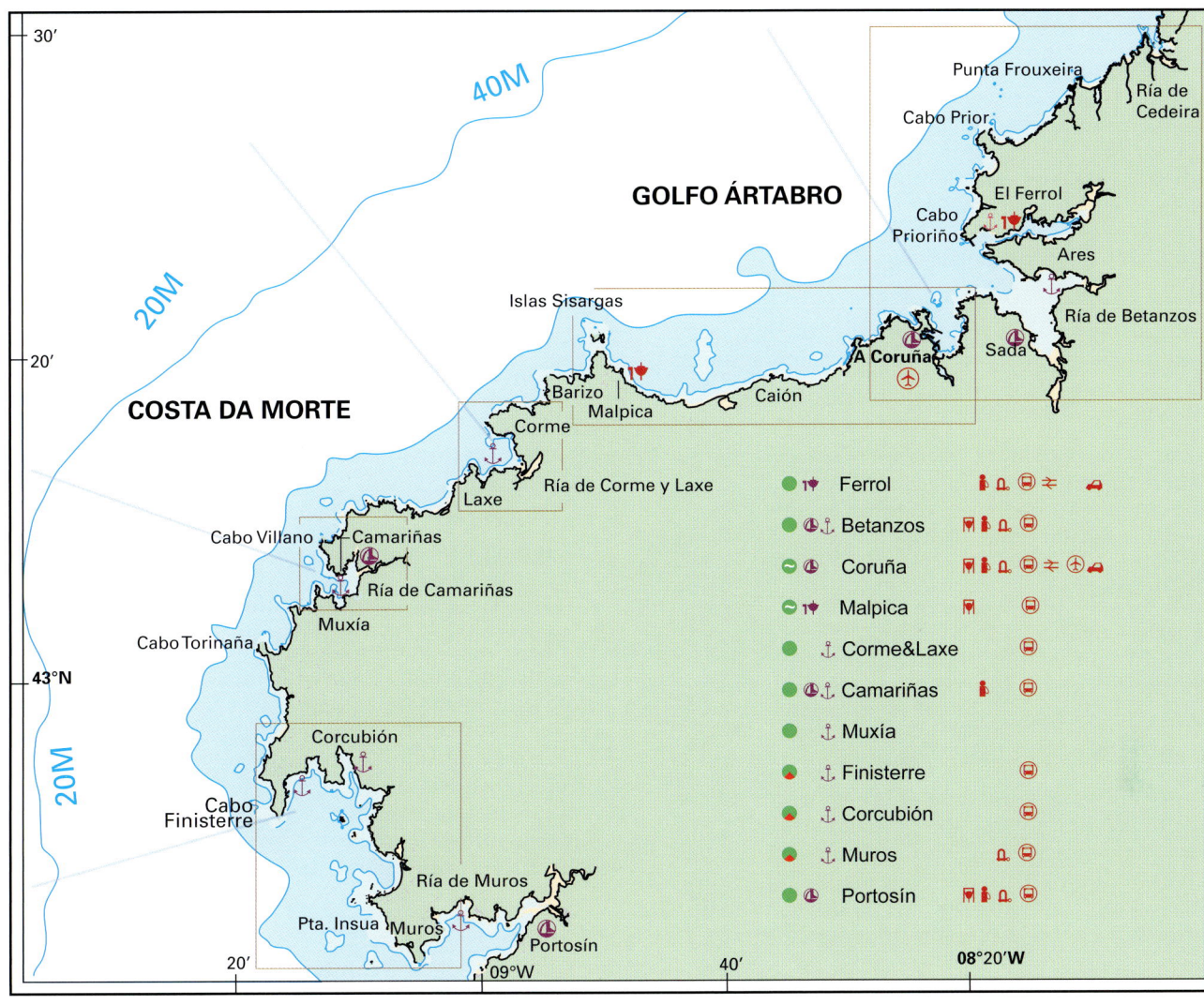

open 2008 at breakwater, all facilities including fuel. Rail, bus, airport. Car hire available from major companies. Seda also has fuel (24hr)

- Malpica: fishing harbour that may be used in bad weather, berth against fishing boats or the harbour wall. Subject to swell

- Corme y Laxe: all weather anchorage providing shelter for northerly (north of ría at Corme between the *bateas* and the breakwater harbour) or southerly winds (south of ría at Laxe, south of breakwater opposite beach)

- Camariñas: all weather marina (subject to swell) and anchorages north and south of the ría. Access to bus transport

- Muxía: anchorage providing shelter from south winds

- Finisterre: anchorage sheltered from north winds. Access to bus transport

- Corcubión (Finisterre): good anchorage shelter for north, east or west winds, best behind the harbour breakwater or towards the Sardiñeiro beach

- Muros: anchorage shelter for all weather conditions

- Portosín: all weather marina, fuel, bus transport.

Emergencies

Lifeboats are based at A Coruña and Muxía. Coast radio stations are based at A Coruña to the north and Finisterre in the south. Timings of weather broadcasts are given in the Appendix. A Coruña, Ferrol and Muros/Noia (near Portosín) in Ría Muros have significant medical facilities.

GOLFO ÁRTABRO / COSTA DA MORTE

Provisioning

Markets, supermarkets, restaurants and bars serving tapas are excellent in Coruña. All the smaller towns near the marinas in the area (Sada, Camariñas) and the anchorages at Corme, Laxe, Muxía, Finisterre and Corcubión have good quality food available from local shops and bars.

Repairs and chandleries

Pompo in Coruña is the best chandlery in this area, extensively stocked and able to obtain any piece of equipment from any major sailing manufactuurer or distributor in Spain and abroad. Staff are well informed and very helpful.

Chandleries are more basic in the smaller towns, where the best source of gear will be from *ferreterías* (ironmongers) that can be found in abundance and often also supply camping gas.

Transport

There is an airport at A Coruña, serving the major Spanish cities as well as London and other European capitals through Iberia and Clickair.

There are main train stations at Ferrol and Coruña, with excellent local and long distance services.

Buses are the best method of transport for access the the coastal towns, all of which have links to Coruña, Santiago and Vigo as well as the smaller cities in the southern rías. The major companies are Arriva and Castromil but several other companies offer services on equivalent or complementary routes. Services are punctual, efficient and very reasonably priced.

Passages

The total **distance** from A Coruña to Ría Muros is 90M. Because of the significant distances between some of the harbours, the emphasis will often be to take advantage of any weather windows to transit the area.

See the main introduction to the book for a description of tides, tidal heights and general weather conditions to be expected.

Swell generated by significant weather systems, sometimes deep in the Atlantic, can build up and stay for days. The best strategy will be to stand offshore into more than 100m. Harbour entrances are deep enough that an entry will not be affected by tidal height. Offlying shallow banks are however best avoided. These are shown on the chart for this section in blue. Some anchorages will become uncomfortable, or in the extreme untenable.

There are **unlit dangers** along this stretch of the coast which must be taken into account when passage planning. The dangers are shown in red in the chart for this section. They can all be avoided by staying in more than 100m depth. This also coincides with a straight line between Islas Sisargas Fl(3)15s23M and Cabo Prioriño Chico Fl.5s23M on a bearing of 255° and 75° respectively.

Tidal flows and height will not generally have an impact on any passage plan which means that the use of daylight hours can be maximised.

The chart of this section of coastline shows the **significant lights** that can be used for passage navigation at night and the unlit hazards more than 0.5M from the coast.

Fishing boats will be present, with their size and type of activity dependent on how far offshore they are found. Expect **fishing pots** in anything up to 150m. These can be all shapes, sizes and degree of visibility and can sometimes have pick-up buoys and floating lines trailing. Spotting them in significant swell will require attention. Some of the large ones have radar reflectors

Shipping will be using Golfo Ártabro (Coruña, Betanzos) for anchorage as well as transit. The Traffic Separation Scheme off Cabo Finisterre is best avoided by use of the inshore traffic zone.

Refuelling along Costa da Morte is difficult, only the harbours at Camariñas and Corcubión have Gasóleo A for yachts. The best and nearest locations outside Costa da Morte are at Marina Seca (Oza, Ría de A Coruña), Sada (Ría de Betanzos) and Portosín (Ría de Muros). From 2008 (planned) Marina Coruña by the breakwater wall at A Coruña will become the best option.

North to south

The coastline from Coruña to Cabo Finisterre (Finisterre) has a number of unmarked offlying dangers up to 4M offshore and it is best to stand off having cleared Torre de Hércules. Bajos de Baldaio west of Caión must be avoided in all conditions.

Cross checking the GPS can be difficult at this range and water depth, but a check on distance run and a focused helmsman should be sufficient downwind. Upwind will be more challenging and probably involve radar ranging on some of the more prominent headlands. Standing inshore for a closer look is not a good alternative. The passage through between Isla Sisarga Chica and the mainland offers an interesting distraction, if conditions allow, as well as a lunch time anchorage. Make sure that the information on IHM Spanish chart 928 is available before attempting the passage.

The distance from Coruña to Corme-Laxe is 40M and the only port that offers shelter in any significant swell is Malpica. While the prevailing wind is likely to be favourable (N or NE) the distance and lack of refuge must be considered when planning.

The journey south from Corme-Laxe can be broken into smaller segments of 20M, to Camariñas, Finisterre and then Muros.

It is worth noting that a number of the lighthouses along this part of Spain are at a considerable height and will remain unseen in low cloud. Some, like Cabo Finisterre, have fog horns to further assist navigation.

When approaching Finisterre from the north, the previous prominent headland (Cabo de la Nave) can be confused for it close inshore.

Ría de Corcubión inside Finisterre offers shelter from the north, east and west (best towards Sardiñeiro beyond the harbour) but the right choice of anchorage has to be made if there is a northerly or southerly component present or predicted. Care should be taken on any approach at night because of the presence of small wooden fishing boats and buoys.

South to north

Most of the information given for the passage going south is applicable to travelling north. However, the **prevailing wind is from the north or northeas**t and could possibly be quite strong for extended periods of time (nordés). With these conditions, rounding Cabo Finisterre can be daunting. By reaching shelter behind the Finisterre headland rather than jumping off from a Ría further south, the distance to Camariñas (the next shelter to windward) can be minimised (20M) and any weather window can be fully exploited. Note that one window could be an early morning departure before the land heats up and the pressure falls over it.

If there is an easterly component to the wind then motor sailing close to the shore until Cabo de la Buitra south of Camariñas could be an option, although the final 4M will be on an unforgiving lee shore unless a tack out to sea is made on starboard first. From Camariñas, Corme (20M) can offer suitable protection overnight from a northerly, leaving a 40M trip to A Coruña. This can be broken by an overnight stop in Malpica, although this may be alongside a fishing boat in a harbour subject to swell. No other harbours along this coastline would be sensible in any significant swell.

Golfo Ártabro

A Coruña, Betanzos, Ares, Ferrol

Golfo Ártabro

Introduction

The Golfo de Ártabro is the area between Rías Altas and Costa da Morte, where Rías de Coruña, Betanzos and Ferrol nestle together offering good shelter from the rigours of the ocean. A Coruña is usually the initial destination for yachts crossing Biscay and also the launch point for long cruises north or south bound.

Ría de Coruña is home to illustrious **A Coruña**, the second largest city of Galicia, a key cultural centre and the location for many large companies. A Coruña combines the old and the new where the most modern of venues are found amidst traditional granite streets. The city's history is long and colourful, as ever in this part of the world entwined with maritime events and wars. Despite its strong Galician feel, it was the first town to clad its balconies in the galleried style, A Coruña is home to a world fashion phenomena. Zara, the company created by Amancio Ortega Gaona, opened its first store here in 1975.

Rías de Betanzos and Ares are the much quieter estuaries further east, with scenery that is a perfect example of why this coast is so attractive. Pontedeume at the end of the Ría is a small, traditional Galician town worth visiting.

Further inland, and set on a hill, **Betanzos** is one of the historic seven capitals of Galicia. It is a delightful town and well worth a journey.

Ferrol is a much underrated city, very busy and in parts needing a serious facelift. It is home to the Spanish Naval Academy and still a large industrial and shipbuilding port that somehow has fallen behind the development and renovation that is obvious elsewhere. The centre of the town, however, retains its class and wealthy outlook, acquired in the past through the privileged position of its natural harbour.

The entire area is full of wonderful places to anchor in quiet and beautiful settings, though berthed at A Coruña you can step from your boat into the heart of vibrant city in just a few paces. From A Coruña you also have easy access to the major sights inland including Santiago, while being able to leave your boat secure in a good marina.

Betanzos

Market at A Coruña

Ferrol

A Coruña street

GOLFO ÁRTABRO

Approach and key facilities

Approach to Golfo Ártabro

The lit, broad, entrance to A Coruña is straightforward in all weather conditions. There are no offlying dangers for yachts, but in bad weather take care of Banco Tarracidos, 9M north (min. depth 10.2m) Cabaleiro, 7M north (min. depth 27m), Laixiñas, 6M north (min. depth 19m) and Yacentes, 2M north (min. depth 7.5m) all shallow areas north of the entrance over which the seas may break.

Breakwater and background lights obscure possible vessel (fishing, pilot vessels, commercial ships and cruise liners) movements. Both approaches given below use the commercial shipping routes, although shoal ground close by may offer temporary protection in case of poor visibility. Beware of fishing pots.

Note prominent Torre de Hércules Fl(4)20s23M and Cabo Prioriño Chico Fl.5s23M guard the west and east side of the entrance respectively.

GOLFO ÁRTABRO

From the north (off Cabo Prior) to A Coruña:

- Turn onto transit on Punta Fiaiteira (182°, front Iso.WRG.2s, rear Oc.R.4s) until the breakwater Fl.G.3s is passed.

From the west to A Coruña:

- Turn onto first set of leading lights on Punta de Mera (108°, front Oc.WR.4s, rear Fl.4s). Note shallow bank (Bancos Yacentes ou Basuril, 9m minimum) to port.
- Pass starboard hand mark Fl(3)G.9s, turn onto second transit on Punta Fiaiteira (182°, front Iso.WRG.2s, rear Oc.R.4s until the breakwater Fl.G.3s is passed.

From either of the approaches above:

- For Real Club Náutico, run parallel to the breakwater (295°). Pass inside unlit wavebreak WNW of Castillo De San Antón Fl(2)G.7s. Beware unlit mooring buoys and anchored boats.
- If heading for Dársena Deportiva, turn to leave Castillo De San Antón Fl(2)G.7s 100m to starboard and pass between port Fl(2+1)R.21s and starboard Fl(3)G.9s arms of inner harbour. There is a row of hammerheads to starboard.

CRUISING GALICIA

Initial shelter

The marinas at A Coruña, Real Club Náutico and Dársena de la Marina are the closest shelter from the entrance to Golfo de Ártabro. Both are located behind the 1km long breakwater wall that protects the harbour, unmissable with its cube-tower structure at the inshore end. Dársena has a lot more space and is a common port of call for Atlantic cruising yachts. There is also plenty of space to anchor in the lee of the breakwater wall (with a tripping line) - some of this space will become the new Mariña de Coruña (2008/09).

The marinas and anchorage are ideally placed, very close to the centre of one of the nicest cities in Galicia, with extensive facilities, services and interesting things to do.

The pontoons at Oza are private but the facilites of Marina Seca, including a 24-hour self service fuel station, are excellent. Marina Seca is run by the same company that is building Marina de Coruña.

Other ports and facilities

Further east, Sada is a large marina with good facilities but it is subject to swell. Fuelling is straightforward but check there are no large motor boats in wait before you as this is the only berth they can use in Golfo de Ártabro. There is plenty of hard standing for dry over-wintering. The initial approach is largely unlit.

Ares is a private marina not designed to accept visitors but the pontoons may serve as a temporary stop if there is space.

Ría de Ferrol has no marinas or facilities dedicated to the leisure sailor, all its pontoons and facilities are private and the area is dominated by Navy and shipbuilding docks. It is possible to dock against the wall at Dársena Curuxeiras, near where tourist boats depart from, with the advantage of being able to step right into the centre of town. There is a self service fuel pump at the quay.

There are numerous anchorages in small pretty bays with good tree cover along Rías de Betanzos, Ares and at the entrance to Ferrol, all quiet with some shops and transport a short walk away once ashore.

Provisioning

Coruña is a haven for food, whether for provisioning or to enjoy at the bars and restaurants. The excellent *mercado* (market) is one of the best places in Galicia for fresh fruit, veg, dairy and fish. The supermarket underneath will deliver to your boat at the marina, an absolute godsend of a service.

Sada is also good for supermarkets and there are good bars come restaurants near the marina. Ares has a number of shops but this will probably require a dinghy trip ashore.

Ferrol, if parked at the harbour wall, has an extensive array of shops and supermarkets as well as bars and restaurants.

Repairs and chandleries

Near the fishing harbour area in A Coruña the chandlery Pombo is among the most extensive you will find, holding all kinds of spares and bits and able to courier parts from anywhere. There are a number of more specialised stores nearby. Dársena has contact with a number of local mechanics, electricians and rigging specialists, all good and most helpful.

Sada Marina has a very good chandlery and a workshop.

Transport

All the towns in the area are linked by an array of bus services, which also connect to locations further away including Cedeira, Santiago, Noia, Vilagarcía, Pontevedra and Vigo, as well as Lugo and Ourense inland.

The Spanish RENFE main train system has stations at Coruña and Ferrol, with local stations at Betanzos and Pontedeume. From Coruña, the high speed western line connects all the coastal towns down to Vigo.

The narrow gauge FEVE train line, quirky and slow but reliable and travelling through beautiful scenery, links the northern coast starting at Ferrol and reaching Oviedo in Asturias. This is a good way to travel on short hops from Ferrol to Ortigueira and Ribadeo, but check timings as it is very much slower than road transport.

Car hire is available from all the major companies. It is easiest to arrange it using the national reservation numbers and collection from Coruña airport (the offices in Coruña and Ferrol are within the rather difficult one way systems).

GOLFO ÁRTABRO

Cruising in the Rías of Golfo Ártabro

There is plenty to do in this part of the world, both ashore and in the water, with plenty of local sites to visit and extensive cruising space for good sails.

One day

If time is absolutely of the essence head for A Coruña, park the boat and step ashore to at least sample the old town. You will not have much time to sail in the Ría other than to arrive and leave.

One week

There is certainly more than enough to do to keep you for a week. Spend two or three days moored in Coruña to visit the town sights as well as feast at the bars and restaurants. Sail to Ría de Betanzos and find a small bay to anchor for a night or two. Visit Betanzos for one of the best traditional Galician towns. If you have time, venture into Ferrol and anchor at the entrance for a complete change of scenery.

GOLFO ÁRTABRO

⚓ Ría de Ferrol

Ría de Ferrol is a long protected natural harbour which serves as one of the major bases of the Spanish Navy. Side by side with the Naval ships and College Ferrol hosts many industrial complexes, no longer in their hay day of shipbuilding but still a strong visual presence. Ferrol city has charm in the centre but several areas are not in good condition or have been built anew without much regard to aesthetics.

Approach & entrance

Straightforward initial approach with prominent breakwater Fl.R.5s. The final approach is in a narrow and winding but deep-sided, river. Strong tides and squalls are possible inside the river. Breakwater and background lights obscure possible vessel (naval, commercial and fishing) movements.

The approach described below assumes fair weather. In bad weather take care of Banco Tarracidos (min. depth 10.2m), Cabaleiro (min. depth 27m) and Laixiñas (min. depth 19m), shallow areas north of the entrance over which the seas may break. Note the new breakwater Fl.R.5s is now present on north side of entrance (Cabo Priorińo Chico, Fl.5s23M). A lit west cardinal Q(9) is now 1M west of the entrance.

From 1M west of Priorińo Chico, Fl.5s on the transit for A Coruña, Punta Fiaiteira 182°, front Iso.WRG.2s, rear Oc.R.4s.

- Alter course to clear new breakwater Fl.R.5s to port
- Alter course to clear starboard hand mark Fl.G.2s. (Note sectored light San Cristóbal Oc(2)WR.10s)
- Follow transit (85°, Front Fl.1.5s, Rear Oc.4s), passing Fl.R.5s to port
- Pass between port and starboard hand marks Fl(2)G.7s, Fl(2)R.7s, Fl(3)G.9s, Fl(3)R.9s, Fl(4)G.11s, Fl(4)G.11s.

⚓ Playa de San Felipe

This small bay on the northern side in the entrance channel is charming and away from the bustle of the port. Anchor in 3-5m, away from small boat moorings. Good shelter but poor holding on rock.

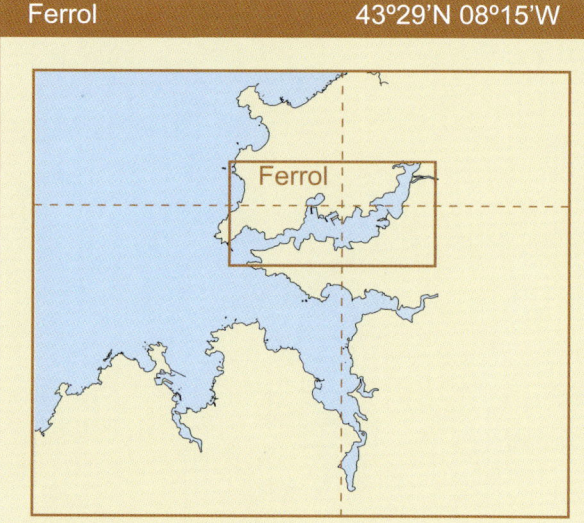

Ferrol   43°29'N 08°15'W

Dársena Curuxeiras
- Straightforward approach in all conditions
- Lie alongside the starboard wall on entry
- Harbour office boat will make contact to collect fees
- ⛽ Fuel in the quay, self service
- Harbour office ☎ 981 308000

⚓ Ensenada do Baño

On the south side of the entrance channel beyond San Felipe, another pleasant location for anchorage. There are pontoons at the shore but it is too shallow there to moor alongside. Good shelter.

🍴 Dársena Curuxeiras - Ferrol

This is the only area of the commercial and naval harbour where you may enter. The pontoons are administered by the Harbour Office (Autoridad Portuaria ☎ 981 308000), but it is not practiced in receiving visitors, so you are likely to be breaking new ground!

You can lie alongside the town side wall ('cortina') without requesting permission. The harbour office boat will come in due course to charge you fees. Again, arrangements are not structured so an element of initiative is required.

There is a self service fuel pump serving Gasóleo A to leisure boats.

Playa de San Felipe

Dársena de Curuxeiras

GOLFO ÁRTABRO

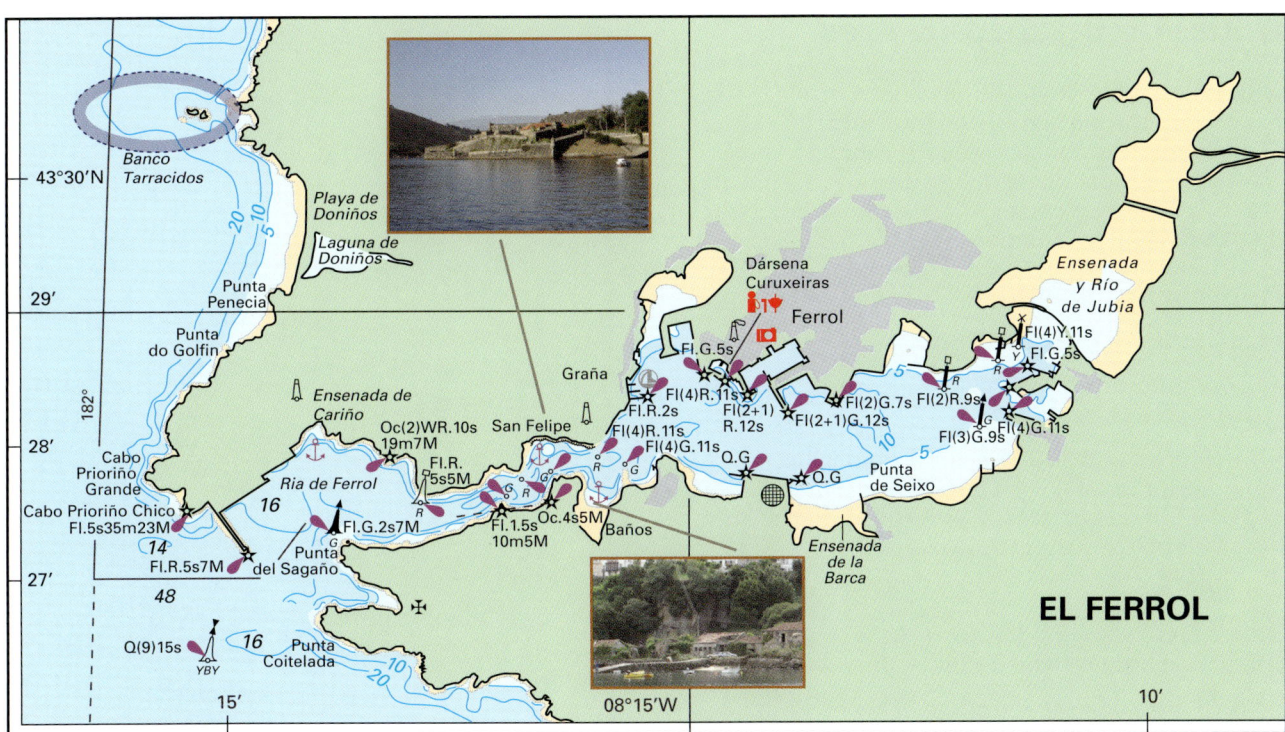

⚓ Puerto Deportivo da Graña

Private pontoons in the very pretty setting of Graña, west of Dársena across the water. Emergency only.

Provisioning & eating

If you reach the dársena at Ferrol you can find bars and restaurants immediately ashore. Walk to Barrio de la Magdalena beyond the Parador above the military academy. The streets between Magdalena and Sol are the main area for good bars and tapas.

Interest

There is more to Ferrol than you may think given the industrial views from a boat or the rather untidy outskirts if coming by land.

The old town, known as Ferrol Vello, is not in good condition and there seems to be little effort in progress to renovate the many buildings that are crumbling. But matters improve from there towards the monumental part of the city, starting with the grand churches and building around the **Parador**. The gardens facing the port provide a more gentile setting than could be expected in the context of the industry at shore level.

Barrio de la Magdalena is a grid of streets designed and built in the 19th century following the principles of urban planning that were being used in the wealthy cities of Spain and Europe. Straight streets at right angles are home to neoclassical buildings that distinguish themselves from other city projects by the extensive use of *galerías*, the trademark of Galician balconies. Calle Iglesia is particularly interesting, with its succession of grand builldings, the fish market, Catedral de San Julián, Teatro Jofre, post office and the Caixa Galicia Foundation (museum) leading to the pleasant gardens at Alameda de Suances.

Ferrol

- Coruña 50, Santiago 100km, Pontevedra 170km, Vigo 200km
- 🚌 Bus station: just north of Plaza España
- 🚆 Train station: by Plaza España
  - National RENFE network, long distance trains (Talgo) and R598 high speed train
  - FEVE narrow gauge train to Rías Altas and Oviedo
- 🛒 Market/Supermarket:
  - Groceries and supermarkets in the centre of town
- 🍴 Restaurants and bars in Barrio de la Magdalena, the neoclasical area of Ferrol
- ℹ Tourist office: Praza C.J. Cela
  ☏ 981 311179 / 337131
- ✚ Centro Saude Fontenla Maristany, Plaza de España ☏ 981 336633
  - Several others in town

Parador de Ferrol

GOLFO ÁRTABRO

⚓ Rías de Betanzos & Ares

Quiet Rías, away from the bustle of Coruña. Sada has a large marina and is straight forward to enter in all conditions. Initial approach is unlit. There is often more space here than A Coruña. There are also several very pleasant, quiet anchorages. Note that ships sometimes moor in Ría de Betanzos.

Approach & entrance

From the north (off Cabo Prior):

- Turn onto transit on Punta Fiaiteira 182°, front Iso.WRG.2s, rear Oc.R.4s.
- Alter course to 120° when Prioriño Chico Fl.5s is on a bearing of 45°. This will put Punta de San Pedro (Perbes pier) Fl(2)WR.7s 3M on the bow (albeit out of sight at 7.5M).

From the west:

Monte San Pedro and the Torre de Hércules (Roman lighthouse) are useful landmarks.

- Turn onto first set of leading lights on Punta de Mera (108.5°, front Oc.WR.4s, rear Fl.4s)
- Alter course and aim for southern most radio mast F.R. south of Monte Faro when it bears 70°. Note special mark Q(5)Y.20s and Banco Yacentes o Bausuril, 9m minimum will be left close to starboard
- Alter course to 120° when Prioriño Chico Fl.5s is on a bearing of 350°. This will put Punta de San Pedro Fl(2)WR.7s 4M on the bow (albeit out of sight at 7.5M).

From either of the approaches above:

- Maintain depth above 20m until Ensenada de Cirro Fl(2)G.10s is on the beam. Punta de San Pedro Fl(2)WR.7s 3M should now be in sight on the bow
- If heading for Ares, the end of the breakwater is marked by Fl(3)R.9s
- If heading for Sada starboard breakwater Fl(4)G.11s should be in sight on the starboard bow. Alter course for it when it bears 160°. Note lit (Fl.Y) area of *bateas* to starboard. Alter course to clear breakwater and pass between starboard Fl(4)G.11s and Port Fl(4)R.11s breakwaters. Breakwater and background lights obscure possible vessel (fishing) movements.

⚓ Ares

The marina at Ares is private and, while there may be space if a berth holder is away, it should be considered only for emergencies. See anchorages.

⚓ Sada

The marina at Sada is modern, large and growing. There are extensive shore facilities and services, a chandler and space for dry berthing. Fuel and a travel lift are at the shore side in front of the marina

---

Betanzos & Ares   43°23'N 08°15'W

Marina Sada
- Straightforward approach in all conditions
- 54 visitors moorings, up to 22m length
- Minimum depth 3m, entrance 4m
- Suitable for winter berth
- Pontoon mooring, subject to swell
- Water & electricity at the pontoons
-
- ☏ 981 619015 Fax 981 619287
- VHF Channel 09
- marinasada@igatel.net
- www.marinasada.com
-
- ⛽ Fuel pontoon at the wall opposite marina office (very easy access)
- 🏗 32ton travel lift
- 🔧 Workshops, chandlery at the marina
- Laundry, showers/toilets basic and a long way from visitors pontoons

Club Náutico Ría de Ares
- Private marina, emergency only
- ☏ 981 468787 Fax 981 468787
- VHF Channel 09

Ares

GOLFO ÁRTABRO

RÍAS BETANZOS AND ARES

offices. Check no large motor boats are due as this is the only fuel point they can access in Ártabro.

Visitors' berths are on the two northerly pontoons, which are subject to swell. Showers are basic and a very long way away from the visitors' spaces.

Anchorages

Sada

- Coruña 20km, Santiago 80km, Pontevedra 150km, Vigo 180km
- Bus station: on AC163 road at the level of the marina
- Supermarket:
  - Gadis, Linares Rivas 29
  - Hypermarket next to Marina
- Restaurants and bars along Avda da Mariña from the Marina
- Tourist office: Avda.da Mariña ☎ 608 073425
- Centro Saude Sada, Rúa Párroco Villanueva ☎ 981 621893 / 621900

Sada

CRUISING GALICIA 85

There are many spots where anchorage is possible, the two main ones are:

- Northeast of Marina de Areas, in Ensenada de Ares, 3-4 m sand
- Ensenada de Redes, 1.5M east of Ares, between the shellfish platforms and the shore at Redes.

There is a small harbour at Miño, opposite Sada across Ría de Betanzos, which dries. It should not be attempted.

Interest

Ares is a small town which comes to life in the summer, well decked with promenade space in which to enjoy the good weather.

The main landmark of interest at Sada is the modernist building **A Terraza**, a striking wooden building which serves as a cafetería in the summer. Sada is not otherwise a very interesting town, although the promenade towards the marina and the various bars and restaurants along it make a pleasant place to stroll and soak the local atmosphere.

At the end of Ría de Ares, Pontedeume is a town that has retained Galician charm and it is set at the end of a magnificent Roman bridge. It can be reached in a small boat, subject to a height restriction at the modern bridge of 8m, but it is probably best accessed by road. A taxi from Sada for an evening out on Friday or Saturday will provide you with plenty of entertainment.

Further away, by road only, the town of **Betanzos** is a star destination. One of the old seven capital cities of Galicia, the streets of the old town set up on top of the hill are a great example of the galleried style of building. Numerous historical buildings and a long history will give you a feel for the importance of the town in the past, while bars and cafeterías serve for a relaxed break enjoying the view. You can reach Betanzos by bus or train from Coruña and Ferrol. From Sada there are buses or taxis.

A Terraza, the Sada Art Deco building

Betanzos & Pontedeume

Betanzos

The towns of Pontedeume and Betanzos are good day trips from A Coruña, both accessible through bus and train from the central station.

Betanzos is one of the seven cities of the old Galician kingdom. The central plaza and the streets that fan out from it and up the hill are a pleasure to walk through, shopping or browsing. Near the Town Hall the old Bank of Spain correspondant building stands, now producing coffee instead of money. Several museums and monuments will entertain you, as will the numerous bars and restaurants. Betanzos should be high on a shortlist of places to visit.

Pontedeume sits at the end of Ría de Areas, accessible by small boats that can clear the height restriction of the modern bridge. A Roman bridge crosses the river and is still used by one of the main roads. The streets have *soportales* and other traditional Galician architecture. The imposing tower that guards the town can be visited, while the market building behind is excellent for fresh fruit, veg and fish. The old part of the town becomes very lively at weekends, the streets full of people feasting on tapas.

Pontedeume

GOLFO ÁRTABRO

⚓ A Coruña

Approach & entrance

The lit, broad, entrance to A Coruña is straightforward in all weather conditions. There are no offlying dangers for yachts, but in bad weather take care of Banco Tarracidos, 9M north (min. depth 10.2m) Cabaleiro, 7M north (min. depth 27m), Laixiñas, 6M north (min. depth 19m) and Yacentes, 2M north (min. depth 7.5m) all shallow areas north of the entrance over which the seas may break.

Breakwater and background lights obscure possible vessel (fishing, pilot vessels, commercial ships and cruise liners) movements. Both approaches given below use the commercial shipping routes, although shoal ground close by may offer temporary protection in case of poor visibility. Beware of fishing pots.

Note prominent Torre de Hecules Fl(4)20s23M and Cabo Prioriño Chico Fl.5s23M guard the west and east side of the entrance respectively.

From the north (off Cabo Prior) to A Coruña:

- Turn onto transit on Punta Fiaiteira (182°, front Iso.WRG.2s, rear Oc.R.4s) until the breakwater Fl.G.3s is passed.

From the west to A Coruña:

- Turn onto first set of leading lights on Punta de Mera (108°, front Oc.WR.4s, rear Fl.4s). Note shallow bank (Bancos Yacentes ou Basuril, 9m minimum) to port
- Pass starboard hand mark Fl(3)G.9s, turn onto second transit on Punta Fiaiteira (182°, front Iso.WRG.2s, rear Oc.R.4s until the breakwater Fl.G.3s is passed.

From either of the approaches above:

- For Real Club Náutico, run parallel to the breakwater (295°). Pass inside unlit wavebreak WNW of Castillo De San Antón Fl(2)G.7s. Beware unlit mooring buoys and anchored boats
- If heading for Dársena Deportiva, turn to leave Castillo De San Antón Fl(2)G.7s 100m to starboard and pass between port Fl(2+1)R.21s and starboard Fl(3)G.9s arms of inner harbour. There is a row of hammerheads to starboard.

⚓ Dársena de la Marina

Berth on the visitors' waiting pontoon, first hammerhead, and walk to office.

This marina is in the old fishing harbour right in the centre of town, with 350 berths for boats between 8 and 30m. The shower and laundry facilities are in portacabins on the quay, a little basic, but the enthusiasm of the staff and the location more than compensate. Water and electricity on all pontoons. No fuel.

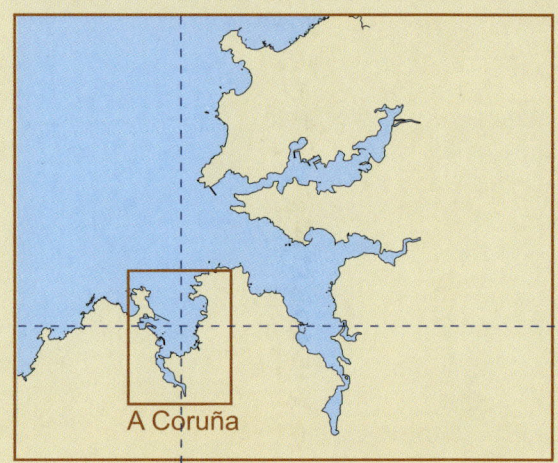

A Coruña 43°22'N 08°24'W

Dársena de la Marina A Coruña
- Straightforward approach in all conditions
- 40 visitors' moorings, up to 30m length
- Minimum depth 4m
- Marina used to receiving boats after long offshore passage
- Can be busy in summer peak periods
- Pontoon mooring, water & electricity
- Office ☎ 981 914142 Fax 981 914144
- Marinero ☎ 650 053130
- VHF Channel 09
- 🔧 Repairs through Marina office
- info@darsenacoruna.com
- Laundry, showers/toilets in temp building
- Marina Coruña (planned 2008/09)
- Extensive new marina along breakwater
- 🚜 50-ton travel lift
- ⛽ Fuel pontoon

Marina Seca (Oza)
- ☎ 981 913651 Fax 981 913649
- marinaseca@marinaseca.com
- VHF Channel 09
- 🚜 30-ton travel lift, hard standing space
- ⛽ Fuel self-service pontoon

Real Club Náutico de A Coruña
- Straightforward approach
- 10 visitors' moorings, up to 12m, 3m depth
- Can be busy in summer peak periods
- Pontoon mooring
- Excellent club building by the dársena (correspondance with foreign clubs)
- ☎ 981 203265 Fax 981 203008 rcnc@arrakis.es
- VHF Channel 09
- 🚜 30-ton travel lift (diffcult to access)
- ⛽ dificult access, only HW+/-2h
- Showers/toilets at sailing club

GOLFO ÁRTABRO

⚓ Marina Coruña (planned 2008/09)

New marina sited along the harbour breakwater. Extensive facilities including a clubhouse, fuel, travel lift and a large amount of space (25%) for transiting yachts. Marina Seca at Oza is part of the same company, offering hard standing and wintering dry facilites.

⚓ Marina Seca (Oza)

Marina Seca is a dedicated yacht service company, with plenty of space for dry winter storage and workshops for repairs. The company is responsible for the new Marina Coruña (planned for 2008, construction begins winter 2007).

A travel lift and fuel berth are ready from 2007, part of an extension of hard standing. Both are very easy to access in comparison to the facilities at RCN.

⚓ Club Marítimo de Oza

Private marina, with a splendid clubhouse built in 2006. It does not accept visitors so use only in an emergency.

⚓ Real Club Náutico

There are no hammerheads or sprigs and some berths are Mediterranean style. If coming alongside one of the pontoons watch out for trailing lines. The RCN also has 10 buoys. The pontoons between RCN and the castle belong to the Marina Seca company but are not in service (2007).

GOLFO ÁRTABRO

Both the RCN, and the Sporting Club near it, have showers and other facilities. Water and electricity in all pontoons. Fuel available but confined approach.

⚓ Anchorages

The area adjacent to the breakwater is sheltered and a short dinghy trip away from RCN or Dársena, near the centre of town. It can get busy in summer. Use a tripping line.

The area opposite Playa de Santa Cristina (sand, mud, weed) is sheltered except in northerlies. It is good half hour walk from the centre of Coruña.

Provisioning & eating

Coruña is one of the best places in Galicia to go out to eat, with streets where your only problem will be which bar or restaurant to choose. From Dársena head up hill toward the old town and sample Galician fair in numerous establishements, always best when you have fish, shelfish or local meat in the form of tapas. For very well selected cured meats go to the excellent bar La Leonesa.

The streets west of Plaza María Pita are full of bars, restaurants and shops, plus, if the weather is reasonable, the entire local population out for a *paseo* - atmosphere like nowhere else.

For the freshest fish, fruit and vegetables visit the Mercado at Plaza de San Agustín, 5 minutes from Dársena. Below the market is a well stocked supermarket (which delivers) and there are also plenty of groceries in the streets adjacent.

Interest

The history of La Coruña is long and colourful. Its natural harbour was used by the Phoenicians and the Romans. It also served as a staging post for the arrival of tribal groups from other Atlantic facing parts of Europe, a connection which links Galicia with the 'celtic' culture. Later Coruña was one of the landfall targets in the English pilgrim route to Santiago de Compostela, the star destination of Galicia which has attracted catholic visitors over the centuries.

A Coruña's history is linked with Britain, in both positive and negative ways. The town of Reading in the UK bears the scallop shell symbol of the apostle as one of the gathering point for the pilgrimage. Drake defeated the Armada that set off from here, and later tried to assault the town.

GOLFO ÁRTABRO

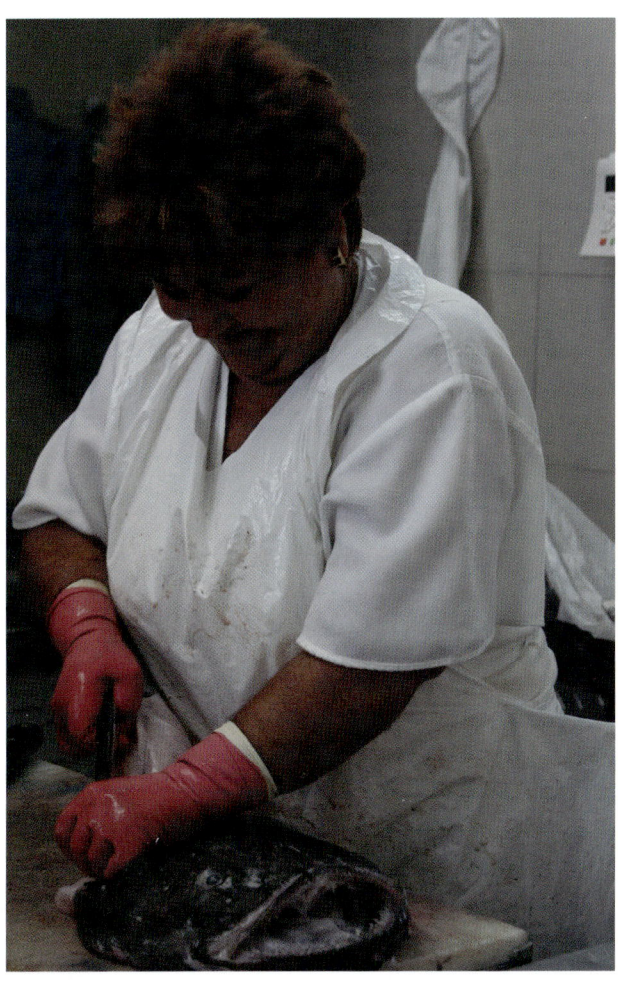
Plaza de María Pita

Local heroine María Pita rescued the day for Spain, repelling Drake's guns, and is remembered today through the name of the grand square in the old town. Further on in time, General Sir John Moore died helping Spain against Napoleon's troops. He is buried at the lovely Jardines de San Carlos at the top of the old town, overlooking the harbour, his fate and courage enshrined in poems by illustrious local writer Rosalía de Castro.

The **old town** up the hill is a delight of medieval streets, the houses built traditionally in granite, solid but graceful constructions, nearly all with galleried balconies typical of Galicia. Granite and glass for the rain! Look at the romanesque churches **Colegiata de Santa María del Campo** and Iglesia de Santiago, sober and solemn but beautiful in their stout style.

Torre de Hércules

Colegiata de Santa María

CRUISING GALICIA **91**

GOLFO ÁRTABRO

A Coruña

- Ferrol 52km, Santiago 60km, Pontevedra 120km, Vigo 155km, Ourense 170km
- Bus station: Caballeros 21 - extensive network with services by several companies
- Train station: national RENFE network, long distance trains (Talgo) and excellent Galician R598 high speed train than links the major towns from Ferrol to Vigo
- Airport: links to all major Spanish cities and some low cost airline connections to UK, France and Germany
- Car hire: all major companies, from airport

- Market/Supermarket:
  - Mercado at Plaza de San Agustín
  - Supermarket below Mercado, delivers
  - Many groceries and other supermarkets in the centre of town

- Restaurants and bars:
  - The old town up the hill from Dársena
  - Rúa Franja from west of Plaza María Pita

- Tourist office: Avda de la Marina west of Dársena ☎ 981 221822

- Chandlers (Efectos Navales):
  - Regata: opposite Dársena de la Marina
  - Efectos Navales Pombo, Avda Primo de Rivera 8, ☎ 981 245 319 / 235 368 www.navalespombo.com - the most extensively stocked chandler in Galicia

  - Numerous ferreterías (ironmongers) in the centre, near Plaza de San Agustín

- Centro Saude Casa do Mar, Avda do Exercito 2 ☎ 981 170358 / 170360 / 170361
  - Several others in town

GOLFO ÁRTABRO

RCN building at Dársena

RÍA DE A CORUÑA

Down at sea level, the San Antón castle is now a Museum. In front of the Dársena catch the tramway, every ½ hour, to visit the **Torre de Hércules,** a lighthouse built by the Romans and refaced in the 18th century which is still used today.

From the grand Plaza de María Pita walk towards the west, along Avda de la Marina admiring the galleried buildings or the parallel streets, all full of restaurants, bars and boutiques. The new museum of Fundación la Caixa is worth a visit.

The walk along the peninsula towards Torre de Hércules is very pleasant, built by the town to provide good views and ample pedestrian space for *paseos*.

Coruña old town

CRUISING GALICIA 93

GOLFO ÁRTABRO

South of the Torre at Paseo Marítimo, reached by the tramway, Aquarium Finisterrae is a must for any visitor. Very carefully put together and centred on the Atlantic marine species, it is informative and entertaining, a good way to spend a morning or afternoon, especially with children.

Eating and drinking is not a problem other than choosing among the extensive choice available. Almost anywhere, particularly along the streets west of Plaza María Pita, will serve the best fish and *tapas*. Try Pulpo a Feira, Empanada, fresh cheese, fish or cured meats with a glass of Albariño white wine or Ribeira Sacra red for a good introduction to local fare.

Coruña park area towards Torre de Hércules

Empanada

The flat pie that is made in Galicia with every type of filling. Tasty and different from other pies because of the olive oil in the pastry.

Ingredients

Pastry

0.5kg flour
1 cup olive oil
1 cup white wine

Filling

1 onion, cut into small pieces
1 garlic
0.5kg fresh tuna, cut into chunks
half a cup of olive oil
2 tins of cut tomato in its juices
Salt to taste

1 egg yolk, beaten

Oven dish, shallow

Preparation

To make the filling, fry the onion and garlic in olive oil until the onion is golden and soft. Add the tomato tins and tuna and cook for 15 minutes, until the sauce is quite thick.

Pastry: mix together the flour, wine and olive oil until it holds and leaves the sides of the bowl. Flour a surface which will allow you to roll the mixture to the shape of your oven dish. Divide the mixture into two, reserving a small amount aside to make decorations. Roll each half independently. Roll the small amount set aside into long strips.

Place the first half of rolled out pastry mixture in your oven dish. Add the filling and spread across the base.

Cover with the second half of the pastry and pinch/fold over the edges to close the empanada. Decorate the top with the long strips, perhaps in a lattice form.

Paint the egg yolk over the top to give the pie a glaze. Cook for 30 minutes at 150ºC.

Serve with Albariño wine.

Costa da Morte

The tougher coastline of Galicia

Costa da Morte

Introduction

Costa da Morte is the chilling name given to the stretch of Galician coastline between A Coruña and the start of the Rías Baixas at Ría de Muros. The rocky coastline sits at the northwestern tip of the Iberian peninsula, giving rise to dramatic and sudden changes of conditions around its major headlands. There are few locations that offer the sailor refuge from difficult weather, and it is this that has given Costa da Morte notoriety.

However, despite its name, this coast is perfectly manageable. Modern weather forecasts and navigation tools make planning a passage along Costa da Morte a simple exercise. The reward is views of a dramatic shore and access to this very remote part of Galicia, beautiful, wild and unspoilt.

Malpica is a feisty port, home to a large fishing fleet and set impressively nestled into the rock. The town is a tourist destination and host to many restaurants.

The islands of **Sisargas** mark a major headland for the sailor. A seabird sanctuary, the narrow passage between the islands and the coast is rewarding in good weather, possibly with a good lunch break at the anchorage.

The rías of **Corme y Laxe** and **Camariñas** offer undeveloped charm and an untouched landscape. It is true that modern construction has destroyed much of the traditional feel of the small towns, but the space, feeling of remoteness and views more than compensate. There are large quantities of windmills, the result of national energy policy about which you will need to develop your own opinion - renewable energy versus a blot on the landscape.

Finisterre is the headland that has captured the imagination of navigators and land settlers for centuries. Named by the Romans as the end of the world (*finis terrae*), it often marks the most significant stage of any sailor's journey in this area. The history of Finisterre is celebrated in an Easter festival that combines ancient rituals worshipping the Sun with Christian traditions.

At Ensenada de Corcubión, the town of **Corcubión** retains a traditional feel and the coast is home to some of the most spectacular *hórreos*, the ancient Galician grain store buildings.

The church of **Muxía** is a rugged building set on the headland facing the onslaught of the ocean. Visit it during the town festival, and you may enjoy passing under the **roca das barcas**, a ritual that is supposed to improve your health.

The land of this region remains an unexploited wilderness, with opportunities for travel through beautiful scenery as well as remote and rewarding treks.

Muxía lighthouse

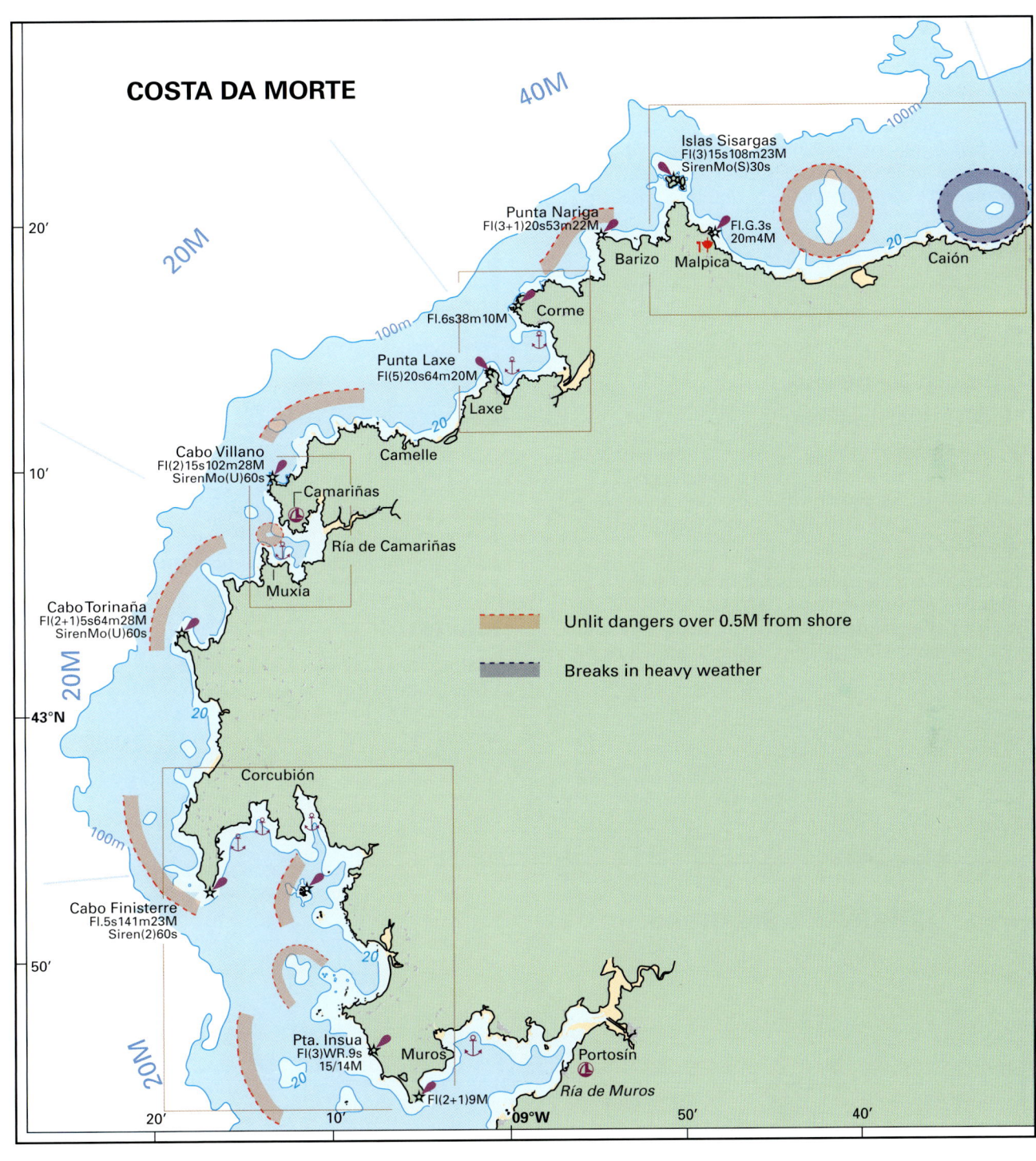

COSTA DA MORTE

Coruña to Sisargas

This is a very unfriendly stretch of coast that should be avoided in anything other than settled weather. Bajos de Baldaio (see Passage Area section Ártabro/Costa da Morte) are dangerous unmarked shallows which should be given a wide berth. They can be avoided by staying in more than 100m depth. This also coincides with a straight line between Islas Sisargas Fl(3)15s23M and Cabo Priorño Chico Fl.5s23M on a bearing of 255° and 75° respectively.

There is a very small fishing harbour at Caión, with a leading light, but the harbour is only an option for a yacht in settled weather and in daylight. The entrance to Caión is very narrow and exposed.

⚓ Malpica

Small fishing harbour, very tight for space but providing some shelter from all but E winds or N/NE swell.

Approach & entrance

Difficult in heavy weather.

Approaching from the east, Bajos de Baldaio (6M east of Malpica) must be given wide clearance. Numerous rocks and shallows stand in an extensive patch covering an area that extends from 1 to 3M from the coast.

The entrance is straightforward, although the wall will hide vessel movements. The sea wall side of the channel is the preferred side as shallows extend from the shore. It may be possible to attach to the very high harbour wall.

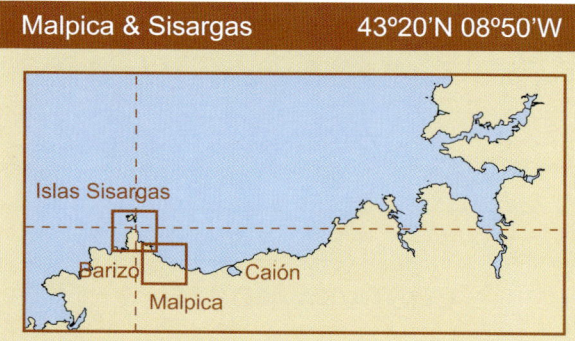

Malpica & Sisargas   43°20'N 08°50'W

Malpica
- Emergency only, busy fishing harbour
- Entrance along the sea harbour wall
- Temporary berthing along sea harbour wall between fishing boats
- Inner harbour hard area changes (2007)

Islas Sisargas
- Settled weather short term anchorage
- Channel passage only in calm weather, otherwise 1M clearance from the islands

⚓ Anchorage

Anchor clear of the fishing boats but inside the protection of the wall. The beach north of Malpica is a possible alternative anchorage, offering shelter from the south, but it is completely open and will not be comfortable in any swell.

Interest

Malpica is a very picturesque fishing village, full of restaurants and bars to look after the visiting tourists. The location is one of the best to admire the rugged aspect of Costa da Morte from the comfortable shelter of a land base.

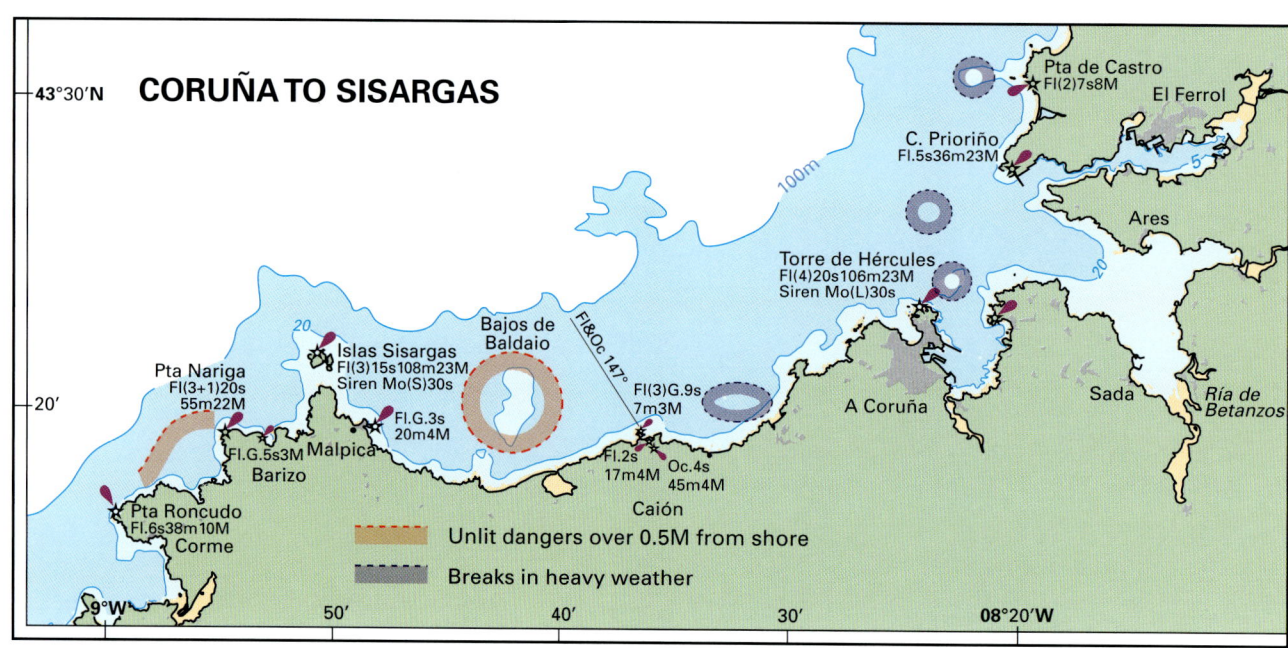

COSTA DA MORTE

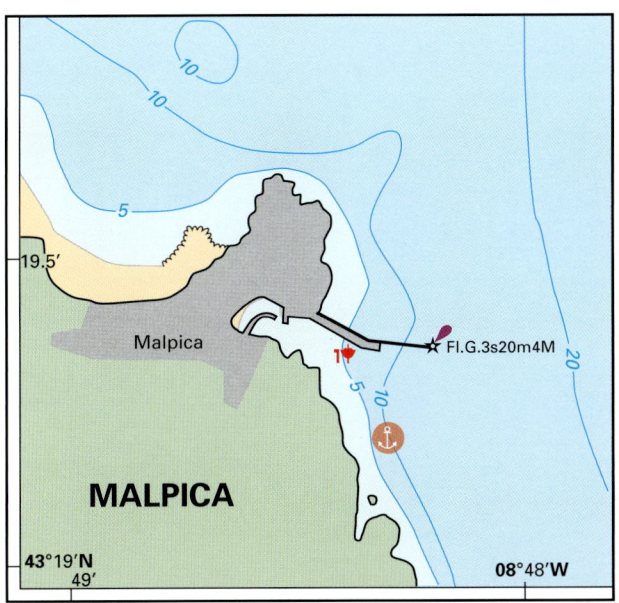

Malpica

Islas Sisargas

⚓ Islas Sisargas

One of the landmarks in any passage along Costa da Morte, a quiet short term anchorage for settled weather only.

There are three bays 3M south to southwest of Islas Sisargas (Playa de Beo, Ensenada de Ceiruga and Puerto de Barizo), all subject to swell and only accessible in settled weather and during daylight.

Approach & entrance

Settled weather only, the channel between the islands and the coastline is narrow and dangerous if the wind and swell build up.

From the east:

- Approach Pedra Do Lobo on course of 270°
- Alter course when Punta del Rostro bears 310°
- Alter course when a back bearing of the southern most part of Isla Sisarga Chica bears 240°.

From the west:

- Approach when the southern most part of Isla Sisarga Chica bears 60°
- Alter course when a back bearing on Punta del Rostro bears 130°

- Alter course when Pedra Do Lobo has a back bearing of 270°.

⚓ Anchorage

Anchor in the small bay between the two islands.

If you are able to anchor the Sisargas islands are a very picturesque, rocky setting. The islands are an ornithological reserve, home to seabird colonies.

⚓ Puerto de Barizo

5M east of Punta del Roncudo (43°19'.21N 08°52'.82W) lies a narrow inlet protected from the east through south to west. There is not much room and the harbour is exposed to swell.

The most eastern inlet before the Sisargas headland is an option from shelter from NE wind and swell. Exit may become difficult if wind direction changes to NW.

CRUISING GALICIA 101

Granite

Granite is the rock that you will see everywhere in Galicia, from the exposed coastal line with its cliffs to the beautiful streets of medieval towns. Granite has created the shape of the rías and gives the towns their Galician feel.

Granite is a rock of plutonic origin, formed by three minerals, quartz, feldspar and mica, although in some varieties the mica is not present. Quartz is a silicon oxide, in pure condition forming transparent rock crystal but normally contaminated by metal oxides that give it white, violet, yellow, pink and other tones. Feldspar is a silicate, of aluminium, calcium, sodium or potassium, generally white or light in colour. In damp environments, with an abundance of CO^2 it can undertake a transformation that leads to Kaolin, or china clay, the basis of porcelain. The Rías Altas have extensive Kaolin deposits and the remnants of a porcelain industry.

Granite is the most abundant rock of the Earth's crust, produced when rocks of high silicon content, in a state of fusion in magma, form underneath the crust and cool gradually under great pressure. The size of the feldspars is an indication of the speed of solidification, larger when pressures were smaller. Through erosion granite reaches the surface, occupying the high parts of mountains due to its lesser density.

There are many types of granite, depending on the nature and quantity of its components. On the whole it is an ideal material for construction given its strength and resistance to atmospheric agents.

Granite is very abundant in Galicia and has been used for centuries as a basic building block for religious and civilian monuments as well as for homes. Until the development of cements and asphalts, granite was used for road building, often in small regular blocks like cobble stones. People called *canteros* worked on the stone by hand, using hammer and chisel to cut and smooth its surfaces. Historic towns of Galicia, such as Santiago, Mondoñedo, Betanzos, Lugo or Pontevedra, show this skilled work at its best, but many less important towns also have the traditional granite streets.

COSTA DA MORTE

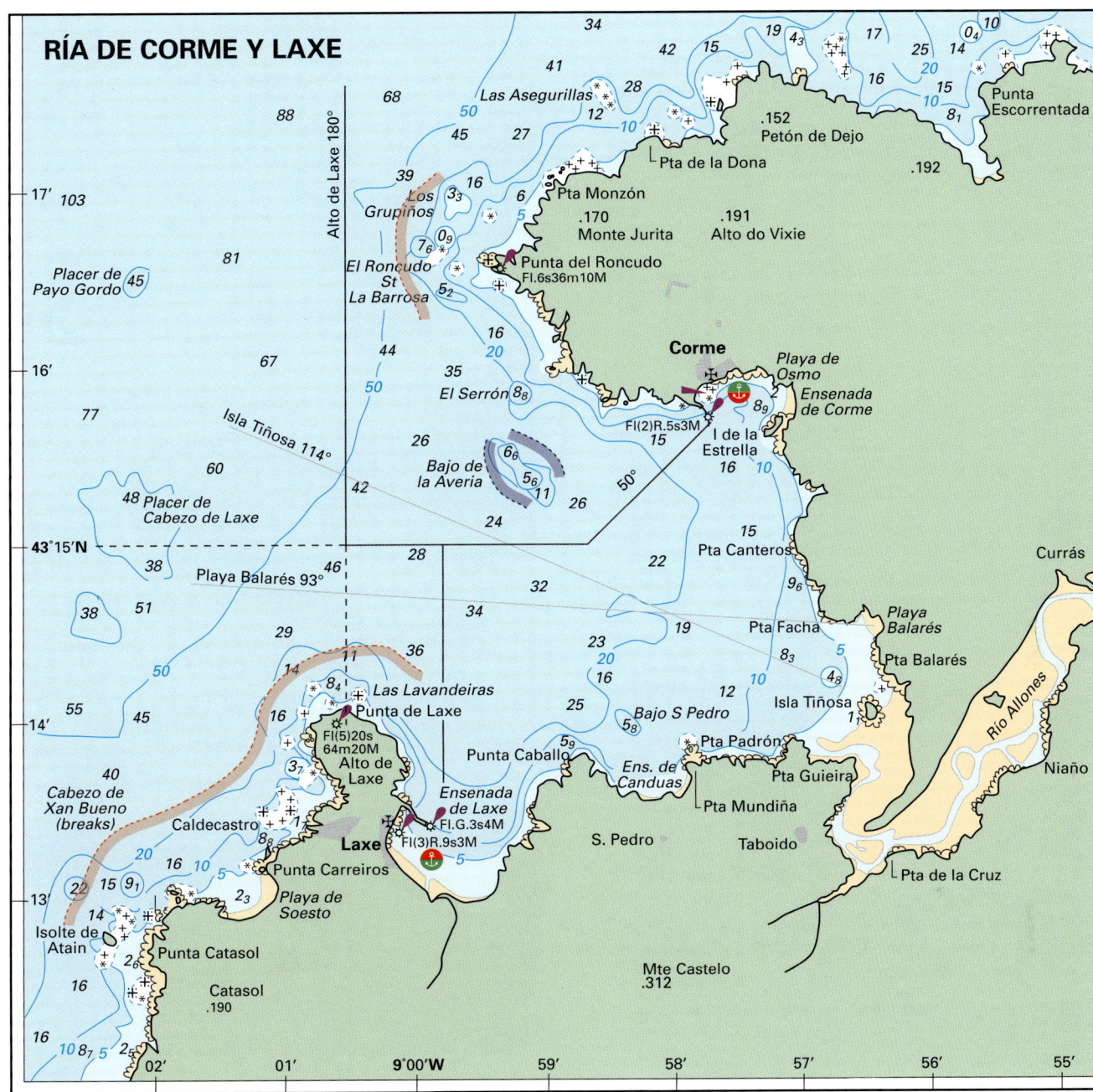

Ría de Corme y Laxe

Approach & entrance

Approach into bay is unlit before lit final approach. Care must be taken to stay outside the grid of *bateas* in Corme at night. Both harbours will have fishing vessel movements.

The nearst long range light is at Punta de Laxe Fl(5)20s20M.

From the north:

- Head due south (longitude 09°00'.68W) for Punta de Laxe Fl(5)20s to clear El Roncudo

- In rough conditions avoid the Bajo de Averia by sailing south of it on latitude 43°15'N which is in line with Punta Canteiros

- For Corme wait until the light on the end of the breakwater Fl(2)R.5s (Playa de Osmo behind) bears 50° before making for the harbour

- For Laxe turn due south when the end of the breakwater bears 180° (longtitude 08°59'.7W).

CRUISING GALICIA 103

COSTA DA MORTE

⚓ Corme

Shelter from NW, N and E, but very exposed for S winds. Anchor between the harbour wall and *batea* grid in 3-5m sand.

Note isolated rock and unlit green post close to NW corner or *batea* grid.

⚓ Laxe

Shelter from W, S and E, but very exposed for N winds unless space is found behind the harbour quay.

Provisioning & eating

The streets along the sea front are where the majority of shops and bars/restaurants are located.

Corme has a market every Friday, at one end of Calle Real (from the little square in the centre of the village).

At Laxe, walk south away from the harbour area towards the beach along Rúa de Rosalía de Castro and Avenida de Cesáreo Pondal.

Interest

Corme is smaller than Laxe at the other end of the ría, a pleasant village located in a picturesque setting which has retained traditional Galician buildings and charm. The little park at Avenida de Marina by the sea front is a good setting to admire the view.

Laxe is slightly bigger, also in a very picturesque setting. The church of Santa María is central to the town, a good point from which to walk along the pleasant Paseo Marítimo. The views of the ría and the ocean from Monte de Insua (Punta Laxe) 1 mile north of the town are excellent.

Out of Laxe, towards the detour to Baio from the Ponteceso road, there are two historics sites woth visiting. **Dolmen de Dombate** is a megalithic monument from around 2500BC. **Cibdá Celta de**

| Corme & Laxe | 43°15'N 08°58'W |

Corme
- Straightforward approach, mussel platform grid in the bay (lit)
- Good shelter from all winds except strong south
- Anchor behind harbour wall or between mussel platforms and shore

Laxe
- Straightforward approach, clearance 0.5M from Punta de Laxe, exposed to N wind
- Anchor behind harbour wall or towards the beach

Cibdá Celta de Borneiro

Ponteceso at the head of Ría de Corme

104 CRUISING GALICIA

COSTA DA MORTE

Borneiro, access through a track from the road is a *castro* settlement from 500BC.

To the south and west of Laxe, the dramatic coast down to Cabo Villano opens up, not developed and endowed with some of the most attractive, wild beaches and natural spaces of Costa da Morte. The coastline is treacherous to sailors but from land it is a small area well worth exploring. The tiny fishing village of Carmelle is a good stopping point. **Laguna de Traba** is among the best spots, for its combination of lagoon, sand dunes and pink granite rock mountains backdrop. If you have the time plenty of little bays will catch your interest, including the notorious Ensenada de Trece, site of the loss of the *Serpent* school-ship from the British Navy.

Corme & Laxe

- A Coruña 100km, Santiago 60km, Pontevedra 100km, Vigo 140km

Corme
- ✗ Bars & restaurants: harbour front and from the village square (Calle Real etc)
- ☐ Market every Friday from the village square at Calle Real

Laxe
- ✗ Bars & restaurants: along the harbour front, Calle de la Rúa Marina
- ⓘ Tourist office: Avda Cesáreo Pondal (sea front southern side) ☎ 981 706903
- 🔧 Ferretería: Sergio Albores Lema, Villa Amparo 53 ☎ 981 735455
- ✚ Centro Saude Laxe, Avda Cesáreo Pondal ☎ 981 735199

Corme harbour

Corme

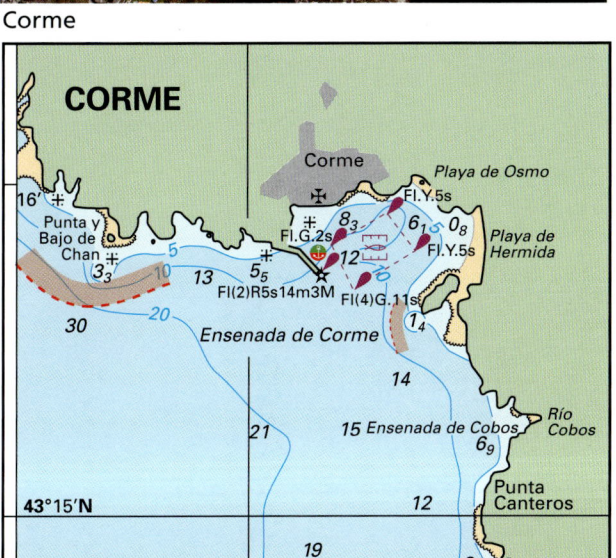

Laxe

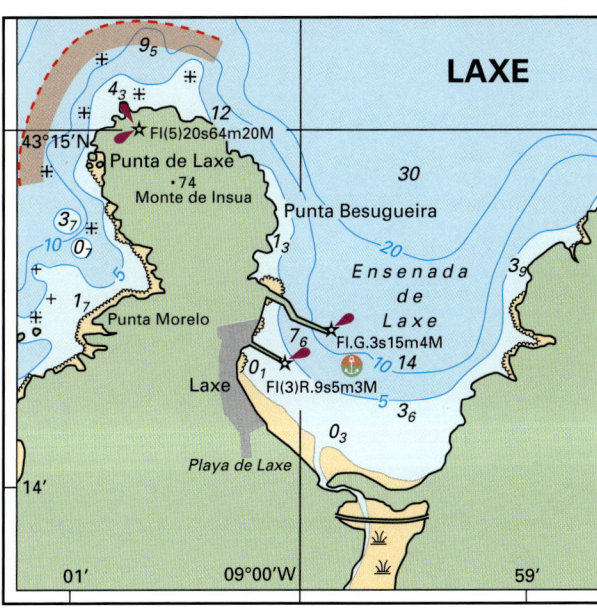

RÍA DE CORME Y LAXE

CRUISING GALICIA 105

COSTA DA MORTE

Ría de Camariñas

Approach & entrance

Day and night time lit approach but must be undertaken with care as there are numerous off lying dangers. The entrance can be locally very windy. The nearest long range light is at Cabo Villano Fl(2)15s28M.

From the north and northwest:

- Keep Cabo Toriñana Fl(2+1)15s bearing no greater than 200° to clear offlying rocks NW of Cabo Villano Fl(2)15s and Las Quebrantas
- Transit Punta de Lago light Oc(2)WRG.6s and tower white beacon (located inside ría on east shore) on 108°.5. Follow this transit until the destination port (Muxía or Camariñas) is visible
- If approaching Caramiñas, alter course when the end of the breakwater Fl.R.5s bears less than 30°.

Alternative approach from the north

Settled weather only:

- From 4 miles out, heading of 135° towards Ermita de Nuestra Señora del Monte Farelo
- Change to transit of Muxía church with Monte Enfesto hill on 179°
- Change to transit Punta de Lago light Oc(2) WRG.6s and tower white beacon (located inside ría on east shore) on 108°.5. Follow this transit until the destination port (Muxía or Camariñas) is visible.

From the southwest:

- Transit Punta Villueira and Punta del Castillo lights (front Fl.5s rear Iso.4s) on 80°
- Change to transit Punta de Lago light Oc(2) WRG.6s and tower white beacon (located inside ría on east shore) on 108°.5. Follow this transit until the destination port (Muxía or Camariñas) is visible.

Camariñas Marina

106 CRUISING GALICIA

COSTA DA MORTE

⚓ Camariñas

Small and friendly marina at northern end of the ría, next to fishing harbour. Can be bouncy in NE to S winds. Camariñas is a small town famous for its embroidery craft.

Approach & entrance

The approach into Ría de Camariñas is described at the start of the section. Once inside the Ría approach into Camariñas marina is straightforward day and night.

From the transit Punta de Lago light Oc(2)WRG.6s and tower white beacon (located inside Ría on east shore) on 108°.5:

- Alter course when the end of the breakwater Fl.R.5s bears 30°
- Ensure at least 300m clearance from the shallows and dangers along the shore west and south of the marina
- Having passed the breakwater Fl.R.5s head to one of the outer hammerhead pontoons.

Berthing & Facilities

Club Náutico de Camariñas is a small and welcoming marina, at a perfect location along this difficult stretch of Galician coast. The pontoon dimensions are designed for boats up to 10m, but yachts up to 15m can be accommodated in the fingers and even larger on the outer hammerhead pontoons. The pontoons can be bouncy in a strong *nordés* (NE wind) common in the summer.

Showers and laundry are basic but of good standard and the restaurant at the clubhouse offers good hearty food.

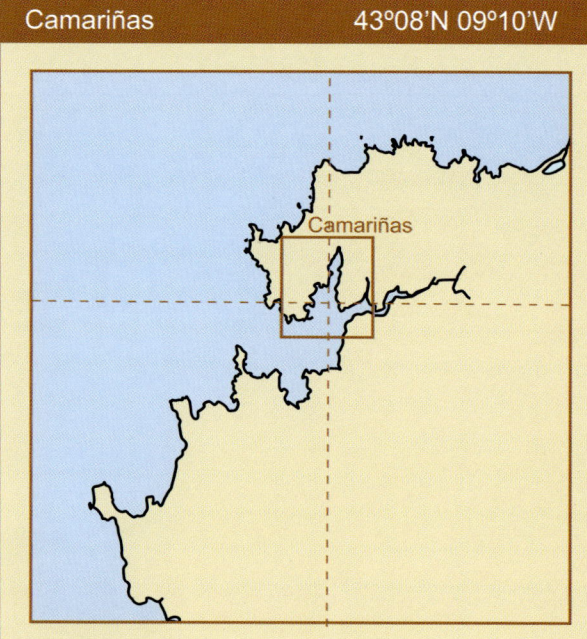

Camariñas   43°08'N 09°10'W

Club Náutico de Camariñas
- Good shelter from S, W, N winds, can be bouncy with strong NE.
- Careful piloting required to avoid dangers on approach (Las Quebrantas and Leixón de Juanboy shallows) at isolated rocks/ shallows at the entrance
- Approximately 60 visitor berths from total of 80
- Depth 3m minimum
- ⛽ Fuel tank on shore at the centre pontoon opposite the marina hut - long hose reaches to third finger

⚓ Anchorages

There are a number of anchorages very near the marina, in 2 to 8m mud or sand with some gravel depending on where you are. Good shelter from the *nordés* can be had using the steep tree-lined hills north of the Río del Puente del Puerto. Exit routes in case of wind change are clear of hidden dangers.

The Camelle harbour 5M northeast of Camariñas is subject to swell and should only be approached in settled weather due to its narrow entrance.

Provisioning

Camariñas is small and remote, this is not a place for large supermarkets. There are a number of shops and restaurants along the sea front by the fishing harbour (Avda Ambrosio Feijóo, Cantón Miguel Feijóo) and the continuation round the headland (Avda da Coruña).

COSTA DA MORTE

Camariñas

Quiet anchorages

CRUISING GALICIA

COSTA DA MORTE

Embroidery at Camariñas

Camariñas

- A Coruña 90km, Santiago 80km, Pontevedra 140km, Vigo 180km
- 🚌 Bus stop: Avda Ambrosio Feijóo (by the fishing harbour quay), buses to Santiago and other major towns
- 🛒 Supermarket: Gadis, Cantón de Miguel Feijóo (seafront, north of harbour)
- 🍴 Bars & restaurants:
  - Marina clubhouse
  - Along the sea front streets by the fishing harbour and around the town headland
- ℹ️ Tourist office: Praza de Insuela ☏ 981 737234 (across the water from fishing harbour quay)
- ✚ Centro Saude Camariñas, Rúa Río do Prado ☏ 981 736200

Interest

The town of Camariñas has been spoilt by careless modern construction, at the expense of the old fishing village feel. The setting of the Ría is, however, beautiful and remote.

You are in a windy, rugged place, as is clear from the amount of wind turbines in the hills behind the town. On the way in you are bound to have felt the strength of the wind which seems to build up even in the calmest day. This is one of many locations along Costa da Morte where wind electricity generation has been given priority encouraged by a generous tax system from the Spanish government.

Camariñas is well known for its traditional embroidery, a craft which continues today and is celebrated in the interesting Museo do Encaixe (Cantón de Miguel Feixó) which holds historic and modern pieces. A statute outside the museum celebrates the women that practice the craft (*palilleiras*).

To the north of Camariñas the coast is the most dramatic stretch of Costa da Morte. A short taxi ride will take you to the *Cementerio de los Ingleses*, the resting place of the 172 English cadets that died when their school ship *Serpent* wrecked in the shallows of Boi by Ensenada de Trece (also known as the English Beach).

The tragedy of the British Navy's Serpent

During the night of the 10th of November 1890, the British Navy school ship The *Serpent* approached Punta de Boi, en route to Sierra Leone from Plymouth. A mountainous ocean swell and very strong onshore wind pushed the ship towards the coast with such strength that nothing those on board could do to prevent her crashing onto the rocks.

Only three of 175 sailors survived, Bourton, Gould and Lacsne, who arrived in the early hours of the morning at the parish of Xaviña. The village rallied to assist but when they reached Ensenada de Trece they found only the wreckage and bodies washed ashore. The villagers buried the dead in what is now known as Cementerio de los Ingleses (The English Cemetery). Nine days later in the presence of the *Lapwing*, another British ship that had arrived from A Coruña, the cemetery was consecrated. The kind actions of the village were acknowledged by the *Lapwing* with a gun salute and the Admiralty gifted a gun to the priest, a gold watch to the Mayor of Camariñas and a barometer to the Council. It is said that, up to 1950, all British Navy vessels saluted as they passed by.

The disaster led to the construction of the lighthouse at Cabo Villano, a new light to assist ships in navigation.

COSTA DA MORTE

COSTA DA MORTE

⚓ Muxía

Small fishing harbour at the southern side of Ría de Camariñas, offering shelter from W, S and E winds.

Approach & entrance

The approach into Ría de Camariñas is described at the start of the section.

Day and night time approach into Muxía.

- From the transit transit Punta de Lago Oc(2) WRG.6s and tower white beacon (located inside Ría on east shore) on 108°.5
- Turn onto light at end of breakwater Fl(2)G.10s when it bears 200°
- Ensure at least 400m clearance from Punta de la Barca peninsula which is surrounded by shallows and isolated dangers. Beware of shallows on the east side of the harbour, and further east above Punta de Chorente.

⚓ Anchorage

It is possible to anchor within the harbour, subject to finding space among the many small fishing boats. Sheltered by the harbour breakwater and moles from all winds.

There is room to anchor outside the east mole, exposed to north winds.

From 2007 there are some pontoons inside the harbour which may be available to visitors. A new marina is planned (2008/09).

The harbour quay is a possibility of last resort, subject to appropriate arrangements with the fishing boats which use it.

Provisioning, eating & transport

Muxía is very small, it won't take you long to find all the action at Calle de la Rúa Marina along the harbour. There are a few small restaurants, shops and chemists. Several small groceries and *ultramarinos* (small food stores) will provide enough for a victualling expedition but there is no supermarket in the town.

There is no scheduled transport from the town. A taxi ride to Camariñas gives you access to a bus stop from which coaches depart to the major towns including Santiago.

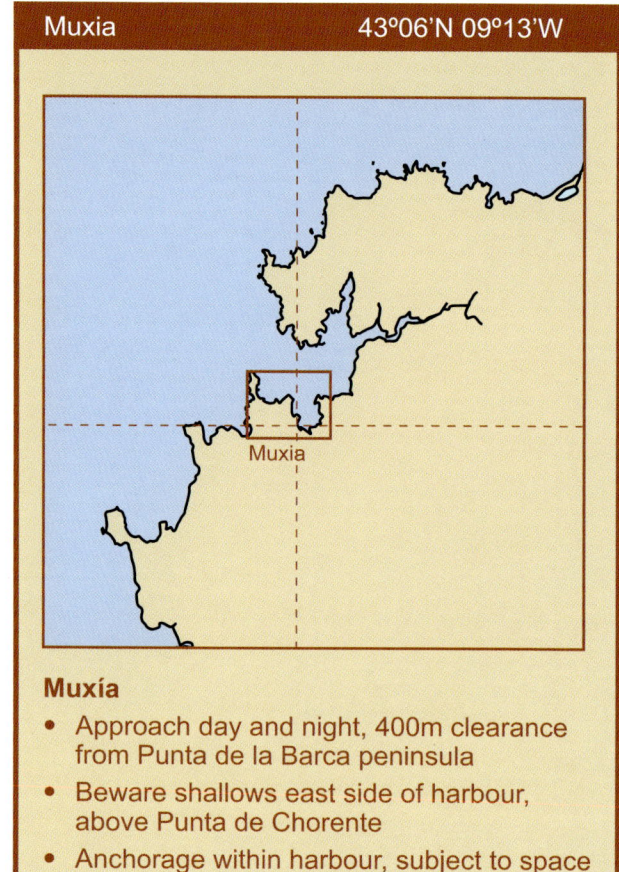

Muxía
- Approach day and night, 400m clearance from Punta de la Barca peninsula
- Beware shallows east side of harbour, above Punta de Chorente
- Anchorage within harbour, subject to space
- Planned marina (2008/09)

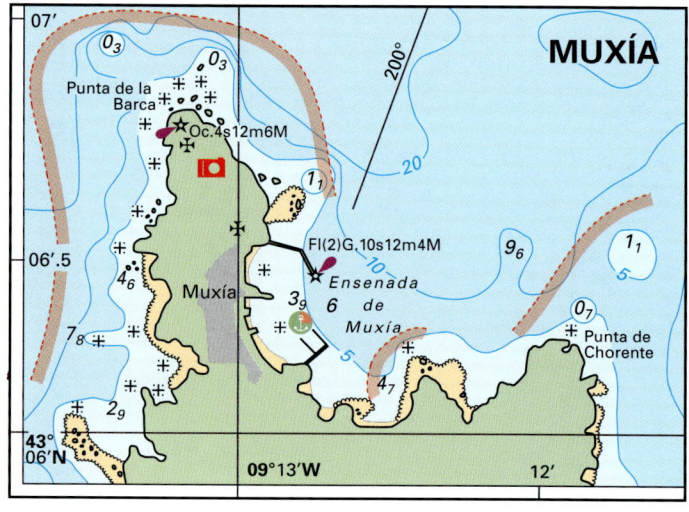

Muxía harbour

112 CRUISING GALICIA

COSTA DA MORTE

Interest

Muxía is yet another Galician fishing village whose traditional houses have been replaced with modern, bland construction. There is still character in the small town, given its location, but little is left of the old charm.

Muxía's highlight is the **Santuario de la Virxe da Barca**, which you can reach walking towards Punta de la Barca along the shore road. It's a pleasant walk and the views are spectacular. Along the way you can see the fish racks in which *congrio* fish is dried.

The church is a sober affair associated with miracles. The stones (**Piedras del Milagro**) have good sailing shapes, one of which resembles a small boat (*barca*) and will cure your various ills if you pass under it.

Along the road to Caramiñas, **Playa de Lago** is a beautiful beach setting, surrounded by trees and adjoining a small lake with a river flowing into the Ría.

> **Muxía**
>
> - A Coruña 100km, Santiago 80km, Pontevedra 130km, Vigo 170km
> - 🛒 Groceries along Calle de la Rúa Marina
> - ✖ Bars & restaurants: along the harbour front, Calle de la Rúa Marina
> - ℹ Tourist office: Virxe da Barca ☎ 981742563
> - ✚ Centro Saude Muxía, Rúa Saude ☎ 981742066

Virxe da Barca sanctuary

Pedra da Barca

Anchorage east of the mole

RÍA DE CAMARIÑAS

CRUISING GALICIA 113

COSTA DA MORTE

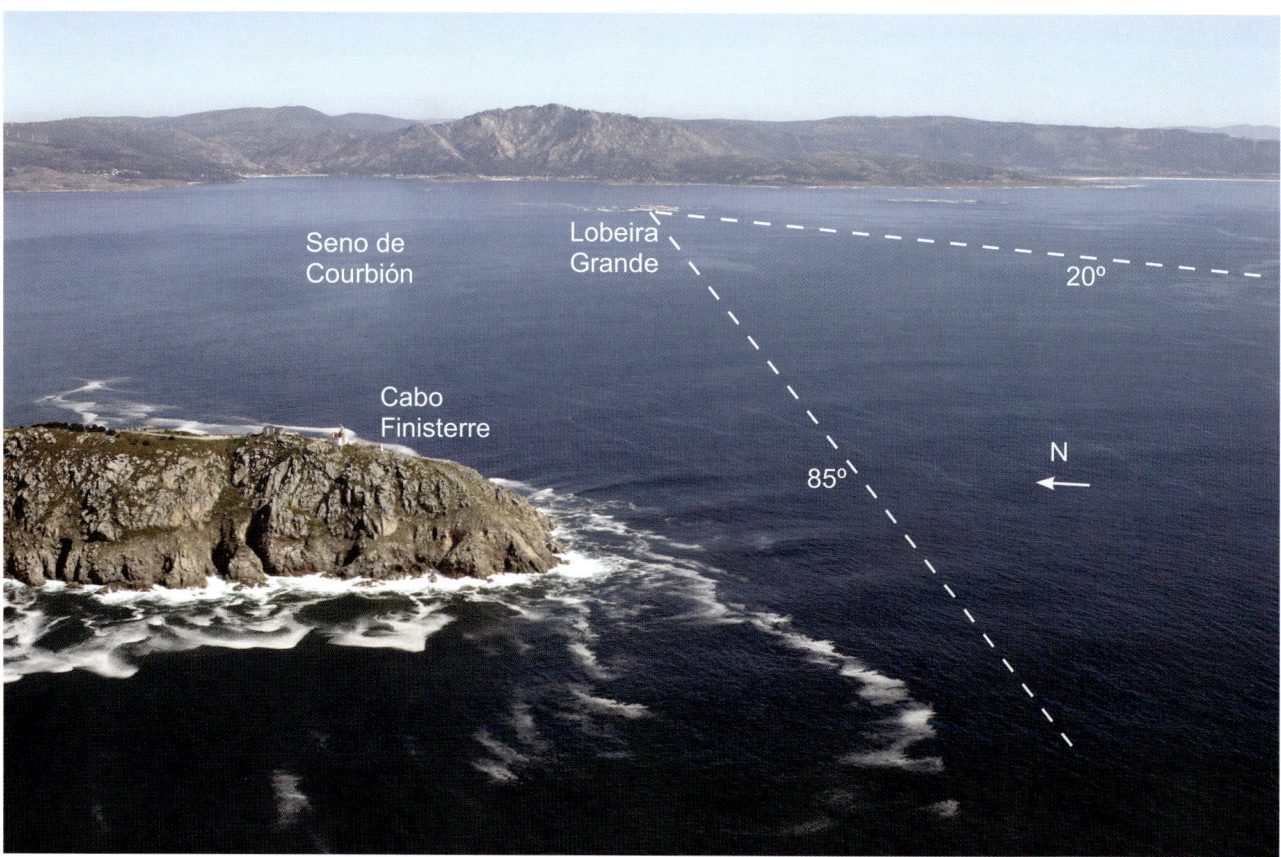

Finisterre - Seno de Corcubión

Approach & entrance

Day and night time approach.

From the north:

- Caution is needed around La Muñiz (4M, 140° to Finisterre light Fl.5s23M) and La Carraca shallows (2M on a bearing of 120° to Finisterre light Fl.5s) and Centolo island. Keep at least 2 miles from the shore in adverse conditions on an approach from the north and even further (4M) if transiting the area
- Turn into the bay once Lobeira Grande FL(3)15s bears less than 85°
- Inside the bay it is possible in good conditions to turn and sail closer to the rocky shore, maintaining 300m clearance towards Finisterre breakwater Fl.R.2s.

From the south:

- In good weather there is a 1M wide passage from Ría de Muroa (Punta Carreiro), on a 315° heading. Clearance of 300m should be given from the coast to clear off lying dangers from Punta Carreiros to Los Minarzos. Bajo De Los Meixidos and Los Buyos are left to the west. The direction of these dangers from Punta Insua Fl(3)WR.9s are indicated by the red sectors of the light.
- Ensure a bearing of at least 20° to Lobeira Grande FL(3)15s is maintained in order to avoid the shallows Las Arrosas and Bajo Duyo (don't confuse it with Lobeira Chica as both are low lying).

114 CRUISING GALICIA

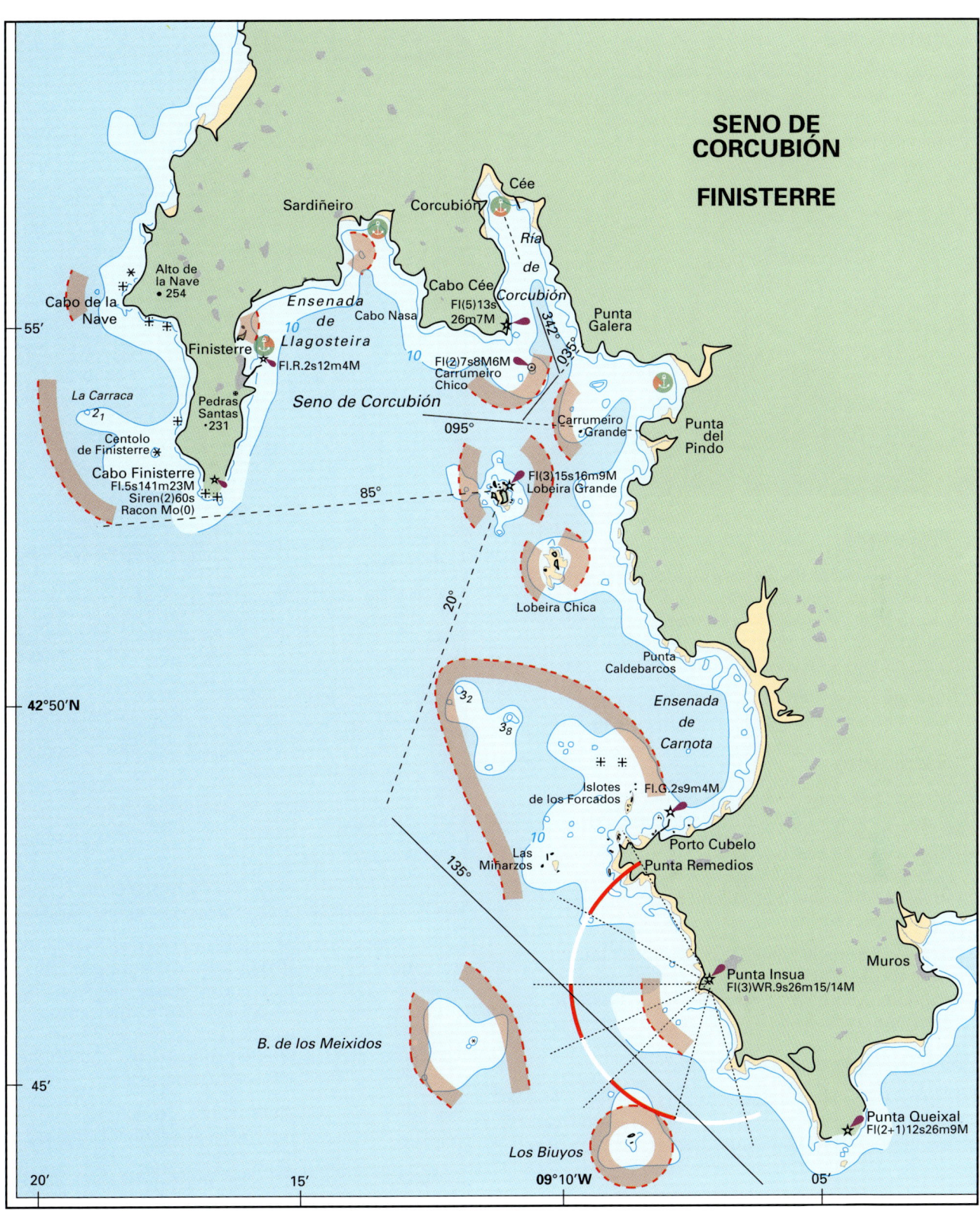

COSTA DA MORTE

⚓ Finisterre

The notorious peninsula that is associated with many dramatic marine episodes. Difficult in bad weather, often a point of significant change in weather conditions for the sailor. Picturesque anchorages inside the bay.

Finisterre lighthouse

⚓ Finisterre

Anchorage beyond the harbour breakwater wall in mud and some stones. The location is exposed to the north and there are many fishing boats within the sheltered area of the harbour, so it may be difficult to find a satisfactory position.

If the wind is northerly Playa de Langosteira offers shelter, slightly further away from the town.

⚓ Sardiñeiro

Very quiet but unlit anchorage in mud and weed sheltered from all winds except from the south.

- Approach the beaches on a track along the east side of Ensenada del Sardiñeiro to avoid the shallows off Eiro. The channel is around 0.5M with ample depth
- Beware the many small boats and their lines close to the beach, many very difficult to see at night. No bateas were present in 2007 but bottom may be foul.

Provisioning and facilities

Finisterre has a large number of bars and restaurants for the size of the town, due to tourism. You will not fail to find somewhere in the area near the harbour and the plaza.

Interest

Finisterre received its name from the Romans (*Finis Terrae*), as the perceived end of the world of their time. It is not in fact the most western point of Iberia, Cabo de la Nave and Cabo Toriñana are both further west, but it is hard to escape the sense of a place at the end of the mainland when standing at the lighthouse.

The shore of Finisterre has been the scene of a number of major sailing tragedies. The British Navy ship *Monitor Captain* collided with the

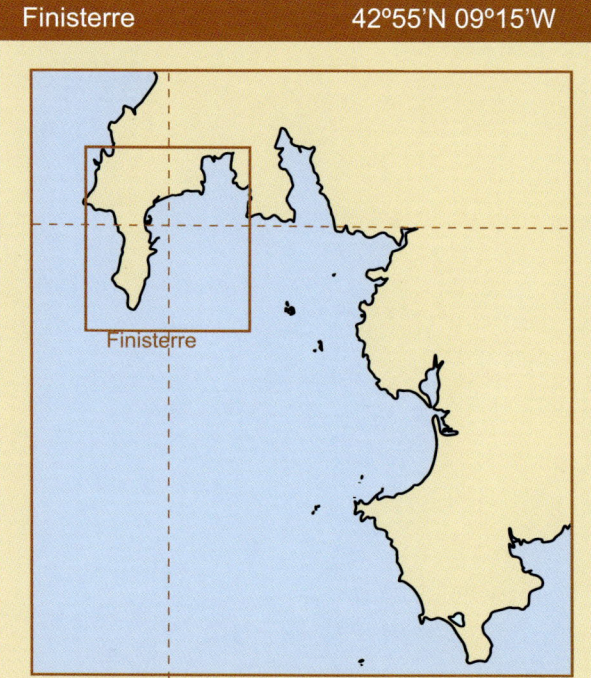

Finisterre   42°55'N 09°15'W

Finisterre
- Behind the harbour breakwater, mud and stones.
- Difficult in poor visibility due to large number of boats.
- Exposed to N wind.

Sardiñeiro
- Difficult in poor visibility, due to many small boats by the beach.
- Approach on the east side to avoid shallows.
- Mud and weed.
- Good shelter from W, N and E winds.

Centolo rock in 1870, unable to recover from a roll caused by very strong westerly winds. 482 crew were lost at this, the most tragic incident of Finisterre's history. More recently, the cargo ship *Casón* was a casualty, beached at Playa del Rostro, loaded with toxic products that caused the evacuation of the local population.

The **lighthouse** was built in 1853, a major construction at the top of the headland. Later a

Finisterre harbour

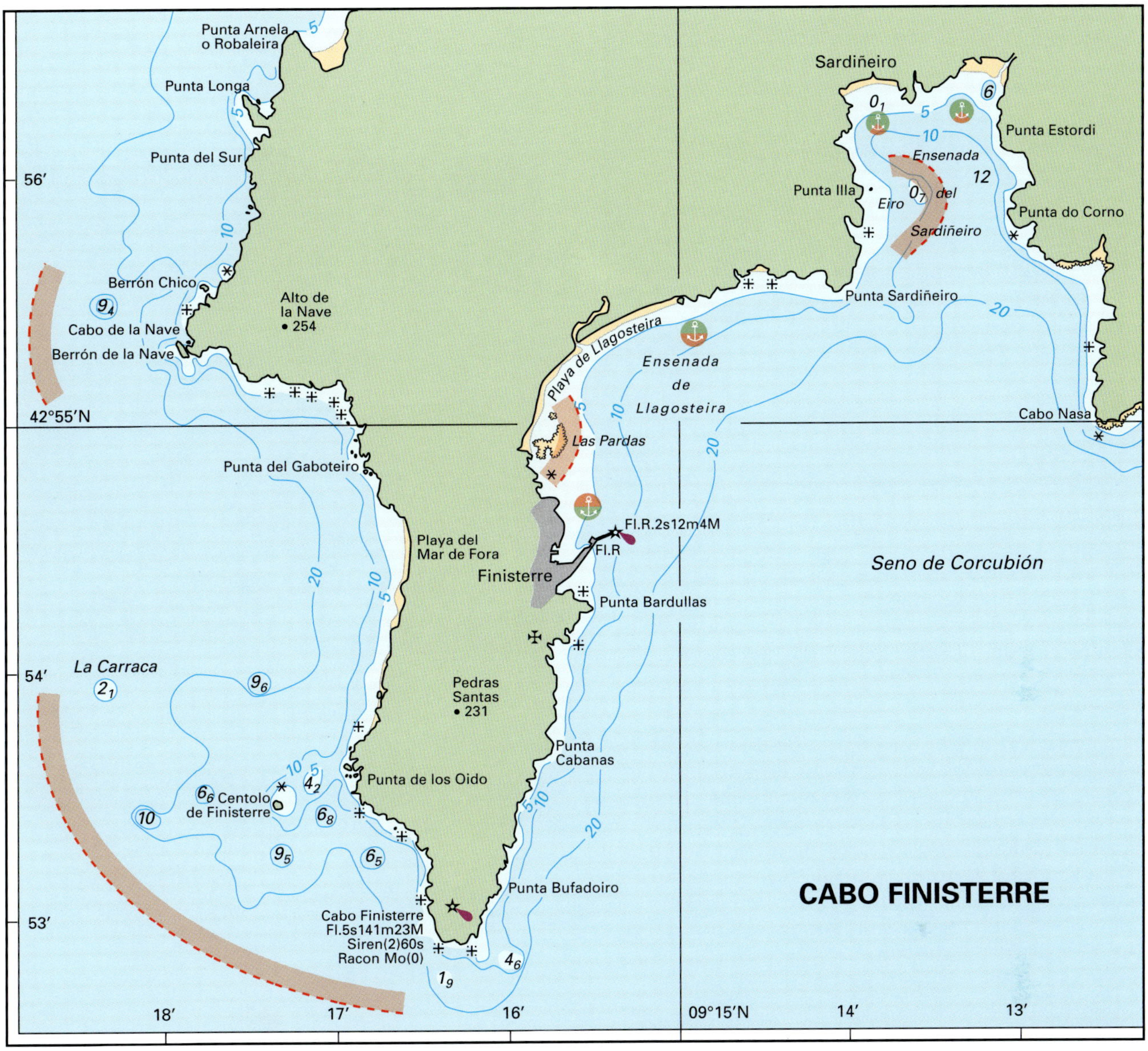
CABO FINISTERRE
Punta Arnela
o Robaleira
Punta Longa
Punta del Sur
56′
Berrón Chico
Alto de
la Nave
• 254
Cabo de la Nave
Berrón de la Nave
42°55′N
Punta del Gaboteiro
Playa del
Mar de Fora
Finisterre
La Carraca
54′
Pedras
Santas
• 231
Punta de los Oido
Centolo
de Finisterre
53′
Cabo Finisterre
Fl.5s141m23M
Siren(2)60s
Racon Mo(0)
Punta Bufadoiro
Punta Cabanas
Punta Bardullas
Fl.R.2s12m4M
Fl.R
Las Pardas
Playa de Llagosteira
Ensenada
de
Llagosteira
Sardiñeiro
Punta Illa
Eiro
Ensenada
del
Sardiñeiro
Punta Estordi
Punta do Corno
Punta Sardiñeiro
Cabo Nasa
Seno de Corcubión
18′
17′
16′
09°15′N
14′
13′

Cabo de
la Nave
Centolo
Cabo
Finisterre
N

FINISTERRE

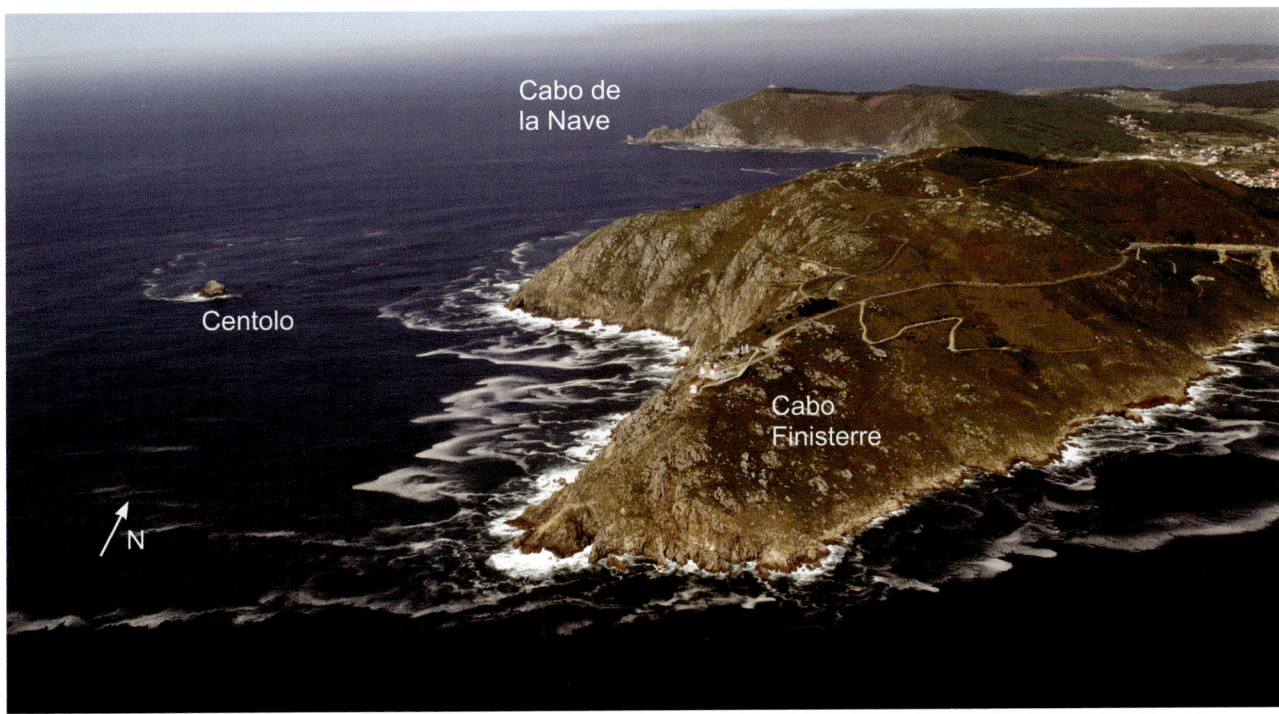

COSTA DA MORTE

> **Finisterre**
>
> - A Coruña 110km, Santiago 80km, Pontevedra 150km, Vigo 180km
> - 🚌 Bus station: Rúa Federico Ávila
> - 🛒 Market: Mercado Municipal, Paseo da Ribeira (harbour front)
> - 🍴 Restaurants and bars: many for the size of the town, close the harbour
> - ℹ️ Tourist office: Rúa Real 2 ☎ 981 740781
> - ✚ Centro Saude Fisterra, Rua Cala Figueira, ☎ 981 712263

siren was added to assist with visibility in the not infrequent fog. This siren bellows two prolonged low pitch blasts that have acquired it the name of *Vaca de Fisterra* (Finisterre cow). Anyone who has heard the sound cannot but agree with the description, of some help in the nervous circumstances of navigating in this area in poor visibility.

Finisterre was one of the pilgrim destinations in the middle ages, associated with apostle Santiago as a transit point in his voyage to Galicia. The numbers of pilgrims led to the construction of a Pilgrims Hospital, long destroyed, near the pretty church of **Nosa Señora das Areas**. Outside the church during Easter the Romaría do Santo Cristo de Fisterra festival re-enacts the passion but also incorporates the ancient cult of the sun.

Romaría de Santo Cristo at Easter in Finisterre

COSTA DA MORTE

Finisterre harbour

Ensenada del Sardiñeiro

COSTA DA MORTE

⚓ Corcubión

Long ría with good shelter anchorages but complex piloting in bad weather or poor visibility. Busy fishing and industrial town.

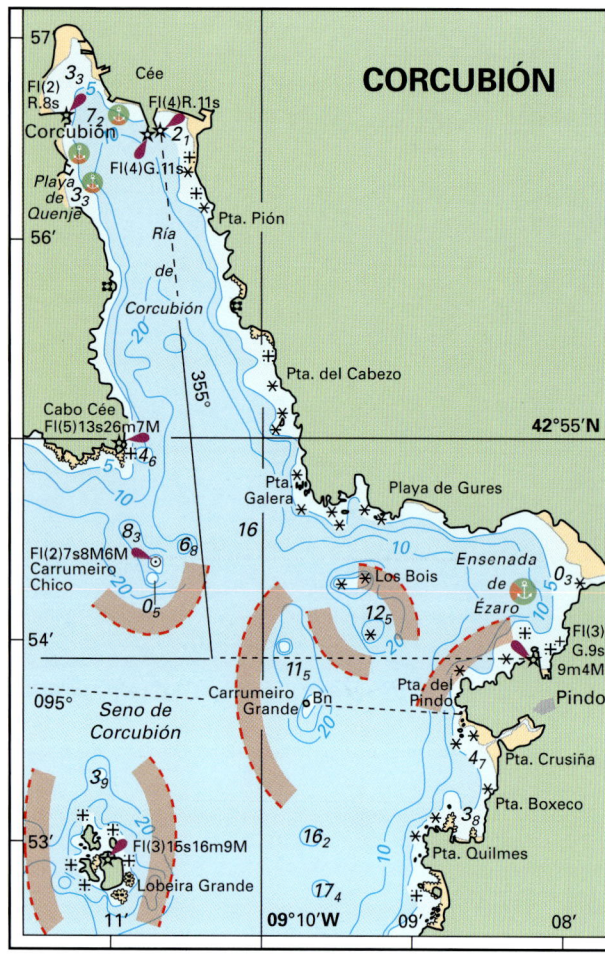

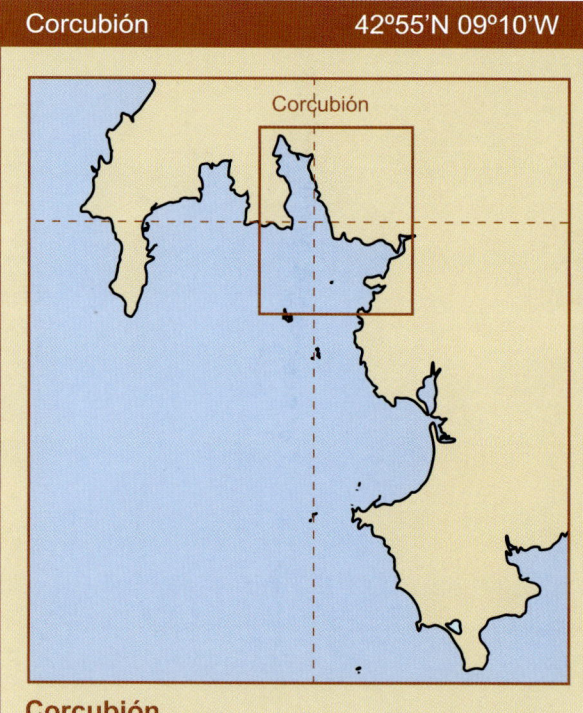

Corcubión
- Good shelter from W, N and E winds.
- Complex piloting in bad weather or poor visibility.
- ⛽ Fuel at fishing harbour.

Ensenada de Ézaro
- Good shelter from N, E and S winds
- Exposed to an air current that can build up from the valley NE.
- Exposed to west with dangerous shallows on west side of bay.

Approach & entrance

Day and night time approach possible but complex piloting around the many dangers in bad weather or poor visibility.

- Having entered Seno de Corcubión, approach on a latitude of 42°54'N with Pindo Pier Fl(3)G on the bow
- Alter course to 355° and head for the pier at Pontella Fl(4)R.11s.

⚓ Corcubión and Cée

Anchorages in 3-10m sand and stones, all good shelter from W, N and E winds.

- In front of Playa de Quenxe. Beware the many small boats near the beach
- Small inlet to the south of Corcubión harbour. The space in the harbour itself is crowded with small boats. beware restricted area for shellfish beds.

Corcubión

COSTA DA MORTE

- To the east in front of the Cée industrial harbour quay.

⚓ Ensenada de Ézaro

- Very quiet and charming anchorage, but exposed to west winds and to a NE air current (common in the summer) that builds up from the valley. Some shelter from swell.
- beware **unmarked shallows** on the west side of the bay.

Corcubión

- A Coruña 100km, Santiago 90km, Pontevedra 130km, Vigo 165km
- 🛒 Market: Mercado Municipal, Rúa de Mártires
- ⓘ Tourist Office: Explanada do Porto 17 (harbour fron) ☏ 981 706163
- Banks and other shops: Plaza Castelao (in Ceé)
- ✚ Chemist: Rúa da Viña
- ✚ Centro Saude Corcubión, Rúa da Viña ☏ 981 745552

Provisioning & eating

Corcubión is a small town but it has a good *mercado* (market) in the centre, near the main square by the town hall. The streets around the square are good for bars and food.

Interest

Corcubión is a very pretty village, with many traditional Galician **galleried houses** looking onto the pleasant promenade by the sea. The village combines the heritage and wealth of past local nobility with the working style of a fishing community.

CRUISING GALICIA 121

Corcubión

The setting is somewhat spoiled by the shipbuilding and industrial Cée across the water, local providers of jobs but not the best for a pretty anchorage background. Look towards Corcubión or the mountains and you will appreciate the charm of this area.

It is worth looking at **Casa Miñones** in the central plaza, an impressive house of past nobility. The Iglesia de San Marcos is romanesque in origin, showing the old pedigree of the village. There are other imposing buildings in the centre which you will quickly come across as you walk around it.

The **Seno de Corcubión** museum at the small boat harbour (Quenxe) has an interesting collection of maritime objects and displays centred on the Ría.

The valley behind Ensenada de Ézaro is the course of the **river Xallas,** a unique feature as it is one of very few that empties into the sea through a water fall. The dam up river greatly reduces the flow, to the point where in summer months it may only last a short time in the day.

The landscape is dominated by the mountains, particularly Ézaro and Pindo. The latter is associated with legends about the Celts.

A walk of 1 mile to the south of Ensenada de Ézaro is the interesting **Playa de Quilmes,** where you can see remains of old salt factories and 19th century abandoned boathouses.

COSTA DA MORTE

⚓ Carnota

Very exposed anchorage in Ensenada de Carnota, with fishing harbour Puerto Cubelo at the south end (many dangers). Spectacular beach.

Approach & entrance

Settled weather daytime only. Unmarked shallows and reefs NW of Puerto Cubelo. No lights other than the Puerto Cubelo wall marker.

- Approach from NW
- Beware unmarked 3.2m shallow Roda Grande in the centre of the bay.

Porto Cubelo

⚓ Porto Cubelo

Busy fishing harbour, some protection may be afforded from swell by harbour wall and the reefs to the NW. Very tight space inside the harbour.

Once inside Ensenada de Carnota, approach end of harbour wall Fl.G.2s on 180°. Avoid shallows and reefs and Roda Grande.

Interest

Playa de Carnota is a spectacular isolated expanse of sand set in a 5km long crescent. The beach, dunes, tidal and wet areas behind form a rich ecological system. If the weather is settled this beach is a delight to walk.

Nearby the *hórreos* (Galician grain stores) at the villages of Carnota and Lira are the second and third largest in Galicia.

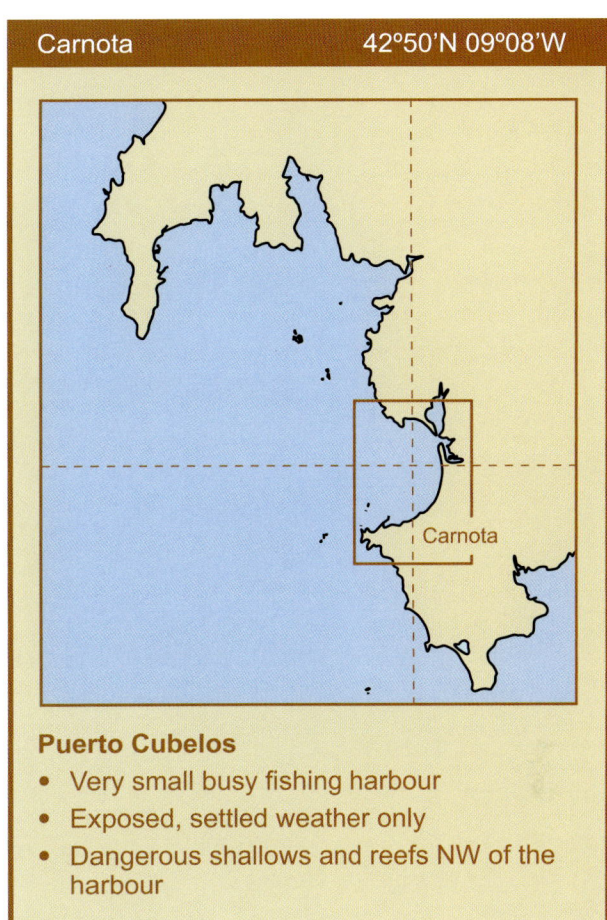

Carnota 42°50'N 09°08'W

Puerto Cubelos
- Very small busy fishing harbour
- Exposed, settled weather only
- Dangerous shallows and reefs NW of the harbour

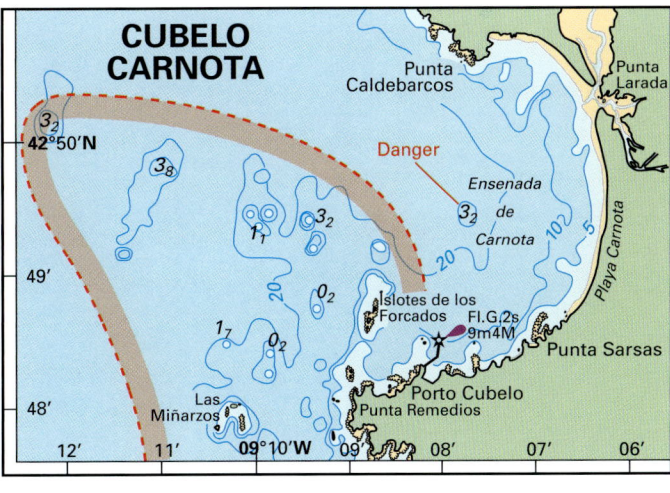

CORCUBIÓN

CRUISING GALICIA 123

Rías Baixas
Protected cruising waters

Rías Baixas

Introduction

The Rías Baixas are the extensive cruising waters of Galicia below Cabo Finisterre. The large estuaries of Muros, Arousa, Pontevedra and Vigo all provide shelter but are very different in character. From the unexploited and wilder Muros to the very industrial and busy Vigo all four have plenty of interesting sailing destinations and sites to visit.

Ría de Muros, unlike the other three Rías Baixas, is not protected by an island at its entrance but the large, gradually shelving bay absorbs the ocean swell. The towns of Muros and Noia are among the prettiest in Galicia, while Baroña is one of the best examples of Castro bronze age settlements. Anchorages are more sheltered on the northern side of the Ría, some with interesting depth contours that will test your surveying skills but will reward you with great locations at which to settle. On both sides of the Ría the hills are wooded and there are plenty of opportunities for walking. Portosín marina is welcoming and very used to accommodating cruising yachts, with a fuel station to add to the attraction. There are plans for a new marina in Muros, but this could take some time.

Ría de Arousa is very large and protected by Isla Sálvora from the ocean swell. While the whole Ría is very busy its character changes as you move towards the centre. Flanked by very exposed and wild Corrubedo and O Grove, the bays of Ribeira, Caramiñal and Vilagarcía together with the islands of Arousa help to shape a complex and interesting cruising area. You will sail among extensive arrays of *bateas*, the wooden platforms which are used to produce a large proportion of the world's farmed mussels. Despite the traffic it is easy to find a quiet sheltered anchorage, all the time remaining close to port facilities, fuel and very easy provisioning spots. The towns of Caramiñal and Rianxo, historic and characterful Cambados, the Catoira towers, the dunes of Corrubedo and Sálvora island, together with mussels, are among the highlights of the Ría.

After Arousa **Ría de Pontevedra** is a much more peaceful setting. Islas Ons and Onza protect it from the Ocean and fishing activity is not intense, largely concentrated in Marín. Development is on a much lesser scale than in Vigo or Arousa, with the exception of Sanxenxo, so the ría feels like a haven. Combarro and its *hórreos* (stone grain stores on toadstool

bases) and historic Pontevedra are among the most visited places in Galicia, both easy to access from a pretty anchorage behind Isla Tambo. The small Ría de Aldán at the entrance is a delightful away-from-it-all setting.

Ría de Vigo, the last before the border with Portugal at Río Miño, is a combination of industry and, at Vigo. city life, with more refined coastal resorts towards Baiona. **Islas Cíes** protect the ría and offer some sheltered anchorages within the National Park, waters that are hard to beat. For scenery Barra and Limens beaches on the northern side and Ensenada de San Simón right at the end of the ría are good destinations. Baiona, at the

RÍAS BAIXAS

Isla Tambo

Ría de Muros

Baiona

Santiago de Compostela

Hórreos at Combarro

CRUISING GALICIA 127

entrance, is a historic town and a convenient stop for fuel and victuals before crossing the ocean.

The Galician fishing industry is very large, providing for a country that consumes as much of it as the rest of Europe put together. Both inside and outside the Rías Baixas this is in evidence, where substantial coastal and offshore fleets catch a large part of the fishing quota and 3.500 *bateas* are used to farm mussels. Fishing is intertwined with the local way of life and is a key ingredient of local colour.

The Rías Baixas are well placed for a visit to **Santiago de Compostela**, the centre of Christian pilgrimage for over 1,000 years. The **coastal towns** of Muros, Noia, Combarro, Pobra do Caramiñal, Cambados, Pontevedra and Baiona are all worth a journey. If you have the time to travel further, **inland destinations** such as Tui or Ribadabia are within easy reach and are delightful trips. With some form of independent transport Ribeira Sacra in the south is not only home to a very good red wine but also to wonderful scenery. Visit the many prehistoric dolmens and petroglyphs, the remains of pre-roman fortified towns (*castros*), Roman roads and buildings, extensive medieval constructions and striking modern architecture, all of which the Rías Baixas has to offer.

Anchor at Islas Cíes, Ons and Sálvora, behind Isla Tambo, at Ría de Corcubión, on the northern side of Arousa and at Ría de Aldán for some of the best settings in the area. **Berth** at Portosín, Pobra do Caramiñal and Baiona for good facilities and pleasant surroundings.

RÍAS BAIXAS

Sailing in the Rías Baixas

Initial shelter

The best harbours for initial shelter in this area are: Portosín (Ría Muros, north), Caramiñal (Ría Arousa, centre), Sanxenxo (Ría de Pontevedra, centre) and Baiona (Ria de Vigo, south). All have lit entrances offering good shelter inside in marinas. More temporary shelter may be found behind the three offlying islands to Ría Arousa (unlit final approach), Ría de Pontevedra (lit final approach) and Ría de Vigo (lit final approach).

Other ports and facilities

- Muros: anchorage shelter for all weather conditions.
- Portosín: all weather marina, fuel, bus transport.
- Isla Sálvora: temporary anchor shelter from westerlies and Atlantic swell.
- Pobra do Caramiñal: excellent all weather marina and anchorage, fuel, chandleries, repairs, lift, bus transport. 8M from entrance to ría.
- Islas Ons: temporary anchor shelter from westerlies and Atlantic swell.
- Sanxenxo: good all weather marina and anchorage, fuel, chandleries, repairs, lift, bus.
- Aguete: small all weather marina, visitor pontoon (breakwater) bouncy in northerly winds.
- Bueu: anchorage shelter from southerly winds.
- Islas Cíes: temporary anchor shelter from westerlies and Atlantic swell.
- Cangas: all weather marina and anchorages nearby, fuel, chandleries, bus transport.
- Vigo: two good all weather marinas, lift, fuel, chandleries, bus transport, rail, airport.
- Baiona: two good all weather marinas, lift, fuel, chandleries, bus transport.

Emergencies

Lifeboats are present at Ribeira, Vilaxoán, Porto do Son, Portonovo and Vigo. There is a Maritime Safety Co-Ordination Centre (MRCC) at Finisterre which monitors Channel 16, MF 2182kHz and DSC Channel 70. Coast radio stations (Coastguard) are based at Finisterre to the north and Vigo to the south. They need to be contacted on their working channels (see Appendix). All the harbours mentioned as initial shelter have significant medical facilities.

Provisioning

There is no shortage of shops and *plazas* (markets) in the local towns and villages, plus a wealth of restaurants and bars at which you can enjoy excellent fresh food.

Repairs and chandleries

There are **boat lifts** at Club Náutico de Portosín (32 tons, Ría de Muros), Pobra do Caramiñal and Vilagarcía (40 tons, Ría de Arousa), Club Náutico de Portonova Sanxenxo (110 tons, Ría de Pontevedra), Real Club Náutico de Vigo (32 tons, Ría de Vigo) and Marina Dávila Sport Vigo (70 tons, Ría de Vigo).

All the main marinas will have information on local mechanic, rigging and electronic expertise. For spares the *ferreterías* (iron mongers) are a good resource, often very well stocked. Near the marinas there are retailers more focused on leisure sailors. The most extensive **chandlers** are in Vigo (e.g. Betanzos) and further north in Coruña (Pombo).

Transport

The excellent **train** line that links all of western Galicia has stops at Coruña, Santiago, Vilagarcía, Pontevedra and Vigo.

Numerous **buses** cover the area, run by a series of private companies (Castromil, Arriva and others) with routes to all the major towns including Santiago, Pontevedra, Vigo and A Coruña as well as the local towns. The main bus stations are at Santiago, Noia, Vilagarcía, Pontevedra and Vigo.

The major airports are at A Coruña, Santiago and Vigo, all three with regular national flight connections. A Coruña and Santiago have flights from international budget airlines.

Passages

The distance from Ría Muros to Ría Vigo is 50M (using the ports mentioned as initial shelter).

See the main introduction to the book for a description of tides, tidal heights and general weather conditions to be expected.

Swell generated by significant weather systems, sometimes deep in the Atlantic, can build up and stay for days. The best strategy will be to stand offshore into more than 100m. Harbour entrances are deep enough that an entry will not be affected by tidal height. Offlying shallow banks are, however, best avoided. These are shown on the chart for this section in blue. Some anchorages will become uncomfortable, or in the extreme untenable.

RÍAS BAIXAS

Tidal flows and height will not generally have an impact in any passage plan which means that the use of daylight hours can be maximised.

The chart of this section of coastline shows the significant lights that can be used for passage navigation at night and the unlit hazards more than 0.5M from the coast. These are best avoided by staying in more than 100m.

Fishing boats will be present, with their size and type of activity dependent on how far offshore they are found. Expect fishing pots close in (indeed in anything up to 150m). These can be all shapes, sizes and degree of visibility and can sometimes have pick-up buoys and floating lines trailing. Spotting them in significant swell will require attention.

Shipping will be using Ría de Pontevedra (Marín) and Ría de Vigo (Vigo), with Marín taking surprisingly large ships. The Traffic Separation Schemes in Ría de Vigo should be avoided.

Refuelling along Rías Baixas can be done at any of the harbours mentioned as initial shelter.

Winds are generally northerly so, for a round tour of this region, it makes sense to get down to Ría de Vigo in as few steps as possible and break up the return to windward by visiting and enjoying the Rías. The distance to go from one Ría to the next will vary, but can be as much as 35M (Ría Muros to Ría Arousa) if using the harbours mentioned as initial shelter. This is because most of the all-weather harbours are some distance up the Rías.

If transiting the area and wanting to break the journey, the following **anchorages** avoid these detours up the Rias, but none of them are completely protected from all directions and any significant swell. Distances given are measured from Baiona entrance south cardinal buoy, Q(6)+LFl.15s, marking the Islote Piedra de la Garza:

- East side of Isla Sálvora 25M
- East side of Isla Ons 15M
- West side of Ría de Aldán 13M
- East side of Isla del Faro 5M

The offlying islands mentioned also provide a suitable lee to adjust the sail plan and read up about any final approach further up the Ría.

The 100m contour line has a certain significance along this coastline. Stay outside it, and there will be no isolated dangers close-by to disturb a transit of this coastline. On the other hand, coming closer in offers some superb views, sails through narrow passages and numerous anchorages close at hand for a lunch-time stop. If beating to windward then these same anchorages will offer welcome relief overnight, but care should be taken in their selection to ensure they offer an undisturbed night.

If caught out by the nordés then an early morning start before the land heats up and the pressure falls over the land may well offer temporary relief.

Because of the distances involved, an alternative may well be to cut your losses and buy a train ticket into Santiago for a few days with the hope that things will have improved on your return.

RÍAS BAIXAS

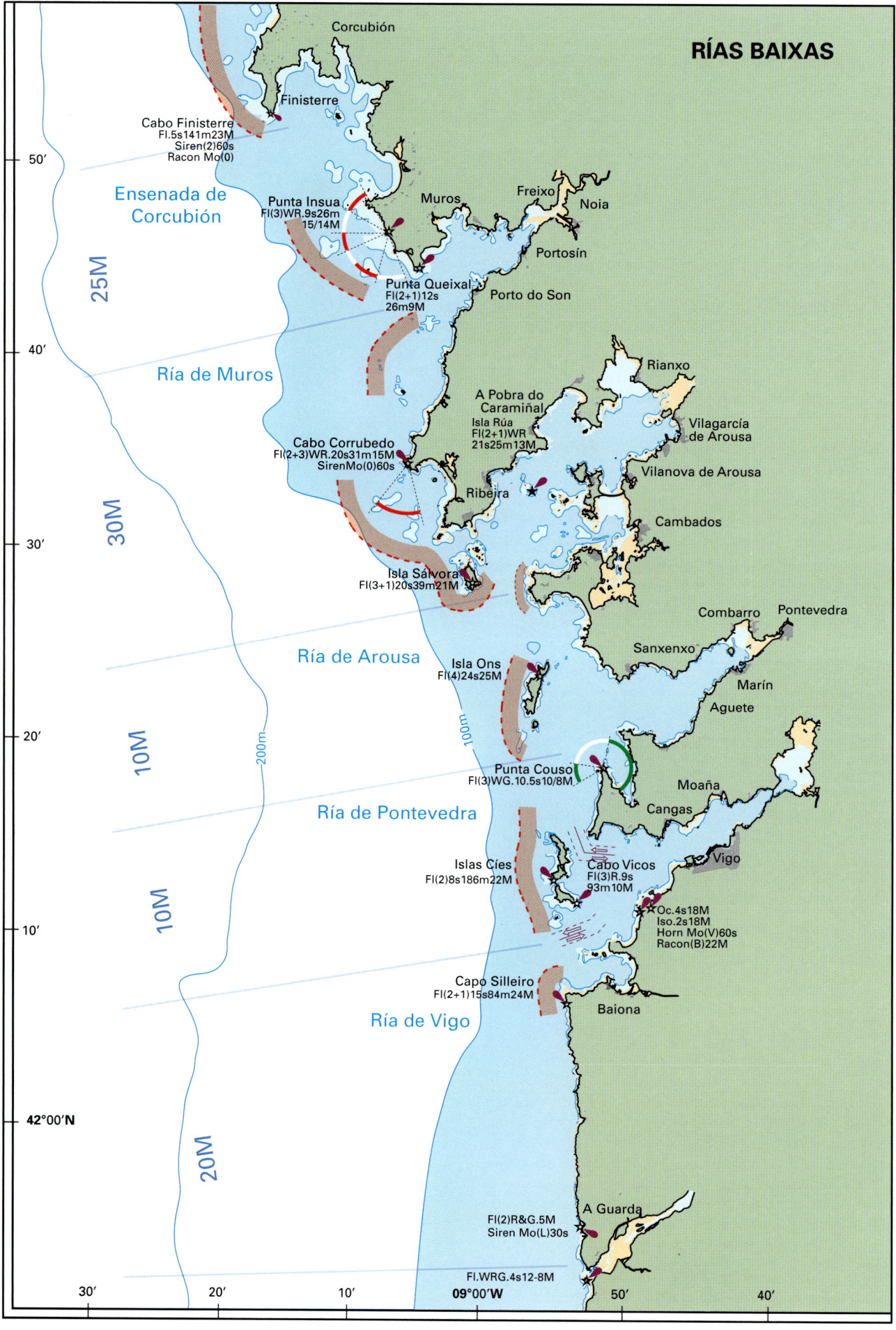

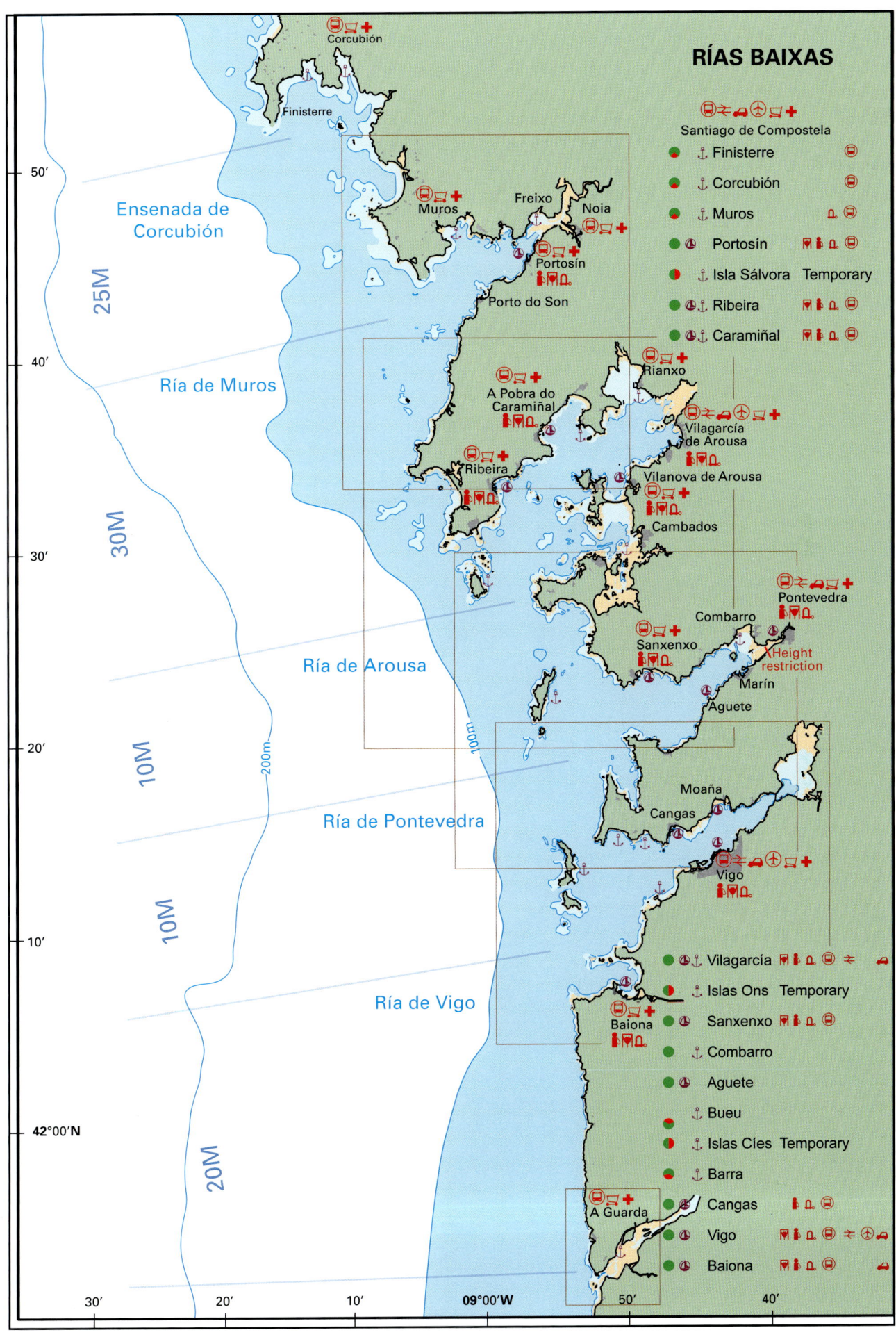

Ría de Muros

Historic and peaceful, the border between wild and industrial Galicia

Ría de Muros

Introduction

Ría de Muros is the most remote of the four Rías Baixas and is the first encountered after rounding Costa da Morte. Unlike the other three Rías Baixas, Muros is not protected by islands from the ocean and the weather is rainier and colder than further south, hence its harbours have not developed as extensively and tourism remains contained. Much of this Ría is very appealing wilderness.

The towns of **Muros** and **Noia** are gems, both steeped in history and retaining all the charm associated with Galician architecture. There are numerous historical sites of interest in each and the bars and restaurants are among the best. Noia is no longer a port due to river silting, but the importance of its position in the past is shown by its impressive streets and monuments. Muros is one of the most attractive Galician harbour towns, pretty and welcoming, full of narrow streets of interest.

Portosín on the south side of the Ría is a welcoming marina, perfectly placed for long distance cruisers wishing to make a stop. The town is not much to speak of but it is in a good location to access other sites in the Ría.

The **Castro de Baroña** is the most spectacular Castro in Galicia, unique for its size and setting. Built on a promontory that juts into the Ría it is easy to see how the village could have defended itself and eaten well from sea food available directly outside the walls.

There are many quiet **anchorages** along the northern coast of the Ría, providing great views of wooded hillsides and unspoilt landscape. The shallows at the northern end and the channel leading to them are also rewarding destinations.

Noia

Castro de Baroña

Muros harbour

RÍA DE MUROS

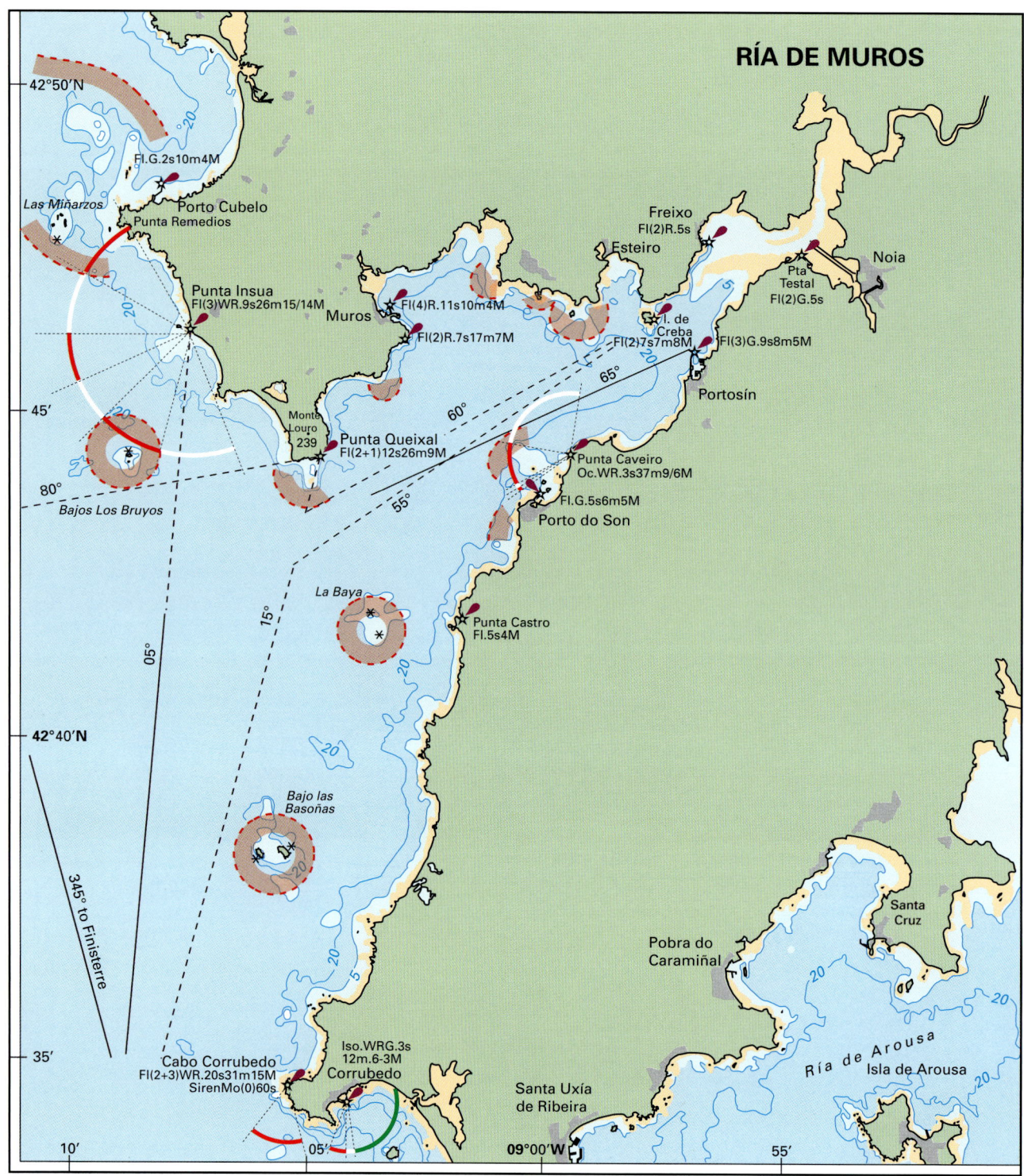

Approach and key facilities

Approach to Ría de Muros

Ría de Muros does not have the advantage of protection from offlying islands as the Rías further south do. It also has a number of isolated rocks well removed from the shore both on an approach from the north or south. All these lie on the edge of a steep seabed, just inside the 50m contour line. Although the approach from the west described below is clean, due attention is required for an extended period of time on the approach to this Ría. Note Punta Cabeiro Oc.WR.3s identifies dangers local to Porto do Son.

From the north to Portosín

Punta Insua Fl(3)WR.9s15M is the nearest long range light marking offlying dangers. A back bearing on Cabo Finisterre Fl.5s of not less than 345° will keep you clear of Bajo de los Meixidos.

- Punta Qeixal Fl(2+1)12s can be used as the apex for a cone of safety to approach the Ría, utilising

RÍA DE MUROS

the following clearing lines: When Punta Qeixal Fl(2+1)12s becomes visible and bears less than 80° (and greater than 15°) an approach can be made towards that light. This ensures the vessel is south of Los Bruyos on the north side of the cone (and north of Bajo las Basoñas on the south side of the cone)

- There are rocks off the headland of Punta Qeixal Fl(2+1)12s which must be given 0.5M clearance. However, by then the next target should have been spotted

- Isla Creba Fl(2)7s8M should be kept on a bearing between 55° and 60° to clear Punta Qeixal Fl(2+1)12s to the north and Bajo el Xorexo to the south

- Once the sea wall at Portosín Fl(3)G.9s is located and is seen to be bearing greater than 65° a direct approach can be made, clearing Bajo el Xorexo to the south

- Round the breakwater Fl(3)G.9s taking due care of moving vessels hidden by the wall and background lights. The marina is located inside inner breakwater Fl(3)R.9s. Note shoal patch beyond end of last marina finger marked by Post Fl.Y.5s and lit buoys.

RÍA DE MUROS

From the south to Portosín

Cabo Corrubedo Fl(2+3)WR.20s15M is the nearest long range light. Dangers 2-2.5M off Punta Falcoeiro and Cabo Corrubedo respectively are cleared by ensuring a back bearing on Punta Besugueiros Fl(3+1)20s is kept below 120°

- If Punta Qeixal Fl(2+1)12s can be identified on a bearing of greater than 15° (and less than 80°) then an approach can be made towards the light. This ensures the vessel is north of Bajo las Basoñas on the south side of the cone (and south of Los Biuyos on the north side of the cone)
- If this isn't visible then approach Punta Insua Fl(3)WR.9s (which is to the north of Punta Qeixal Fl(2+1)12s) on a bearing of 5°, until the latter is identified
- There are rocks off the headland of Punta Qeixal Fl(2+1)12s which must be kept 0.5M off. By then, however, the next target should have been spotted
- Isla Creba Fl(2)7s should be kept on a bearing between 55° and 60° to clear Punta Qeixal Fl(2+1)12s to the north and Bajo el Xorexo to the south
- Once the sea wall at Portosín Fl(3)G.9s is located and is seen to be bearing greater than 65° a direct approach can be made, clearing Bajo el Xorexo to the south
- Round the breakwater Fl(3)G.9s taking due care of moving vessels hidden by the wall and background lights. The marina is located inside inner breakwater Fl(3)R.9s. Note shoal patch beyond end of last marina finger marked by Post Fl.Y.5s and lit buoys.

From the west

The major light local to Ría Muros is Punta Insua Fl(3)WR.9s which has a 14M range. The red sectors identify offlying dangers up to 4M off.

- Head south until it bears less than 50° (and more than 5°) in more than 50m of water
- Once Punta Qeixal Fl(2+1)12s can be identified, approach on a bearing of between 15° and 80°
- Follow previously described approach from the south.

Initial shelter

Portosín is an all weather marina, with a straightforward day and night entrance. The only consideration is a distance of 10M from the entrance to the Ría. The bay behind Punta Queixal offers initial respite from westerly winds and swell.

Other ports and facilities

Ensenada de Muros is a good bay offering protection from W, N and E winds at various anchorages. Tucked behind the harbour is good for all winds, and space is generally not a problem.

Provisioning

Muros and Noia are excellent for provisions, both with a *mercado* (market) and good supermarkets. The small town of Portosín has a few shops to get you by.

Bars and restaurants are in abundant supply in Muros and Noia. Elsewhere, you should have no problem finding tapas at any of the bars in Bornalle, Esteiro, Portosín and Porto do Son.

Repairs and chandleries

Portosín marina is the best location in the Ría to find assistance and some spares, although it does not have a chandlery. Muros has a number of *ferreterías* with a marine bias that should look after your basic needs. For more complex spares you may need the services of larger chandleries further afield in Arousa or Coruña.

Transport

Muros and Noia both have bus stations with services to all major destinations. The nearest train stations are in Santiago and Vilagarcía de Arousa. The closest airport is Santiago.

Cruising in Ría de Muros

Ría de Muros is a wide open estuary, easy to cruise but exposed to the west, unlike the other three Rías Baixas all of which are protected by islands at the entrance.

Swell decreases significantly towards the northern side of the river, absorbed by the gradually shallowing bottom. Wind from the NE funnels through the Ría valley and can be very strong at times - the anchorages at Ensenadas de Muros, Bornalle and Esteiro offer protection.

One day

If you only have one day do not miss Muros. It is one of the nicest traditional Galician towns.

One week

With more time to explore, the northern coast of the Ría has several good bays that offer protection and anchorage in very pleasant settings. Ensenada de San Francisco at the west entrance, Ensenada de Muros, Ensenada de Esteiro and Freixo are all good anchorages on the northern side. The southern coast offers the friendly and well equipped Portosín marina and Playa de Aguieira (subject to swell) for a quiet anchorage.

RÍA DE MUROS

CRUISING GALICIA 141

RÍA DE MUROS

Monte Louro

The beaches to either side of Monte Louro offer picturesque anchorages with some shelter from W, N and E winds.

Approach & entrance

Apart from Punta Qeixal Fl(2+1)12s, the coast is unlit and should be considered as approachable in daylight only. From west to east: Punta de Lens, Punta Qeixal and Punta Bouga all have offlying dangers and should be stood off at least 0.5M.

⚓ Playa de Louro

Very exposed anchorage for settled weather only in sand.

⚓ Ensenada de San Francisco

Shelter from W, N and NE winds in gravel and sand. A tripping line is advisable in case of stone snags.

Interest

The peninsula on which Monte Louro is located is a delightful, if exposed, wilderness. Due to its location it has been the site of defensive fortifications to guard the entrance to Ría de Muros. There are paths that will take you round the mount and the views from the top are spectacular if you can brave the climb.

Laguna de Louro (also known as Laguna de Xarxas) to the north of the peninsula is a pretty lagoon which serves as a stop for an abundance of migratory birdlife.

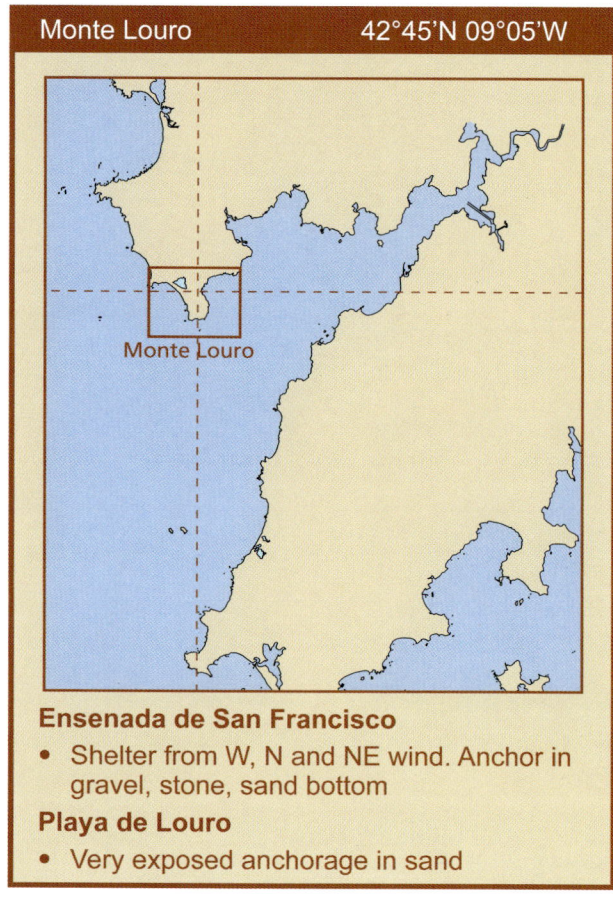

Monte Louro 42°45'N 09°05'W

Ensenada de San Francisco
- Shelter from W, N and NE wind. Anchor in gravel, stone, sand bottom

Playa de Louro
- Very exposed anchorage in sand

Laguna de Louro

142 CRUISING GALICIA

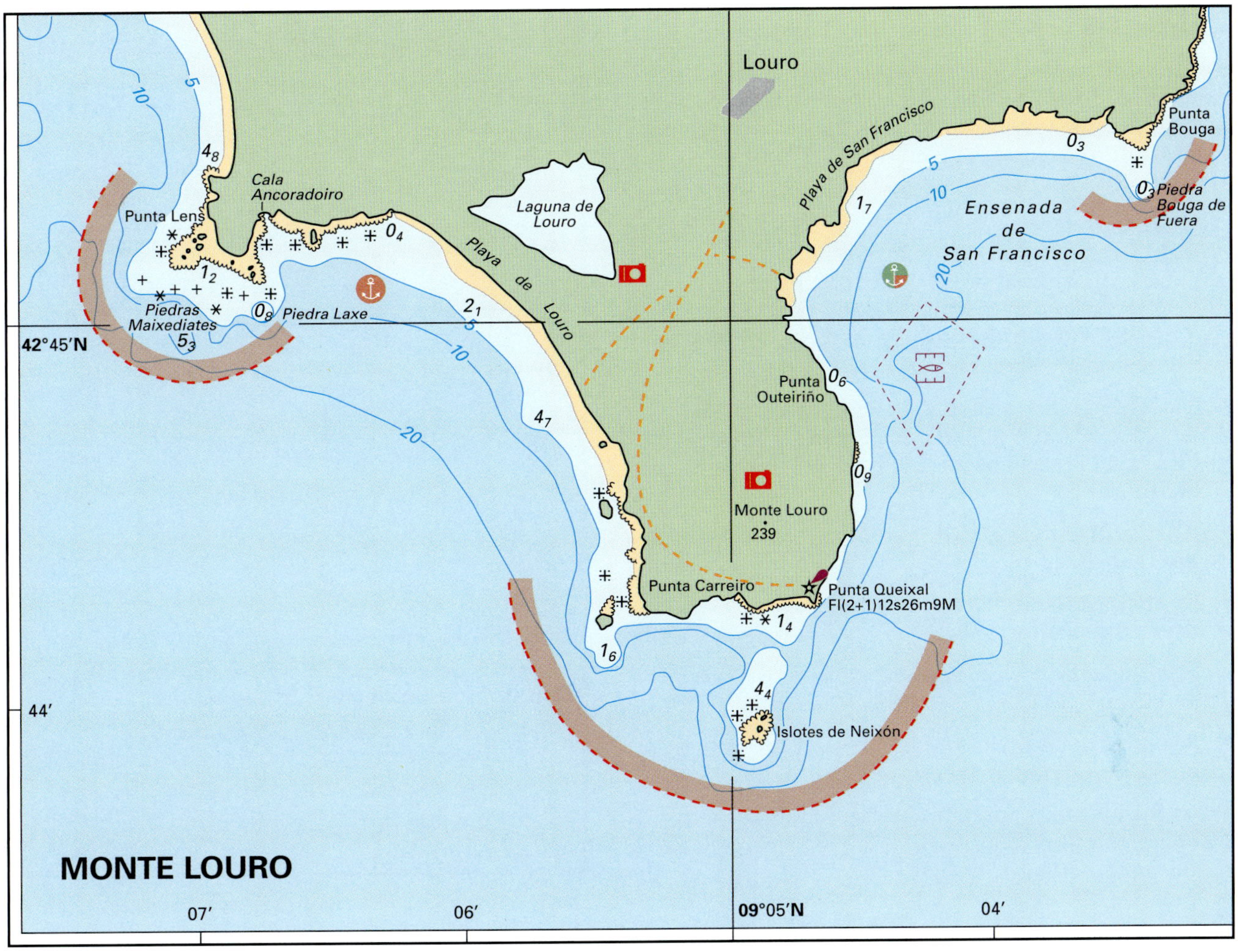

RÍA DE MUROS

MONTE LOURO

Pimientos de Padrón

These little sweet peppers are traditionally grown in the valley of Padrón, and used to be the best kept Galician secret before their delicious taste led to mass production. Today they can be bought year round in Spanish supermarkets, supplied from all kinds of non gallego places. The best continue to be from Padrón itself, during July and August. Occasionally you will get a fiery one, typically the large or later specimens.

Ingredients
Olive oil
1kg fresh pimientos de Padrón
Salt to taste

Preparation
Fry the peppers for about 5 minutes or until soft.

Serve immediately with *pan gallego*.

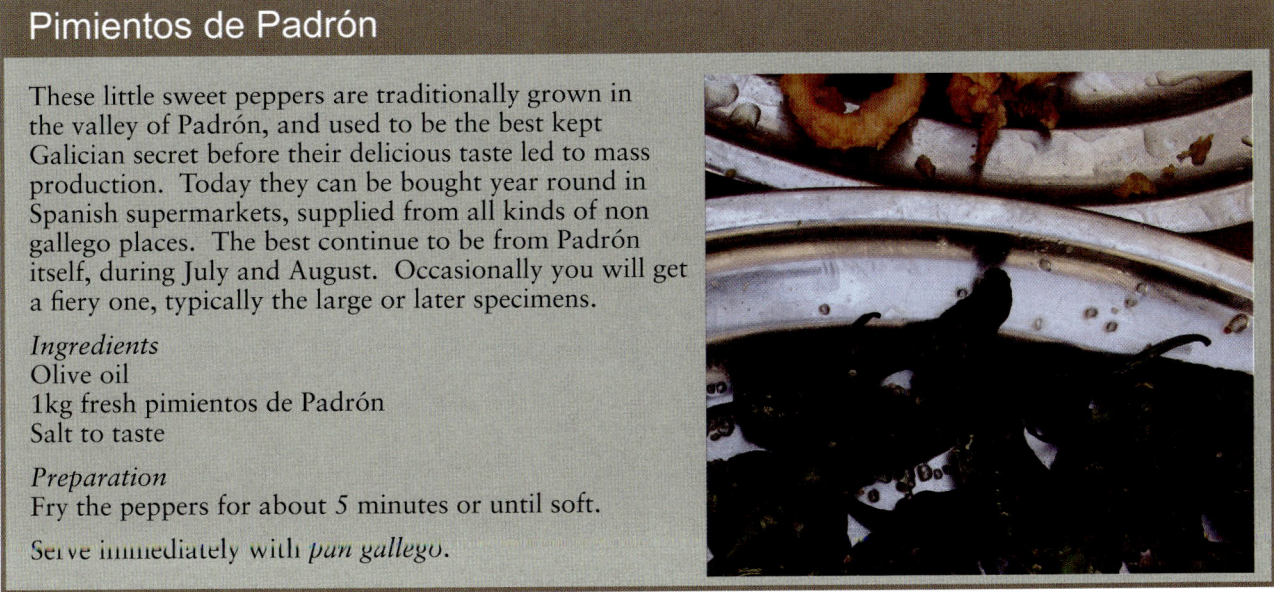

RÍA DE MUROS

⚓ Muros

Sheltered bay which can be approached in all conditions. Muros is one of the most attractive historic seaside towns of the Rías. Shelter available from west, north and east only.

Approach & entrance

Straightforward approach in all conditions, although care should be taken of moving vessels hidden by background lights and the unlit *batea* grid in the centre of the bay. From the west, 1M south of Punta Qeixal Fl(2+1)12s.

- Isla Creba Fl(2)7s should be kept on a bearing between 55° and 60° to clear Punta Qeixal Fl(2+1)12s to the north and Bajo El Xorexo to the south
- Alter course for Cabo Rebordiño when it bears less than 10°
- Round headland more than 400m off and greater than 20m depth
- Head to offer a wide berth to the end of Muros breakwater Fl.R.5s when it bears less than 300°
- Beware fishing boats and breakwater obscuring possible vessel movements.

From the east the shoreline between Punta de Santa Catalina and Punta Borneira should be cleared. Stay in more than 20m.

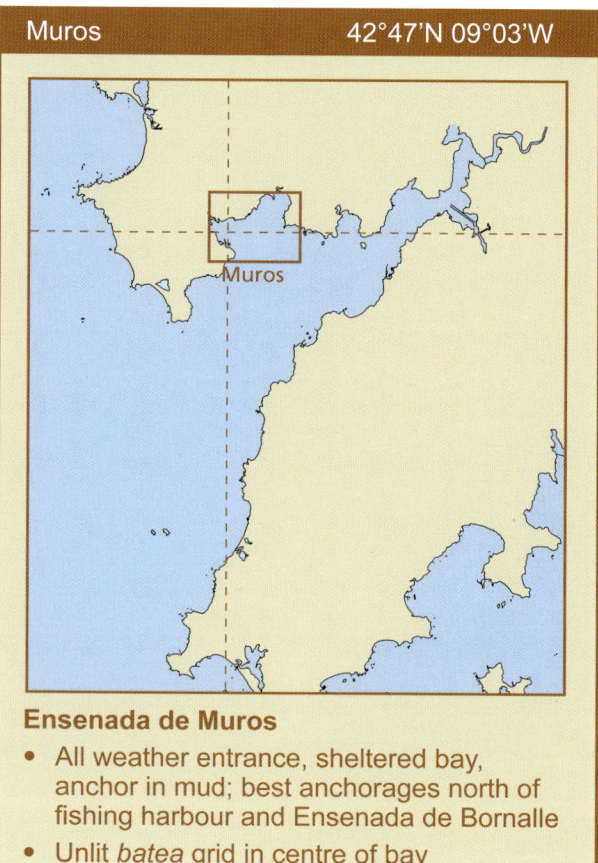

Muros   42°47'N 09°03'W

Ensenada de Muros
- All weather entrance, sheltered bay, anchor in mud; best anchorages north of fishing harbour and Ensenada de Bornalle
- Unlit *batea* grid in centre of bay

Ensenada de Muros

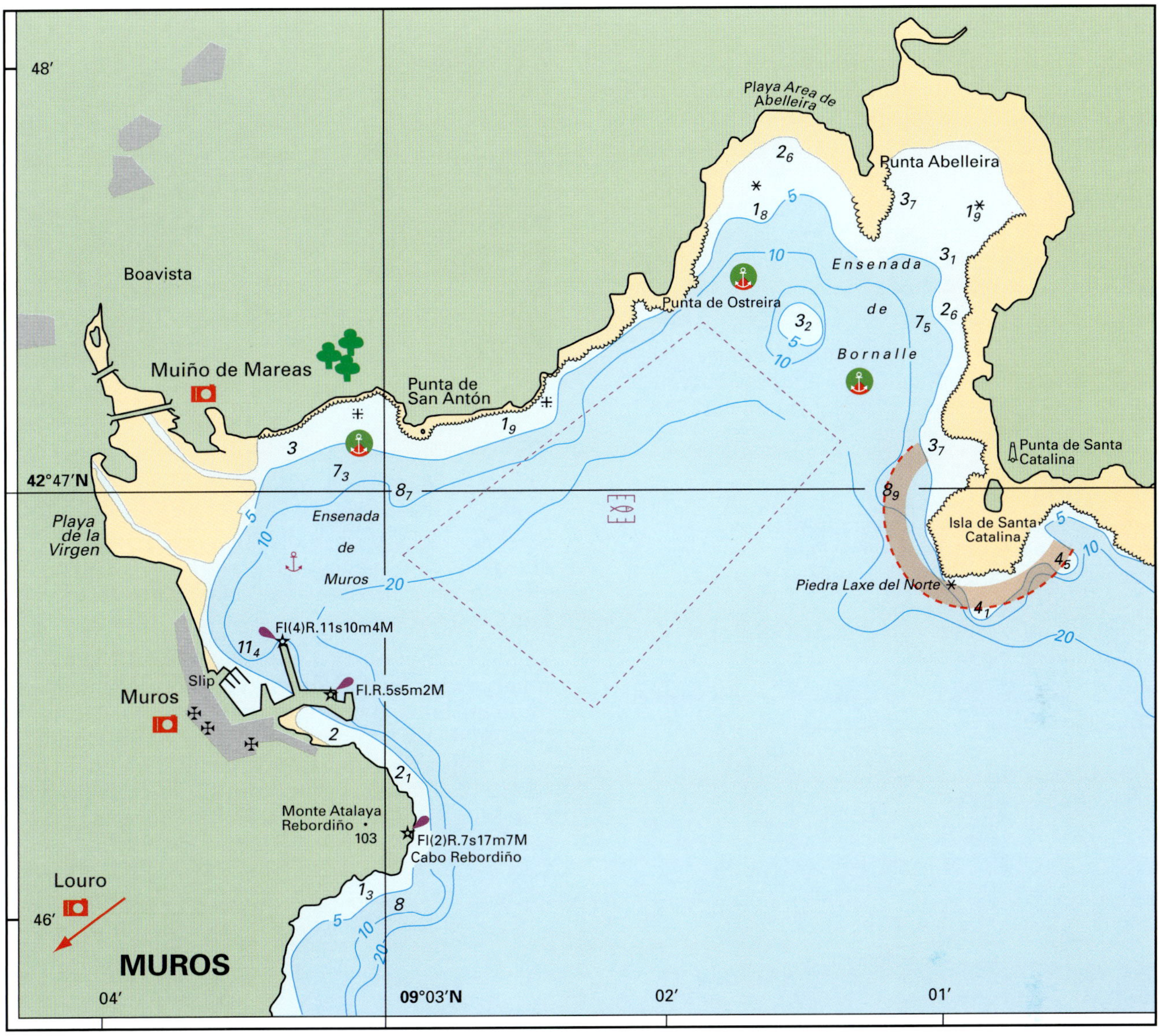

RÍA DE MUROS

Ensenadas de Muros, Bornalle, Esteiro and Isla Creba

CRUISING GALICIA 145

⚓ Anchorages

To the north of the fishing harbour of Muros anchor in mud at Ensenada de Muros at either end of the bay in 5-10m. Note that in a strong northeasterly shelter will be available at the eastern end inside Isla de Santo Antón, under a steep, tree lined, shore.

It is possible to anchor inside the fishing harbour but it is crowded with fishing boats and very easy to get the anchor line fouled.

Ensenada de Bornalle, opposite Muros across the bay behind the shellfish platforms, is a quiet and very pretty spot. Bottom is mud and weed. Note isolated rocks and reef extending from Punta Abelleira inside 5m contour.

Provisioning

There are many bars and restaurants everywhere in Muros, particularly along Avenida Castelao. For the best ambience head for one of the bars underneath the *soportales* (covered walkways) and order Albariño white wine with the local speciality *caldeirada de peixe* (fish stew).

The Gadis supermarket to the north is well stocked, but there are numerous groceries along the way. For the best fresh produce head for the market (*Mercado de Abastos*), as always in Galicia a provisioning paradise.

Muiño de Mareas mill

Interest

Muros has been a prosperous harbour since it received a royal concession as a trading port in 1452. Its location and status underpinned illustrious development. The wealth of the town also attracted pirates and attacking fleets from European nations.

The old stone houses in the town are flanked by *soportales*, colonnaded covered walkways similar to those of Santiago that shelter the promenader from the rain that is common in this part of the world. In earlier times the *soportales* would have been used to secure small boats during storms. These walkways give Muros a distinct character that attracts tourism.

Muros

RÍA DE MUROS

Muros

- A Coruña 105km, Santiago 71km, Pontevedra 98km, Vigo 132km
- 🚌 Bus station: Castromil (Monbus), Avda Calvo Sotelo, ☏ 982 292900; also Rúa del Río further north
- 🛒 Market: Mercado de Abastos, Praza do Mercado (historic building)
- 🛒 Supermarket: Gadis, Porteliña 64
- 🍴 Restaurants: best area along Avenida Castelao, many bars and restaurants set under the *soportales* (covered walkways) throughout the old town
- ℹ️ Tourist office: Curro da Praza 1 (at the Town Hall) ☏ 981 826050
- ⚓ Chandlers:
  - Efectos Navales O' Redero, Edificio Fábrica de Hielo ☏ 981 826851
- ✚ Centro Saude de Muros, Avda de Bilbao, ☏ 981 867616 (near Calle Rosalía de Castro)
- Banks, chemists and other shops: Avenida Castelao

The **stone built narrow streets** in the old town reveal the strong religious connections, their names (Calvario, Amargura, Sufrimiento etc) reading like names taken directly from the Bible. Several churches are worth visiting to round off your appreciation of the religious past of Muros, Colegiata de Santa María and Capilla Virgen del Carmen the best. Walk along Rúa Real for some of the prettiest typical Galician street images.

At the northern end of Ensenada de Muros, **Muiño de Mareas** is one of the longest Galician mills, powered by the Valdexeira stream and tidal flow. It no longers functions as a a mill but it is worth visiting as a short walk from Muros.

Outside Muros, the peninsula of Monte Louro and Laguna de Louro are worth visiting, as walking excursions from the town.

As to fiestas, the celebrations of the patron San Pedro host an *empanada* competition on the first Saturday of July, a good venue to try the Galician pie. As in other fishing harbours the seaborn procession on 16 July (Virgen del Carmen) is a great spectacle. Ashore, *Procesión de los ofrecidos de San Roque* on 16 August is a solemn occasion.

RÍA DE MUROS

⚓ Esteiro

Sheltered bay anchorage for daytime entry only. Esteiro is a small summer beach holiday town. The coves nearby offer small, quiet anchorages.

Approach & entrance

Daytime entry only as there are no navigation lights and the bay is populated with unlit shellfish platforms. The bay has numerous shallow patches to the west of its entrance up to 0.5M offshore. These are best avoided by staying in more than 20m until standing into the bay. You will be met by the *batea* grid which can be passed through.

⚓ Anchorages

Opposite Playa de Esteiro at the northern end of the bay. A good survey of the anchoring spot is recommended to avoid swinging to a shallow patch.

Playas de Tal and Punta Uía, near Isla de Creba Fl(2)7s, are very picturesque anchoring spots but they should not be used in anything but the best conditions. A trip line for the anchor would be a good precaution as there are rocks along the bottom. Inside the eastern end of Isla De Creba is a possibility, there is sufficient space between the *bateas* and shallow ground.

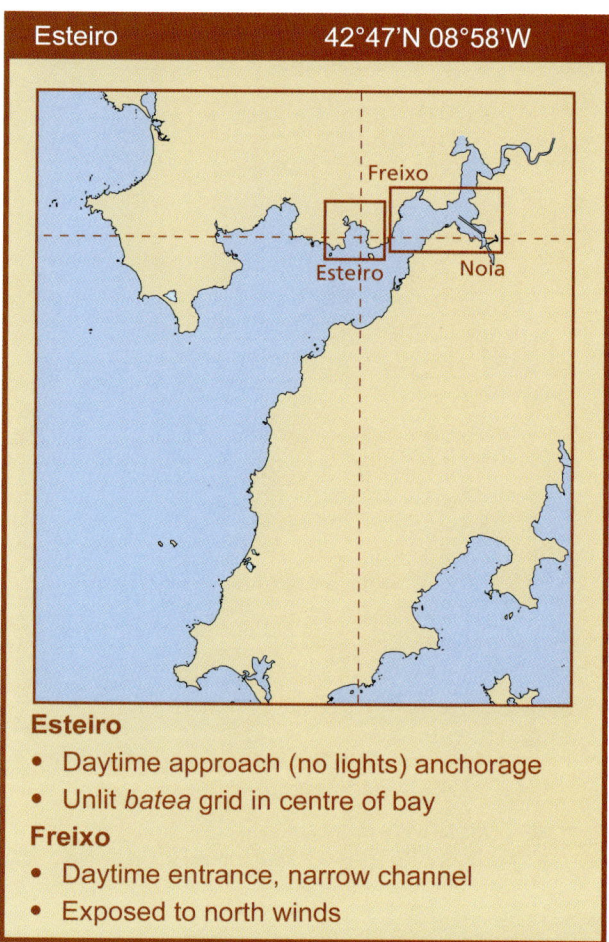

Esteiro
- Daytime approach (no lights) anchorage
- Unlit *batea* grid in centre of bay

Freixo
- Daytime entrance, narrow channel
- Exposed to north winds

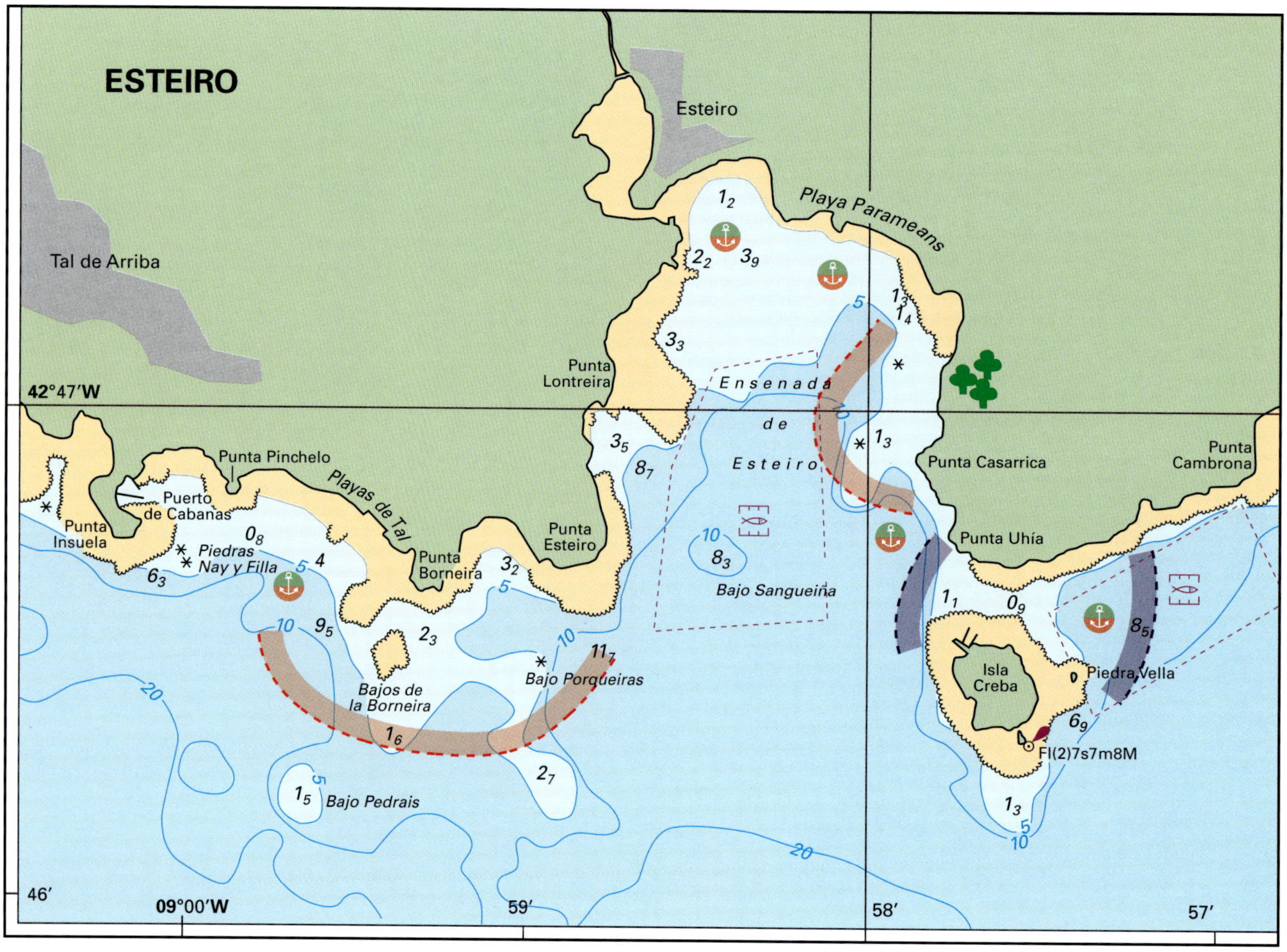

148 CRUISING GALICIA

RÍA DE MUROS

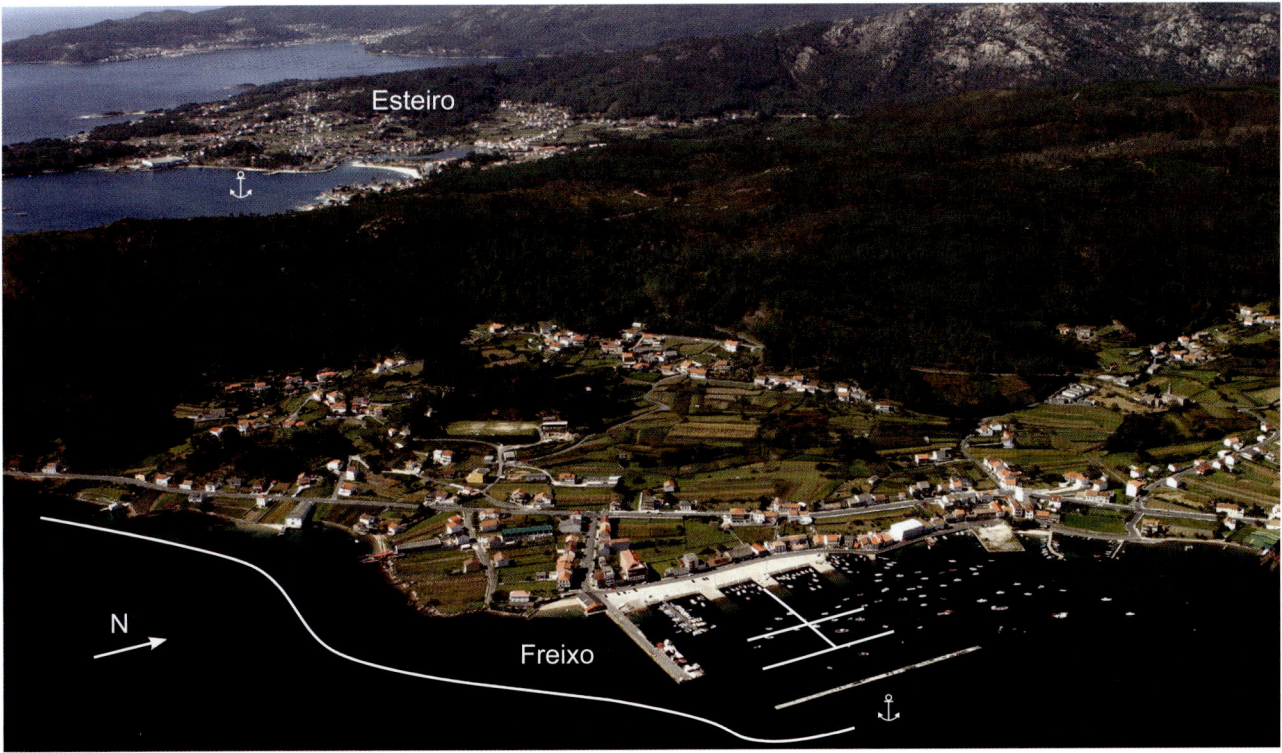

⚓ Freixo

Narrow channel entrance to small, but busy, shipbuilding and fishing harbour only. Rural surrounds and town of Noia reachable by dinghy. The entire bay is silted with sediment from Río Tambre and most of it is navigable only at high tide. The harbour quay of Noia dries most of the time.

Approach & entrance

Depths and areas of shallows will alter, so due care is required navigating in the upper reaches of the Ría. Taking the simple precaution of ensuring the crew are seated could save a headache. Tidal flows are not strong. Although partially lit, a daylight approach is strongly recommended. From south of Isla de Creba Fl(2)7s:

- Head northeast past the *batea* grid.
- Once due south of the eastern end of he quay (between Punta Pequena and Punta Soagro), head due north towards it
- Alter course to 45° alongside the quay
- Head to pass east of Freixo harbour wall Fl(2)5s when due south of it.

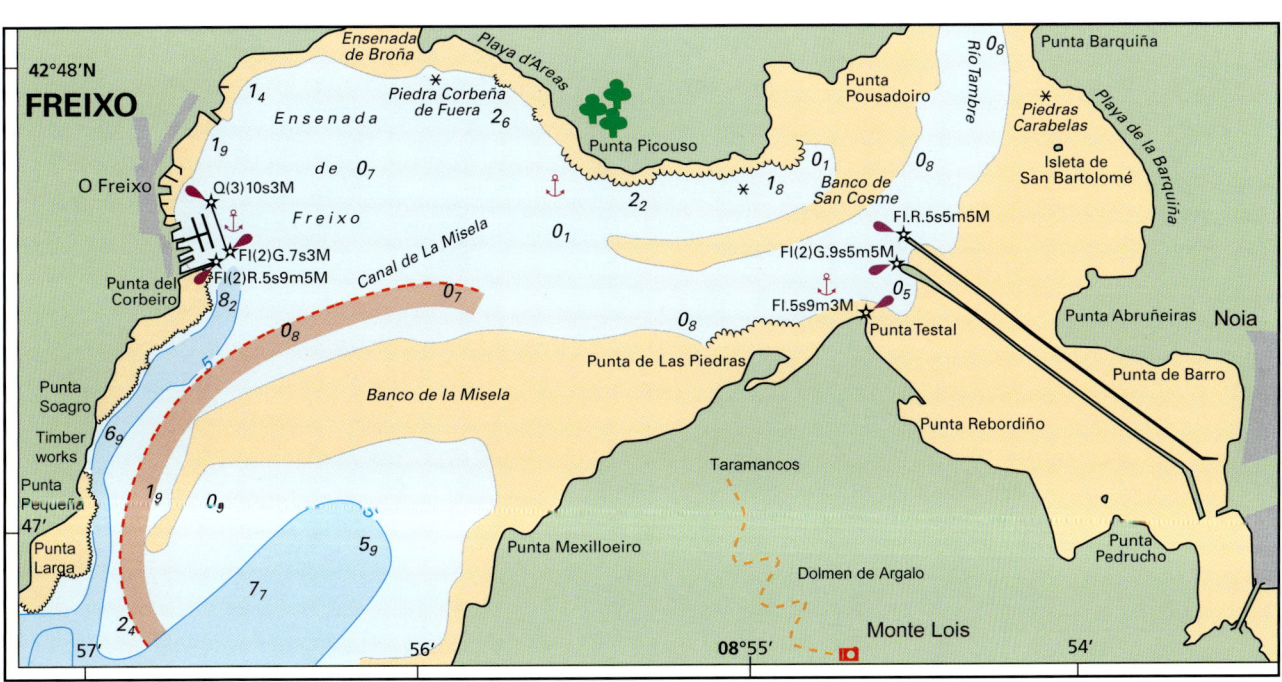

CRUISING GALICIA **149**

RÍA DE MUROS

Approach close to the west shoreline and keep a constant watch on the depth gauge.

⚓ Anchorages

Opposite **Freixo harbour**, best outside the N-S floating pontoon in 3-5m mud. It is possible to berth to the pontoon for a short time. The area inside the harbour is very busy with fishing boat traffic. The anchorage is exposed to north winds.

Off **Punta Picousa** 1M to the east of Freixo there is a deep pool which would allow a boat to remain afloat at all states of the tide. The approach should be on a rising tide from Freixo. A minimum charted depth of 0.7m is recorded on the approach.

Off **Punta Testal** Fl.5s.1.5M to the east of Freixo and at the entrance to the channel up to Noia. A boat could remain afloat here at neaps (0.5m charted depth recorded) to allow an excursion to Noia by land or sea. The Río Tambre has created a north bank extending to a point south of Punta Picousa which could be rounded before making directly for Punta Testal, ensuring maximum depth (0.1m charted depth recorded). Anchor between Punta Testal Fl.5s and the end of the training wall Fl(2)G.9s.

Provisioning

Esteiro has a number of shops but Freixo is very small, not a place for provisioning.

Noia is a much larger town, with all kinds of amenities and shops, but you need to consider the

RÍA DE MUROS

Clam collection rakes in Muros

practicalities of an expedition in a dinghy, at a distance of 1-2M. A taxi ride will be needed for major victualling.

Interest

The little town of **Esteiro** is primarily a summer tourist destination. Away from the beaches the best of this part of the Ría is the simple remote feel of the coast. The great expanses of sand that are uncovered by the tide are home to large quantities of cockles and clams (*berberechos* and *almejas*).

Freixo used to be the port of Noia, a natural harbour of some importance for trade and production of bulky goods including wood. The silt from Río Tambre has made it impossible for larger boats to enter the port but it continues to be a busy harbour, today dedicated to boatbuilding and shellfish farming. Astilleros Armado at Punta Corbeira continues to produce traditional boats, although GRP has now substituted the old wood

Shallows — Shellfish farm — Freixo

CRUISING GALICIA 151

RÍA DE MUROS

craft. On the other side of the harbour larger yards specialise in modern steel and fibre boat construction.

Noia is a historic town, very wealthy in the past due to its privileged position at the end of the Ría. Illustrious buildings remain from Noia's noble past, particularly along the Alameda (promenade) at Rúa de Rosalía de Castro and the older town around the magnificent Iglesia de San Martiño. At the Museo das Laudas Gremiaís (Iglesia de Santa María a Nova) a fascinating collection of tombstones from as early as 10th century record, in drawings and words, the status and profession of each person buried, from Knights to guild craftsmen.

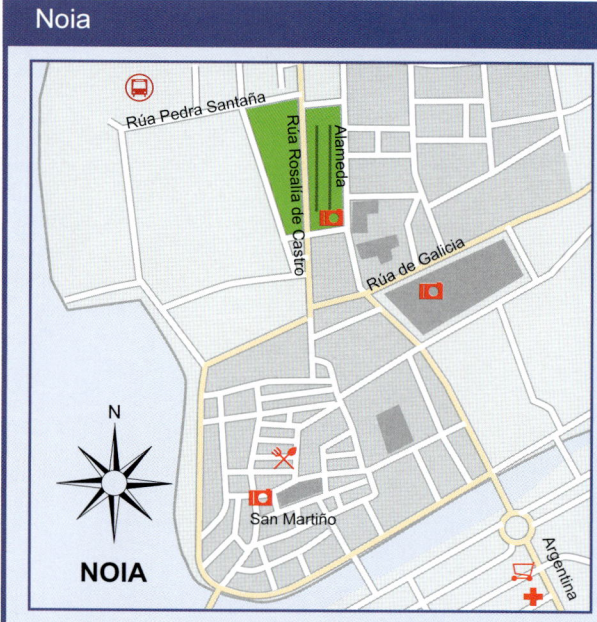

- A Coruña 100km, Santiago 40km, Pontevedra 100km, Vigo 130km
- 🚌 Bus station: Rúa de Pedra Santaña
- 🛒 Supermarket:
  - Gadis, Rúa República Argentina
- 🍴 Bars and restaurants: best areas the old town near San Martiño church and along the Alameda (Rosalía de Castro)
- ✚ Centro Saude Noia, Rúa República Argentina, ☏ 981 842180

Noia old town

Iglesia de Santa María a Nova

RÍA DE MUROS

Puerto de Cabañas

For the adventurous, the track from the village of Taramancos to the top of **Monte Lois** (363m) is a rewarding 3 hour trek. On the way, admire the Dolmen of Argalo, a prehistoric circular burial ground, and Pazo de Peña del Oro together with the views at the top.

Chipirones en su tinta

The colour of this dish is very striking but should not put you off, it's delicious. The taste comes from the squid ink which you add at the end.

Ingredients

One onion, cut small pieces
Olive oil
One tin of cut tomatoes in their juice
One red pepper, cut into small pieces
1kg squid, cleaned and mouth removed; separate tentacles and cut body into strips
One small bag of squid ink (you can buy them from the fishmonger)
Rice, cooked separately

Preparation

Fry the onion until soft and golden. Add the tin of tomatoes and reduce for 10 minutes. The tomato sauce should be quite thick.

Add the squid and cook for five minutes.

Add the ink from the little back and enjoy the dramatic colour change from red to black. The sauce will thicken further.

Serve on a bed of rice.

RÍA DE MUROS

⚓ Portosín

Excellent and friendly marina with an all weather entry. Portosín is a small town set by wooded hills, close to Noia and Santiago de Compostela.

Approach & entrance

All weather day and night entry. Swell if wind from the north. Note shoal patch beyond end of last marina finger marked by Post Fl.Y.5s and buoys.

From the west:

- Punta Qeixal Fl(2+1)12s can be used as the apex for a cone of safety to approach the Ría. When Punta Qeixal Fl(2+1)12s becomes visible and bears less than 80° and greater than 15° an approach can be made towards that light. This ensures the vessel is south of Los Buyos on the north side of the cone (and north of Canco las Basoñas on the south side of the cone)

- There are rocks of the headland of Punta Qeixal Fl(2+1)12s which must be given 0.5M clearance. However by then the next target should have been spotted

- Isla Creba Fl(2)7s should be kept on a bearing between 55° and 60° to clear Punta Qeixal Fl(2+1)12s to the north and Bajo El Xorexo to the south

- Round the breakwater Fl(3)G.9s taking due care of moving vessels hidden by the wall and background lights. The marina is located inside inner breakwater Fl(3)R.9s. Note shoal patch beyond end of last marina finger marked by Post Fl.Y.5s and buoys.

From the direction of Freixo, the approach is clean.

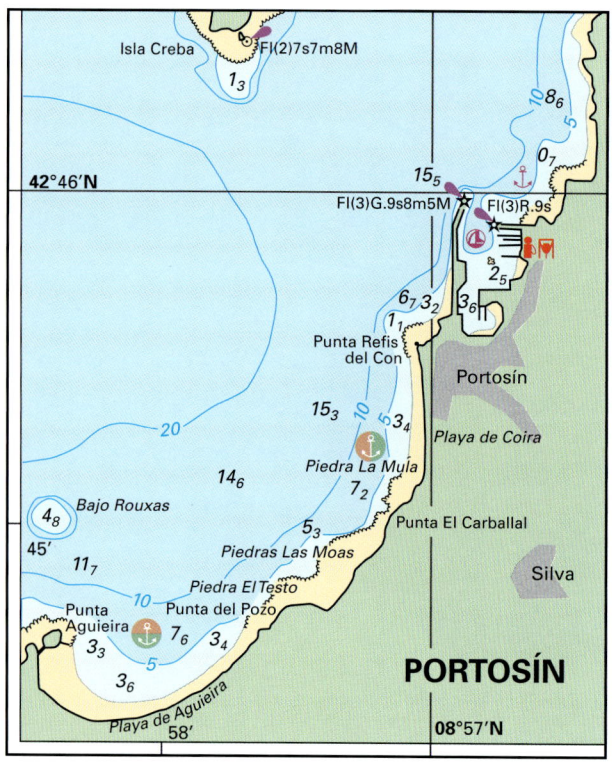

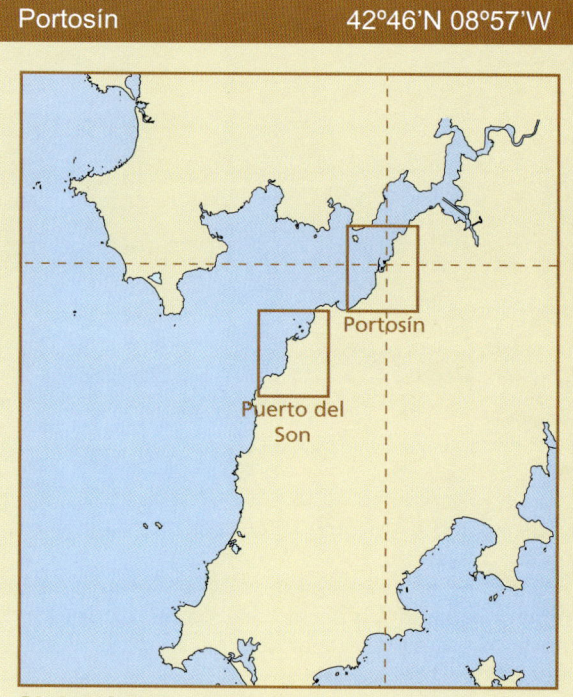

Portosín 42°46'N 08°57'W

Club Náutico de Portosín

- Straightforward approach in all conditions
- 69 visitors' moorings, up to 16m length
- Minimum depth 2m, 9m at the entrance
- Marina welcomes offshore passage arrivals
- Pontoon mooring
- Water and electricity at pontoons

- ☎ 981 766583 Fax 981 766389
- VHF Channel 09
- nfo@cnportosin.com
- www.cnportosin.com

- 🚢 32-ton travel lift
- 🔧 Repairs workshop at marina
- info@darsenacoruna.co
- Excellent facilities (showers, laundry)
- Restaurant
- Sailing Club

Berthing & facilities

Portosín is a welcoming marina, used to receiving yachts that have made long passages. It is set in a quiet part of the Ría, but close to the larger and historic Noia. Approach the second of the outer pontoons if you have not arranged a berth prior to arrival.

Many of the berths are Mediterranean style moorings.

RÍA DE MUROS

Portosín Marina

Water and electricity at the pontoons. Fuel at the refuelling berth alongside the marina wall next to boat lift. There is a 32-ton lift and space ashore for dry standing.

⚓ Anchorages

North of the marina entrance wall in sand, good shelter from all but north winds.

To the south of Portosín, the beaches offer good holding in sand in picturesque settings. The best spot is in front of **Playa de Aguieira,** a small bay that attracts many seabirds to a small estuary just inside Punta Aguieira.

Portosín

- Santiago 45km, Noia 10km
- 🚌 Transport: no major links in Portosín, Noia is nearby and has a bus station
- 🛒 Provisions: very small town, some shops near the south fishing harbour
  - Supermarkets at Noia and Port de Son
- ✚ Consultorio Portosín, Lugar de Mariño (between marina and fishing harbour)
  ☎ 981 766772

Portosín Marina entrance

Playa de Aguieira

CRUISING GALICIA 155

RÍA DE MUROS

⚓ Porto do Son

A lit confined approach to an anchorage in front of busy fishing harbour. Daytime only, many dangers and shallows. Although the approach is lit, the anchorage may be difficult to locate and swimming area may restrict options.

From the east:

- Approach on a heading of 180° on the Puerto do Son sea wall Fl.G.5s to clear the rock patches to starboard (Isla Filgueira) and port (Pieras Figueriñas). A depth of more than 5m should be maintained. Note this brings you within 100m of Piedras Figueriñas.

From the west:

- Approach Punta Cabeiro Oc.WR.3s in the white sector on a course of 60°. Alter course when the Puerto do Son sea wall Fl.G.5s bears 140° (or, if visible, the church behind the beach bears 130°).

From either of the approaches above:

- Clear end of breakwater, taking due care of moving vessels hidden by the wall and background lights
- Head for church on shoreline
- Anchor in 2.5m sand directly in front of the church.

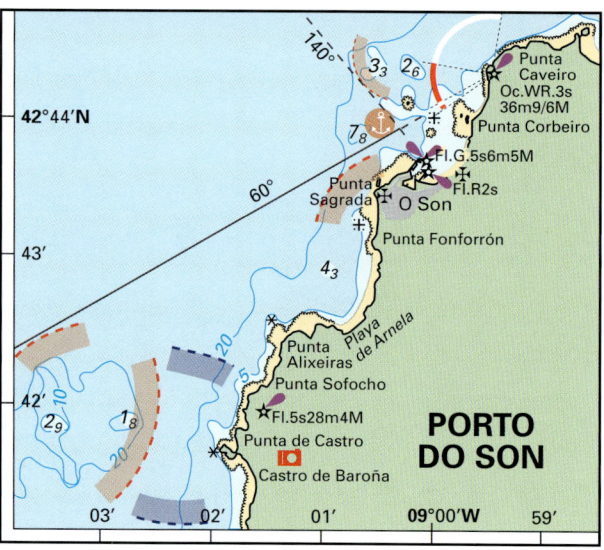

Provisioning

Porto do Son is a small harbour with a few shops adequate for provisioning. There are a number of bars and restaurants which are very popular in the summer.

Portosín is a small friendly town, with a few shops for provisioning, in the street south of the fishing harbour. Noia is a better choice for major provisioning, but it needs a 10km taxi ride. The marina Restaurant is a good place to settle for a nice meal.

Interest

The *lonxa* (fish auctions) at Portosín is a lively place when fishing boats come in, worth seeing the action in the mornings.

The town has some history, used by the Romans and later the Catalans as a centre for salting and fish production. None of this industrial context spoils the setting today.

There is none of the high rise development of some areas in the Rías, the coast is quiet and dotted only with individual homes. See the house at **Punta Aguieria**, built in an old salt factory, for a perfect holiday home location.

The main attraction of Porto do Son is the Centro de Interpretación del Castro de Baroña, a small place where you can see some of the objects recovered from the Castro and a good guide to the significance of the site.

Porto do Son church

Porto do Son harbour

156 CRUISING GALICIA

Percebeiros collecting barnacles near Baroña

Castro de Baroña itself is a pre-Roman settlement located 4km south of Porto del Son at Punta del Castro. Set in a spectacular location, it is one of the most striking remains of such type of settlement which was the norm in Galicia during "celtic" times. The extraordinary location of the Castro is probably related to the availability of tin nearby combined with ample supply of fish. The archeological discoveries support the theory of a group taking advantage of the site for trading, while deriving ample nutrition from sea produce.

From Porto do Son to Corrubedo

This stretch of coast, known as Costa Sagrada, needs to be given a wide berth as there are many dangers and it is very exposed. The shore is largely a rock face.

If intending to look at Castro de Baroña from the sea then, from the west (and having rounded Punta Laxe Brava), a course of 15° from Cabo Corrubedo Fl(2+3)WR.20s will clear both the isolated rocks to seaward and those off the shoreline. A close eye should be kept on the boats position as many of the dangers are close to the 30m contour.

All the beaches on this coastline will be subject to swell which is likely to make a landing by dinghy a wet experience.

The Castro settlements

Pre-historic Galicia evolved through the iron age towards a society that was organised around individual settlements. There was cultural uniformity, and trade in common with other Atlantic regions of Europe, but only when the Romans arrived was the region brought together politically.

Castro settlements started to appear in the late Bronze age from around 1000BC and survived well into the 2nd century, standing side by side with Roman infrastructure and new towns. It is estimated that there are 3,000 castros in Galicia, the north of Portugal and the western edge of Asturias. Local names often beginning with "Castro de" relate to ancient settlements even when there are no obvious remains.

Castros were commonly small, rarely extending beyond a few hectares. Their location was chosen with defence and access to food as priorities. Many were built on hilltops surrounded by a defensive earth bank. During Roman times castros were built near to the mines that were exploited for gold and tin.

At the coast, a promontory surrounded by the sea could be defended easily across a narrow isthmus, while the sea was a source of food.

Initially houses were round or oval though later Roman influence led to rectangular layouts. In the end the villages were abandoned in favour of more advanced urban designs for larger towns with modern infrastructure and services.

For some of the most spectacular locations visit Santa Tecla near A Guarda, Viladonga between Ribadeo and Lugo, and Baroña in Ría de Pontevedra.

RÍA DE MUROS

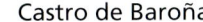
Castro de Baroña

CRUISING GALICIA 159

Ría de Arousa

The largest Galician ría, home of mussels

Ría de Arousa

Introduction

Ría de Arousa is the largest of the Rías Baixas that reach from Finisterre to the border with Portugal. Protected by Isla Sálvora at its entrance it is home to half of the 3,500 *bateas* that are used to farm mussels in this part of Spain. The Ría is constantly busy with the activity of the mussel boats but it is possible to find numerous anchorages that feel remote and the towns along the shore will not disappoint, for provisioning and for a taste of real Galician food and character.

Supported by the Galician Regional Government through Portos de Galicia the marinas have been developed and offer very secure facilities to leave a boat for a long period. The summer season is busy but space is still always available. The majority of local leisure craft are motor boats, from fishing launches to very opulent motor cruisers. Despite an obvious increase in prosperity the more hard nosed commercial approach of marinas further north in Europe does not seem to have reached this area. Like the rest of the Galicia coast Arousa is focused on the sea. While some facilities are below par there is a genuine desire to be helpful to anyone in a boat.

Arousa's location and coastal features mean its history is connected with naval events and trade. Various Viking, Norman and Arab fleets have attempted invasions through its wide waters. The defensive fortifications at Catoira were built to block such advances. In their time Phoenicians established bases for trade (see remains at Aguiño) and the Romans located garrisons along the coast here. The highlight of Arousa's naval history is its contribution to the story of apostle Santiago. Reputedly this was the landing place for the craft that brought his body to Galicia.

Ría de Arousa is an attractive, self-contained cruising ground that could easily keep you interested for a week or more. It is ideal for short sailing trips, each destination having an interesting town with a *plaza* (food market) for provisioning together with good food in any number of bars and restaurants. There are many opportunities for hill walking and fiestas to entertain you at every village worthy of a name. Visit the old town of Cambados, home town of Albariño wine, and the pretty Pobra do Carabiñal, anchor at Isla de Sálvora, visit the lagoons and sand dunes of Parque Nacional de Corrubedo, walk the nature paths in the hills behind Vilagarcía and of course do not leave without trying some mussels.

RÍA DE AROUSA

Parque Natural Dunas de Corrubedo

Isla de Cortegada opposite Carril

Cambados, home of Albariño wine

Rianxo

Mussels

RÍA DE AROUSA

Approach and key facilities

Approach to Ría de Arousa

Inside the Ría beware of the extensive *vivero* areas full of *bateas*. The edges of the allocated *vivero* areas along the main channel are generally marked with standard G or R buoys as well as Fl.Y.5s special marks.

Entrance to Ría de Arosa should be made to the south of Isla de Sálvora Fl(3+1)20s21M through the Canal Principal.

- **From the north** keep 3M off Cabo Corrubedo Fl(2+3)WR.20s15M to clear Bajo la Praguiña (within Bajos de Corrubedo) and Isla Sálvora Fl(3+1)20s21M by 1M to clear Piedra Pegar

- **From the south** keep 1M (or not less than 20m depth) off Penisula de O Grove and clear Roca Pombeiriño Fl.G.5s

- If approaching from Ría de Pontevedra inside Isla Ons then clear Bajo Picamillo Fl.G.5s to starboard and leave Bajo los Camoucos Fl(3).R.18s and Bajo Fagilda buoy Q.R.1s to starboard

- Once in the Canal Principal use the Isla Rúa light Fl(2)WR.7s as the apex for a cone of safety between 010° and 025°. The major hazards outside this cone (Sinal del Castro Fl.R.5s to port and Los Esqueiros Fl(4)G.11s and Los Mexos Fl.G.5s to starboard) are all lit.

To Pobra do Caramiñal

- From the entrance to the Ría proceed on a course that avoids rock dangers and the main mussel bed sections, between Islote Jidoiro FL(3)G.15s and Isla Rúa Fl(2)WR.7s

RÍA DE AROUSA

- Proceed between Bajo Las Touzas Fl.R.5s and Bajo Ter Fl.G.5s heading for the mussel bed lights at Sinal de Ostreira Fl.Y.5s. If this isn't visible then the alternative, until closer in, is the red channel marker Fl(3)R.9s

- When the mussel bed lights at Sinal de Ostreira Fl.Y.5s are abaft the beam, alter course towards the end of the starboard breakwater Fl(3)G.9s. Follow the 10m contour.

Initial shelter

Initial shelter can be found from the Atlantic swell and westerly winds behind **Isla de Sálvora**.

For a quieter berth, the marina at **Pobra de Caramiñal** is modern and sheltered, very easy to access even in difficult weather and has alternative nearby anchorages.

Note that the marina at **Santa Uxía de Ribeira** is closer to the entrance but the majority of berths are Mediterranean style moorings which may be difficult to manage in adverse conditions. The outer pontoon is likely to be untenable with a strong northeast but because of this may well have free space.

Other ports and facilities

The marina at **Vilagarcía** is 12M up the Ría but has access to significant facilities and communications ashore.

Rianxo marina is limited and only appropriate for smaller boats (up to 8m) but it does have facilities ashore.

A new (2006) marina has been built to the north of the fishing harbour at **Vilanova**. It offers good

CRUISING GALICIA 165

RIA DE AROUSA

shelter from all conditions but careful navigation is required east of Isla de Arousa to get to it. Only limited shore facilities were available at the time of publication.

The fishing harbours on the north coast of **Isla de Arousa** are difficult as well as unpicturesque, given the amount of fishing activity and small boats on buoys. There are a few buoys available to visiting yachts at **San Xulián** but arrangements are not always the easiest to organise. A knowledge of Spanish would help to find the correct authority responsible.

There are numerous and pleasant anchorages throughout the Ría, which will depend on wind and weather conditions for their suitability. Some need careful navigation around coastal and other dangers but the destinations are often very rewarding.

Provisioning

There is no shortage of local shops and *plazas* (markets) in the towns and villages, plus a wealth of restaurants and bars at which you can enjoy excellent fresh food.

Repairs and chandleries

Vilagarcía and Pobra do Caramiñal both have boat lifts and all the main marinas will have information on local mechanic, rigging and electronic expertise. There are no chandleries focused on leisure yachts but, given the size of the local fishing industry, there should be no problem in finding a suitable way forward for a repair. The *ferreterías* (iron mongers) are plentiful and well stocked. Ferretería del Río at Caramiñal and those in Vilagarcía are particularly extensive. For more complex spares you may need the services of larger chandleries further afield such as Betanzos in Vigo or Pombo in A Coruña.

Transport

The excellent **train** line that links all of western Galicia from A Coruña to Vigo serves the station at Vilagarcía. The high speed R598 trains stop there.

Numerous **buses** cover the area, run by a series of private companies (Castromil, Arriva and others) with routes to all the major towns including Santiago, Pontevedra, Vigo and A Coruña as well as the local towns. The main bus stations are at Vilagarcía, Cambados, Pobra do Caramiñal and Ribeira and there are local stops at the majority of the smaller towns. Further away there are main bus stations at Noia and Pontevedra. See the local tourist office for schedule details.

Cruising in Ría de Arousa

Ría de Arousa is the largest of the Rías Baixas and too big to simply visit for a one day tour. It is a reasonably well sheltered area and distances inside are not large so it is an ideal day sailing cruising ground.

One day

If you only have one day to get a taste of the Ría it will not be worth travelling further than Isla de Arousa. Depending on weather conditions, try anchoring at Isla Sálvora, La Lanzada or near Isla La Toxa further in. Alternatively you could simply sail in the outer area and enjoy busy fishing boat activity against the rural wooded background. You can find a pretty anchorage on the south side of the isthmus of Isla de Arosa at Ensenada Sur de San Xulián where you can land and sample local life. To get any better than this you will need to sail to the northern end of the Ría.

One week

The anchorages at Ensenada de San Xulián, Isla Sálvora (settled weather), Santa Cruz, Punta del Chazo, La Toxa and Corrubedo (settled weather) are very scenic, showing the best of Ría de Arousa's natural beauty. These anchorages and the marinas at Ribeira, Caramiñal, Vilagarcía and Cambados will give you enough options for overnight stops. A suggested itinerary in settled weather is as follows:

Anchor at Corrubedo or Aguiño if conditions permit to visit the **Dunas de Corrubedo**, a striking national park which you see from well marked paths. Take binoculars to look at the migratory birds in the lagoons.

Anchor at **Isla Sálvora** for one of the best day settings you will find.

Stay at **Pobra de Caramiñal,** a pretty town with a pleasant sea front, some history and the natural pools in the hills behind. A good place for provisioning, shelter and repairs.

Anchor near **Santa Cruz** or **Rianxo** for very scenic, quiet locations.

Stay at **Vilagarcía** from where you can make easy land journeys to many of the Ría southern highlights and further afield. Vilagarcía is also the best for facilities, night life and spares.

Visit **Cambados**, a town of imposing aristocratic buildings and the home of Albariño, the fruity white wine which competes with Ribeiro for primacy among Galician wines. Either find space in the fishing harbour pontoons or travel there by land.

Anchor to the south of **San Xulián** and go ashore to enjoy some of the best restaurants and bars. Isla de Arousa can be very touristy but the Ensenada de San Xulián retains charm.

Anchor near Isla **La Toxa** for a great view of this once unspoilt island. If you do go ashore during the high season you will meet the tourist crowds that now arrive in volume.

Anchor opposite **La Lanzada** beach to see a vast expanse of sand and the flooded area of Ensenada de O Grove full of seabirds.

Passages from Arousa

Leaving Arousa is most easily done using the Canal Principal between Isla Sálvora and Península de O Grove. This is a very broad channel which is well marked.

From Arousa to Ría de Muros, a more interesting passage navigational exercise (calm conditions, daylight only) can be made by passing inside Isla Sálvora using Paso de Carreiro and Canal de Sagres as described in the Aguiño section. A lunch time anchorage can be found in Ensenada de Corrubedo (see Corrubedo section) before travelling north to Ría de Muros taking care of Bajo las Basoñas and La Baya.

From Arousa to Ría de Pontevedra there is a well marked passage between Isla Ons and the mainland. Shelter for lunch can be found off the east coast of the island (see Ría de Pontevedra section) before making for the picturesque Ría de Aldán or the harbours and anchorages within the main Ría (Sanxenxo, Aguete, Combarro).

RÍA DE AROUSA

⚓ Ensenada de Corrubedo

Ensenada de Corrubedo is a very scenic bay on the west entrance to Ría de Arousa, but it is exposed to the west and southwest. Daylight and good visibility approach only recommended, although Cabo Corrubedo and the harbour have sectored lights that ensure dangers are cleared.

The beaches to the north of Corrubedo (Ensenada de Valeiras) are a popular destination for surfers, which gives an indication of the Atlantic swell that beats the cape.

Approach & entrance

This wide bay offers numerous approach routes but all pass close to submerged rocks. The options below assume good visibility and sea conditions. Beware small fishing floats and pots.

From the northwest:

- Pass within 0.5M of Cabo Corrubedo (Fl(2+3) WR.20s) in 30m depth on a course of approximately 130°

- Note the extending reef from Punta Posalgueiro, 0.5M to the SE of Cabo Corrubedos, and isolated rock Bajo Marosa, 1M south of of Cabo Corrubedo

- When Islote Ferreira, a prominent rock on the beach bears less than 60° turn and head for it, into the bay.

From the south:

- Pass close to Islas Sagres (Fl.5s) in greater than 30m depth

- Stay in at least this depth until well into the bay to clear Banco del Pragueiro and offlying isolated rock (Bajo de la Dianteria) to seaward

- If Cabo Corrubedo Fl(2+3)WR.20s is in sight, ensure bearing doesn't increase above 345° to keep clear of Banco del Pragueiro

  or and when

- The breakwater at Corrubedo Iso.WRG.3s is visible keep the light on a bearing of 356° (centre of white sector). This will clear all dangers to the entrance

- Ensure bearing on breakwater doesn't drop below 330° to clear Bajo Paremo and offlying isolated rock.

Anchor either off Playo do Prado, the beach to the west of the entrance, in 3-5 m or off the sandy section of beach to the east. For the latter ensure that Islote Ferreira, a prominent rock on the beach

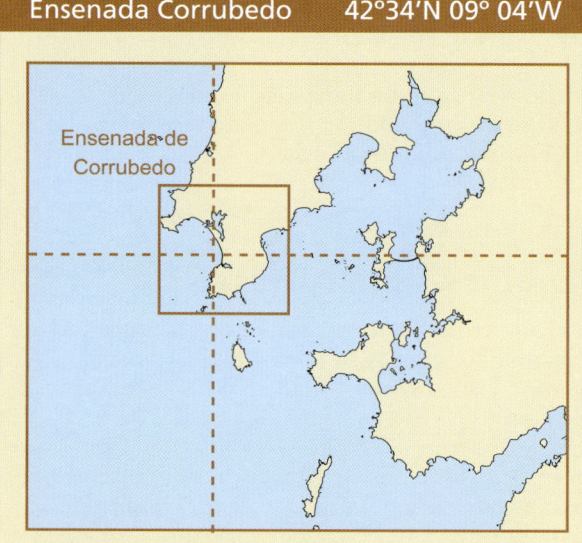

Ensenada de Corrubedo
- Only day entrance recommended. Anchor NW at Playa do Prado or off sandy beach to east
- Shelter: exposed to SSW, very open to sea swell

(see photo) remains on bearing greater than 40° to clear Bajo Paremo and offlying isolated rock.

Provisioning & facilities

Corrubedo has a few shops for basic provisioning.

There is a health centre at Casa do Mar.

Dolmen de Axeito

RÍA DE AROUSA

Interest

Myth has it that locals lit fires to guide sailors towards Cabo Corrubedo. Once the boats were close to the rocky shoreline the fires were extinguished and the ensuing wreck became a profitable pillage. But let this not deter you!

Cabo Corrubedo is home to *percebeiros*, the collectors of *percebes*, a very strange claw-like delicacy plucked from the rocky shoreline (see Percebes interest box). Attached to the rocks in their wetsuits, *percebeiros* can be observed about this precarious business from Faro de Corrubedo (lighthouse).

The highlight of the bay is *Parque Natural de Corrubedo* (*Parque Natural do Complexo Dunar de Corrubedo e Lagoas de Carregal e Vixán* is the full name). An area of outstanding natural beauty, it comprises impressive sand dunes and two lagoons (Vixán and Carregal) that host extensive wildlife. Orchids grow in the flats near the northern entrance close to the town of Oliveira. Well marked paths cover various routes through the park. The entrance near the village of Vilar to the south includes a good information centre. Playa do Vilar is a pleasant sandy beach with showers and cabins, as well as a beachguard. Unless it is a very calm day your best option to enjoy the park is to arrange transport from Ribeira.

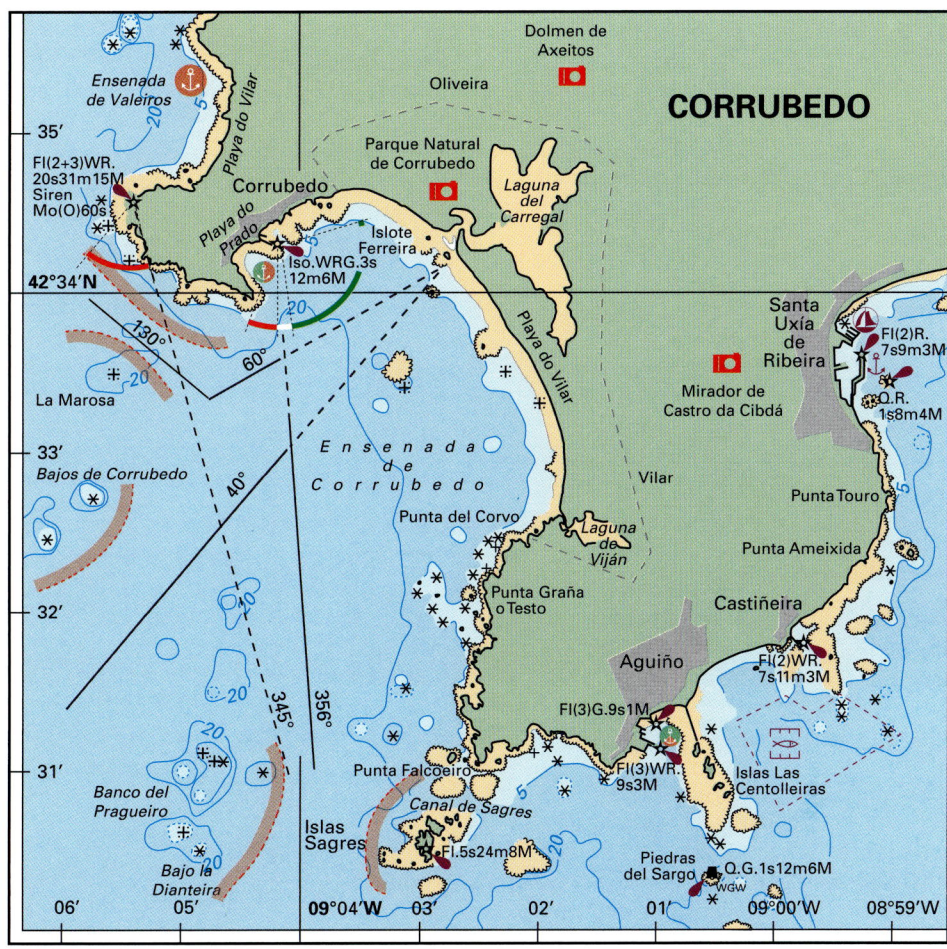

Nearby visit the prehistoric and well preserved *Dolmen de Axeitos*, one of many important remains from the stone age in Galicia.

Mirador Castro da Cibdá, up 250m, is a great spot for a view over the national park and the sea bay below. You will need transport, as it is a long stretch up hill on main roads.

Playa de Corrubedo

RÍA DE AROUSA

⚓ Aguiño

Daylight approach only recommended, although Aguiño breakwater is lit with a sectored light.

Aguiño is a busy fishing harbour which hosts one of the largest fleets in the area, and is a major centre for *percebe* and clam.

Aguiño & Isla Sálvora   42°31'N 09°00'W

Aguiño
- Only day entrance recommended
- Open to the southwest
- Anchor between the harbour and the reef/causeway to the east

Isla Sálvora
- Use only in calm conditions, avoid with easterlies, only suitable as a temporary anchorage
- Anchor in front of Playa dos Bois

Approach & entrance

The approach is through a rock strewn bay which offers numerous routes but all pass close to submerged rocks. The options below assume good visibility and sea conditions. Beware fishing boats and floats. The breakwater at Aguiño harbour obscures possible vessel movements.

From the southwest:

Canal Principal is the main approach for large fishing vessels.

- Approach in the white sector (26°- 40°) of the light on the end of the breakwater Fl(3)WR.9s.

From the west:

Canal de Sagres is a 250m wide passage, in 7-10m, which is not recommended except on a calm day, using detailed charts and preferably with local knowledge.

- Approach from well inside Ensenada de Corrubedo with Islas Segres (Fl.5s) bearing between 130° and 150°
- Alter course when Piedras del Sargo (Q.G) bears 105° and head for them
- The south side of the 250m wide channel is the preferred side as there are offlying isolated rocks from Cabo Falcoeiro
- Stay on this course once through the passage to clear Piedra de Barlovento to the south
- Approach Aguiño in the white sector (26°- 40°) of the light on the end of the breakwater Fl(3) WR. 9s.

From the east:

- Paso del Carreiro is a 200 m wide passage in 5-10m which is not recommended except on a calm day, using detailed charts and preferably with local knowledge.

Beacon at Piedras del Sargo

RÍA DE AROUSA

- Approach from south of the Red cardinal buoy / mark (Fl.R5s) marking Bajos Sinal del Castro on a course of between 240° and 250°

- When 250m from the beacon at Piedras del Sargo turn onto 270°

- Approach Aguiño in the white sector (26°- 40°) of the light on the end of the breakwater Fl(3)WR.9s.

From any of the approaches above, when close to the breakwater, stay in more than 5m until north of the quay (this gives you clearance from the reef and off-lying rock).

⚓ Anchorage

Anchor north of the Aguiño quay in 4m depth, sandy bottom.

The area northeast of the Centolleiras reef appears tempting but the bottom is full of stones so it is not recommended.

Provisioning & Servides

Aguiño has a few shops for provisioning and a ferretería where basic materials for repairs can be found.

✚ Health centre at Casa do Mar, Estrada Xeral, Aguiño.

⚓ Isla Vionta, Isla Sálvora, Cabo

Aguiño harbour

Isla de Sálvora

CRUISING GALICIA 171

RÍA DE AROUSA

Arousa Dorna boats

Falcoeiro

At **Isla Vionta** anchor in front of the beach on the northeastern side, very pleasant location. Some shelter from a westerly swell but only suitable for a stop in calm conditions.

The inlets **west of Cabo Falcoeiro** offer remote settings for a stop in calm conditions.

Isla Sálvora is a delightful anchorage. Calm weather is best and it is exposed to the *nordés* wind from the northeasterly common in the summer months. The approach and anchorage need to be undertaken with care given the very many rocks. The **Paso Interior** between Sálvora and Vionta is often a calm haven from the Atlantic swell. The anchorage shown feels almost like a pool, perfect if you are the only boat.

Interest

It is worth seeing the *lonxa* (fish auction hall) of Aguiño as wholesale trading of clam and *percebe* is quite a spectacle. The town is not very attractive despite its claim to Phoenician origins (see Cala de A Covasa for the stepped large blocks that reputedly formed the Phoenician quay).

The town's **Fiesta del Percebe** on 22 July is a celebration of the local product, a fun event regardless of your taste in seafood.

Look out for the distinctive *dorna* boats used by local fishermen. They are reputedly a small version of a *drakar*, the boat used by Viking fleets for successive attempts at invasion of Santiago. The bow is round and rising while the stern is small and flat. Dornas are about 4.5m in length and 1.5m beam. They are normally sailed with only one main sheet, large for the size of the boat but possible because of the keel.

Isla de Sálvora is the third largest island of Galicia's *Parque Nacional das Illas Atlánticas*. Legend links the island with the Mariña de Lebeira dynasty, reputedly engendered by a siren. In the past it was home to a small settlement dedicated to salt production (see the buildings near Playa do Almacén, in the 20th century converted into a large *pazo*) before being requisitioned by the Spanish army who built the small quay. It is now privately owned by an aristocratic family, but since the late 1970s there have been no permanent inhabitants. The island is picturesque, well worth a walk ashore to see the lighthouse at the southwestern end and the abandoned village in the centre.

Percebes (barnacles)

Percebes are a delicacy in Spain, regarded and prized as an expensive treat. However, they are not to everyone's visual or culinary taste, and prying the edible tentacle away from its shell undoubtedly requires some dexterity.

Barnacles are shellfish that live in the most exposed coastline, thriving on rock faces that are battered by waves yet also soaked in sunshine and freshwater from rain when the tide is out. The larva of the young animal drifts in the sea until it strikes a suitable rock to which it sticks using a special gland that secretes a glue like substance.

Collecting *percebes* is a dangerous enterprise as the locations are generally very hazardous. Fishermen tie themselves to the rocks in order to avoid being dragged into the sea by the waves, in modern times wearing wetsuits to withstand the cold. The value of the catch is astronomically high and licencing is very tightly controlled.

The rocks on the western shore of Corrubedo are a good quality harvesting ground. Other star locations are Costa da Vela near Cangas, near Baroña and Porto do Son, Cabo Roncudo near Corme, the Costa da Morte around Sisargas and the immense cliffs near Cabo Ortegal.

Cooking percebes

Buy the *percebes* fresh from the market and aim to eat them within a day. One kilo should be enough for four people.

Boil water, enough to have the shellfish covered and not packed together. Some recipes advise seawater but this can produce a very salty dish. When the water is boiling add the percebes. Wait for the water to boil again and cook for five minutes.

Serve hot with boiled potatoes and good Albariño wine. To eat open from the bottom side to get at the edible meat. Beware of possible liquid splash.

RÍA DE AROUSA

⚓ Ribeira

A larger bustling town, home to a large fishing fleet. A good spot for stocking up and shelter. The majority of berths at the pontoon are Mediterranean style moorings with lines for bow or stern attached to the pontoons.

Approach & entrance

Straightforward and well lit day or night approach in all conditions although commercial ships will be using the channel up the Ría. Fishing boats cross the same channel at speed attending to *bateas*.

From the west:

- Enter the Ría through the main channel (Canal Principal) between Isla Sálvora Fl(3+1)20s21M and O Grove, keeping a northerly course. Note that all the isolated dangers on the east side are lit

- Sail north between the beacons at Bajos de los Esqueiros Fl(4)G.11s to starboard, Bajos Sinal del Castro Fl.R.5s. to port, both marking rock dangers as well as being main channel markers

- The west side of the wide approach to Ribeira is bounded by offlying dangers to the shore starting at Islote Airó Chico. These are avoided by staying in 15m depth or more until beyond Llagareas Q.R.1s light. The east side is bounded by the bateas, whose area is marked by a special mark Fl.Y.5s3M at its SW corner

- Leave Llagareas light Q.R.1s in front of the harbour wall, to port

- Leave the commercial harbour main wall to port and head for the S side of the marina breakwater Fl(2+1)G.15s. Enter marina from the NE.

From the east:

- If coming from the eastern end of the Ría, round Isla Rúa leaving it to N (this avoids unlit rocks further north) and beware *bateas*, whose area is marked by a special mark Fl.Y.5s3M at its SW corner and Bajo Camouco (unlit beacon).

Santa Uxía de Ribeira   42°34'N 08°59'W

Club Náutico Deportivo de Ribeira

- Entrance night and day, waiting pontoon
- Shelter all directions but waiting pontoon exposed to NE
- Depth minimum 3m inside marina, 5m at the northern visitor pontoons
- Visitors up to 16m (few spaces): stern/bow-to mooring and some pontoons
- ☎ 981 874739 Fax 981 873801/290
- VHF Channel 09
- secretaria@nauticoribeira.com

- Water, electricity at the pontoons

- 🔧 Repairs: local mechanic, electrician, diver & general boat work, enquire at marina office
- 🛥 only small vessel slipway

- Good facilities: launderette, showers
- Bar-restaurant
- Saliing club, diving club

Ribeira marina

174 CRUISING GALICIA

RÍA DE AROUSA

- Leave Llagareas light, Q.R.1s in front of the harbour wall, to port

- Leave the commercial harbour main wall to port and head for the south side of the marina breakwater Fl(2+1)G.15s. Enter marina from the NE.

Berthing & facilities

The moorings are stern or bow to except for the north side of the first pontoon directly inside the entrance. The latter will be uncomfortable in a strong northerly.

⚓ Playa Corosa

At the east end of the beach north of Piedras Minateiras with trees offering some shelter from the NE. Anchor in 3-5m of sand and weed.

⚓ Ensenada de Palmeira

Ensenada de Palmeira 2M further northeast provides another stop for anchoring, between the area occupied by small boats and the beach Playa do Corna north of the small harbour. The harbour is too shallow for yachts (and guarded by rock dangers) but the pontoon offers a good landing spot for a dinghy. Anchor towards the west end of the bay clear of isolated rocks in 5m-6m in sand and weed.

Provisioning & eating

Bars and restaurants are towards the fishing harbour, along Avda de Malecón and the streets parallel. There are several well stocked supermarkets including Haley near the marina.

Transport

Ribeira does not have a dedicated bus station but buses do stop, with links to other local towns. Enquire at the tourist office. For many journeys a local taxi is the easiest option.

Interest

Santa Uxía de Ribeira is home to around 12,500 people, one of the larger towns in the area and also the centre for the third largest fishing fleet in Galiicia, behind those of Vigo and Coruña. The town is not the most attractive but there are some genuine streets and squares behind the modern constructions. As always, food in any of the local bars and restaurants is excellent and fresh.

RIA DE AROUSA

Ribeira was a popular point of attack for Moorish and pirate fleets, in the 16th and 17th century becoming a target for British assaults. In 1921 it received the title of Noble for the dedication of its inhabitants to the rescue of survivors of Santa Isabel, a Spanish steamer that sank at the rocks of Isla Sálvora.

The Ría enjoyed an economic revival in 18th century, when various Catalan investors established salt factories, 12 of these based at the now less prosperous Palmeira further north. Many Catalan names survive and there is still an area of Palmeira called Catalan Quarter (*Barrio Catalán*). The more permanent legacy comes from the 19th century when new technologies for conservation and tin canning established an industry which is still large and successful in the Rías. Palmeira itself was a point of emigration, many of its local people can talk of relatives in the US and Latin America.

Visit **Parque Periurbano de San Roque**, an interesting assembly of reconstruction of megalithic, *castro* (pre-romanic buildings) and a Roman amphitheatre, with excellent views of the town and Ría below. The group gives you a taste for the history of this area, home to extensive pre-historic remains and subjected to many invasions each leaving some kind of legacy.

At **Artes**, around 5 km north of Ribeira, the **Centro del Grabado Antiguo y Contemporáneo** is an excellent centre whose collection includes work by Rembrandt, Goya, Picasso and Dalí.

Look out for the *fiesta* at Ermita de San Alberto, a romanesque church on whose grounds young people follow tradition breaking roof slates in the hope of finding partner.

Both Ribeira and Palmeira have good events centred on flowers. The streets of Palmeira are covered with **flower carpets** during *Corpus* (May/June) and Ribeira sports a *Fiesta da Flor* in June.

Santa Uxía de Ribeira

- Vigo 40km Santiago 60km Coruña 120km
- Bus station: Avda Malecón by the end of the fishing harbour wall
- Supermarkets:
  - Gadis, Rosalía de Castro 25
  - Haley, Avda de a Coruña
  - Mercadona, Rúa Carlos Casares
- Restaurants:
  - Bars and restaurants towards the fishing harbour, along Avda del Malecón and old town
- Tourist office: Avda del Malecón 3, 981 873007
- Chandlers (efectos navales):
  - Alvarez e Hijos, Efectos Navales Tres, Av Malecón 34
  - Náutica Barbanza, Avda Malecón 44
  - Martínez Pardavila, Avda Malecón 73
  - Pérez Queiruga, Pr. Lonxa 56
- Banks, chemists and other shops along Avda General Franco, Avda del Malecón, Avda Rosalía de Castro.
- Hospital da Barbanza, Parroquia de Oleiros, around 5km north of the town. 981 835901

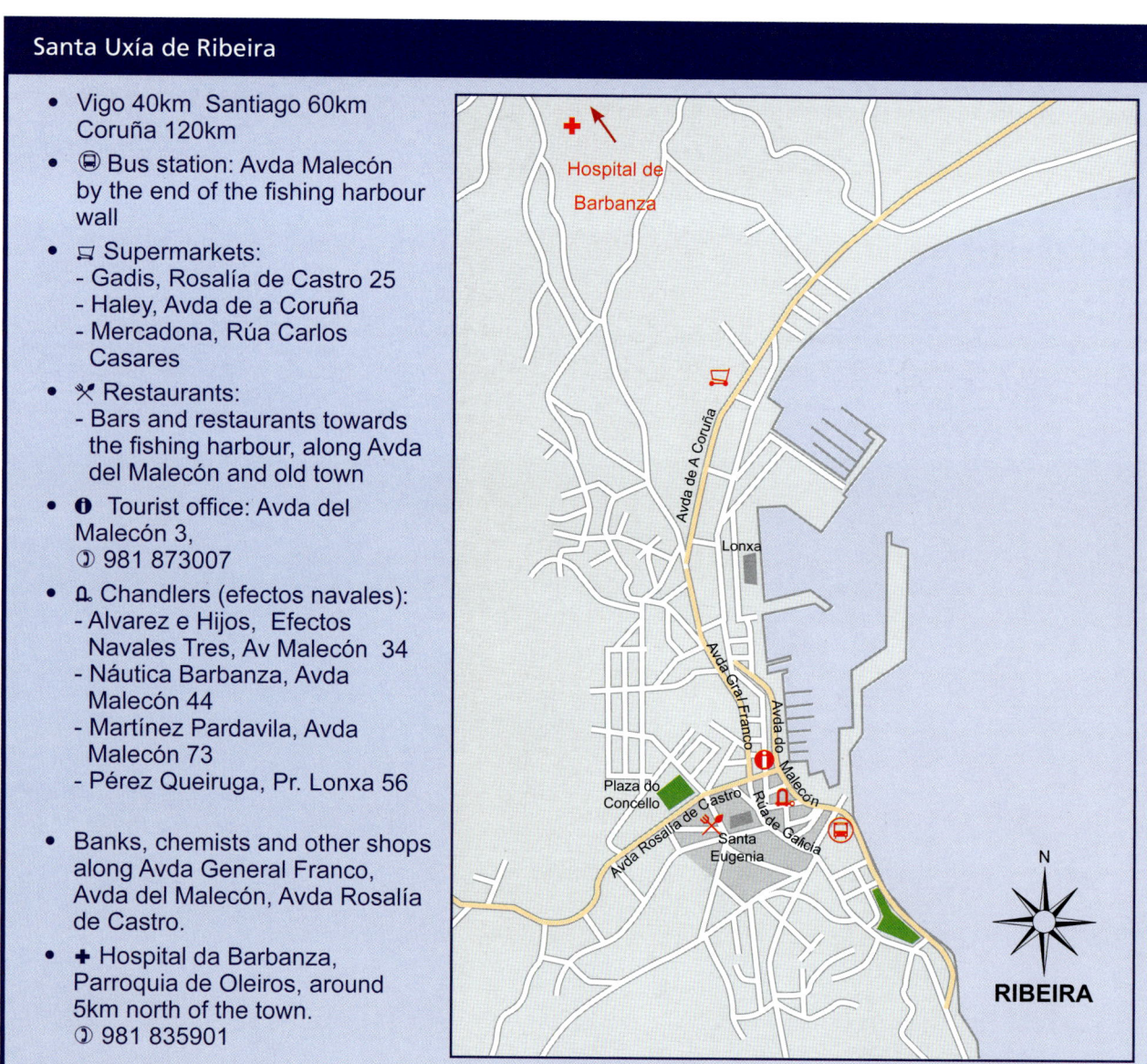

RÍA DE AROUSA

Mussel trading

Mussel fishermen hold a licence from the regional government and are also members of a producer association ('*Organización de productores mexilloeiros de Galicia*'). The association has built shore side facilities that serve to unload the mussels for sale, a common scene at many fishing ports. A boat arrives with its deck laden with mussels collected that morning. The boat docks to the quay near where the association facilities and collecting crane are located. The welcoming party will consist of buyers, typically including a cannery owner accompanied by some of his staff backed by a large lorry. The crane moves back and forth between the boat and the lorry, unceremonuously opening and closing its jaws to collect and dump mussels, about 200kg at a time.

A sample of 50kg is taken early on, to assess the quality of the mussels. After cleaning two pressure cookers are lit with the same precise weight of uncooked mussels in each. Steaming takes five minutes after which the remaining weight is measured. Price paid depends on the plumpness of the mussel itself and in 2006 €0.2 per kg was paid for the leanest and €0.6 for the meatiest. Only the fat ones are sold directly to the public and that summer the price in the market was €3.5 Euros per kg.

RÍA DE AROUSA

⚓ Pobra do Caramiñal

One of the nicest small towns in Arousa, with places to explore, interesting local trips and good places to eat. This is probably the best shelter destination in the Ría, The marina is excellent with finger pontoons of generous proportions, a good place for long term mooring only let down by the lack of better showers.

Approach & entrance

Broad, straightforward and lit entrance. Accessible in day or night with one well lit isolated danger to the SE. Watch for shipping and fishing vessel movements.

- From the entrance to the Ría proceed on a course that avoids rock dangers and the main mussel bed sections, between Islote Jidoiro Fl(3)G.15s and Isla Rúa Fl(2)WR.7s25m12M

- Proceed between Bajo Las Touzas Fl.R.5s and Bajo Ter Fl.G.5s heading for the mussel bed lights at Sinal de Ostreira Fl.Y.5s. If this isn't visible then the alternative, until closer in, is the red channel marker Fl(3)R.9s

- When the mussel bed lights at Sinal de Ostreira Fl.Y.5s are abaft the beam, alter course towards the end of the starboard breakwater Fl(3)G.9s. Follow the 10m contour.

The entrance to the marina is located at its SE corner, at the northern end of Playa Arenal, occupying the space between the large fishing harbour quay and the town.

Caramiñal marina fuel, entrance in the distance

Pobra do Caramiñal   42°36′N 08°56′W

Club Náutico do Caramiñal

- Entrance night and day, outside waiting pontoon
- Shelter all directions but waiting pontoon exposed to NE

- Depth minimum 3m inside marina
- Visitors' berths 15, others available if owners away
- ☏ 981 877317 Fax 981 878455
- cncaraminal@wanadoo.es, cncaraminal@hotmail.com
- VHF Channel 09

- Water, electricity at the pontoons
- ⛽ Fuel at the marina inner breakwater wall, starboard side on entry

- 🔧 Repairs: Esmar at the northern quay of the fishing harbour, some chandlery
- 🏗 40-ton travel lift at the northern end of the fishing harbour

- Basic showers and WC
- Bar-restaurant
- Saling club

- Secure marina for winter storage, space ashore for hard standing

Berthing & facilities

Pontoons are well spaced and of reasonable length. Either communicate on CH09 or tie up temporarily at the outer pontoon until you can establish a more permanent arrangement.

RIA DE AROUSA

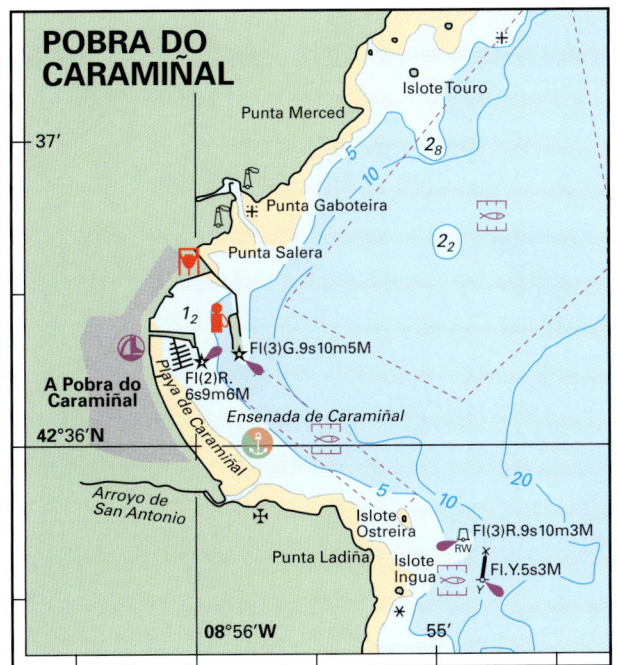

There are 15 visitors' berths on the southern pontoons and often space in the permanent moorings. As with other marinas in Galicia, many of the berths are privately 'owned' and the local habit is to protect the owner's space: you may find reluctance on the part of the *marineros* to let you occupy an empty space ('owner may get upset') and you will certainly jump onto pontoons that are covered with mooring lines left by the berth-holders, so watch your step.

Facilities (toilets, showers) are currently (2007) in portacabins. Water and electricity on pontoons.

Diesel and petrol from refuelling berth alongside the marina wall. Lift out facilities (40 ton), administered by the club, at the northern quay of the main fishing harbour.

⚓ Anchorages

Anchorage outside the marina opposite Playa del Arenal offers good holding in sand. It is exposed to the *nordés* wind (northeasterly) which can set in for a number of days, particularly from May to July.

Provisioning & eating

There is an excellent *plaza* (market) in the new building facing the marina that also hosts a very modern glass front cafetería, between Paseo del Arena and Rúa Castelao. Fish is in excellent supply (except Mondays), straight from the fishing boats that deliver to the *lonxa*. At the fishing harbour, northern side there is a shellfish wholesaler which sells directly to the public. Prices are very good and the produce is the freshest possible.

The Gadis supermarket at Paseo del Arenal is well stocked including fresh fruit and veg.

The bars in front of the marina, near the trees of the Valle-Inclán gardens, all serve good tapas. There are some restaurants further back from the harbour, along Rúa Fernández Varela.

Pobra do Caramiñal

RÍA DE AROUSA

Pobra do Caramiñal

- Vigo 40km Santiago 55km Coruña 120km
- 🚌 Bus station: corner of the fishing harbour pier and the main road
- 🛒 Market: between Rúa Castelao and Paseo do Arenal (modern glass cafetería front of the building)
- 🛒 Supermarkets:
  - Gadis, Paseo del Arenal, 7
- ✕ Bars and restaurants: old streets opposite marina
- ℹ Tourist office: promenade towards fishing harbour
- ⚓ Chandlers: several small *ferreterías* (some have gas bottles) in streets behind the market opposite the marina
  - For a full range of materials see Ferretería del Río on Rúa Gasset
  - Some chandlery in the stores at the main fishing harbour key, near Esmar
- Banks, chemists and other shops along Calle Castelao and Rúa Gasset as well as in streets behind the market
- ✚ Health Centre (Centro Saude), Rúa Venecia, ☎ 981831561, 981832478

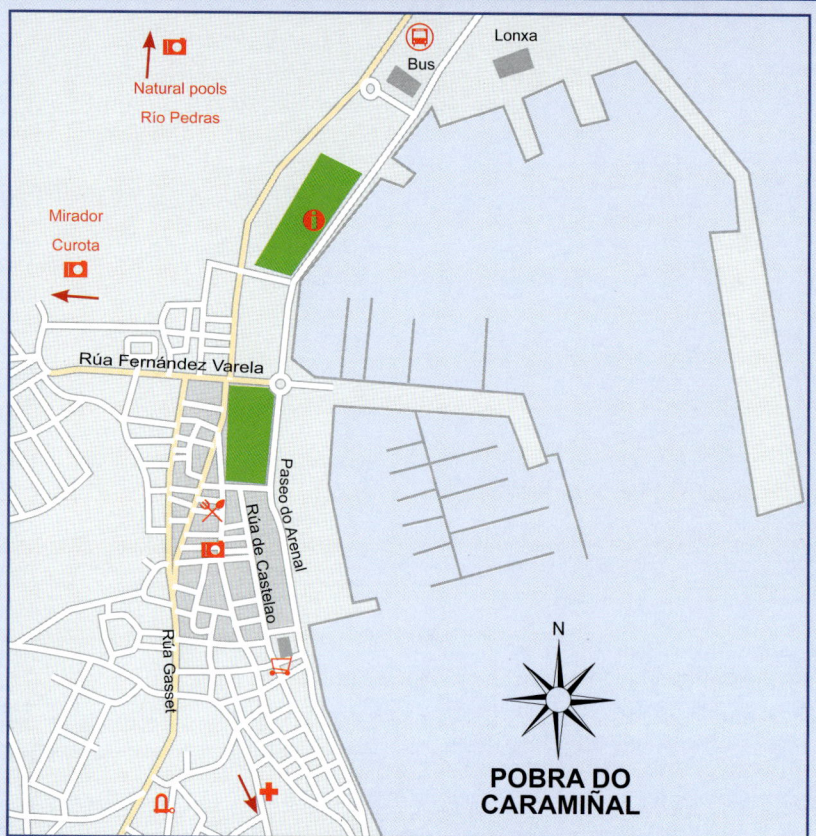

Interest

Pobra do Caramiñal is a town born of the union in the late 19th century of Pobra de Deán, a centre of nobility and church holdings, and the fishing village of Caramiñal. The old divisions have disappeared but the town retains a mixture of grand buildings, see the many coat of arms on walls, and a gutsy fishing community busy at its job.

In modern times Spanish writer **Ramón del Valle-Inclán** made Pobra do Caramiñal his home. Visit the tourist office to obtain a guide to an interesting walk that will take you along some of the key buildings associated with his legacy, of which the most interesting are the Torre de Bermúdez, which used to belong to his grandparents and is now a museum dedicated to his work, and the Farmacia de Tato, Rúa de Paz, a traditional chemist shop.

The streets behind the market up to Rúa de Gasset host a number of buildings associated with nobility. The most imposing are the Town Council, Pazo de Couto and Casa Grande de Aguiar.

Pobra do Caramiñal is located at the foot of the Barbanza hills, a beautiful backdrop to the town setting. The **Curota** mountain offers excellent views over the Ría below, at the *Miradores de Curota*. These are well sign posted from the town centre through Rúa Fernández Varela.

To the north of the town the **natural pools** at Río Pedras (*Piscinas Naturales do Río Pedras*) are a popular destination, worth a visit and a dip in the water.

The scene at the **fishing harbour** is interesting, especially at the *lonxa* during auctions (check at marina for likely times) and when mussel boats

Outer waiting pontoon at Pobra do Caramiñal

CRUISING GALICIA

dock up to unload their cargo (see Mussel Trading for details of how this works). There are numerous canneries in the town itself and to the north of Pobra do Caramiñal which take the mussel product in large quantities. You can get a taste of the scale of this industry by seeing the action.

View from Miradores de Curota

The beach of Arenal used to be the setting for many salt factories, hence the beach is sometimes called 'of the Catalans' making reference to the salt investors that established them. The factories, now long gone, have been replaced by a pleasant promenade and well planned low rise buildings.

Arenal beach is one of many that are used for collecting clams. You will see licence holders early in the morning up to their chest in the water raking the bottom with their toothed wire cages.  Their treasure is well protected, policed by the licencees themselves, who will not take kindly to anyone usurping their rights or breaking the rules for harvesting which give the beaches periods of respite. Buy the clams from a bar to taste the delicacy, or cook them yourself but be sure to learn the technique as they can be very salty if inadequately soaked.

The beaches at Xobre peninsula to the south of Pobra do Caramiñal are nudist, definitely a rarity in this area of fairly conservative and religious traditions.

The most important celebration is the **Procesión de las Mortajas** on the 3rd Sunday of September. The procession commemorates events in the 16th century when a judge due to pass the death sentence on four criminals became gravely ill. When prayers resulted in his recovery he commuted the death sentences and led a procession through the town of Pobra, the four prisoners carrying what would have been his coffin. In modern times people who have survived serious illness head the procession.

Curro Chan das Canizadas in mid July is a traditional gathering centred on the many **horses** that roam the Curota hills behind Pobra do

Caramiñal. The horses are gathered and their mane and tails tidied among the actions of this fiesta.

The *Fiesta del Carmen* (patron virgin of the sailors) takes place in August and involves a parade of boats following an image of the Virgin through the water.

Valle-Inclán Museum

RÍA DE AROUSA

Mussels

The Galician Rías generate 95% of the total amount of mussels grown in Spain, which itself produces 60% of the world's production. Three thousand five hundred licensed *bateas* (in areas named *viveros* on the charts) contribute to the 230,000 tons produced each year, taking advantage of the unique conditions of the rías. Clear Atlantic water flows with the tide, bringing food to the 20m lines hanging down from the floating platforms. Fifty percent of the *bateas* are located in Ría de Arousa alone.

Fishermen use purpose built boats, powerful but arranged with ample clear deck space to work in as well as carry the mussel harvest. The boats moor up to the *bateas*, a common scene you will notice, particularly early in the morning. The boat's crane is used to lift the very heavy ropes that hold the mussels, some at an early stage seeded with small animals gathered from the rocks threaded into self dissolving netting. Others will be fully laden with a one foot wide veritable sausage of molluscs and an assortment of weed and other hangers on. The screw gear and sorting table on deck assists the sorting and cleaning on deck. A typical working morning will load the boat with a pile taller than a man.

The Rías are monitored by the maritime agency of La Xunta, the regional government. Given the size of the industry it is vital that the marine environment is maintained, a positive force for conservation in the ongoing balancing act between fishing, tourism and other industry. This area does not suffer the overcrowding of Mediterranean resorts, though looking at Sanxenxo from your boat would make you think otherwise, but there are issues brought from the increase in summer visitors. Some of the local industries, like the paper plant in Marín, are also sources of at least debate, if not pollution.

RÍA DE AROUSA

Mussels

The marine biology department of the Xunta (regional government) monitor the condition of the mussel population, each day taking samples at numerous locations and running tests on the levels of the phytoplankton ceratium which, if unbalanced, create toxicity in the mussels. Occasionally the marine authority will close a Ría due to toxins, but this is generally short lived and the mussels recover.

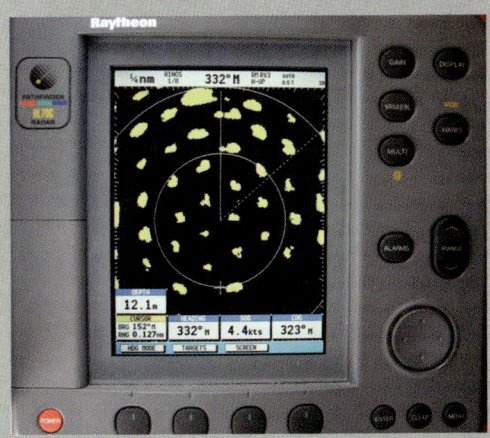

The *bateas* are 10x10m floating platforms, grids of wooden beams arranged atop large man-made floats. A single anchor holds the *batea* in place, typically a very large lump of concrete, sited in the centre. The mussel ropes are very heavy so they hang vertically, not presenting a hazard to navigation. It is perfectly safe to travel between the *bateas*, arranged in clear rows and columns, as indeed do the fishing boats that work them. The platforms are very stable, turning like boats to face waves and even serving to dampen some of the sea swell.

The Rías produce other fish and shelfish, such is the nutrient richness of the environment. Times have changed, as you can hear from any local's tales of earlier times when kids could playfully retrieve *nécoras, pulpos, berberechos, almejas* (velvet crab, octopus, cockles, clams) from the water or sand. Despite the decrease in stock brought by modern times the Rías support 1,143 other shellfish farms, mainly clams, and 16 fish farms, mainly turbot, bream, dorada and salmon delivering 300,000 tons of fish to the Spanish market every year.

CRUISING GALICIA

RÍA DE AROUSA

⚓ Ensenada de Cabo Santa Cruz

Small and busy fishing harbour with neighbouring anchorage offering protection from W to NE. The village of A Pesqueira next to the harbour is dedicated to fishing, the houses painted in bright colours and a few grand houses remaining.

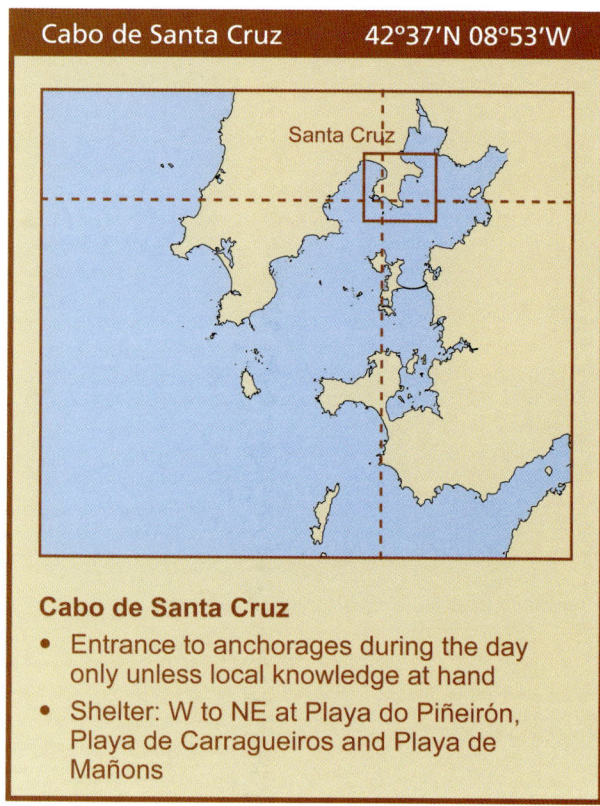

Cabo de Santa Cruz   42°37'N 08°53'W

Cabo de Santa Cruz
- Entrance to anchorages during the day only unless local knowledge at hand
- Shelter: W to NE at Playa do Piñeirón, Playa de Carragueiros and Playa de Mañons

Approach & entrance

Straightforward approach in daylight, but made difficult at night due to the presence of *bateas*. Anchorage is protected from the N and NE.

- Approach Cabo Cruz sailing between Isla Benencia and red channel marker at Bajo Moscardiño Fl(2)R.7s to the east and the lights marking mussel beds at Sinal de Ostreira Fl.Y.5s and Fl(3)R.9s 2.5M to the west

- Work your way between the *bateas* to the anchorage in Ensenada Cabo Cruz. The area between Isla Benencia and the coast is not well marked for dangers, only navigate with local knowledge.

⚓ Anchorages

The anchorage, directly east of the harbour, in front of Playa do Piñeirón, is protected from W to NE and has no isolated dangers, with good holding in sand covered with some weed.

The harbour itself and the area immediately to the north are packed with fishing boats so they are not recommended.

The SE corner of **Playa de Carragueiros** offers an alternative if there is no room available elsewhere, but beware isolated rocks.

The small bay SW of **Punta Porto Mouro** in front of Playa de Triñanes is a very pleasant anchorage spot, sheltered from west to north and for much of the time from the east as well. Beware rocks east and west of the bay. The beach is quiet and sometimes used to repair *bateas*, providing a small amount of local entertainment.

RÍA DE AROUSA

It is possible to anchor at the northern end of **Ensenada de Boiro**, off the Playa de Barraña (beach holiday destination of Galicians), but it is not recommended to approach at night as there are unmarked dangers and *bateas*.

Escarabote, at the W end of Playa de Barraña has a quay that can be used for landing with a dinghy.

From the anchorage at Ensenada de Cabo Cruz

Provisioning

There are some basic shops in A Pesqueira but no supermarket or chemists. For better supplies the nearest larger town is Boiro, north of Playa de Barraña.

Interest

The walk behind **Playa de Carragueiros** towards Punta do Chazo and round north is rural and pretty.

There are prehistoric markings at Laxe da Cabras in Ferreiros, north of the Abanqueiro peninsula that ends in Punta Porto Mouro.

Abanqueiro is known for its **oysters**, food of Kings and Cardinals in the past, a perfect substitute for meat during Lent. The *bateas* in this part of the Ría hold long strings of oysters, not mussels.

Santiago landing in Arousa

Ría de Arousa and the Ulla river are key to the Xacobean legend. According to myth the remains of Apostle Santiago (St James) were brought from Palestine to this part of the world by his two disciples Teodoro and Anastasio. They entered Ría de Arousa and followed the course of the Ulla until they reached the old town of Iria Flavia. They tied their boat to a large stone, a pagan altar, which by an evolution of words (*piedrón* would be the Spanish for large stone) gave rise to the current name of the town, Padrón, otherwise known for its small sweet peppers.

The disciples had to contend with local Celtic queen Lupa and the Roman garrison. Lupa permitted the landing of the remains as long as they were carried on a cart pulled by her bulls. She converted to Christianity when her bulls became tame under the influence of Santiago.

The remains stayed untouched in the Libredón forest until in the 9th century they were 'discovered' by Bishop Teodomiro of Iria Flavia, soon attracting the attention of the King. The legend became a rallying point for the Christian kingdoms of Spain, skillfully used by nobles and Kings as a spiritual buttress in the ongoing wars against the invading Moors. The grand Cathedral of Santiago de Compostela was started in the 11th century and the town became one of the wealthiest in Europe, a focus of pilgrimage which continues today.

The story is told in the Codex Calixtinus, written with Papal blessing in the 12th century. One of the copies is kept in the Santiago Cathedral Museum.

ENSENADA DE CABO DE SANTA CRUZ

CRUISING GALICIA **185**

RÍA DE AROUSA

⚓ Rianxo

Fishing harbour with some pontoons for small leisure boats at the southern (to change to northern) side, and quiet anchorages nearby. Rianxo is a pleasant Galician town in the more rural end of Ría de Arousa.

Approach & entrance

Straightforward and broad approach in daylight, but made difficult at night due to presence of *bateas* and associated fishing boats on the way into Ensenada de Rianxo.

- Starting from the special mark Fl.Y.5s (located on the north side of the main channel half way between the red channel markers at Bajo Moscardiño Fl(2)R.7s and that at the southwest of Isla Cortegada Fl(4)R.11s)

- Proceed north in the channel through the *bateas*

- Once through the *bateas*, the west cardinal Q(9)15s marking the end of the harbour wall at Rianxo will bear 005°

- If making for the harbour, proceed past the west side of the harbour wall

- The entrance is lit by Fl(3)G.9s and Fl(3)R.9s.

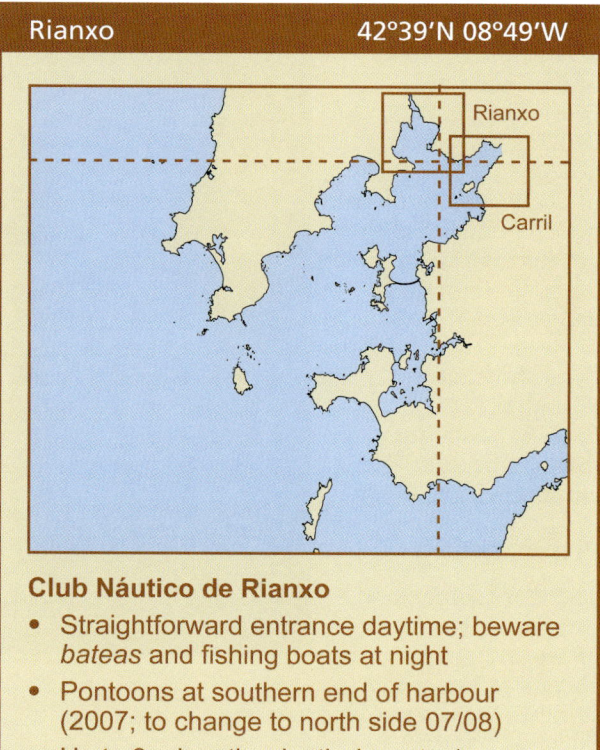

| Rianxo | 42°39'N 08°49'W |

Club Náutico de Rianxo
- Straightforward entrance daytime; beware *bateas* and fishing boats at night
- Pontoons at southern end of harbour (2007; to change to north side 07/08)
- Up to 8m length, depth down to 1m
- ✆ 981 866107 Fax 981 860620
- Showers and toilets in sailing club portacabin

Berthing & facilities

Significant work is being carried out on the harbour (2007) with the fishing boats being provided with more facilities, dredging to 4m and the private pontoons planned to move to the north side. The entrance has moved from that shown on some charts to the north. Care should be taken on entering as the harbour layout shown may have changed.

In 2007 Rianxo harbour had two pontoons set out for leisure boats, but these were not suitable for anything longer than 8m and the depth in the harbour could drop to 1m. The pontoons have water and electricity.

The Club Náutico has showers and toilets as well as a bar-restaurant. There is no fuel for private use or travel lift. Ask at the Club for locally available services if you need repairs or other assistance.

⚓ Anchorages

The area **south of the town** provides shelter from the north, good holding in mud in the vicinity of Playa de Tanxil.

Some anchorages can be found to the north of the harbour and the many fishing boats on moorings, but beware the Lobeiras rocks. There is a pontoon north of the harbour which is suitable for landing your dinghy.

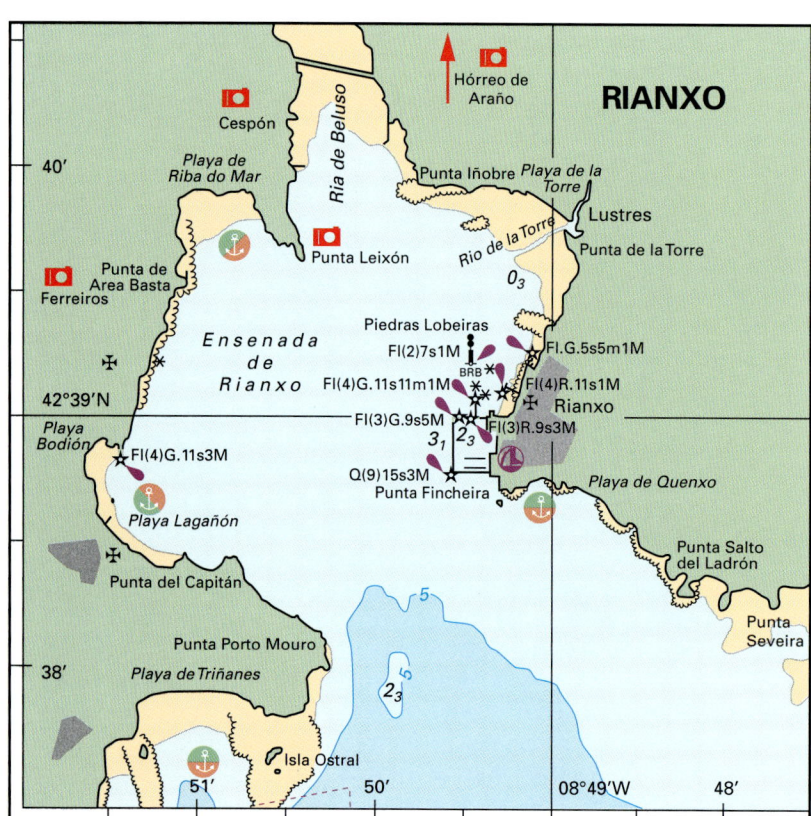

186 CRUISING GALICIA

RÍA DE AROUSA

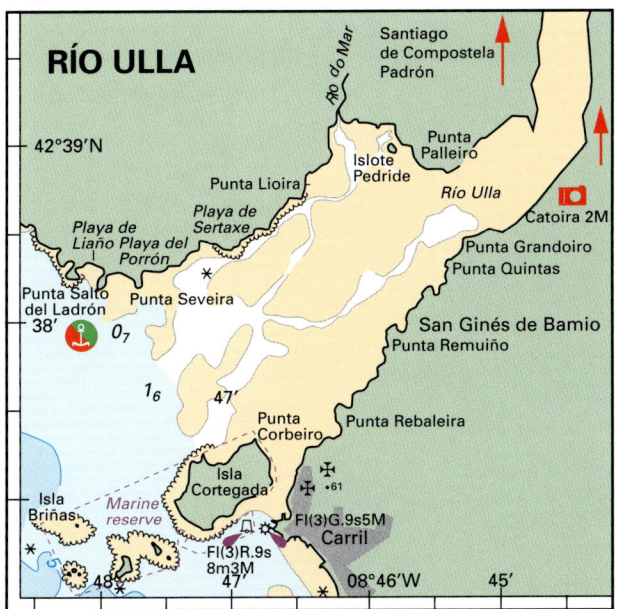

Pontoons in Rianxo harbour

West of Punta Leixón, at the western side of Playa San Vicente is a good very pleasant anchorage, sheltered from anything but southerly winds.

Away to the southeast of Rianxo, opposite the **beaches near Punta Sereira** can also be a good place to anchor with north winds, but pick your spot carefully as this is the Río Ulla delta into the Ría. The river deposits form ever changing banks, making any journey beyond Punta Sereira impossible for any but very shallow draught boats.

Provisioning & eating

The streets between Plaza Rafael Dieste (Santa Columba church) and Virgen de Guadalupe chapel will probably be the focus of your expeditions into this small town. There are grocery shops, a couple of banks, chemists and *ferreterías* as well as a few bars/restaurants in this area. A market takes place on Sundays.

Interest

Rianxo is a small town with a place in Galician folklore due to the song *A Rianxeira* ('A Virxen de Guadalupe, cuando vai para Rianxo...'), composed by two homesick migrants in Buenos Aires. Rianxo was also the home of Alfonso Castelao, who enshrined modern Galician nationalism in the first half of the 20th century through his book *Sempre en Galicia*. Castelao was exiled from Franco in Buenos Aires where he died.

The town did not share in the economic boom brought by salt factories and canneries, yet another place in Galicia where many emigrated to make a living. Today mussel boats are the focus of activity as is obvious looking at the harbour.

The old streets retain charm, many of the buildings in traditional Galician granite. In some of the streets facing the Ría you will notice the narrow houses, named *casas do remo* because they are only the width of an oar (*remo*).

Visit **Capilla de la Virgen de Guadalupe**, **Pazo de Martelo** (now cultural centre) and **Santa Columba** church for a taste of Rianxo's grander past. The church of San Bartolomeo served as a refuge for cholera victims in the past, and the virgin statue (La Morenita) is paraded in a water procession on 8 September.

Either from Rianxo or some of the anchorages nearby you can visit the petroglyphs at Laxe da Cabras near Ferreiros and **Cespón** a small village with interesting churches and a large *romería* (procession and fiesta) on 31 August.

The walk between Cespón and Punta Leixón is set in wooded surrounds, excellent views from the point.

Patron celebrations in Rianxo

CRUISING GALICIA 187

RÍA DE AROUSA

Rianxo

- 🚌 Bus stop: small square just north of harbour, Paseo Manuel Antonio. Buses link to all the major destinations including Vigo, Santiago and Coruña.

- ⚓ Chandlers: several small *ferreterías* around Plaza Rafael Dieste

- 🍴 Restaurants:
  - Several bars and small restaurants along the harbour front and the parallel street and promenade

- Banks, chemists and other shops in the central streets around Plaza Rafael Dieste

- ✚ Health Centre: Centro Saude Rianxo, Rúa Rosalía, ☏ 981 860169

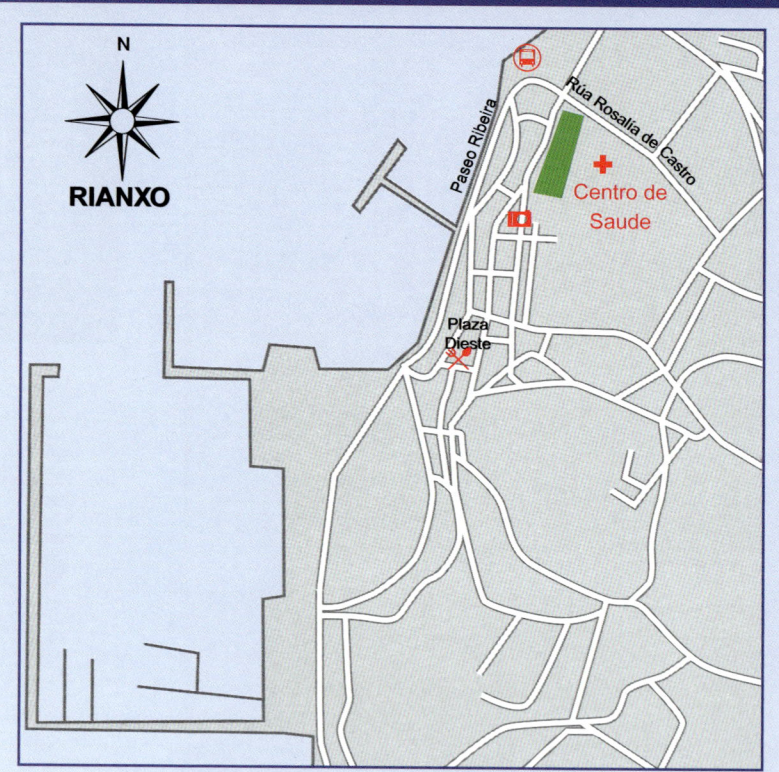

Take a taxi to visit the *hórreo de Araño*, at 37m the longest of these now protected grain stores of Galicia.

The mouth of the Ulla river, despite the unfortunate road bridge location, feels very rural and is a haven for seabirds. The little village of Leiro to the north is interesting for its medieval crosses which serve as the setting for Easter processions.

Catoira is home each 1 August to a re-enactment of a Viking invasion, with replica boats and ample dressed up locals ready to take part in both the mock battles and the drinking celebrations that follow.

The Catoira Towers, two of seven original remaining, were built in 11th century by the the King to guard this port of entrance against the Vikings at the time. In the 18th century they proved their worth once more against a British invading force against Padrón, a first step to an attack on Santiago.

Church of San Bartolomeo

Viking re-enactment at Catoira

188 CRUISING GALICIA

RÍA DE AROUSA

Old windmills near Catoira

Catoira towers

The Catoira replica Viking boats

RÍA DE AROUSA

⚓ Vilagarcía de Arousa

Day and night entrance into well sheltered marina. Berths are a mixture of finger and stern to moorings. Vilagarcía is the largest town in Arousa, bustling with activity and convenient for provisioning, activities and transport.

Approach & entrance

Straightforward and well lit day or night approach in all conditions, although commercial ships will be using the channel up the Ría. Fishing boats cross the same channel at speed, attending to *bateas*.

- Enter the Ría through the main channel (Canal Principal) between Isla Sálvora Fl(3+1)20s21M and O Grove, keeping a northerly course. Note that all the isolated dangers on the east side are lit

- Once in the Canal Principal use the Isla Rúa light Fl(2)WR.7s as the apex for a cone of safety between 010° and 025°. The major hazards outside this cone (Sinal del Castro Fl.R.5s to port and Los Esqueiros Fl(4)G.11s and Los Mexos Fl.G.5s to starboard) are all lit.

- Proceed between the following pairs of channels markers:
  - Isla Rúa lighthouse Fl(2)WR.7s and Islote Jidoiro FL(3)G.15s.
  - Bajo Las Touzas FL.R.5s and Bajo Ter Fl.G.5s.
  - Fl(2)R.7s to the south of Isla Benecia and Fl(3)G.10s to the NW of Isla de Arousa.
  - Fl(4)R.11s to the SW of Isla Cortegada and Fl.G.5s on the end of the commercial harbour wall

Vilagarcía de Arousa 42°36'N 08°46'W

Marina de Vilagarcía

- Entrance night and day
- Shelter all directions
- Depth minimum 3m inside marina
- Berthing: pontoon and stern-to mooring
- Visitors' berths 45, others available if owners away

- ☎ 986 511715 Fax 986 512792
- VHF Channel 09
- marinavilagarcia@marinavilargarcia.com
- www.marinavilagarcia.com
- Administrative centre for the PdG marina consortium ('passport' discount)

- Water, electricity at the pontoons
- ⛽ Fuel at the marina inner breakwater wall, starboard side on entry
- 🔧 Chandlery: numerous *ferreterías* in town
- 🔧 Repairs: contact marina for mechanics, electricians, divers and other specialists
- 🏗 70-ton travel lift at the Astillero (shipbuilders) next to marina

- Showers, laundry, restaurant at the marina building, all excellent quality
- Good local and tourist information
- Sailing club

- Secure marina for winter storage, space ashore for hard standing

- The marina entrance is flanked by Q.R and Q.G. Beware vessels (commercial, and private ribs, jet skis, dinghies from the sailing school) sometimes moving at speed.

There is little room once inside so preparations are best made clear of the entrance.

RÍA DE AROUSA

Entrance to Marina de Vilagarcía, fuel pontoon

Pontoons at Vilagarcía

Berthing & facilities

Vilagarcía is busy in the summer and there is no advance booking for a night. Either communicate on VHF Ch09 or come alongside the 30m berth pontoon directly opposite the entrance, if free, and talk to staff after tying up.

There are 45 berths allocated to visitors in theory, in a variety of locations along the fingers. Berths are a combination of finger and Mediterranean style. Pontoons are well spaced and of reasonable length. Rarely are there any free 'visitor' pontoons.

If Vilagarcía Marina is full then the closest alternative would be the new marina (2006) at Vilanova de Arousa 4M southwest.

Water and electricity at the pontoons. Fuel at the refuelling berth alongside the marina wall, to starboard on entrance. There is a 70 ton lift at the shipbuilders south of the marina.

⚓ Anchorages

The anchorage to the **north of Vilagarcía** Marina opposite Playa del Arenal (S end near wall) offers good holding in sand but has limited protection from the west. Beware the extensive area of clam farming opposite the beach, a set of individual plots which you may disturb. Anchor in sand keeping clear of El Porrón beacons and fishing areas indicated by yellow post.

There is an anchorage that at first looks appealing south of Isla Cortegada if waiting entry to Vilagarcía. In reality you are squeezed for space between obstructions, fishing areas and the channel to Carril (a crowded and confined fishing harbour) as well as being exposed to northeasterly winds and strong ebb tide. Not recommended.

CRUISING GALICIA 191

RÍA DE AROUSA

Isla Cortegada

At Carril it may be possible to lie alongside the southern harbour wall for a short period of time. This is an exposed berth in windy conditions.

The areas to the south of the **main harbour wall** at Vilagarcía and the south of **Vilaxoán** harbour offer shelter with good holding in sand.

Provisioning & eating

The *Praza da Pescadería* (fish market) along Avda da Mariña to the south of the marina is excellent, as is the *Plaza de Abastos* (market) in Rúa Alexandre Bóveda a short distance along.

The Mercadona at Avda de Rosalía de Castro is well stocked including fresh meat, fish, fruit and veg.

The area in front of the marina hosts a number of bars and restaurants, lively in the evenings.

There are better quality of restaurants at Carril next to the port, specialising in product from the Ría (fish and shellfish).

Interest

Vilagarcía is the largest town in Ría de Arousa, home to 35,000 people and comprising within its municipal bondaries the towns of Carril to the north and Vilaxoán to the south. Parts of the town have an industrial feel, particularly around the main harbour and further south around the canneries and fish factories of Vilaxoán. Having acquired pre-eminence as a harbour from Carril during the change from sail to power driven boats, Vilagarcía has continued to grow as a major centre of commerce and trade.

Carril is a pretty spot to the north which makes a claim to the lion share of clam production, harvested in the extensive patchwork of underwater plots that surround it. Clams are celebrated during the *Fiesta de la Almeja* in mid August. Carril has a medieval past as a port for the route towards Santiago through Padrón as well as a destination for Vikings, whose legacy includes the *dorna* boat design you can see in the harbour. As late as the 19th century the port had favour through a royal decree that put it at the level of Cádiz in the south, and this attracted foreign maritime companies.

Carril was also the place of birth of Rosalía de Castro, the writer of the 19th century who did much to promote Galician culture, and Camilo José Cela, winner of the literary noble price in the late 20th century (author of *The Hive*).

Evidence of wealth can be seen in the various **pazos** (large homes of nobles or wealthy merchants), of which the most noteworthy are Pazo de Rúa Nova, home of the Valle-Inclán family (see Caramiñal), and Vista Alegre, both in Vilagarcía, Rubiáns and Rial (now a pleasant hotel).

The **churches** of San Martín at Vilaxoán and Santiago in Carril, together with the splendid **Convento de Vista Alegre** in Vilagarcía provide evidence of grandeur during 12th to 17th century. The stone cross at Carril is a very good example of this type of Galician monument, often used to mark the route to Santiago.

Isla de Cortegada boasts the only laurel forest of its kind in western Europe, legacy of a semi-tropical warmer past of this region. The island was given to King Alfonso XIII in 1907, and was sold by his exiled father after the country chose to be a republic in 1931. The buying development consortium had plans to turn the island into a second elite resort in the area, following the model of La Toxa further south, but plans have not materialised due to local popular objection, resulting lately in a declaration of 'special interest' for the island. For the time being the forest and pretty beaches are home to horses, goats and other happy wild residents.

Vilagarcía Town Hall

RÍA DE AROUSA

Vilagarcía de Arousa

- Vigo 45km Santiago 30km Coruña 100km
- ⌁ Train station at the end of Rúa Doctor Moreira Casal
- 🚌 Bus station: Avda López Ballesteiros

- 🛒 Markets: south along Avda da Mariña *Praza da Pescadería* (fish market), *Plaza de Abastos* (market) in Rúa Alexandre Bóveda
- 🛒 Supermarkets:
  - Mercadona, Avda Rosalía de Castro
- ✕ Restaurants:
  - Marina complex, several restaurants/bars
  - Avda da Mariña and streets parallel towards the town hall
  - Harbour side at Carril

- ℹ Tourist office: Avda Juan Carlos I, 37

- ⚓ Chandlers: various *ferreterías* near the marina, for full chandlery or more complex kit may need Coruña or Vigo
  - Port Sanm, Avda da Mariña, 76
  - Ferro Ferretería, Avda Cambados 20
  - Various services and some materials in the buildings around the main fishing harbour

- Banks, chemists and other shops along Rúa da Mariña and parallel streets behind

- ✚ Hospital Comarcal do Salnés, Lugar Estromil-Ande, Vilagarcía ☎ 986 568000
- ✚ Ambulatorio San Roque (health centre), Avda das Carolinas ☎ 986 507448

Islas Malveiras to the south of Cortegada have their charm but are difficult navigation spots. Malveira Pequeña has the dubious honour of hosting a population of large rats from whom it inherits the nickname of *Isla Ratera*.

The fish industry is evident around Vilaxoán, a large shellfish processing plant at Punta Saiñas and several conserving warehouses very visible. Vilaxoán is home to research centres concerned with the productivity and wellbeing of the Rías, the most noteworthy the *Centro de Investigaciones Pesqueras*.

Compostela beach to the north of Vilagarcía is very popular as a summer holiday destination. Playa das Sinas to the south is the pre-eminent location for night life, but the area in front of Vilagarcía Marina can also get busy.

Inland the **Monte Lobeira** top is a great spot from which to admire the view of the Ría. This hilltop and the area north of Carril are good places for walks. The **petroglyphs** at A Pedra dos Ballores, Bamio are a good representation of pre-historic art (circular and deer drawings).

Fiesta de San Roque in Vilagarcía on 16 August is a good opportunity for *fiesta* fun. The statue of the saint is paraded to the church to the beat of a *pasodoble*, while water is poured over the spectators from balconies along the streets. On the 16th of July fishermen parade their patron (Fiesta del Carmen) in the water. There are of course ample opportunities for other fiestas if you should miss these.

RÍA DE AROUSA

⚓ Vilanova de Arousa

New marina (2006) which is a good alternative to Vilagarcía if this is full. The marina is a good 10 minute walk from the town. Vilanova is a quiet, pleasant harbour village.

Approach & entrance

Straightforward and well lit day or night approach in all conditions although commercial ships will be using the channel up the Ría. Fishing boats cross the same channel at speed, attending to *bateas*.

- Follow the directions up the Ría for Vilagarcía up to the Fl(3)G.10s to the NE of Isla de Arousa near Bajo el Seijo

- Leave the Fl(3)G.10s to the NE of Isla de Arousa close to PORT to allow passage down through the *bateas*. From this light:

- Steer 180° (longitude 08°50'.8W) for 1.2M until the commercial harbour entrance lights Fl(4)R.11s and Rl(4)G.11s are abeam

- Turn for Fl(4).R.11s when it bears 100°. When close to the entrance turn to port, parallel to the breakwater in 5-6m.

- When north of the commercial harbour pass between the marina entrance lights Fl.R.5s and Fl.G.5s.

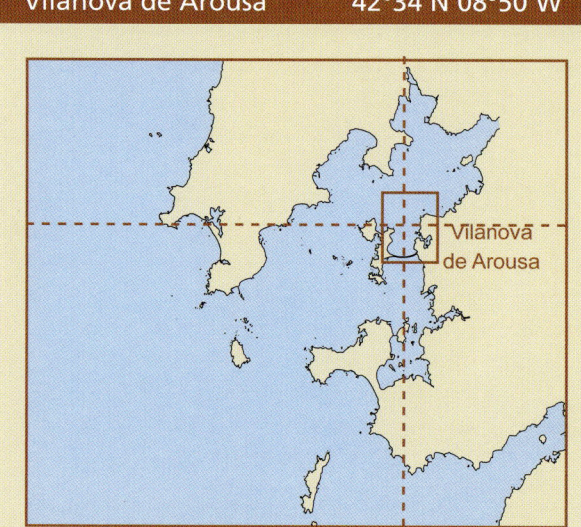

Vilanova de Arousa   42°34'N 08°50'W

Marina Arousa
- Entrance night and day
- Shelter all directions
- Beths for around 200 boats from 8 to 15m in good wide pontoons
- Electriciy and water at the pontoons
- ☎ 670 623084 / 986 554113
- VHF Channel 09

- ⛽ Fuel scheduled (2007) to be accessed at pontoon immediately to starboard on entrance
- 🛠 Travel-lift scheduled 2007
- Showers, restaurant scheduled 2007

Beware Bajo el Seijo about 1M north of the harbour marked with an unlit beacon. Follow the channel south through the *batea* grid and then east when in line with harbour entrance. The main harbour to the south of the marina is a busy fishing harbour and not suitable for leisure boats.

Vilanova marina

RÍA DE AROUSA

Vilanova de Arousa

- Vigo 45km Santiago 30km Coruña 100km

- 🛒 Market: Plaza de Abastos (main street from fishing harbour past police station)
- 🛒 Supermarket: Froiz in main street from fishing harbour
- 🍴 Restaurants:
  - Several bars and restaurants in the plaza near the town hall and police station

- ℹ Tourist office, Casa da Cultura
  ☎ 986 554845
- Bank, chemist and other shops in the main street from the fishing harbour
- ✚ Centro Saude Vilanova Arousa (health centre), As Rodas, ☎ 986 561068

Berthing & facilities

Marina Arousa is the result of an extension to the fishing harbour, built in 2006. The pontoons are wide and manoeuvring is easy. Facilities are being built (2007/08) including a fuel berth, travel lift and showers plus a restaurant.

Provisioning & eating

Vilanova does not have large supermarkets but the Plaza de Abastos (market) has a number of small shops that will be more than adequate for provisioning. Several restaurants and bars will look after you, around the main plaza near the town hall.

Interest

Vilanova is a well kept small town, busy with fishing boats at the harbour but with a pretty centre. Writer Ramón del Valle-Inclán was born here at **Casa del Cuadrante**.

South of the town and the flooded lagoon, the wooded area of Monte Terrón is a good place for a stroll. A pedestrian bridge has been built that gives access across the harbour.

The beaches in this area facing Illa de Arousa are unexploited and full of charm.

Nearby visit the Monte Lobeira hilltop viewpoint for an excellent panorama of the Ría.

Planned lift

CRUISING GALICIA **195**

RÍA DE AROUSA

⚓ Isla de Arousa

Various anchorages around the island, of which only Ensenada de San Xulián Sur is recommended for an overnight stay. Isla de Arousa is one of the main tourist destinations in the Ría, its northern part very busy in the summer and still in the process of substantial development.

⚓ Ensenada de San Xulián South

Approach is best done in daylight with caution, given the large number of off-lying hazards and *bateas*.

To reach the very picturesque **Ensenada de San Xulián Sur** from the main channel of the Ría:

- Enter the bay proceeding in the channel between the rows of *bateas*. Leave Islotes Jidoiro, Pedregoso Fl(3)G.15s first then Areoso (unlit) to starboard

- The islet (Piedra Touza) is steep to all round and can be passed close either to port or to starboard. The area close to the shore in the north of the bay (beyond the isolated rock awash) is full of small boat moorings

- Holding is good in sand and offers shelter for west, north and east winds. There are plenty of restaurants facing the bay and the land either side is wooded with a rural feel to it, despite the tourist hotspot beyond it.

Anchor on the outer edge of the moored boats. Use of a tripping line is advisable.

⚓ Other anchorages

It is possible to anchor at **Ensenada de San Xulián Norte**, north of the island, in front of the main O Xofre harbour (fishing boats and breakwater wall, small boat pontoons and mooring buoys) but this is a very busy area. You may be able to negotiate a buoy mooring but you will be quite exposed wherever you end up. The fuel jetty is at the breakwater wall.

Anchorage **west of Punta Caballo** lighthouse is better, generally quieter in the water but quite a distance from all facilities and you will be competing with *bateas* for space and depth. Exposed to winds with NW component.

The **south of the Island** is a natural paradise but needs care to navigate and anchor.

Provisioning & eating

There is no shortage of restaurants, shops and supermarkets in Arousa, indeed making a choice in the summer is probably the greatest challenge.

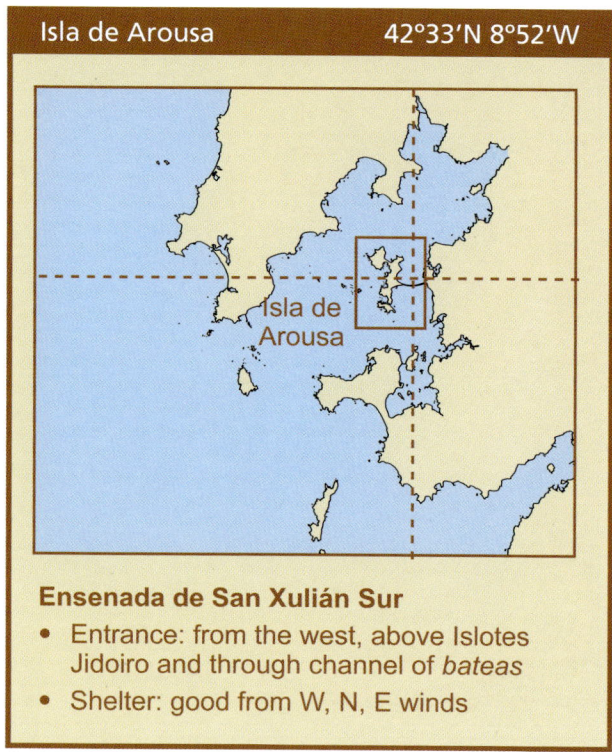

Ensenada de San Xulián Sur
- Entrance: from the west, above Islotes Jidoiro and through channel of *bateas*
- Shelter: good from W, N, E winds

Interest

Isla de Arousa has become one of the major tourist destinations in the Ría, extensively developed and attracting many holidaymakers in the summer. There is still plenty of construction happening, largely of flats marketed as second homes to the wealthier Galicians.

The island was the location chosen for the **Goday** cannery, the first major modern facility of this new industry built in the Ría. Completed in 1879 it set the new standards for fish preservation which up until then had been based on salt-drying. The factory is in the northwestern part of the Island, not a great tourist site but interesting for its role in the development of the area.

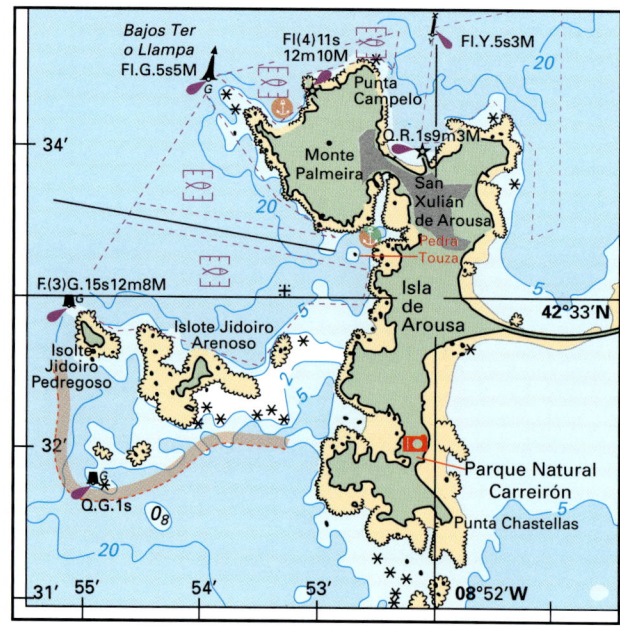

RÍA DE AROUSA

Esenada de San Xulián from Arousa looking south

Isla de Arousa

- 🛒 Various groceries in town for provisioning
- 🍴 Large quantity of restaurants, very busy in the summer tourist season, best area at Ensenada San Xulián Sur
- ⚓ Chandlery:
  - Efectos Navales Arousa, Paseo Cantiño, Arousa (opposite main fishing harbour) ☎ 986 527 330
- ✚ Consultorio Illa de Arousa (health centre), Lugar Laxes, ☎ 986 527363

Isla de Arousa O Xofre main harbour in the north

CRUISING GALICIA 197

RÍA DE AROUSA

⚓ Cambados

Private pontoons have been installed (2006) in the large harbour Puerto de Tragove, the only possible permanent berth in this part of the Ría. Cambados is a historic town, one of the nicest in the area and also the home of Albariño wine.

Approach & entrance

This is an area that needs to be navigated with care due to extensive shallows, rocks and bateas. Use informatio from IHM chart ES415C. Limited mooring opportunities close to town.

To reach Cambados follow the channel marked by red and green beacons between Isla de Arousa and O Grove.

From the main channel to the west, to reach Porto Tragrove:

- Pass between Islote Corbeiro Q.G.1s and Bajo Los Mezos Fl.G.5s with Pragueiro Fl(4)G.11s bearing 100°. Alternatively pass to the south of Bajo Los Mezos Fl.G.5s wtih Pragueiro bearing 70°. Beware Pedras Umías SW of Pragueiro

- Leave Pragueiro Fl.G.5s close to starboard

- Alter course for Bajo Lobeira de Cambados Fl(3)R.9s (120°). Pass between it and Pedra Golfeira Q.G

- Alter course to 80° and head for the Port hand light Fl(3)R.9s on the end of Porto Tragrove. Note Bajo Orido to port and very steeply shoaling ground to starboard within *bateas*.

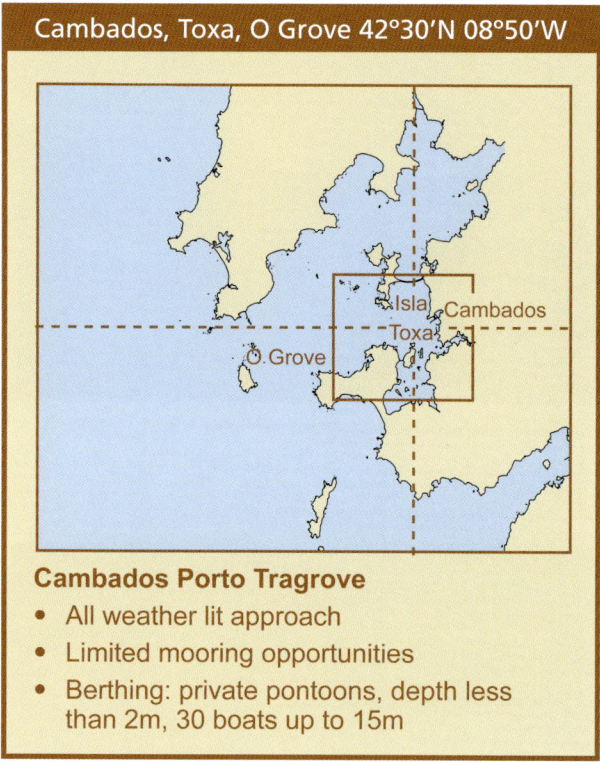

Cambados Porto Tragrove
- All weather lit approach
- Limited mooring opportunities
- Berthing: private pontoons, depth less than 2m, 30 boats up to 15m

Berthing & facilities

Single L-shape sprig from shore on the south wall of Porto Tragrove, convenient if only some distance away from the town. Pontoons are private.

The best option is to moor alongside the outer pontoon or anchor clear of the route to and from the fishing quay. In either case you may have to use the dinghy to land.

Porto Santo Tomé is not suitable for larger boats, maximum length 8m and depths below 2m. It may be possible to berth with the fishing boats.

198 CRUISING GALICIA

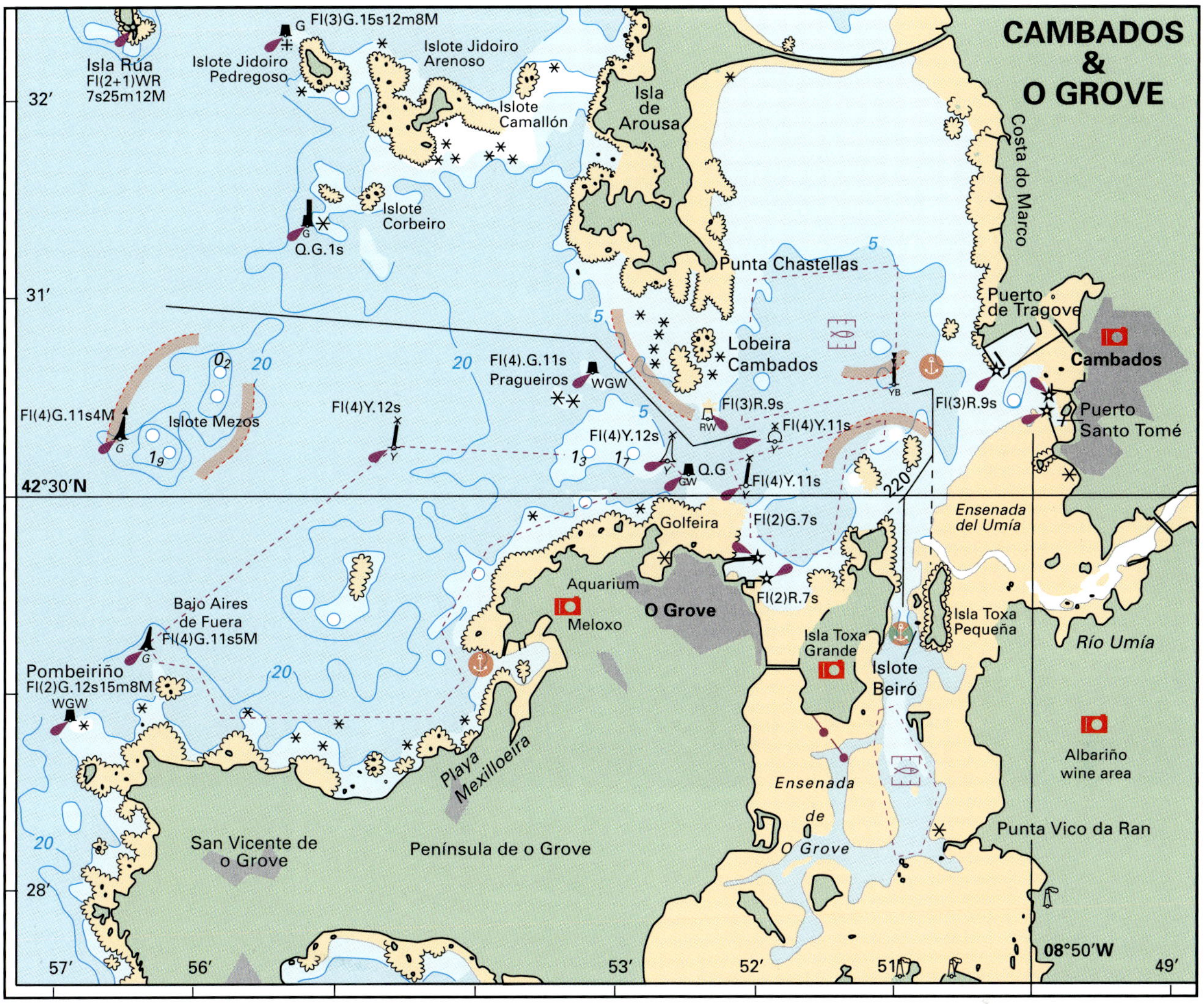

CAMBADOS AROUSA O GROVE

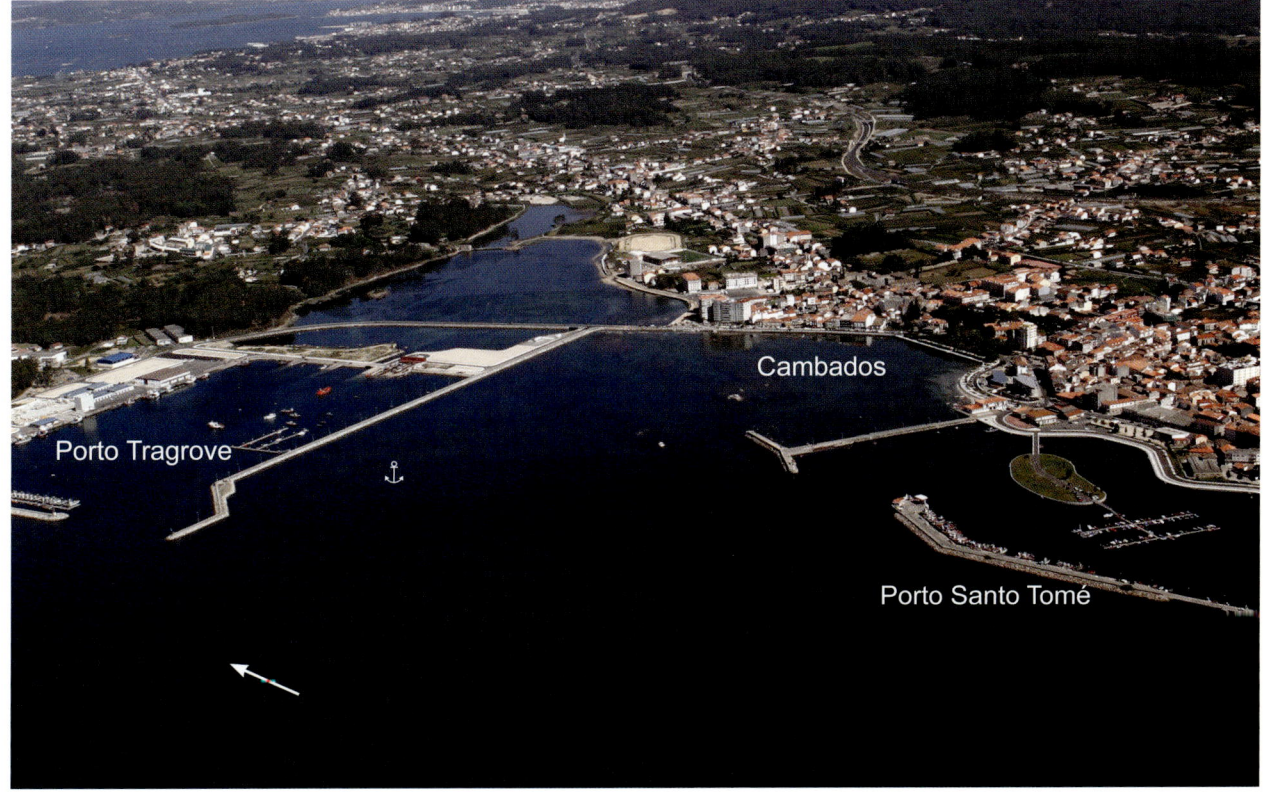

RÍA DE AROUSA

⚓ La Toxa

There is limited anchorage space off Isla Toxa Grande (east of small quay at the hotel in La Toxa Grande) and further NE off Islote Beiró in 2.2m. The spot is very pretty but difficult to navigate given the shallows and silt from Río Umía.

The following describes a route with a minimum charted depth of 0.7m and should therefore be attempted with due caution on a rising tide. A neap tide with a range of 1.5m will offer benefits.

- Follow the route already described for entry into Cambados until 0.3M from the entrance, where the last *bateas* are left to starboard
- With Isla Toxa Pequeña bearing 180° head due south for the top of the island
- Head for the north end of Isla Toxa Grande when it bears 220°
- Head due south when the channel between the two islands opens up. The 0.7m depth is on this leg.

Beware possible issues with traffic around *bateas* to the south and limits on swinging room space.

⚓ O Grove

O Grove is a very busy harbour for fishing and tripper boats, and exposed. Anchoring outside is an option but you will be exposed to any northerly wind. The town is very busy with tourists in the summer. There are some buoys within the breakwater of the harbour which are used by yachts, arranged through the Capitanía if you manage to locate their staff (mornings only office).

The approach is from the north between lines of bateas to the east of Piedra Golfeira Fl(3)G.9s with the end of the breakwater of O Grove Fl(2)G.7s bearing no less than 175°.

⚓ Meloxo

The harbour to the west at **Meloxo** is less busy than O Grove. The daylight only (unlit) approach through *bateas* from the main channel of the Ría is from Bajo Aires de Fuera Fl(3)G.10s and straight to the entrance.

The pontoons are for boats up to 8m. There is some space in which anchorage is possible plus some buoys used by yachts. Not very pretty all round but it is sheltered from all winds except W and the harbour wall may offer some additional protection. No fuel available for yacths.

O Grove harbour

RÍA DE AROUSA

Cambados

- Vigo 40km, Santiago 45km, Coruña 120km
- 🚌 Buses stop in the Paseo Marítimo just north of Porto Santo Tomé
- 🛒 Supermarkets:
  - Froiz/MercaMás, Rosalía de Castro 24
- 🍴 Restaurants:
  - Many throughout, along the promenade, the sea front and the old part
- ℹ️ Tourist office: Praza do Concello, ☎986 520786
- ⚓ Chandlers:
  - Efectos Navales Lita, Valbanera 1, ☎ 986 543 061
- Banks, chemists and other shops along Rúa da Mariña and parallel streets behind
- ✚ Centro de Saude Cambados (health centre), Rúa de Galicia, Cambados ☎986 524211 / 524264

Dorna boats

Provisioning & eating

The supermarket Froiz/Mercamás at Rosalía de Castro in Cambados is well stocked including fresh produce.

Cambados is a key tourist destination and so it is well served by restaurants and a lively night scene in the streets of the old town (Plaza Ramón Cabanillas, Plaza Fefiñáns). O Grove is a summer tourist spot, full of bars and restaurants.

Albariño wine

Interest

Cambados is one of the key tourist destinations of Galicia, endowed with a historic past and a medieval old town housing many monuments of interest. **Plaza de Fefiñáns** is framed by the imposing Palacio on one side and the San Benito 18th century church on the other, a space for past grand parades.

The old streets lead to various imposing grand Galician houses (*pazos*), of which **Pazo de Bazán** (now a high standard Parador hotel) and **Pazo de Ulloa** are the most impressive. The ruins of **Santa Mariña Dozo** 16th century church are worth a visit as are those of the **San Sadurniño tower**, a 10th century structure for defence against Viking raiders and later of imprisonment for various Spanish medieval royals.

Cambados is the home town of **Albariño**, a delicious fruity white wine. The *fiesta* that takes place the first Sunday of August is a fun event, plenty of enjoyable wine at its core but also plenty of folklore and even an election to the Order of the Wine.

Isla **La Toxa** (Grande) is a popular destination for tourists who come to look at this once exclusive resort island, with a pretty shell covered church and the luxurious Gran Hotel. The island is home to a spa, offering a range of water and mud based treatments using water from the various springs in the island, reputedly health giving because of the

Pazo de Fefiñáns, Cambados

minerals dissolved in it. The soap is still a major brand, and it may give you a taste of the luxury available, but at a lesser cost. While the hotel still holds its own, the island is now in full swing, new holiday homes and other hotels springing up everywhere. During the summer it is very busy.

The *Ruta del Vino* on the mainland east of La Toxa Pequeña is a good trail for learning more about, and tasting, Albariño. Visit the tourist office in Cambados for a current list of open cellars who conduct tours and tasting sessions.

O Grove is a summer tourist destination with plenty of action and entertainment. The peninsula is best known for its beaches, of which **La Lanzada** is a very impressive long stretch of white sand facing the Atlantic. You can get a sense of scale of the beach visitor numbers from O Grove, Sanxenxo and San Vicente just by looking at the size of the car park.

The quietest part of the O Grove peninsula is the area south of Meloxo, the wilderness and lagoon behind Playa Mexilloeira a good place for a nature walk if you are anchored nearby. Meloxo also hosts **Aquarium Galicia**, a very interesting display of marine ecosystems.

The isthmus that connects the O Grove peninsula, with La Lanzada to one side and the Ensenada de O Grove mudflats to the other. is a very striking natural feature, good for watching nature exposed to the elements.

Cambados

RÍA DE AROUSA

Cambados

San Benito church in Cambados

Mejillones a la marinera

Galicia is the largest producer of mussels in the world, its farming *bateas* a constant feature in the waters of the rías. They are the simplest seafood to prepare and you will never taste any as good if you buy them fresh at a *mercado* or even get them directly from a fisherman's boat.

Ingredients
One onion, cut small pieces
Olive oil
1kg fresh mussels, clean and beards removed
White wine, one cup

Preparation
Fry the onion until soft and golden. Add the mussels and white wine and steam with the lid on the pot for five minutes. Discard any mussels that have not opened.

Serve immediately with pan gallego.

The **Ermita de Nosa Señora da Lanzad**a is a romanesque church in a unique setting. Visible from the sea, it is set in a promontory at the southern end of the bay.

Puerto Deportivo Pedras Negras

RÍA DE AROUSA

⚓ San Vicente de Mar

The village of Pedras Negras (adjoining San Vicente de Mar) has a small very new marina, most likely without space but with places nearby to anchor. Pedras Negras and San Vicente are holiday tourist destinations with many hotels, bars/restaurants and Spanish holiday homes.

Approach & entrance

From N keep at least 0.5M clearance from the coast to avoid the many rock dangers that surround the headland.

- Approach marina on a 310° heading, passing between Red Fl(3)R.9s and Green Fl(3)G.9s, in the white sector of harbour light Fl(4)WR.11s.

Berthing & facilities

The Pedras Negras marina is very new and well equipped but small and often full. Minimum depth 2m, 10 visitor spaces for boats up to 14m.

Fuel is at the shore wall in front of the car park. There is a chandler shop at the harbour and the marina can arrange mechanics, electricians and divers. Showers are reasonable.

Interest

San Vicente and Pedras Negras are holiday resorts, largely built up with Spanish second homes. The town has a supermarket and shops for victualling.

| San Vicente de Mar | 42°27'N 08°55'W |

Puerto Deportivo Pedras Negras
- Lit entrance
- Shelter: good
- Depth minimum 2m inside marina
- Visitors' berths 10 (but often full) up to 14m
- ☎ / Fax 986 738325 / 430
- VHF Channel 09
- club.nautico.s.v@wanadoo.es
- Water, electricity at the pontoons
- ⛽ Fuel pontoon (1.5m) at the shore wall next to lift
- 🔧 Repairs: contact marina for mechanics, electricians, divers and other specialists
- 🏗 30-ton travel lift
- Diving and sailing club

The **beaches** are the reason why tourists come, of which La Lanzada is a spectacular expanse of sand.

Nearby the remains of a Roman necropolis at Cacheiras and the viewpoint at the top of the hill (views towards the rocky coast line and Isla Sálvora) are worth a visit.

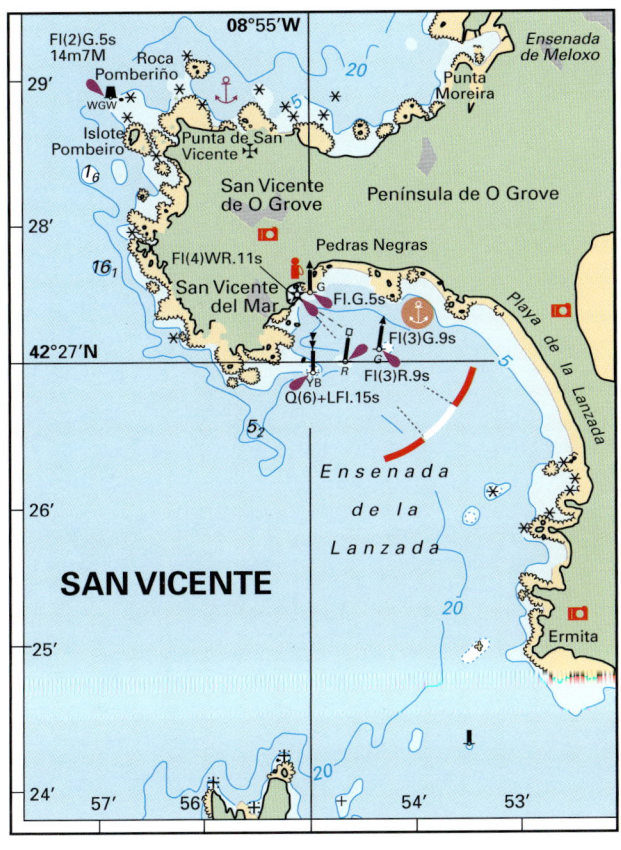

CRUISING GALICIA 205

Ría de Pontevedra

Historic harbours, quiet beaches and summer tourists

Ría de Pontevedra

Introduction

Coming from Arousa or Vigo, Ría de Pontevedra and its smaller sibling Ría de Aldán can feel like a haven of tranquillity. The Ría is not lacking in activity, indeed it is home to the large tourist resort of Sanxenxo and the busy port of Marín, plus a large part of the Galician frozen fish industry and the Spanish Naval Academy. The feel of the Ría is, however, very much quieter than that of its immediate neighbours. It is protected by Isla Ons and Isla Onza, part of the Atlantic Islands National Park, sheltered by them from the rigours of the ocean.

The Ría is home to **Pontevedra**, one of the historic cities of Galicia and still today capital of the province despite the much larger size of Vigo, with whom it maintains an old but firendly rivalry. Although it is no longer the major port of the past the city maintains its prominence and is one of the most beautiful towns in Galicia.

Ría de Pontevedra was one of the locations where the canning industry was developed by entrepreneurs from Catalonia, amongst whom the Massó family became very prominent and the first to adopt modern technology to increase production volumes. The **Massó museum at Bueu** is a very good introduction to the maritime history of the Ría and the seafood preservation industry that developed here.

Ría de Aldán is one of the prettiest settings for anchoring in Galicia with a very sparsely populated and thickly wooded coast. There are good walks on the western side and along the wilderness of Costa da Vela. The village of **Hío** to the south is host to one of the best examples of a *cruceiro*, the stone cross that is dotted throughout Galicia.

Aguete was the base for some of the more notorious Spanish corsairs, among them the four Gago de Mendoza brothers who in the 18th century were notorious for harassing enemies of the Spanish crown. Today Aguete has a delightful small marina, while Mogor nearby has some stone age carvings easily accessible from the pretty beach.

At the entrance to the Ría, **Isla Ons** is a delightful place for anchorage, part of the Atlantic Islands National Park and good destination for walks. Smaller Isla Onza (also known as Onceta) is a nature sanctuary closed to visitors.

On the northern shore Sanxenxo is the primary beach destination of the Rías Baixas. Built in the style of large scale Mediterranean resorts it becomes very busy in July and August. Portonovo immediately west has a much more traditional

Ría de Aldán

Pontevedra

Hío

Portonovo

Isla Tambo

character and the smaller beaches nearby are attractive for anchoring.

Towards the top of the Ría, **Combarro** is one of the highlights of Galicia. The village, built to the shore, has narrow streets carved into rocks and is host to a large quantity of *hórreos* that are still used to store grain and other foodstuffs. The village is a destination for most tour groups but crowds can be avoided if you anchor in front of the harbour or near Isla Tambo.

Combarro

RÍA DE PONTEVEDRA

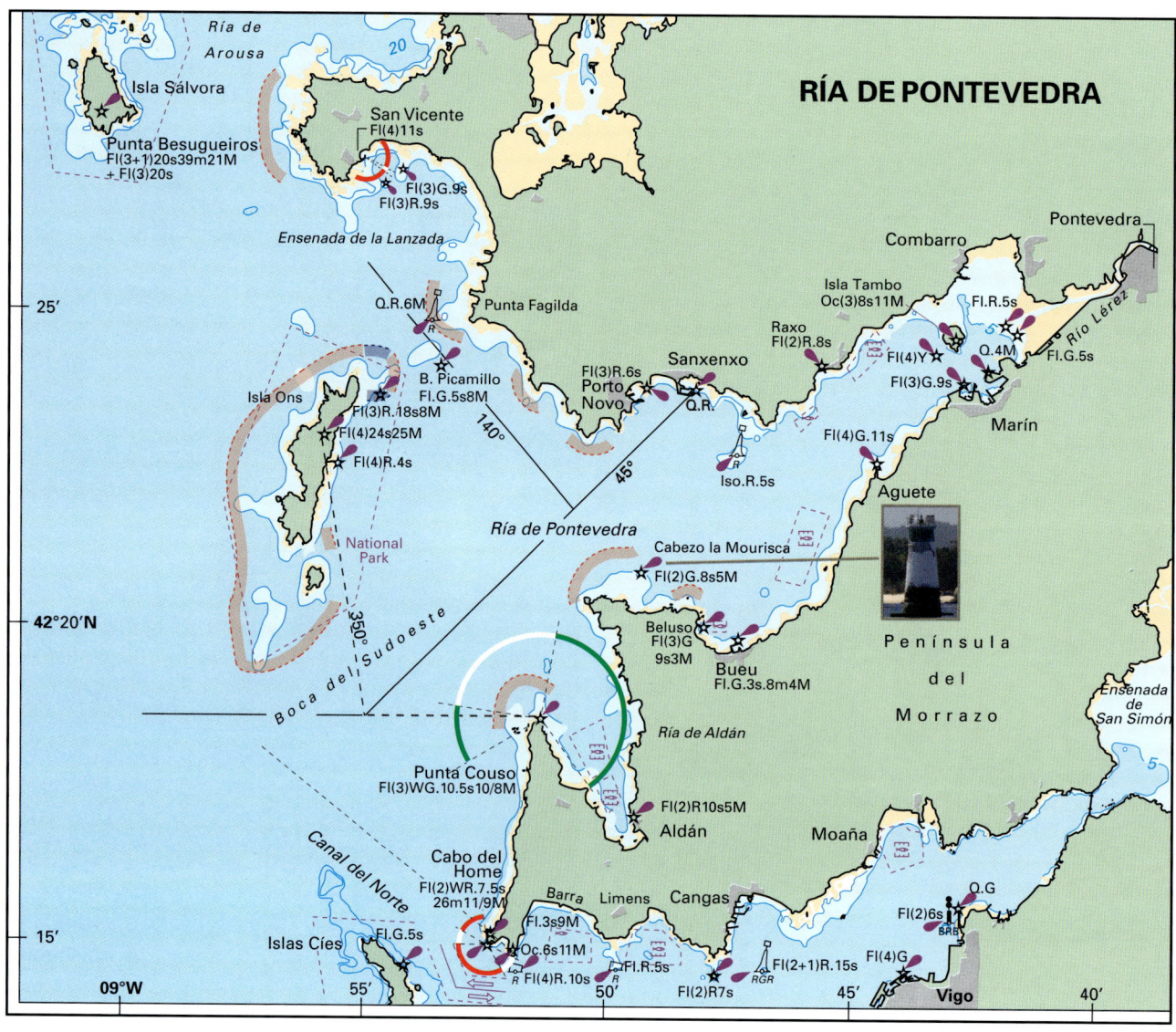

Approach and key facilities

Approach & entrance

The entrances, to the north and south of Isla Ons and Onza are straightforward. In adverse conditions of significant swell or sea, care should be taken to take a suitably deep route through the Paso Fagilda between Isla Ons and Onza and the mainland. When using the main route to the south (Boca del Sudoeste) be aware of possible shipping movements into either Ría de Pontevedra or Ría de Vigo. Ferries also operate from Sanxenxo to the islands. Isla Tambo Oc(3)8s with an 11M range at the top of the Ría has useful light for orientation at night. If coming from offshore, then Isla Ons Fl(4)24s25M identifies the Ría.

From the north (Arousa) to Sanxenxo

- Keeping a respectful distance off Península de O Grove (in 30m or more) head for Bajo Fagilda buoy Q.R.

- Leave Bajo Fagilda buoy Q.R. close to port. (Note Los Camoucos Fl(3)R.18s is left well to starboard).

- A course of 140° from Bajo Fagilda buoy Q.R (back bearing 320°) will leave Bajo Picamillo Fl.G.5s to starboard and put Cabezo de la Mourisca Fl(2)G.7s on the bow, when it is sighted.

- Head for Sanxenxo when the port hand breakwater light Q.R. bears 45° or less.

- Follow the breakwater round and pass between port hand breakwater light Q.R. and starboard hand mark Fl(3)G.9s. Take care of ferries.

An alternative between Isla Ons and the mainland, in good conditions and for a closer look at Isla Ons, is to pass Los Camoucos Fl(3)R.18s close to port, between it and Isla Ons.

RÍA DE PONTEVEDRA

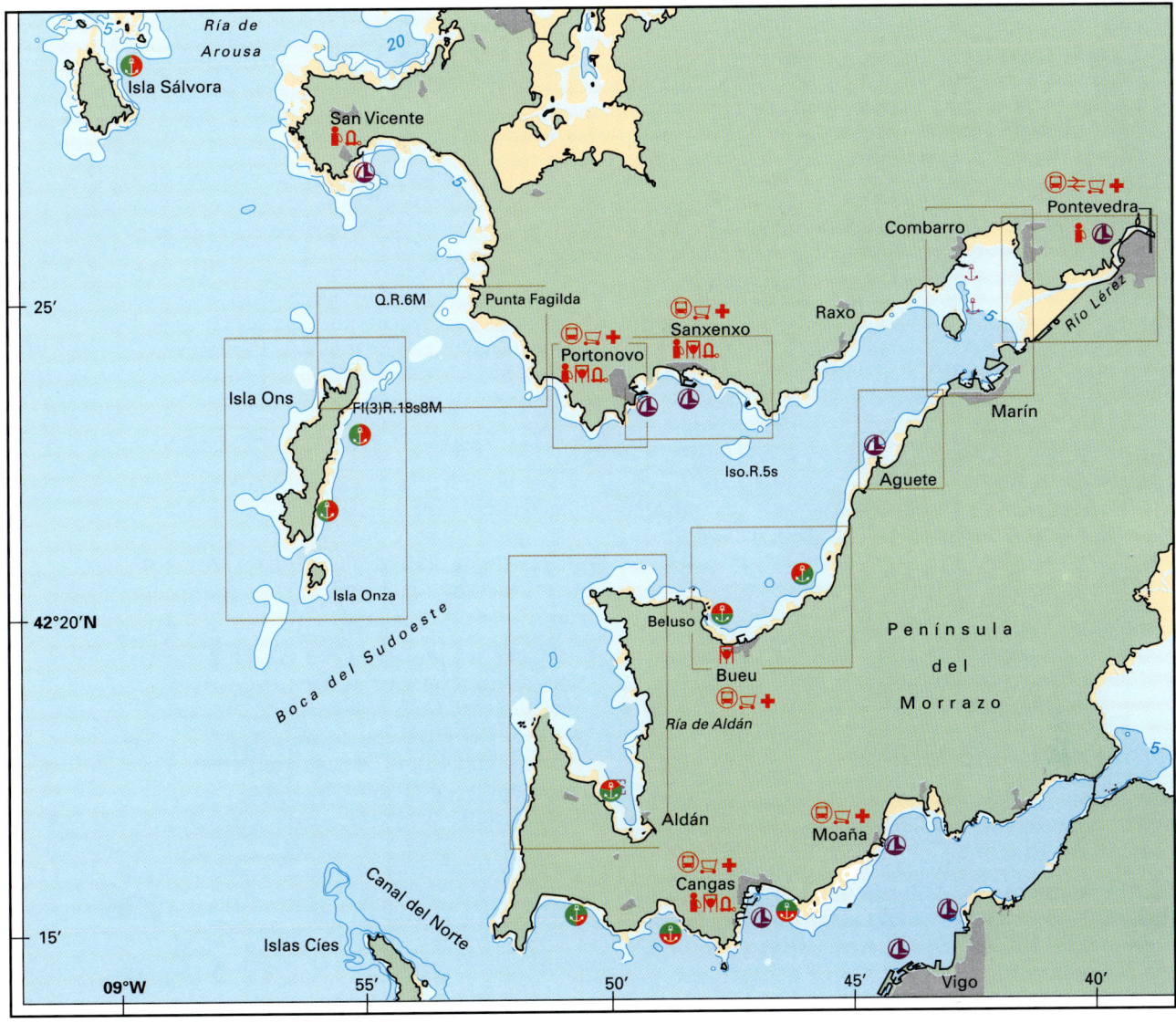

From the west to Sanxenxo

The Boca del Sudoeste is the main deep water route and may well have shipping present. Ría de Aldan on the south side of the entrance has a significant number of *bateas* with attendant craft transiting it and Ría de Pontevedra.

There are no lights to bring you into the Ría directly from long range, although Islas Ons light Fl(4)24s25M will indicate the general direction of the Ría.

A wide berth (1.5M) should be given on the north side to Isla Onza due to offlying dangers. Stay in more than 50m. A berth of more than 0.5M should also be given to Punta Couso Fl(3)WG.10.5s. The following achieves this:

- Head 90° towards Punta Couso Fl(3)WG.10.5s (latitude 42°18'.5 N), staying in its green sector. (Note: the white will take you close to the Isla Onza offlying dangers)

- Alter course to 45° when Isla Ons light Fl(4)24s bears 350°. This will put Sanxenxo port hand breakwater light Q.R on the bow when it becomes visible. (Note Cabezo de la Mourisca Fl(2)G.7s will also become visible on the starboard bow)

- Follow the breakwater round and pass between port hand breakwater light Q.R. and starboard hand mark Fl(3)G.9s. Take care of ferries.

From the south (Ría de Vigo) to Sanxenxo

With Cabo del Home Fl.3s on the beam:

- Head due north up the 8°53'W longitude with Cabo del Home light remaining in the visible sector (90° to 180° towards the light). Beware shipping movements from astern from Ría de Vigo

CRUISING GALICIA

- Alter course to 45° when Punta Couso Fl(3)WG.10.5s bears 90°. Note the light will turn from green to white soon after this. This will put Sanxenxo port hand breakwater light Q.R on the bow when it becomes visible. (Note Cabezo de la Mourisca Fl(2)G.7s will also become visible on the starboard bow).
- Follow the breakwater round and pass between port hand breakwater light Q.R. and starboard hand mark Fl(3)G.9s. Take care of ferries.

Initial shelter

Coming **from the north**, Ría de Pontevedra offers good initial shelter close to the entrance. The lee of the Isla Ons provides a temporary respite from westerlies and ocean swell. Sanxenxo is the best port on a first arrival at the Ría, less than 5M from the north or south entrance to the Ría. The marina is large and easy to access with extensive facilities ashore.

Coming **from the south**, Ría de Aldán is a good anchorage destination in winds from west, south and east. At night or in poor visibility the *bateas* present a barrier and there are isolated dangers close to anchorages.

Other ports and facilities

The marina at Portonovo is a good alternative, albeit much smaller, to Sanxenxo on the northern coast of the Ría.

On the southern side Aguete is the only marina if there is space in the visitors' outer pontoons, but these can be bouncy in any swell. Beluso and Bueu are not geared for visitors and only anchoring nearby is possible.

At the end of the Ría, behind Isla Tambo 10M from the entrance to the Ría, Combarro is a good anchorage destination.

Pontevedra is a restricted entrance due the road bridge (clearance 12m).

Note that many of the beaches have buoyed swimming areas which can restrict the shelter available compared to that found on the charts. Buoys are unlit.

Provisioning

The best locations for provisioning and restaurants are the larger towns of Portonovo, Sanxenxo, Bueu, Combarro and Pontevedra.

The *plazas* (markets) in Pontevedra and Bueu are excellent for fresh produce.

Repairs and chandleries

Sanxenxo is the only marina geared for major yacht services, and has a good chandlery on site. Elsewhere the marina staff and fishing harbour authorities are your best point of contact for access to local expertise.

For complex spares you may need the se[rvices of] larger chandleries further afield such as [in] Vigo or Pombo in A Coruña.

Transport

The excellent **train** line that links all of w[estern] Galicia from A Coruña to Vigo serves th[e] Pontevedra. The high speed R598 trains

Numerous **buses** cover the area, from bu[ses] and stops at Portonovo, Sanxenxo, Com[barro,] Pontevedra, Marín and Bueu. The best l[ocation] for connections to the major towns of Ga[licia is] Pontevedra.

Cruising in Ría de Pontevec[ra]

The wide Ría is a very pleasant cruising [ground] with few, well marked, offlying dangers s[et] by good scenery and with a number of a[nchorages] that are good destinations for short stops traffic to and from the port of Marín but less busy than Vigo or Arousa.

In one day you can get a taste for the Ría exploring the area at the entrance beyon[d.] With more time in your hand, you could good 3 or 4 days anchoring at Ría de Al[dán,] beach and Combarro, staying at Aguete [as] a friendly quiet shore base away from th[e] Sanxenxo.

RÍA DE PONTEVEDRA

CRUISING GALICIA 213

RÍA DE PONTEVEDRA

⚓ Portonovo

Pleasant anchorages for settled weather or north wind and a sheltered marina. The area feels remote, a good break from Sanxenxo further east.

Approach & entrance

Straightforward lit approach and entrance, avoid shallows extending 200m offshore from Punta Cabicastro 2M to the WSW of the entrance and, if approaching from the east, the isolated 0.3m patch 500m SW of Punta Festiñanzo (1.5M to the ESE of the entrance).

Beware moving vessels obscured by the harbour walls. A ferry service runs to Isla Ons.

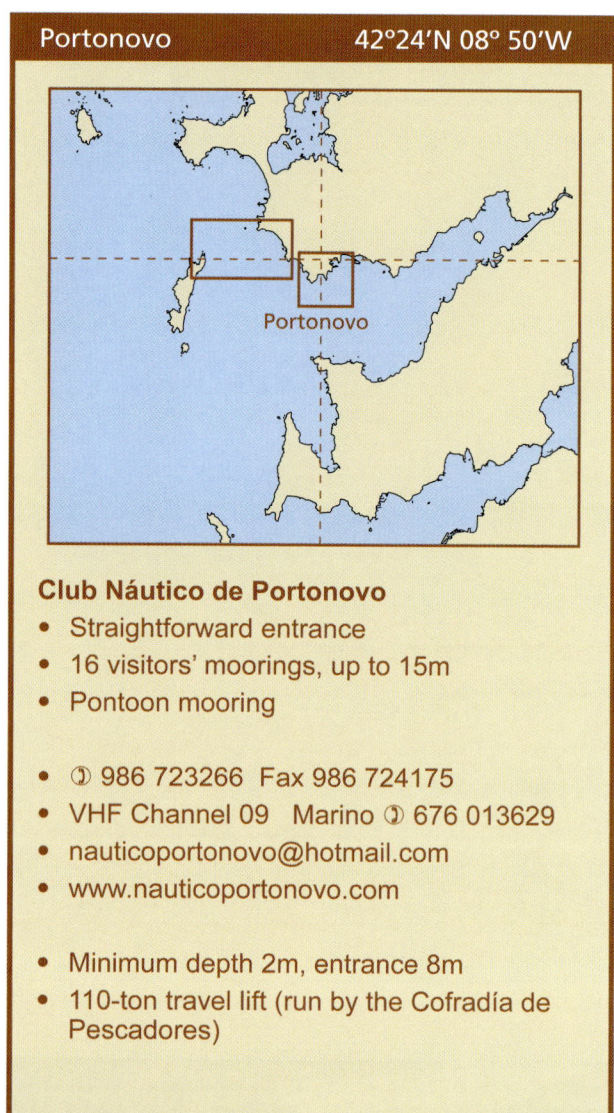

Club Náutico de Portonovo

- Straightforward entrance
- 16 visitors' moorings, up to 15m
- Pontoon mooring

- ☎ 986 723266   Fax 986 724175
- VHF Channel 09   Marino ☎ 676 013629
- nauticoportonovo@hotmail.com
- www.nauticoportonovo.com

- Minimum depth 2m, entrance 8m
- 110-ton travel lift (run by the Cofradía de Pescadores)

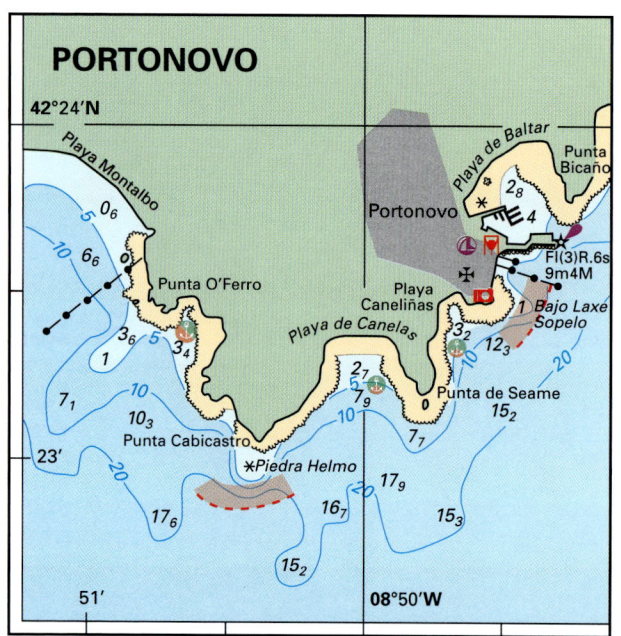

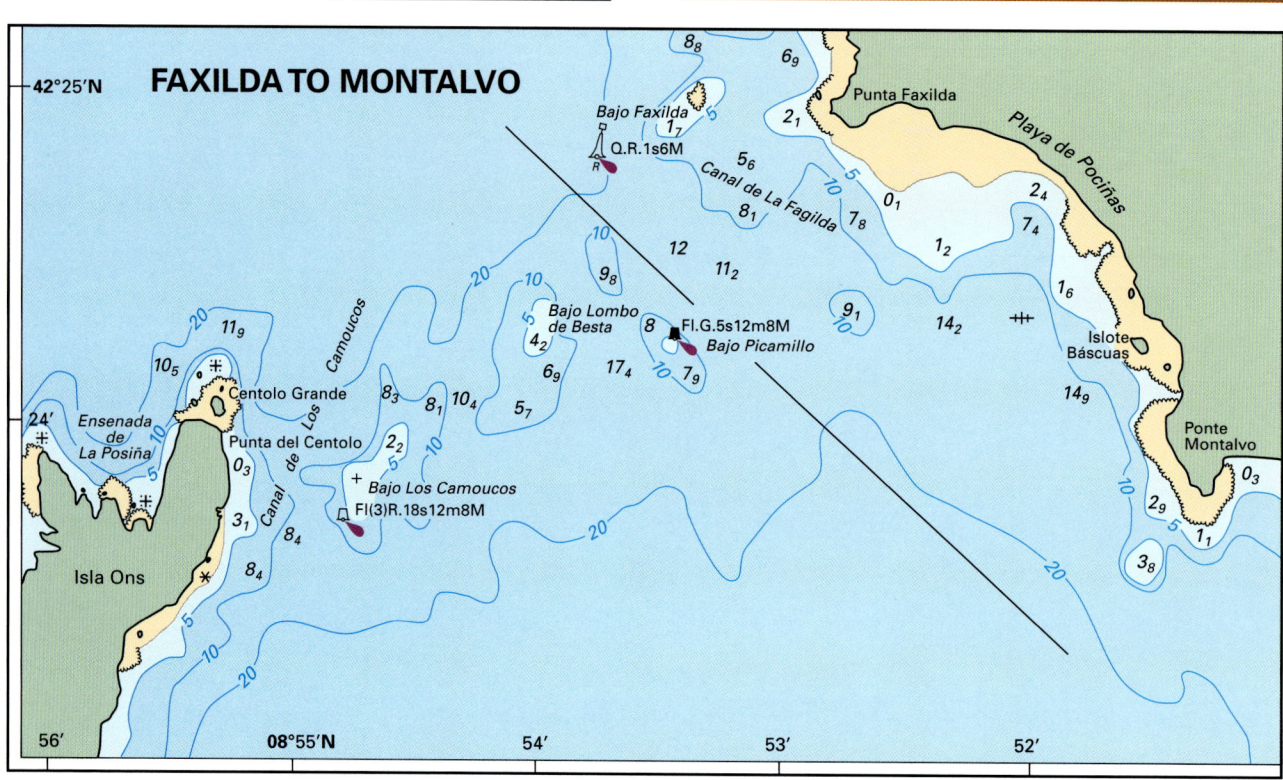

214 CRUISING GALICIA

Berthing & Facilities

Portonovo Marina accepts visitors but there are no facilities ashore (2007). If advance communication has not been possible then berth alongside the hammerhead pontoons at the entrance and then discuss where you should go.

Anchorages

The beaches of Caneliñas (immediately west of the town) and Canelas (next along) offer shelter from W, N, E winds. Paxariñas and Montalbo further west are more exposed. All anchorages are in sand and without isolated dangers.

Interest

Portonovo is set at the quieter end of this area popular with summer tourism, with pretty bays and a good rural backdrop. The town has retained its fishing village charm, still looking Galician and without large apartment towers to spoil it. It is nevertheless a tourist destination, well endowed with bars and restaurants. The fishing heritage is celebrated by the Monumento a Peixeira (fishing woman statue) at the southern of the town.

To the north, the wilderness of La Lanzada with its medieval Ermita de Nosa Señora da Lanzada is worth a trip (see Arousa section).

Near Portonovo, Punta Montalbo is one of the best locations from which to admire the ría. Below, the beach of Montalbo was used as a location for luring ships to disaster. Fires would be lit that would attract boats and their crews to a miserable end.

The beach of Paxariñas is a pleasant relaxing spot, while the track in the forest from the beach to Punta Cabitastro is worth doing for the view.

Ferries to Ons depart from the harbour quay.

Portonovo

Portonovo harbour

RÍA DE PONTEVEDRA

Portonovo

- Pontevedra 20km
  Santiago 50km   Coruña 130km
- Ferries to Islas Ons from the harbour quay
- 🛒 Provisioning:
  - Nearest supermarket: Froiz, Fonte de Ramos, Sanxenxo
  - Small shops in harbour area
- ✗ Restaurants:
  - Bars and restaurants up the hill from the harbour area
- ℹ Tourist office: Rúa Baltar ☏ 986 723044
- ⚓ Chandlers:
  - Todopesca Portonovo, Carretera Lanzada 36, ☏ 986 691452
- ✚ Centro Saude Baltar, Lugar Baltar, Portonovo ☏ 986 723128

Playa Caneliñas

Playa Canelas

Homage to the fishwoman at Portonovo

216 CRUISING GALICIA

Corsairs, privateers, pirates

The rías of Galicia and the Atlantic to the west were cruised during the 16th to 19th century by all manner of ships with dubious credentials. As a major sea voyage crossroads the waters of this part of the world were the scene of attacks on cargo ships and skirmishes between armed boats.

The line of distinction between proper and illegal attacks on sailing ships is very faint, but from the 15th century there was a procedure for nations to sanction the activities of private adventurers in pursuit of national interests. Corsairs would be given licence to harass the trading routes of specified 'enemy' nations, their reward the cargo of the unfortunate victim boats. While not officially at war, Britain, France, the Low Countries and Spain saw fit to provide such licence to privateers, simply to keep a check on the competing empire. Spain was the target while it was the dominant world power in 16th and 17th century, later launching its own corsairs against the other European nations once dominance at sea was lost to Britain.

Corsairs in Spain were given licence under a system called *patente*, a form of debenture that required the private buccaneer to deposit a sum of money. The state could resort to this money in case the acts committed were deemed to be illegal and compensation should need to be paid to the aggrieved ship or nation. Copies of *patentes* can be found in the archives of Pontevedra, which also hold notary records called *protestas*, certified statements made by sea captains with respect to misadventure in the water or loss of cargo. Some of the *protestas* were made by foreign vessels complaining about being assaulted and detained despite not being an 'enemy'. Procedure allowed cases to be referred to a high court, but lucky the ship owner that recovered property once on foreign soil, as an enemy flag could always be 'found' within the sealed ship.

Famous corsair characters abound, some of them entering romantic literature. Francis Drake began his career under an informal corsair licence from Queen Elisabeth, using five ships to play havoc among the convoys returning to Spain with treasure from the Americas. He took a price off the coast of Perú that was equal to half the yearly budget of the Queen, albeit it only represented a minor amount to the dominant empire of the time. Another notorious character, William Dampier, in the late 17th century combined pirate actions against Spain with a worthy intellectual passion for exploration and scientific research, publishing the first international best selling travel book '*A new voyage around the world*'.

In Spain, the Gago de Mendoza brothers acted with zest from their base in Aguete, Ría de Pontevedra, against British and French ships, sometimes for pure profit, sometimes in defence of the Galician coast, acquiring local hero status for their actions. Benito Soto, another Galician, strayed beyond the bounds of 'proper' privateering and was considered a pirate by both the Spanish and the British and he was finally executed by the latter in Gibraltar.

The corsair arrangements served at least to draw the line with respect to piracy, a curse that plagued European waters from time immemorial. Berber boats from northern Africa attacked the harbours of Galicia with dreadful efficiency, most often to capture people that would be traded as slaves or exchanged for ransom. Spanish writer Cervantes, author of Don Quijote, was a victim of one such attack and spent 5 years in captivity while his family and contacts navigated the dubious mechanisms of recovery. The British Navy put an end to piracy from the Med in the 19th century, using its power to destroy the remnants of the feared industry in Algeria.

RÍA DE PONTEVEDRA

⚓ Sanxenxo

Excellent marina but crowded summer beach tourist location.

Approach & entrance

Straightforward lit approach and entrance. Avoid shallows extending 200m offshore from Punta Cabicastro 2M to the WSW of the entrance and, if approaching from the east, the isolated 0.3m patch 500m SW of Punta Festiñanzo (1.5M to the ESE of the entrance). Enter between end of harbour wall and starboard hand mark Fl(3)G.9s.

Beware moving vessels obscured by the harbour walls, especially ferries.

Berthing & Facilities

Very good marina with ample space for manoeuvres, wide pontoons and excellent facilities. It gets crowded in the summer so finding space may not be easy.

⚓ Anchorages

Playa de Silgar, Playa de Areas: both beware of wind/swell from S and scattered rocks.

3M to the east it is possible to anchor in sand at Ensenada de Raxó, near the small fishing quay. Exposed to S and E winds.

Interest

The village was developed in the early 20th century as *Balneario de Sanxenxo*, attracting high society. From 1960 enormous tourist development, leading to the current overcrowding in summer.

Sanxenxo   42°24'N 08°48'W

Real Club Marítimo de Sanxenxo

- Straightforward entrance day and night
- Crowded in summer
- Shelter in winter (exposed to S winds) improved by high defensive wall
- Berthing: pontoon mooring, 50 visitor spaces (from 370 total), up to 18m
- Depth minimum 3m, with 7m at entrance
- Water and electricity at pontoons

- ☎ 986 720517 Fax 986 720578
- VHF09
- ⛽ Fuel at entrance
- 🏗 Travel lift 64-ton at entrance

- Showers, toilets, laundry good
- Restaurant in marina club house

Club Marítimo de Sanxenxo

The trekking route **Ruta dos Muiños** follows the river of the same name that climbs through the forest behind the village of Samiera, 4 miles north of Sanxenxo. This part of Ría de Pontevedra is delightfully rural. The 10km route takes the walker past many watermills, some restored, and offers excellent views of the Ría below from viewpoints set in the forest.

Playa Silgar

Sanxenxo

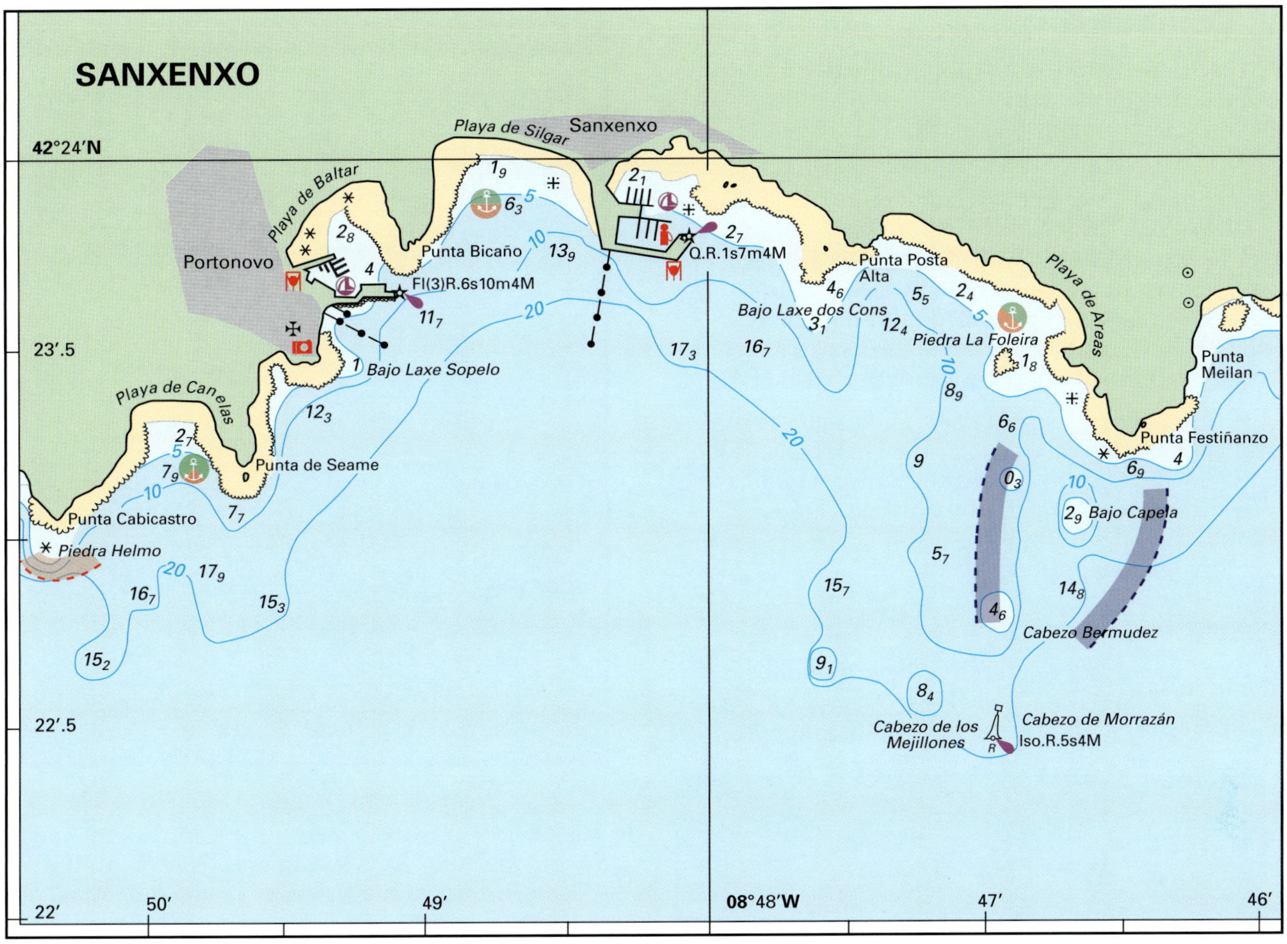

RÍA DE PONTEVEDRA

Sanxenxo

- Pontevedra 20km
  Santiago 50km
  Coruña 130km
- 🚌 Bus station: Estr. Circunvalación
- Ferries to Islas Ons from the harbour quay
- 🛒 Supermarket:
  - Froiz, Fonte de Ramos, Sanxenxo
- 🍴 Restaurants:
  - Bars and restaurants along the modern tourist resort area of Playa Silgar
- ℹ Tourist office: Puerto Deportivo (marina), ☎ 986 720285
- ⚓ Chandlers:
  - Davila Sport, Augusto Besada, Puerto Deportivo (marina)
- ✚ Centro Saude Sanxenxo, Rúa Progreso 59, ☎ 986 691995

CRUISING GALICIA 219

RÍA DE PONTEVEDRA

⚓ Combarro

Sheltered anchorage at the top of Ría de Pontevedra, in the setting of one of the most picturesque locations in Galicia, the village of Combarro.

Approach & entrance

The approach is straightforward although it is advisable to pass around the south side of Isla Tambo Oc(3)8s at low water (1.3m minimum depth). Beware any unlit *bateas* anchored for repair if approaching at night or poor visibility.

A slow transit of the area between Isla de Tambo and Combarro is advisable as the area is shallow and may differ from the charted depth. Holding is good in 2 to 5m mud, towards the quay at Combarro or in front of the north beach of Isla de Tambo (landing not permitted).

Marín

A commercial and naval port which should be avoided, although it is possible to anchor in **Playa dos Praceres**, to the north of the industrial port.

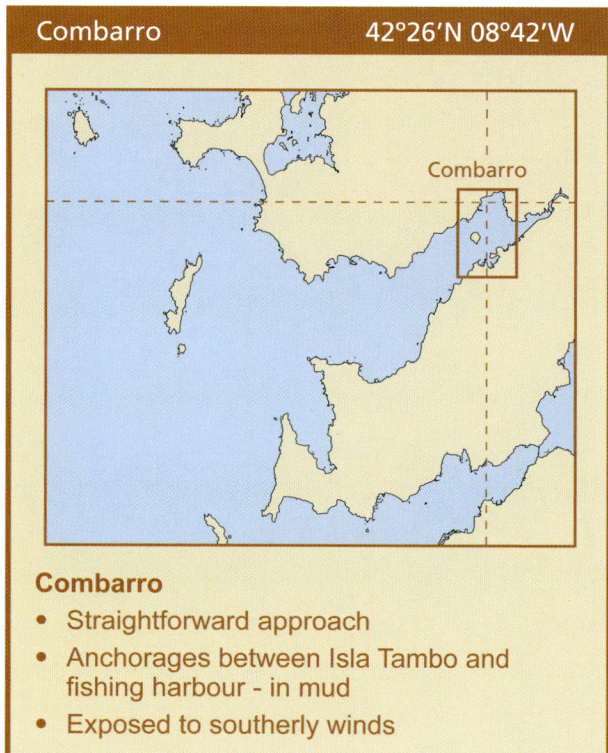

Combarro
- Straightforward approach
- Anchorages between Isla Tambo and fishing harbour - in mud
- Exposed to southerly winds

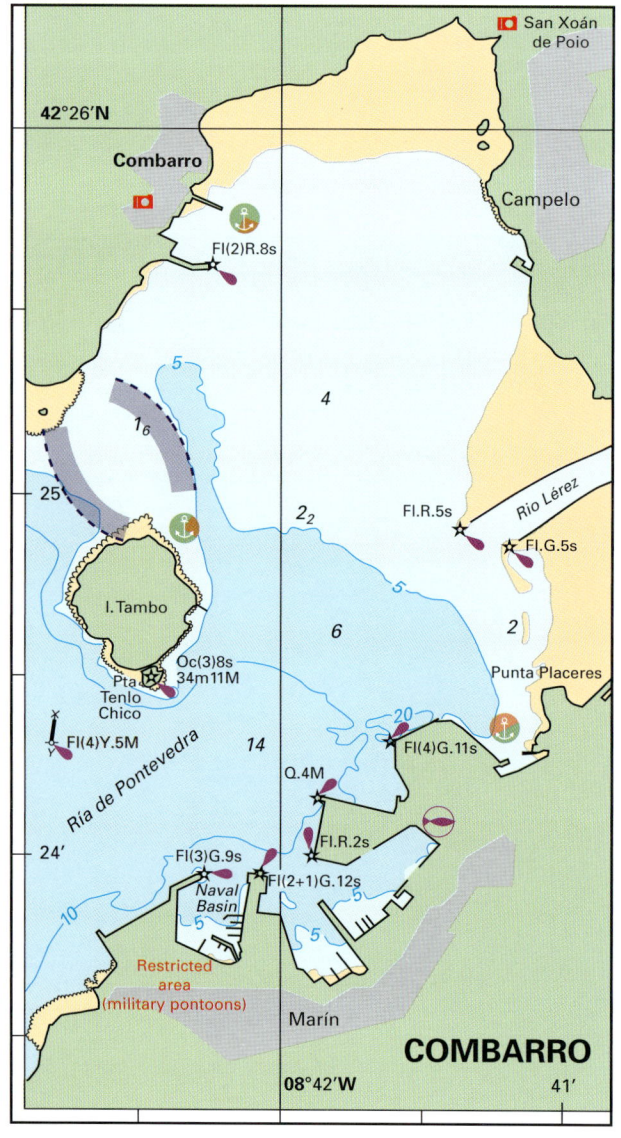

Anchor in the space between the outside wall and the tiny harbour for small boats. The area to the south of Marín is the Spanish Navy Academy, so access is restricted.

Provisioning

There are two supermarkets, some small shops and a chemist on the main road that passes through the modern part of Combarro.

Various provisioning vans (charcutery, conserves, fruit, vegetables) often set up in the small plaza by the harbour.

Restaurants by the sea wall are unbeatable for location, though rather touristy.

Interest

Combarro is one of the most scenic of Galician villages. Set right on the water's edge, the close-knit network of stone houses line the narrow streets of this small community. The village is transformed

RÍA DE PONTEVEDRA

Isla Tambo

Combarro

through conservation and tourism, but its houses retain their traditional character with balconies that resemble grander *pazos*. Thirty *hórreos*, unique in Galicia for their shore side setting, continue to be used. At various crossing points *cruceiros* (stone crosses) tell about the past of this pretty town.

Opposite your anchorage you will not fail to notice the paper mill next to the naval port of Marín. Now scheduled for closure in 2018, the factory has been a source of local controversy due to pollution. The location of the plant was a source of local joy when it was first opened in 1963 as it created many jobs but the smell and contamination of the Ría have in the long run set the local population against it. Pollution is controlled but the sight does not compare well with what is in view to the north.

Across the bay the **Monasterio de San Xoán de Poio** was established in the 10th century and is associated with the legend of Santa Trahamunda, who was captured by the moors and miraculously escaped to return. The episode is symbolised in the Poio town coat of arms.

Isla de Tambo used to be occupied by Benedictine monks, but their monastery and settlement was destroyed by Francis Drake on his way back from wreaking havoc at Vigo with his 20 ships. The island became a hospital in 19th century finally to be taken over in 20th century by the Defence Ministry, and the naval officers from Marín can make use of the cottages ashore. The island cannot be accessed but the anchorage opposite its northern beach is among the most pleasant in the whole of the Rías.

Marín is a modern town with good facilities but difficult to access from a boat. A taxi ride is needed. The town is one of the key industrial centres for the major Spanish frozen fish companies, Pescanova among them. The commercial harbour is dotted with fish processing and fishing warehouses.

Tambo lighthouse

Old street and *hórreo* in Combarro

COMBARRO

CRUISING GALICIA 221

Hórreos

The *hórreo* most distinctly identifies rural Galicia. It can be traced back to the Romans, from whose word *horreum*, signifying grain store, its name has evolved. *Hórreos* are storage places for grain and other agricultural produce, keeping them safe from rodents and birds but also providing a dry environment above the ground which allows air to circulate.

The basic structure of an *hórreo* sits upon a series of pillars that end in round or square platforms, designed to make it impossible for a small animal to climb to the top. No mouse or rat could easily overcome the challenge presented by a horizontal surface a metre or so above the ground. Typically these toadstools are made of granite but some have wooden pillars or cheaper arrangements made more recently with bricks.

The main chamber walls have vents that are small enough to prevent access by animals or birds while permitting a free flow of air to keep the grain or fruit fresh. There are a number of standard granite blocks that are used but towards the north many walls are built with

wooden slats or slate tiles. The roof protects the chamber from rain, normally made with more durable terracotta tiles though sometimes with wood.

The apex at each end of the roof is often crowned with stone decorations. Some are religious, such as crosses or saints, but others represent animals or buildings. Yet others tell the time through sun dials.

Access is along portable steps, otherwise a ready path would be left behind for the creatures they are intended to exclude. There is normally a single door at one end.

No farm in Galicia, Asturias or northern Portugal would be without an *hórreo* given the amount of rain that falls. Size is an indication of wealth, from small basic structures to very large affairs such as at Carnota, which can accommodate the needs of an entire village. Many *hórreos* are protected buildings and such is their appeal that they are often now added to enhance the Galician character of new homes.

RÍA DE PONTEVEDRA

⚓ Pontevedra

Excellent pontoons right in the centre of historic town but only accessible if draft below 2m and mast height less than 12m. The reward for overcoming these barriers is the proximity to the centre of Pontevedra.

Approach & entrance

Approach limited by shallow channel (1m) in Río Lérez and bridge (12m).

Provisioning

The town is well supplied with small grocers and supermarkets. For fresh produce visit the *Mercado de Abastos* at Avda. de Buenos Aires by the river to the north of the old town.

Restaurants and bars for anything from tapas to formal meals are abundant in the old town.

Interest

Pontevedra is the smallest of the seven Galician cities. The old town has been completely closed to traffic and is second only to Santiago for its traditional setting of domestic and noble buildings. The stone streets in the centre are a delight to walk and get lost in, never very far from a good restaurant or something interesting to see. Numerous events throughout the year, from classical music to popular fiestas, exceed what could be expected for the size of the city.

Pontevedra is the capital of the province, a position won in competition with Vigo and which still today is the subject of controversy. Its location as a key step in the Portuguese route to Santiago gave it pre-eminence but an illustrious past from pre-roman times also support its status.

It is very easy to visit the sights of Pontevedra given the compactness of the centre. The monumental highlights include **Iglesia de Santa María**, a Galician masterpiece whose contruction in the 16th century was sponsored by the powerful Guild of Seamen, hence it is often called Iglesia de los Pescadores.

The *cruceiro* (stone cross) and the excellent Museo Provincial at **Eirado da Leña** (wood market) are a good stop to admire the centre of the town, where individual markets used to be located.

Pontevedra 42°26'N 08°39'W

Club Naval de Pontevedra
- Entrance restricted by bridge (12m height) and channel low water depth (2m) - means unlikely port for sailing yachts longer than 10m
- Berthing: pontoon, up to 5 visitors
- Depth at marina 2m
- Excellent shelter.
- ☎ 986 861022
- VHF Channel 09
- Water, electricity at pontoons
- ⛽ Fuel pontoon on town side wall (depth 2m, silted 2007 due to winter wash after mountain fires)
- 🛥 12-ton travel lift

Club Naval de Pontevdera

Pontevedra

224 CRUISING GALICIA

RÍA DE PONTEVEDRA

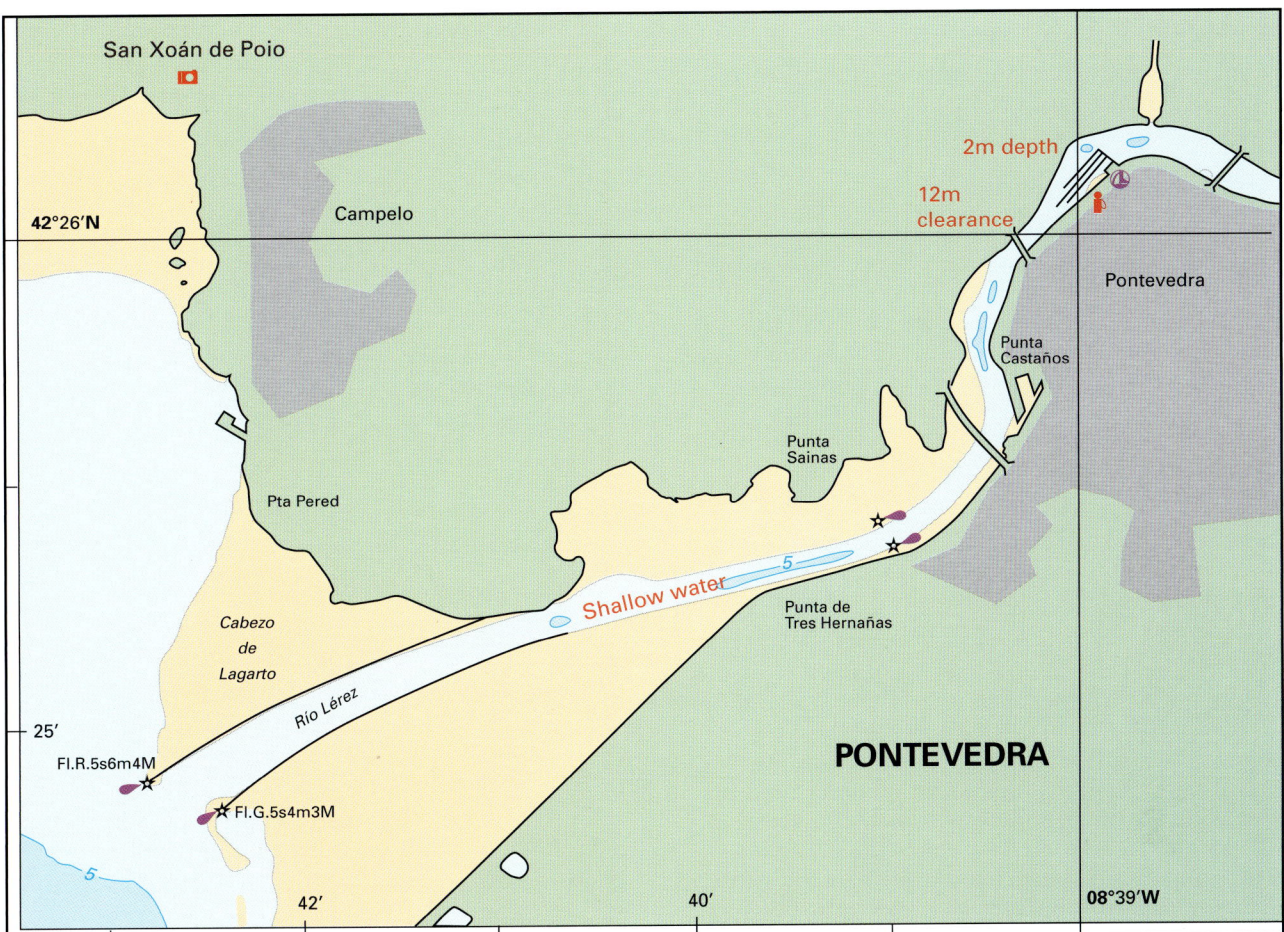

The **Santuario de la Peregrina** is notorious less for its architectural perfection than the story of the Virgin which it hosts. The statue was brought to Pontevedra as a pilgrim image and competed for a long time with the resident image at its original hosting church, Nuestra Señora del Camino. The issue was resolved through the construction of the Santuario in the 18th century. The Pilgrim Virgin is associated with Galicians and their history of emigration, often becoming the patron of centres abroad.

Pontevedra

- Santiago 60km   Coruña 120km, Vigo 30km
- Bus station: Calle de Calvo Sotelo ☎ 986 852408
- Market:
  - Mercado de Abastos, Avda. de Buenos Aires
- Restaurants:
  - Bars and restaurants in the old town, best around Museo Provincial
- Tourist office: Oficina de Turismo de Pontevedra, Calle Gral. Gutiérrez Mellado 1, ☎ 986850814
- Hospital Montecelo, Rúa Mourente, ☎ 986 800000

CRUISING GALICIA 225

RÍA DE PONTEVEDRA

⚓ Aguete

Small and very welcoming marina with good facilities ashore. Not much space and exposed to swell. Coast nearby is a delight.

Approach & entrance

The lit approach to Aguete marina is straightforward during the day. The final approach is via a starboard hand mark Fl(4)G.11s (which marks offlying rocks to the southwest) and the end of the wave break Fl(2)G.7s. The berths available can be seen from outside, allowing final arrangements to be made in the space of open water. Arrival at night can be difficult but not impossible as there is only one light at the end of the breakwater.

Note if you are caught out by a change of wind direction around to the northeast then the anchorage inside Isla de Clemente 2.5M to the southwest could offer an alternative. (See Bueu & Beluso).

Berthing & Facilities

Aguete is a small private marina with a strong sailing club. Space is limited and you may end up alongside the outer pontoons, which also act as a breakwater. These can be bouncy in NW to NE winds and are unconnected to the shore. Beware the condition of some of the cleats on the outer pontoons which can also be slippery. VHF is well attended, but your best bet may be to park and then communicate. The marina maintains a local 'taxi' boat that will collect you from your berth.

Showers and toilets are to a dinghy sailing club standard. Transport (taxis) is best arranged through the club.

Provisioning

The clubhouse of Real Club de Mar has an excellent restaurant and bar with splendid views of Ría de Pontevedra.

For provisioning the only shops nearby are at the tiny village of Aguete or the slightly larger Montecelo. Both need a walk up to the road of about half a mile.

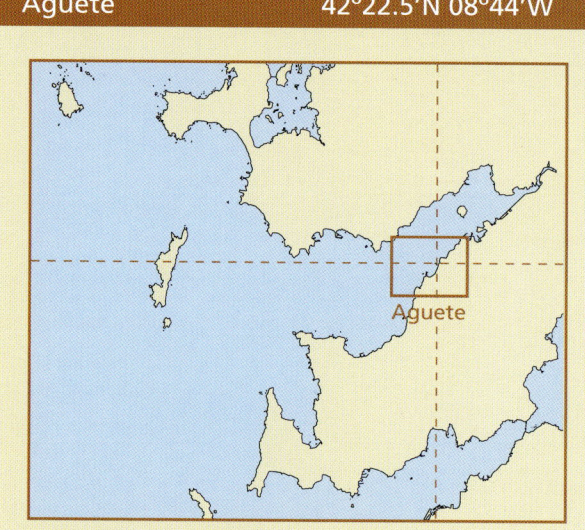

Real Club de Mar de Aguete

- Straightforward approach during the day, clear north green beacon; limited navigation lights for night approach
- Floating breakwater leaves outer marina berths exposed to swell - can be bouncy in N/NW winds
- Berthing: pontoon mooring, visitors in the first channel to starboard on arrival
- Water and electricity: only in shore connected pontoons
- ☎ 986 702373   Fax 986 702708
- VHF Channel 09
- rcma@ctv.es
- Fuel at the harbour wall
- Showers and toilets good
- Good restaurant with excellent view

Aguete

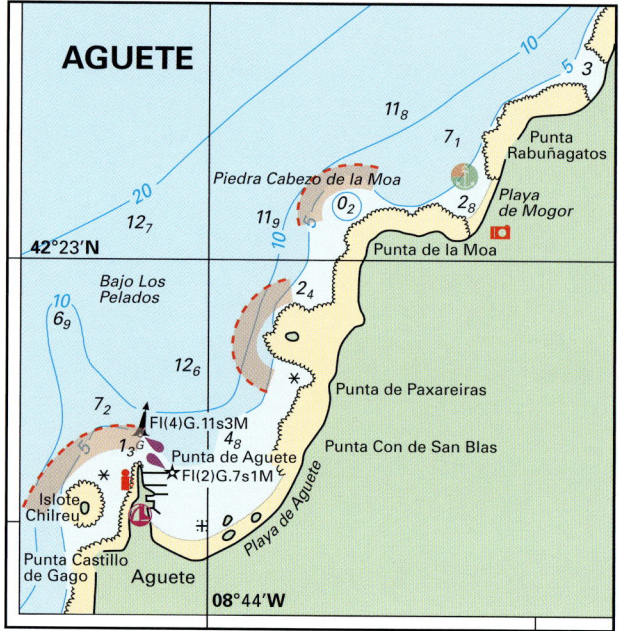

RÍA DE PONTEVEDRA

Aguete marina outer pontoons

⚓ Playa do Mogor

1M to the northeast, this anchorage opposite a beach is very picturesque and gives access to the petroglyphs ashore. Use of a tripping line is recommended in case of snags with rocks.

Interest

Aguete is one of the friendliest marinas you will find anywhere, welcoming and devoid of any commercial undertones. Founded in the early 70s by a group of local prominent people, it has grown from its small beginnings. The grand **clubhouse** was built in the style of a boat, with a terrace that is the perfect spot for a good set of tapas and views over the ría.

Aguete was the base for local sea hero **Juan Gago de Mendoza**, who during the latter 18th century and early 19th century used his small fleet to harass the attacking British boats. He later defeated the French at Marín during the invasion of Spain by Napoleon. During his life he was a key player in the local warring for control of the important ports that Spain used for trade with the Americas. His participation in 1820 in the liberal movement led to his downfall and death in poverty when the Bourbon royals regained absolute control. It is worth walking the street named after him to look at the grand coat of arms at one of the large granite houses.

Mendoza's house at Aguete

To the north of Aguete the **petroglyphs of Magor** are a legacy of Galician prehistory, possibly connected with the cultures of Atlantic facing Europe further north. Lines carved in stone give a sense of mystery and will leave you free to interpret their possible meaning.

Mogor petroglyphs

The trees of Punta de Moa and the small beach of Magor provide a very pretty setting. It is possible and pleasant to walk along the small road from Aguete to Playa de Mogor.

A short taxi ride from the clubhouse can take you into **Pontevedra**, one of the highlights of Galicia.

Mogor beach

CRUISING GALICIA

RIA DE PONTEVEDRA

⚓ Bueu & Beluso

A bay at the entrance to the ría which offers shelter from west, south and east winds. The small marina at Beluso and temporary pontoons in the summer at Bueu can provide berths. Bueu is a small town steeped in the fish canning history of the area, full of character and activity.

Approach & entrance

Straightforward approach during the day. At night care must be taken with the unlit *batea* grids. If approaching from the **west**, use the beacon at Cabezo de la Mourisca Fl(2)G.7s for its intended purpose and give Islote el Caballo, an unlit isolated rock 1M to the ESE, a comfortable berth before making your way south outside the *bateas* towards Bueu. If heading for Beluso, approach parallel to the shore inside the *bateas* from the direction of Bueu.

If approaching from the **east** between the *bateas* and the shore then note quickly shoaling headland at Monte Gordo with offlying rocks 1M to the northwest of Bueu.

⚓ Anchorages

The area is quite exposed so shelter is not the best. The beaches east and west of Bueu offer anchoring in sand. Near Beluso space in front of the harbour is very tight with small boat moorings. The little

Bueu & Beluso 42°20'N 08°47'W

Beluso
- Small fishing harbour, no space reserved for visitors; sailing club has very basic facilities
- Expansion plans in progress, may provide additional space for sailing club

Bueu
- Fishing harbour
- Ponttons are private, no facilities for visitors
- Travel lift 110-ton, space ashore

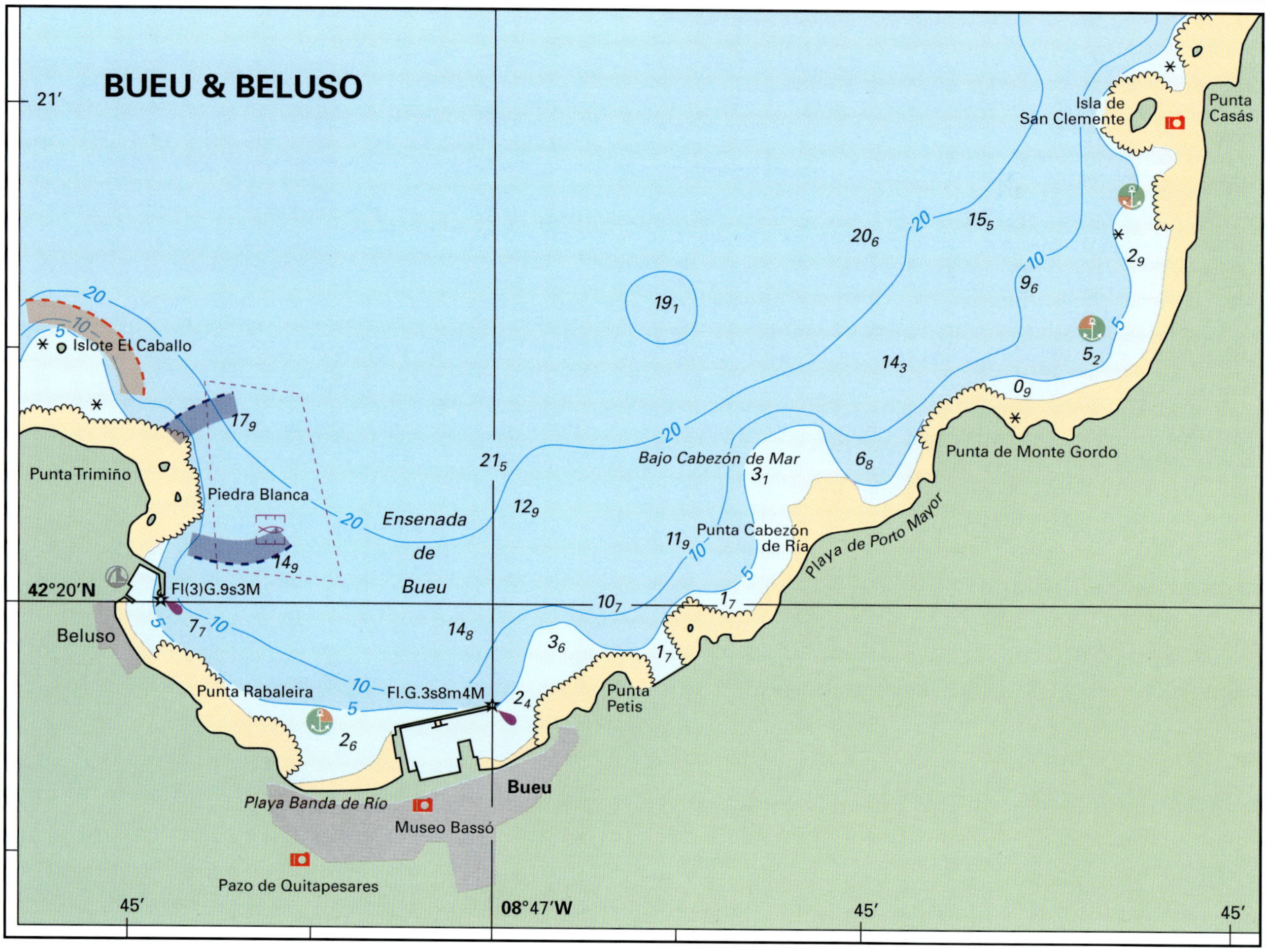

cove immediately north of the harbour may be the best choice with the right wind direction and the use of a tripping line.

⚓ Isla De San Clemente

2.5M to the south west of Aguete, this anchorage could offer an alternative if the berth at Aguete becomes untenable due to a change in wind direction to the northeast. Anchor as close to the Island as depth permits to gain the best shelter. Note offlying rock to the south of the island and anchorage.

Provisioning

Bueu town is the only practical location for provisioning, but distances are short and the walk pleasant from where you are in the bay. The *mercado* along the sea front at Calle Montero Ríos is well stocked with fresh produce and the best of fish.

Interest

The highlight of Bueu is **Museo Massó**, sited in the old factory of the illustrious pioneer of fish canning and conservation in Galicia (Calle Montero Ríos by the harbour). The museum is very well appointed and gives a good introduction into the history of the area, from the *castro* pre-roman tribal societies to the modern large scale fishing industry. Good examples of boats and machinery will take you through the hardships and innovations of Galicia, culminating in the enormous changes brought by *fomentadores catalanes* (Catalan entrepreneurs) encouraged by the liberalisation of fishing through a marine act in 1748. New fishing techniques (the *xábega* fishing net) and technology for salting and canning (presses) greatly increased the sardine production volumes. In a world involved in increasing maritime trade with the Americas these advances revolutionised victualling.

It is worth visiting **Pazo de Quitapasares** at Carrasqueiras, a short walk east of Bueu, a grand 17th century building which sports a stone carving of an orchestra at the entrance, including a Galician *Gaiteiro* (bagpipe player). **Isla de San Clemente** is linked to the coast by a sand strip that uncovers at low water. Galician legend links the San Clemente chapel built at the island with the reconquest of

RÍA DE PONTEVEDRA

Museo Massó

Seville in November of 1248. The Castillian King Fernando III entered the capital of Al-Andalus in a key historic event for Spain, aided by a fleet of boats from Santander, the Basque Country and Galicia. The King succeeded having taken the risk of a large attack to the heart of the Muslim world in the south of Spain rather than continue a policy of small advance against the numerous Taifas (local Muslim enclaves). This military success set the scene for the final period of the Christian Reconquista. The chapel on the island, according to legend, was built in honour of the Galician participants in the campaign.

As with all other towns in Galicia, there are plenty of fiestas throughout the year. The key, and colourful, events of the year are the **Fiesta del Carmen** on 16 July celebrating the fishermen's patron and **Corpus Christi**, in late May or early June, when the town is covered with colourful flower carpets, in the tradition of the towns of Pontevedra.

Beluso is a very picturesque small harbour.

Anchorage under trees to the north of Beluso

Bueu harbour

Beluso

RÍA DE PONTEVEDRA

⚓ Ría de Aldán

Ría de Aldán is a remote part of the Morrazo peninsula. Quiet and very picturesque, it sits at the entrance to Ría de Pontevedra and in the right conditions offers a useful, convenient and possibly therapeutic break after a transit along the Rías Baixas.

Approach & entrance

Ría de Aldán is exposed to Atlantic swell and any wind from the north/northwest.

The Ría is relatively small and full of *bateas* on the western side with both shores dotted with submerged reefs up to 500m from the shore. It is not well lit. Because of this it should not be attempted in bad weather or at night. Detailed local charts are advised for this Ría.

The only light is at the southern end of the Ría at Aldán (Fl(2)R.10s) with a 5M range. A course of 160° will clear the dangers mentioned above, or more likely its reciprocal, 340°, will aid an early start to the day.

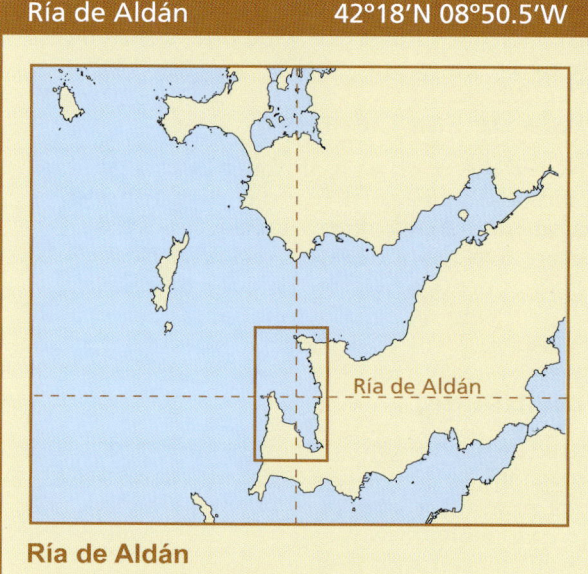

Ría de Aldán   42°18'N 08°50.5'W

Ría de Aldán
- Exposed to N/NW winds and ocean swell. Do not attempt in bad weather.
- Best aprroach by day.

It should be noted that although the regimented *batea* grids allow straightforward navigation through the floating platforms, they are unlit. It should not be assumed that because you are within one of these grids you are in deep water.

⚓ Anchorages

There are many places along the southern part which are suitable for anchoring. In all cases proceed with care as there are a number of isolated dangers.

Mussel boat in front of the old factory in Aldán

230 CRUISING GALICIA

RÍA DE PONTEVEDRA

Playa Castineira is approached through the mussel beds. Submerged and drying dangers lie to the south of the beach (Bajo Con de Manuel and Punta Pintens).

Playa de Bon on the eastern shore is a small secluded little bay offering protection from east winds. Playa de Arnelas and Playa de Vilariño to the south are also quiet, take care at Punta Testada and Pedra Con de Arnelas in the SW corner of the Ría.

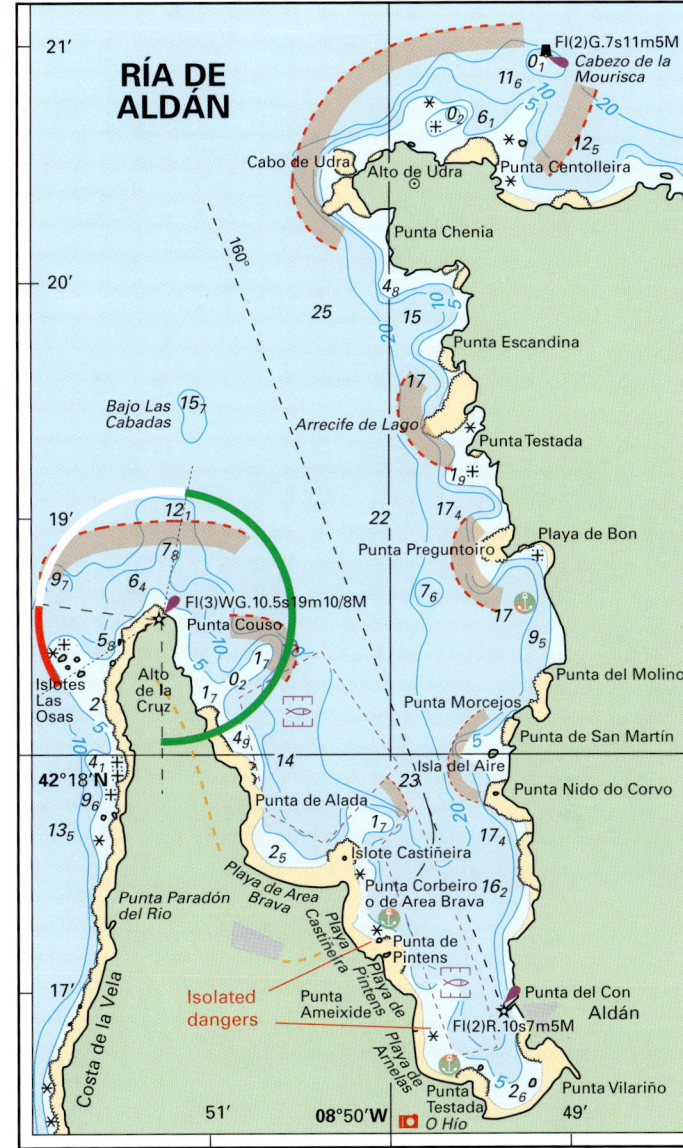

Cruceiro de O Hío

Provisioning

The little towns of Aldán, Vilariño and Pintens have some shops but they require a trip ashore in the dinghy followed by a short walk.

Interest

Ría de Aldán is very pretty and quiet. There are good **walks** towards Punta Couso, from which the views of the dramatic Costa de la Vela and Ría de Aldán are excellent.

Near the bottom of the ría the **Cruceiro de O Hío** is one of the best stone crosses in the whole of Galicia. It is a splendid example of this type of monument, relatively modern (19th century) but nevertheless magnificient. The settting of San Andrés church, house and *hórreo* is very pretty.

Playa Castineira

CRUISING GALICIA 231

Ría de Aldán

Isla Ons north side

Lighthouse Fl(4)14s

Playa Mellide

Almacén

N

⚓ Isla Ons

A popular and pretty island which protects Ría de Pontevedra from the ocean swell. The anchorages offer protection from the east and north. An evening visit or avoiding the weekends would miss many of the visitors that come on the ferry.

The western coast is uninviting and very exposed to ocean swell and should not be approached.

Approach & entrance

Straightforward daylight approach from the east. The quay at Almacén Fl.R.4s, could be used at night for an approach to this anchorage, although there could well be other unlit vessels and buoys present.

Do not attempt Canal de los Camoucos in bad weather.

⚓ Anchorages

Playa de Melide is the more sheltered of the two eastern anchorages, offering protection from west to north winds. Sand with some stones.

Punta de Almacén offers protection from the west. Anchor well clear and to the north of the quay as the tourists' ferries land there. The bottom is gravel and stones. There are some visitors' moorings.

There is a bay at the south end of Isla Ons, between the two islands, which could offer protection from the north but will be subject to swell. If approaching from the east stay close to steep sided Isla Onza to avoid Piedra La Loba (isolated rock off Isla Ons).

Provisioning

There are a couple of stalls in the summer that sell drinks and snacks, otherwise Isla Ons is not a place for provisioning.

Interest

Isla Ons is a pretty, quiet island, worth exploring as a walking expedition. The Buraco do Inferno **cave** at the southern end is a striking blowhole worth walking the mile or two from your landing.

Isla Onza is a restricted bird sanctuary, inhabited principally by cormorants. There are good views of the birds from Isla Ons.

Isla Ons
- Anchorages with shelter from west winds on the eastern shore of Isla Ons. Daytime approach only.
- Landing at the southern Isla Onza is not permitted.

RÍA DE PONTEVEDRA

CRUISING GALICIA

Ría de Vigo

The economic powerhouse of Galicia

Ría de Vigo

Introduction

Ría de Vigo is the most southern of the Galician Rías, benefiting from a slightly better climate as a result of its location. As in Pontevedra, immediately to the north, the weather attracts tourism, with some of the coastal spots like Baiona and Cangas among the classic summer holiday destinations. Protected by Islas Cíes at the entrance, the Ría provides excellent shelter which, together with its convenient proximity to Portugal, has led to its development into a large harbour. Vigo is one of the fastest growing European cities in the 20th century, reaching a population today of 750,000.

The history of the Ría is colourful. As the first harbour after a voyage along the Portuguese coast it became host to many of the traders that travelled between the Mediterranean and northern Europe. Phoenecian, Roman and Nordic boats stopped here to exchange linen, corn and other items from the north and salt, oil and prestige goods from the south. The Ría has also been the scene of many battles between the Turkish, French, British and Spanish empires, many of them played out by commissioned privateers, and also of pirate activity.

Fishing and industry are the modern driving forces. The port of **Vigo** is one of the largest shipping centres in Spain and the biggest fish handling destination for offshore boats. A large **shipbuilding** industry is based in Vigo, still very active and supplying the demands of the Spanish fishing fleet. Travelling the coastal road into Vigo and observation from the water reveals extensive installations used for building and repairing ships.

Vigo is also the birthplace of modern frozen seafood. It was local Pepe Fernández who in the 1960s first established freezing fish at sea and his Pescanova enterprise continues to be one of the biggest companies in the world dedicated to fish production.

The general context is thus busy and industrial, and the Ría the most densely populated in Galicia. This does not mean that you cannot find quieter areas however, among which **Baiona** is one of the best harbours for the leisure sailor in this stretch of the Atlantic coast. The town's history, traditional streets and the character of its own small Ría have made it one of the favourite summer destinations of the well to do citizens of Vigo. From the sea, Baiona is an excellent stop when cruising in the area, typically used by Atlantic crossing yachts for fuelling and victualling before the long voyage.

At the entrance, the eastern coastline of **Islas Cíes** is a delightful area for anchorage, part of the Atlantic Islands National Park and protected as a result.

RÍA DE VIGO

Costa da Vela and Islas Cíes

Ponteareas street flower carpets

Castillo de Gondomar, Baiona

Old town of Vigo

Cangas

At the end of Ría de Vigo, **Ensenada de San Simón** is a peaceful haven away from the busy shipping lanes further out. If you have the time to make the journey there (12M) the reward is a calm and rural setting beyond the road viaduct.

The coast to the west of Cangas is very dramatic, both inland in the forested areas of **Península del Morrazo** and along the cliffs of Costa da Vela. Transport is needed to reach most destinations, even if the goal is walking along the tracks. The beaches of Barra and Limens are good targets for anchoring in rural surrounds, although they may be busy with holidaymakers.

The best destinations on land apart from Baiona are **Cangas** and the **old town of Vigo**, both of which have preserved a traditional feel which has disappeared in the less than well planned industrial and residential construction of the Ría. Vigo has many interesting sights to visit, several good museums, including the excellent Museo del Mar and the intriguing Museo de la Palabra (Word Museum) at Samil, all of which compensate for the busy feel of the place. If you like football, Celta de Vigo plays in the first division of the millionaire Spanish league.

A Guarda has charm, set near the mouth of Río Miño on the border with Portugal. The river valley further inland is one of the most beautiful parts of Galicia. Historic Tuy and Castro de Santa Tecla nearby are excellent tourist destinations. During Corpus Christi (May/June) the flower carpets along the streets of Ponteareas are a magnificient sight.

Oysters are the speciality of the Ría, sold in the streets of Vigo and grown at San Simón. Food is excellent everywhere and what better way to enjoy it than in Baiona, where the first caravela of Christopher Columbus landed in 1493 having discovered America.

CRUISING GALICIA 237

RÍA DE VIGO

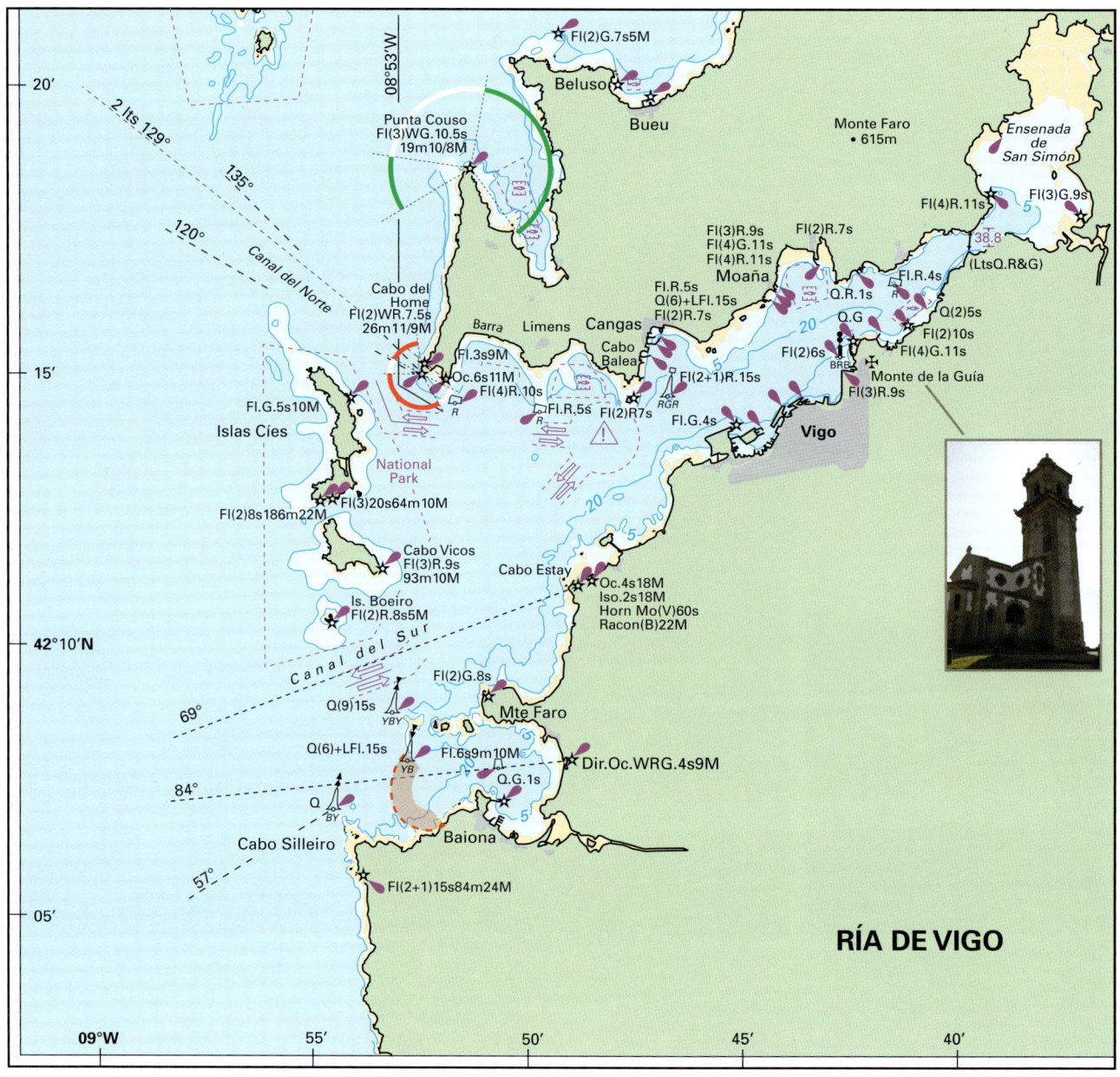

Approach and key facilities

Approach & entrance

If coming from offshore then Monte Faro and Islas Cíes FL(2)8s22M will identify the Ría.
Note: at night there may be additional lights from moored ships seeking shelter behind Islas Cíes.

Ría de Pontevedra to Cangas

This route avoids the main shipping lanes but brings the yachtsman closer to rocky, and potentially, lee shores at the entrance to Ría de Vigo.

- Clear dangers off the entrance to Ría de Aldán
- Approach down the 08°53' W longitude with the front leading light Fl.3s on Cabo del Home remaining in its visible sector (90° to °180°). Note the red sector of Punta Ronaleira Fl(2) WR7.5s becomes visible and then obscured on the approach
- With Punta Ronaleira Fl(2)WR.7.5s becoming visible abeam again, alter course to 120° for channel marker Fl(4)R off Punta Subrido
- Leave red lateral marks Fl.R.5s and Fl(2)R.7s, off Salaiños and Piedra Borneira respectively, close to port (course 90°). Beware commercial shipping movements obscured by background lights to starboard
- Alter course towards the south cardinal Q(6)+LFl.15s on Cangas breakwater when it bears due north, leaving Bajo Salgueirón Fl(2+1)R.15s, isolated rock, to starboard
- Follow NE track around end of breakwater Fl.R.5s. Beware fishing boat movements

238 CRUISING GALICIA

RÍA DE VIGO

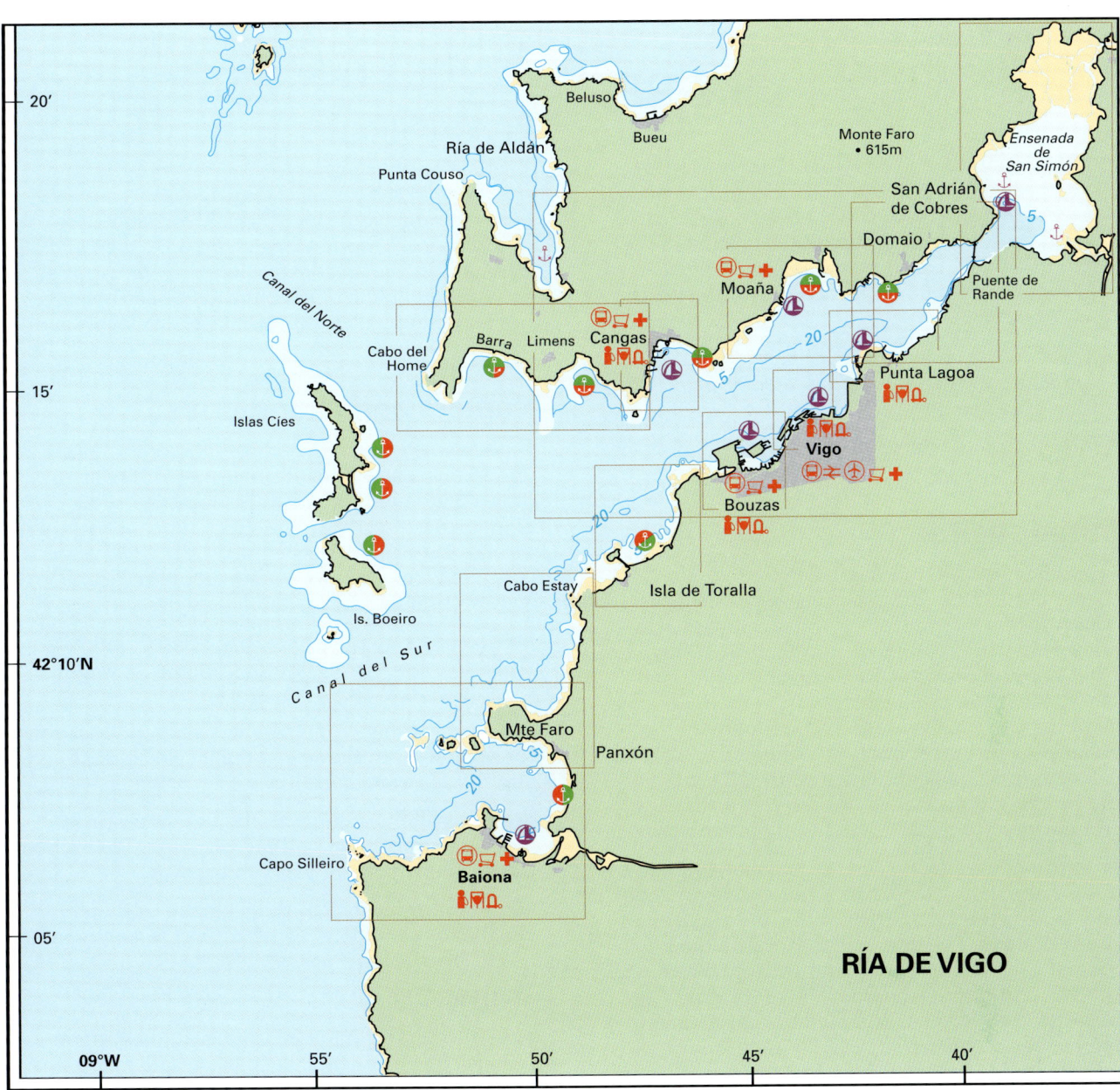

- When clear of end of breakwater Fl.R.5s, pass between arms of inner harbour Fl(2+1)R.15s, Fl.G.4s.

Northwest of Islas Ons and Cíes to Cangas

The following description avoids the main shipping routes where possible and also enables traffic separation schemes to be crossed at approximately right angles.

- The transit, front Fl.3s, rear Oc.6s (129°) is for the commercial ships. A safe cone exists from the front Fl.3s light between 120° to 135° to clear isolated dangers to the north of Islas Cíes and south of Isla Onza respectively
- Head for Isla del Norte Fl.G5s once it bears between 190° and 200°
- Before depth drops below 20m, head for channel marker Fl(4)R. off Punta Subrido (course 100°, crossing the TSS at right angles)
- Leave red lateral marks Fl.R.5s and Fl(2)R.7s, off Salaiños and Piedra Borneira respectively, close to port (course 90°). Beware commercial shipping movements obscured by background lights to starboard
- Alter course towards the south cardinal Q(6)+LFl.15s on Cangas breakwater when it bears due north leaving Bajo Salgueirón Fl(2+1)R.15s, isolated rock, to starboard
- Follow NE track around end of breakwater Fl.R.5s. Beware fishing boat movements
- When clear of end of breakwater Fl.R.5s, pass between arms of inner harbour Fl(2+1)R.15s, Fl.G.4s.

CRUISING GALICIA 239

RÍA DE VIGO

From south and west to Baiona

- Stay in more than 50m of water until past Cabo Silleiro. Note the two yellow buoys SW of this headland (1.8M)
- The transit (084°, Fl.6s front, Dir.Oc.WRG.4s rear) is hard to pick out in daylight. Instead, from the north cardinal Q, off Cabo Silleiro, head for the south cardinal Q(6)LFl.15s (57°), off the reef of Las Serralleiras. This will clear the shallow patch (4.1m) 0.6M E of the north cardinal (Q)
- Alter course to 85° to clear Punta del Buey (north of the Parador, illuminated at night) when due west of it.
- Steer south for the ed of the Baiona breakwater Q.G.

Initial shelter

From the north, Ría de Vigo offers good initial shelter close to the entrance. The lee of the Islas Cíes provides a temporary respite from westerlies and ocean swell, and the Península del Morrazo from northerly winds. The channel is wide, well marked and free of all dangers apart from possible shipping movements in the TSS. From there the distance to several marinas at Cangas and Vigo is less than 5M. For the latter, Marina Davila in the southern Bouzas area of Vigo city is the most straightforward and the most likely to have space.

From the south, the marinas of Baiona (Club de Yates and Puerto Deportivo) offer excellent facilities and are a favourite destination for the majority of ocean cruisers. The entrance to Ría de Baiona is dramatic, exposed to swell and with extensive reefs both to port and starboard. The shore marks can be difficult to identify in daylight or poor visibility, but the channel is well marked with lit buoys. It is at least 0.5M wide, which makes entry possible in all conditions. The final approach and berthing is sheltered from the west, has plenty of manoeuvring room and comprehensive facilities when you get in. Puerto Deportivo de Baiona is likely to have spare berths, even in the holiday season.

Other ports and facilities

There are numerous marinas and pontoons along both sides of the Ría, but several are private and not designed to accept visitors. On the northern side beyond Cangas, Moaña half way up and San Adrián de Cobres in Ensenada de San Simón are small but appropriate destinations for visiting yachts. Only Cangas has fuel for private yachts (2007) and shore facilities for repairs are not extensive.

The southern shore has several large marinas in Vigo city: Davila at Bouzas, RCN in Vigo centre, Punto Lagoa in Vigo north, all with good facilities and fuel. RCN entrance is a tight dogleg through the outer walls. Bouzas also has the Liceo marina, smaller but being developed (2008).

Provisioning

There is no shortage of local shops and *plazas* (markets) in the towns and villages, plus a wealth of restaurants and bars at which you can enjoy excellent fresh food. Cangas, Moaña, Vigo and Baiona host the most extensive range of shops and services, while the quieter anchorages at Limens or San Simón will require walks to the local small towns.

Repairs and chandleries

Vigo has several extensive chandleries at Bouzas and in the centre, plus the marinas of Davila and Punto Lagoa have good workshops and some equipment directly on the shore. Any of these will be able to provide parts immediately or have them couriered from the main manufacturers. See the Vigo section for details and locations.

Baiona has a number of marine related outlets along the shore front but they are not as well stocked as in Vigo.

Elsewhere, Cangas and Moañas are good locations for repairs given the size of the local fishing fleets and the associated services.

For general bits and pieces the *ferreterías* (iron mongers) are a good destination, several in each of the locations you are likely to berth at.

Marina staff have local skill contacts and will always advise and help with respect to any repair.

Transport

The excellent **train** line that links all of western Galicia runs to Vigo. The high speed R598 trains stop there.

Vigo airport is served by the Spanish airlines and some budget airlines with destinations in Europe. Check up to date information on precise airlines and routes.

Numerous **buses** cover the area, run by a series of private companies (Castromil, Arriva and others) with routes to all the major towns including Santiago, Pontevedra, Vigo and A Coruña as well as the local towns. The main bus stations are at Baiona, Vigo, Redondela and Cangas. See the local tourist office for schedule details.

Cruising in Ría de Vigo

Ría de Vigo is the most southern of the Rías Baixas, sheltered by Islas Cíes which are part of the Atlantic Islands National Park. The Ría is open to the Ocean in the southern areas in front of Baiona but shelter is generally good. The main destinations of Baiona, Vigo, Cíes and Cangas can be cruised in two or three days from the sea but considerably

RÍA DE VIGO

more if you take time over the local attractions. The distance to Ensenada de San Simón is significant (12M from Islas Cíes), which needs to be considered when making plans.

One day

If you only have one day to get a taste of the Ría then visit Islas Cíes and Baiona. They are two of the more scenic destinations in the Rías so it will still be worthwhile.

One week

The anchorages at Islas Cíes, Limens and Ensenada de San Simón are good, quiet, destinations. Go ashore to explore the beaches and tracks at Islas Cíes within the national park, with stunning views and abundant birdlife.

Stay at the marina in Cangas or anchor nearby to explore the charm of this traditional town, known for its *casas de patín* (external stairs to main entrance).

The marinas at Vigo will give you access to the historic old town centre and the elegant planned streets near Plaza de Compostela. Several good museums and other sites will keep you entertained and extensive shopping attend to any need you may have.

Baiona is a must for any visitor to the area, historic and set in a beautiful bay. The town gets very busy in August with Spanish tourists and the restaurant charges are higher than elsewhere, but the visit is still worthwhile and the marinas are placed right in the old part.

CRUISING GALICIA 241

RÍA DE VIGO

⚓ Barra and Limens

Two pleasant anchorages on the south side of Cabo Home at Ensenada de Barra and Ensenada de Limens, in front of the beaches of the same name. The cape is part of the protected Home-Costa da Vela natural space, well worth a detour for its beautiful walks and dramatic coastal views.

Approach & entrance

The approach directions are straightforward, but a wide berth is advised from the coast on the western side of Cabo Home which is unwelcoming in difficult weather or swell. The anchorages are quiet, for winds from west round to northeast but avoid in conditions with any southern component.

From the north and west:

- Follow the same directions as would be used to enter Rías de Vigo, which is a wide, well marked (lit) channel free of all dangers apart from possible shipping movements. Pass south of the channel marker off Punta Subrido Fl(4)R.10s.

From the east:

- Straightforward approach
- Dangers and shallows marked south of Piedra Borneira Fl(2)R.7s and Salaiños Fl.R5s.

Barra and Limens   42°15'N 08°51'W

Barra and Limens
- Straightforward entrance.
- Best anchorage NW corner at Playa do Barra.
- Shelter: from W round to N winds at Ensenada de Barra; from W round to E winds at Ensenada de Limens; both open to swell if S wind.

Anchor in sand at Ensenada de Barra in front of the beach. The best shelter from west is found to northeast, in the lee of the wooded hill at the northwest end.

Ensenada de Limens is good for winds from the west round to east, but north northwest winds can channel through the lowland beyond the beach. Anchorage is also in sand.

For both anchorages beware of any change to wind from the south and make preparations so as to be able to make a prompt exit if the situation changes as the coast has rock dangers.

Both beaches will have swimming areas marked out in the summer.

Costa da Vela and Islas Cíes

RÍA DE VIGO

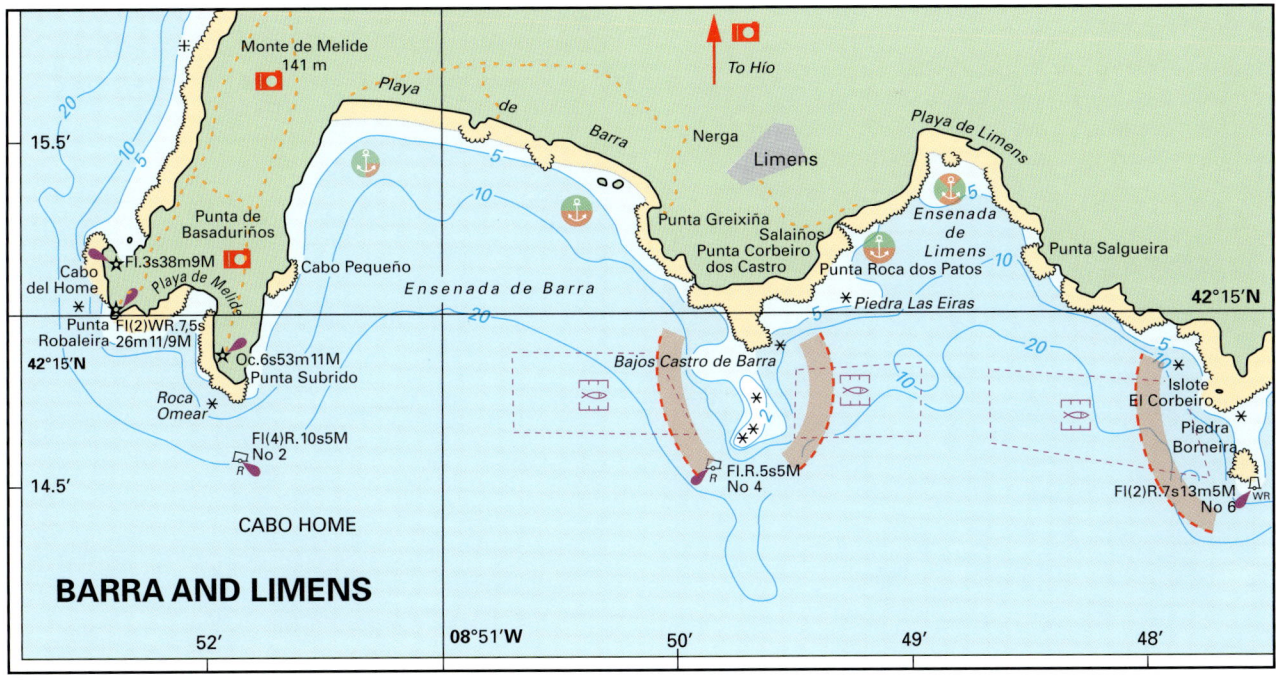

Interest

The area to the west of Playa Barra is the **protected natural space of Home-Costa Vela**, set in woodland with a number of tracks that reach the lighthouse. You can walk quite close to the sea facing dramatic rock escarpments on the western side and reach the peak of Monte de Melide (140m climb) for good views of Islas Cíes, the northern coastline and Ría de Vigo itself. Playa de Melide to the south of Cabo Home is a windswept but attractive spot which you can also reach by a forest track. The Costa da Vela to the west is a rugged rock face, unfriendly to boats but interesting for walks along the west coast of Ría de Aldán.

Playa de Barra, between the Cabo Home woodlands and the Punta Promontorio rocks, is a nudist beach.

Ensenada de Limens

Ensenada de Barra

CRUISING GALICIA 243

RÍA DE VIGO

⚓ Cangas

Cangas is set in a bay that offers shelter from southwest to northeast, with a small marina that can host visiting yachts. The town is a bustling summer resort and a tourist attraction during Easter because of the processions.

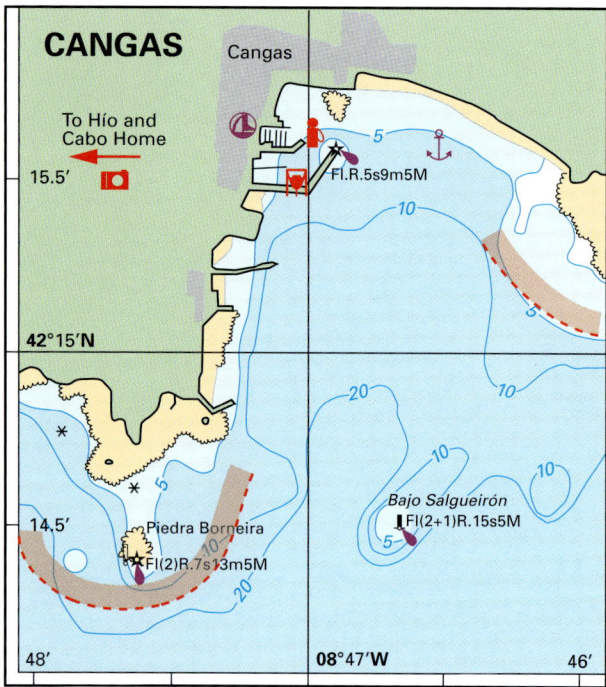

Approach & entrance

Straightforward entrance, given sufficient clearance from the Salgueirón shoal.

From the northwest side of the Ría, and beginning from the channel marker Fl(4)R.10s off Punta Subrido:

- Leave red lateral marks Fl.R.5s and Fl(2)R.7s, off Salaiños and Piedra Borneira respectively, close to port (course 90°). Beware commercial shipping movements obscured by background lights to starboard
- Alter course towards the south cardinal Q(6)+LFl.15s on Cangas breakwater when it bears due north, leaving Bajo Salgueirón Fl(2+1)R.15s, isolated rock, to starboard
- Follow NE track around end of breakwater Fl.R.5s. Beware fishing boat movements
- When clear of end of breakwater Fl.R.5s, pass between arms of inner harbour Fl(2+1)R.15s, Fl.G.4s.

From the direction of Baiona and starting from the west cardinal mark Q(9)15s off Las Serralleiras:

- Aim for the front Iso.2s transit at Cabo Estay on a bearing of 60°. Stay in more than 30m. Note the rear transit Oc.4s on the starboard bow and take care of shipping astern

Cangas 42°15′N 08°47′W

Club Náutico de Rodeira
- Entrance night and day
- Shelter all directions but can be bouncy in the outer pontoons in east wind
- Depth minimum 3m inside marina
- Berthing: pontoon mooring
- Visitors' berths 24

- ☎/Fax 986 305618 – 300165 – 303688
- VHF Channel 09
- nauticorodeira@navegalia.com

- Water, electricity at the pontoons
- ⛽ Fuel at the marina wall entrance, outside
- 🔧 Repairs: contact marina for mechanics, electricians, divers and other specialists
- 🏗 64-ton travel lift at the fishing harbour wall

Playa de Rodeira anchorage
- Good holding mud
- Shelter W to NE

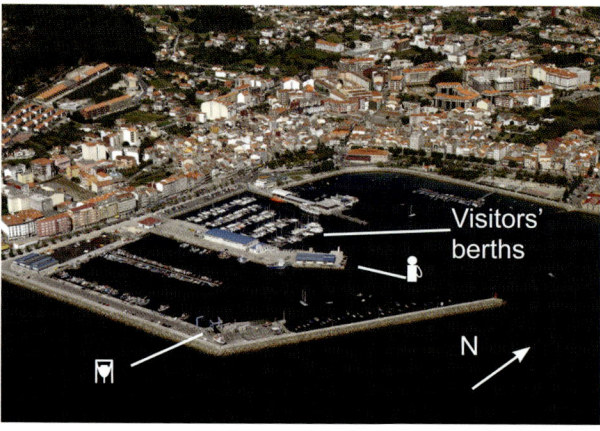

Cangas harbour and town behind

244 CRUISING GALICIA

RÍA DE VIGO

View from the east of Cangas and Playa Rodeira, scene of the Turkish landing of 1617

Cangas marina entrance

- Head towards the starboard hand mark off Isla de Toralla Fl(3)G.9s when it comes into sight to the northeast,. Stay in more than 20m
- Head towards the starboard hand mark off Cabo de Mar Fl(4)G14s (2.0M, 45°). Stay in more than 20m up to the buoy
- Cross shipping lane heading for south cardinal Q(6)+LFl.15s on Cangas breakwater when it bears 355°, leaving Bajo Salgueirón Fl(2+1)R.15s isolated rock to starboard
- Follow NE track around end of breakwater Fl.R.5s. Beware fishing boat movements.
- When clear of end of breakwater Fl.R.5s, pss between arms of inner harbour Fl(2+1)R.15s, Fl.G.4s.

Berthing & facilities

Club Náutico de Rodeira is a welcoming marina, very close to the main part of the town, excellent for going ashore and provisioning. However, there are no showers or other facilities at the marina.

Depth minimum 3m, space for up to 24 visitors, recommended for boats up to 10m but larger yachts can often be seen at the pontoons. Water and electricity at the berths. There is a travel lift for up to 64 tons on the south harbour breakwater wall. Fuel at the entrance to the marina, pier wall.

The port is a busy fishing harbour so take care of boat traffic.

⚓ Anchorage

Playa de Rodeira to the east of the town offers good holding in sand and gravel, opposite the gently sloping beach. Shelter is good for W to NE.

Provisioning & eating

Cangas has good, characterful bars and restaurants in the old town and the streets parallel to the harbour. Mercado Central to the north of the harbour is best for fresh supplies.

Transport

The bus station is located adjacent to the marina and offers extensive services.

Interest

Cangas is a bustling town with much history as a port attacked by foreign fleets for its position in the ría. A turkish invasion in 1617 landing at Playa Rodeira, in front of the church of San Pedro

Casa de Patín

RÍA DE VIGO

Cangas

- Vigo 20km Santiago 50km Coruña 130km
- 🚌 Bus station: Avda Montero Ríos: Autobuses Cerqueiro and others, frequent services to Pontevedra, Vigo
- Ferries to Vigo and Islas Cíes (in the summer) from the northern side of the harbour.
- 🛒 Markets: *Mercado central* (market) in Paseo Marítimo to the north of the harbour
- 🍴 Restaurants:
  - For bars and tapas visit the old town and the area around Alameda (park)
- ℹ️ Tourist office: Paseo Castelao 2, ☎ 986 392023
- ⚓ Chandlers - Efectos Navales (marine supplies):
  - Ibericamar, Fomento 38, ☎ 986 392 026
  - Efectos Navales Ocaña, Magdalena 11 ☎ 986 300 727
  - Central de Efectos Navales Cangas, Arrecife 8, ☎ 986 300 978
  Ferreterías:
  - Antonio Fernández Chapela, Avda Eugenio Sequeiros 14, ☎ 986 300 164
- Banks, chemists and other shops along Avda Montero Ríos, Real and Paseo Marítimo
- ✚ Centro Saude Cangas (Health Centre), Rúa Antonio Jalda ☎ 986 392028

Colegiata de Santiago

Mercado

de Domaio, caused much devastation and also led to subsequent witchcraft trials by the Inquisition, largely against local women. **Witchcraft** folklore is a feature of the town, nowadays given a light character not least through the bonfire night of San Juan on 21 July at the beaches of Barra, Nerga, Limens and others nearby.

Cangas is the major tourist destination of this northern coast of Ría de Vigo because of the town traditions, its beach and natural setting. The wooded hillside of the Peninsula de Morrazo to the north offers very pleasant walks.

Cangas old town is known for its *casas de patín,* a type of building erected by wealthier citizens in the 18th century. The houses have an external staircase that leads to the entrance on the first floor. The old town is also the location of the old Colegiata de Santiago, while in the *Alameda* (park) on the northern side of the harbour it is worth looking at the Meteorological Station donated to the town fishermen by a captain of the Navy early in the 20th century.

Easter is a major occasion in Cangas. The street processions are solemn affairs attended by many

RÍA DE VIGO

As Meigas, the Turks and the Inquisition

Galician myths include many about magic and women that possess knowledge of the occult, called *As Meigas* in Gallego. It is important to know that *Meigas* are different from witches, who dress in black and don a conical hat, act always with bad intent and can even enter into pacts with the devil. *Meigas* by contrast fit the image of a village woman, capable of divination, enchantments and bad eye but benign in character. If you are in doubt follow the local wisdom '*non creo en nas meigas, pero habelas hainas*' ('I don't believe in *Meigas* but exist they do').

The invasion of a Turkish fleet in December 1617 set off a tragic chain of events that would forever enshrine the plight of the poor in Galicia and the abhorrent powers of the Inquisition. 'A fleet of 11 large corsair Turk and moor ships anchored at Islas Cíes ... using artillery... sent a large number of barges to land at the parish of San Pedro de Domaio...' writes the official in Cangas at the time. The pirates killed, looted and took prisoners, leaving a scene of devastation and many widows. In the years that followed, between 1619 and 1628, many newly impoverished women were prosecuted by the Inquisition for being witches. As members of the family that had first sponsored a church or sanctuary many of the women prosecuted had rights of 'presentation', a legal prerogative to propose the successor to the management of a parish church. The associated income is what drew them to the attention of the authorities, also impoverished but able to use their power to ensure they were left the better off.

Popular culture stands on the side of the women, as can be appreciated through the many local tales and songs that defend the wretched victims. One such song tells the tale of María Soliña, who could not be carried through the streets in the traditional gruesome rituals of the Inquisition as she had died from torture. '*Polos camiños de Cangas, a voz do vento xemía: ai, que soliña quedache, María Soliña*' ('Through the streets of Cangas, the voice of wind screamed; how lonely you were left, María Soliña') is one of the verses in the popular song (included in the compilation '*Os amores libres*' from modern Galician singer Carlos Núñez).

In a modern light-hearted celebration beaches along the northern side of Ría de Vigo, between Barra and Limens, host bonfires on the 21st of July aimed at placating enchantments and other bad spirit that may be affecting you. Tradition requires the participants to jump over embers while three wishes written on paper are thrown into the fire. This plus a meal of sardines and bread topped with ample doses of *queimada* will protect you.

thousands of people. Richly crafted religious sculptures are paraded through the streets, like in many other towns of Spain but with a local character given the particular histories of the images, some of which survived burning by the Turks. The best of these works were crafted by Cerviño, also the author of the magnificent **stone cross of O Hío**.

The **Iglesia de San Salvador de Coiro** is worth a trip along the PO 320 road towards Bueu and Pontevedra. It is a grand building in a beautiful mountain setting with good views Ría de Vigo.

For a view of the native woodlands before pines and eucalyptus were introduced visit the **Carballal de Coiro**, a splendid thicket of oaks, full of the right plants and wildlife which the new planted forests no longer host.

The beach of Rodeira is a major summer tourist destination, because of which building has proceeded apace. Thankfully none of the towers of other less fortunate locations have been erected and so the resort retains charm and a local character.

Casas de Patín in Cangas

RÍA DE VIGO

⚓ Ensenada de Moaña

This stretch of the northern coast of Ría de Vigo is very busy, with a few locations for anchoring. There is intense fishing boat traffic servicing the *bateas* moving to and from Porto do Con, Puerto de Meira and Puerto de Domaio.

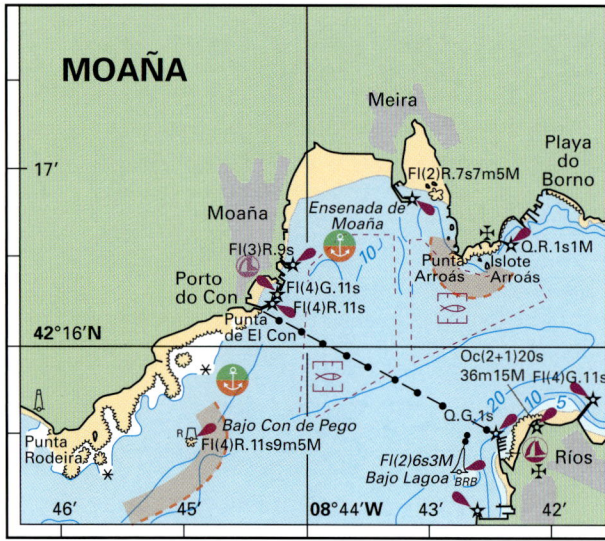

Approach & entrance

The approach to the harbours of Porto do Con, Moaña and Puerto de Meira in Ensenada de Moaña is straightforward if coming from the main channel. The only obstacles are *bateas* in the middle of the bay. The marina at Puerto de Moaña is located to the northeast of the breakwater Fl(3)R.9s with the entrance at the northeast end.

Berthing & facilities

The marina at Moaña opened at the end of 2005 and offers some space for visitors, up to 16m in length. There is no convenient waiting pontoon for new arrivals so communication ahead is advised, otherwise it is a case of finding a free space and then making arrangements with the office.

There is no fuel or a nearby travel lift.

Showers and toilets are a temporary affair while licence for the shore club building is granted.

⚓ Anchorages

The areas around Porto do Con and Puerto de Meira at Ensenada de Moaña can be used for anchoring, subject to appropriate depth and clearance from the main channel for fishing boat traffic. It may also be possible to secure a yacht against the harbour walls.

It is possible to anchor in front of Playa de Vilela, just west of Porto do Con, in around 5m sand, but beware the submerged rock and drying patch.

The anchorage at **Playa do Borno** just east of the factory quays at O Latón and A Borna is a welcome quiet location, with good shelter from W to N winds.

Puerto Deportivo Moaña

- Entrance night and day
- Shelter all directions
- Depth 6m inside marina outer pontoons, very shallow towards the shore side
- Berthing: pontoon mooring, up to 16m
- Visitors' berths 17 (sizes 8 to 16m)
- Planned expansion (2007/8) of additional 15 berths

- ☏ /Fax 986 311140
- VHF Channel 09
- www.moanamar.es

- Water, electricity at the pontoons

- Showers very basic; planned restaurant/social club (2007 subject to planning approval)

Interest

The setting of the wooded hills offers impressive views to the sailor. If you venture inland you will come across rural village locations and get a good taste of what Galicia was like (and still is in more remote regions) before recent development that is so noticeable in the industrial and heavily populated Ría de Vigo.

Ferries to Vigo and to Islas Cíes depart from the quays at Pasaxe. This is a very convenient way to reach Vigo sites without locating your boat at Vigo itself.

For the more adventurous walkers a good trek is to follow the Río Fraga that feeds into the Ensenada de Moaña from behind the sports field. The 6km path towards the **Fraga viewpoint** (400m climb) will reward the walker with very good views as well

RÍA DE VIGO

Puerto Deportivo Moaña

as encounters with horses and other wild animals, and a succession of restored water mills.

The town of Moaña organises a Celtic festival in July, an enjoyable and impressive gathering of musicians and other artists offering performances of the so called 'Celtic' tradition, bagpipe music among others.

Ensenada de Moaña

RÍA DE VIGO

⚓ Domaio

The marina at Ensenada de Mouro is private, run by the La Tella association. There are no facilities or pontoons for visitors. Emergency only.

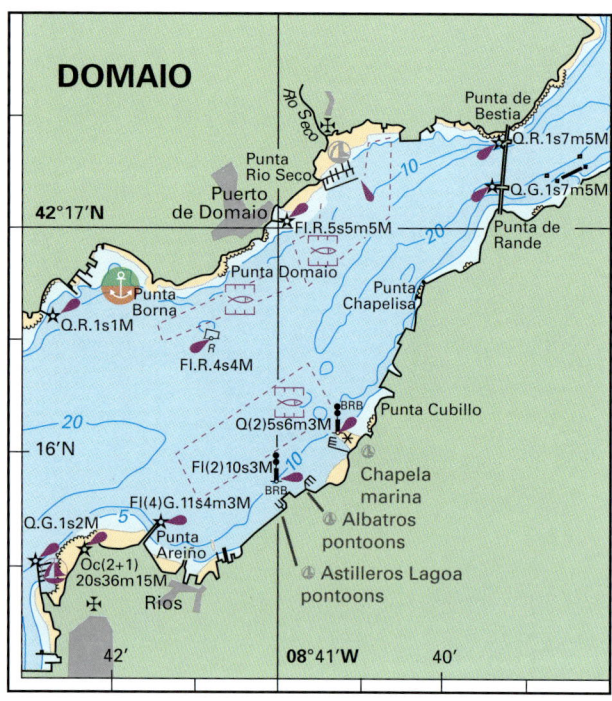

Puerto Deportivo Domaio
- Private marina run by the La Tella association, no access to visitors
- Emergency only

Interest

Faro de Domaio, at 620m the tallest peak of the O Morrazo range, is an impressive backdrop to the northern section of the Ría. From the top of the peak, given good visibility on a clear day, it is possible to see a long way north and south to all the Rías Baixas. A taxi or a hire car is needed to get there.

The entrance to San Simón through the Rande straight is today framed by a motorway bridge but was the scene of the greatest naval battle in the Ría in 1702. An Anglo-Dutch fleet proceeded up towards the entrance, during the international conflict that arose after the succession to the Spanish throne threw the royal family alliances for the Habsburgs (England, Holland and Austria) and the Bourbons (Spain and France) into war. The Anglo-Dutch fleet was greatly superior and easily overran the defences, destroying the forts at the entrance to San Simón. By coincidence a Spanish colonial fleet had just arrived, but its commander threw the treasure into the waters and burnt his ships rather than have either captured.

Rande bridge

Private Domaio pontoons, in Ensenada de Mouro

RÍA DE VIGO

⚓ Ensenada de San Simón

The large bay at the northern end of Ría de Vigo is a haven of peace in a rural setting, sheltered from all winds. The Ensenada is very shallow, as well as being a good 12M from Islas Cíes at the entrance to the Ría. The best time to explore this area is close to neap tides.

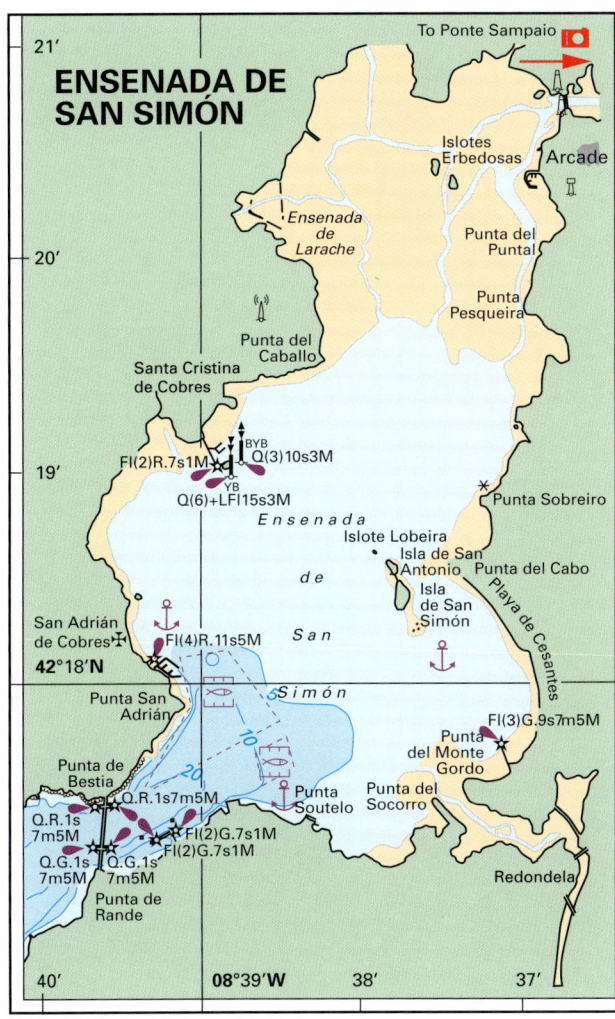

Approach & entrance

The approach to the marina in Ensenada de San Simón is straightforward. After passing under the motorway bridge of Rande sail through the area of *bateas* on the north side. The entrance to the marina faces south.

Berthing & facilities

Puerto Deportivo San Adrián de Cobres is a friendly, quiet marina with excellent showers and a good restaurant. There is no fuel available in the whole of the Ensenada de San Simón because it is a protected area.

Free berthing is provided on the outside of the outer pontoon (clear of piles and therefore straightforward) if coming for a short visit, to eat at the restaurant or to go ashore victualling.

Puerto Deportivo San Adrián de Cobres
- Straightforward entrance day and night
- Electricity and water at pontoons
- ☎ 986 874007 Fax 986 87 41 35
- VHF09
- Good showers and restaurant
- Free berthing (external side of pontoons) if coming for lunch or short victualling stop at village

Puerto Deportivo San Adrián de Cobres

CRUISING GALICIA 251

RÍA DE VIGO

⚓ Anchorages

Ensenada de San Simón is a shallow tidal lagoon. There is plenty of quiet space but a good survey of the anchorage with tide table in hand is necessary to find enough water.

The area around the marina and fishing quay at **San Adrián** is probably the best location in the bay for anchoring, at least 4m deep in mud.

To the south of the bay, the area near **Punta Soutelo** offers sufficient depth, but beware not to approach too far towards Redondela and the shallow sediment banks from Río Maceira.

The space between **Isla de San Simón and Cesantes** should provide at least 2m. There is a quay at Cesantes beach which can be used as a landing spot, the train station is close by.

Further north, the pontoons at Santa Cristina de Cobres (W) and the quay at Arcade are good access points but depth is limited.

Provisioning & eating

Ensenada de San Simón is the more remote area in the ría. There are a few shops and bars at the very small villages of San Adrián (also a restaurant at the clubhouse) and Santa Cristina on the west side, which are also the places where an expedition ashore will be easiest.

The larger villages are on the east side Cesantes and Outero das Penas, on the other side of the railway. The easiest trip is to the quay at the bottom of Playa Cesantes.

Transport

There is a train station at **Outero** das Penas, opposite Isla de San Simón, with transport to and from the island. Trains are on the main Coruña-Vigo line. **Redondela** also has a train station.

Interest

Ensenada the San Simón was the scene of major battle at Ponte Sampaio in June 1809 between Napoleonic troops and a mixture of Galician regulars and volunteers who managed to surprise the French and thus prevent them becoming established in the region. This incident is connected with others in the war that was fought in Spain between a weak monarchy allied to Napoleon and national resistance, brilliantly illustrated in harrowing paintings by Goya. The bridge was also on the route of the Portuguese *Camino de Santiago* (pilgrimage route to Santiago).

Salt and shellfish have been an important part of the local economy. The salt pans stopped being used in the 18th century but the history of Villaboa and Valle de Ulló to the north of the bay is bound with the wealth they brought and the various groups, including the Jesuits, who exploited them. The shellfish industry continues to thrive, the harvest fed by the nutrients brought into the bay by

Ponte Sampaio

the rivers, particularly Río Otaivén at Redondela, hence the large numbers of platforms in that area.

The highlight of the bay is **Isla de San Simón**, the small island to the east of the bay, at low tide almost connected to the shore. The history of the island is long and complex, involving numerous monasteries and orders (Benedictines and Franciscans most prominent), even the Templars, each settlement destroyed by successive attackers, from the moors under Almanzor in the 10th century to the English in the 16th century. A hospital was created in the latter 19th century, which Franco turned into a prison during the civil war then into a training base for his guard. Today the island is being turned into an art centre. The beautiful Castillo de Soutomaior can be visited every day but Monday.

The town of **Redondela** is notorious for its viaducts, one of which is still in use by the main train line. The Easter celebrations of Corpus Christi are renowned for the particular dances that take place (Coca about good vs evil represented by a dragon, Danza de las Espadas and Baile de las Penlas, or angels).

The Carnaval de Cobres, around Ash Wednesday, is known for its processions to the tune of *gaitas* (bagpipes) and Bailes de Madames y Galantes (traditional dances).

For a nature treat visit Parque Natural de Cotorredondo (500m climb) with its Laguna Castiñeiras lake and the Mirador de Cotorredondo, a great spot for views of both Ría de Pontevedra and Ría de Vigo.

Isla de San Simón

Salt, canning, Vigo and the Galician fishing industry

Modern development of the large port of Vigo and the industry of the Ría is connected, with fishing and with Catalan immigrants. Attracted by the abundance of sardines along the Galician coast, numerous enterprising families from Catalonia brought with them Mediterranean technology and know-how that changed fishing in this area for ever, from a low scale subsistence occupation by local fishermen to an industrial mass-production process that could harvest the sea in greater quantity and process fish in volume.

In the 18th century the Catalan families, often in conflict with the local communities because of the change they were introducing, brought with them the *xábega* fishing net, of Arab origin. The net could be up to 600m long and would be gathered from the beach by ox and men, bringing ashore large quantities of sardines. Salting techniques long used in the Mediterranean were used to preserve the fish and thus the link between fishing and immediate consumption was broken, opening the door to a specialised industrial process. Salt had been used for preserving fish in much earlier times by Norse traders who would bring their salted fish to this part of the world and return to northern Europe laden with salt acquired in Galicia and Portugal, but such traditions and trade had been lost before the arrival of the Catalans.

Various salting factories would be opened at Barrios de los Catalanes in El Arenal at Vigo, named so because of the association with the new immigrants to the area. The surnames of many local people tell of their Catalan origins. A local associated industry developed at Arenal, from barrel making to ironwork, dedicated to the packaging and supply of this new long lasting food product.

The Catalans also developed trade, some of the families specialising in the transport of sardines to the Mediterranean and the return of olive oil and wine. The market for this range of goods included not only Spanish regions but also France and Italy.

In the decade of 1880 canneries emerged, set up by illustrious families like Barreras i Casellas (in Alameda), Massó Palau (Bueu) and Hermanos Curbera (Vigo) whose businesses survive to this day. The key to the new leap in productivity was the Nantes canning process, a technique and machinery imported from Brittany and put to use in these new enterprises. Durox presses together with tin from Bilbao and the UK were used to manufacture the tins which, after being filled with the preserved product, would be soldered shut by hand. Some of the factories could produce more than 1,000 cans per day, a revolution in efficiency.

Turgalicia

By the early 20th century many new salting and canning factories were serving an ever growing international market, such was the value of food that could be stored long term, vital for maritime fleets and useful at home.

Advances in boat size were brought in by use of the design of the Santander *traiña* at first to lenghts of 12m. The first shipworks opened in Arenal at the end of 19th century, producing a 20m boat powered by British steam engines and capable of 8 knots, which became known as the *Vapor de Vigo* (Vigo Steamer) and was even used during the first world war as a coastal patrol boat in France. The new boat revolutionised the industry once again, this time extending the distances that could be reached by the fishing fleet. The combination of better boats and improved techniques such as pairing gave an enormous impetus to the whole industrial cycle after the end of the first world war, to a point where more than 5,000 people were employed locally salting and canning, supplying more than 60,000 tons of product to Europe and the Americas from Vigo. From 1927 the introduction of steel trawlers opened the rich seas in SW Ireland to Galician fishermen, expeditions which continue today in the midst of much argument about EEC quotas.

The Vigo boatyards continued extending the capabilities of ever larger boats, from 1940 capable of taking part in cod fishing at the Grand Banks off Newfoundland. There are many stories in the Canadian and US shores which intertwine the local communities with Gallego fishermen, many of whom stayed ashore while others became part of the yearly tragic losses in the treacherous conditions of the Banks.

In the 1960s freezing on board was introduced by pioneer Pepe Fernández supported by Conservera Massó, a technique that would change the techniques used by the worldwide fishing industry. His initial four boats exploited South America and South Africa but the 100 strong fleet of huge company Pescanova now fishes in all the world, supported by a large array of processing plants along the shores the Rías. The frozen seafood companies are a distinct feature of Vigo and Marín but can be seen anywhere along the coast of Galicia.

RIA DE VIGO

⚓ Vigo

Vigo is the largest city in Galicia, a major port and industrial centre which takes advantage of the shelter provided to the Ría by Islas Cíes and the more benign climate of its southerly location. There are several marinas around the city and a wide variety of shops, equipment outlets and attractions.

As a busy city, Vigo combines a heavy industrial feel with old town charm. Not all of Vigo is pretty and you can't escape the dominating presence of cranes and large industrial buildings. This is part of the city's character. Real Club Náutico de Vigo (RCN) partly isolates you in the marina whilst still being close to the centre of town, but some people prefer to be based elsewhere and visit Vigo using the many transport links available.

Approach & entrance

From Ría Pontevedra to Marina Davila Sport:

- Follow the same directions as would be used to enter Ría de Vigo (see Ría de Vigo introduction), through a wide, well marked (lit) channel free of all dangers apart from possible shipping movements. Pass south of the channel marker off Punta Subrido Fl(4)R.10s

- Leave red lateral marks Fl.R.5s and Fl(2)R.7s, Bajo Salgueirón Fl(2+1)R.15s, Fl(3)R. off Salaiños, Piedra Borneira, Canagas and Punta Rodeira respectively, close to port

- When at Punta Rodeira Fl(3)R lateral mark head for the marina breakwater Fl(2)G.7s (140°), the seaward end of which is marked by Fl(2+1)G.15s. The entrance in on the northeast side of the marina

- Beware commercial shipping movements at night obscured by background lights and harbour walls.

From the direction of Baiona to Marina Davila Sport and starting from the west cardinal mark Q(9)15s off Las Serralleiras:

- Aim for the starboard hand mark off Isla de Toralla Fl(3)G.9s on a bearing of 50°. Stay in more than 30m. Note front and rear transits Iso.2s Oc 4s on the starboard bow and take care of shipping astern

- Head towards the starboard hand mark off Isla de Toralla Fl(3)G.9s when it comes into sight to the northeast. Stay in more than 20m

- At Cabo de Mar Fl(4)G.14s, the lights of the shore facilities will be clearly visible. Follow a track that takes you parallel to the outer quay (1M, 60°)

- Head for the marina breakwater Fl(2)G.7s (160°), the seaward end of which is marked by Fl(2+1)G.15s. The entrance in on the northeast side of the marina.

Note that in daylight Monte de la Guía Oc(2+1)20s with its church on the summit is a useful target to guide the navigator up the Ría.

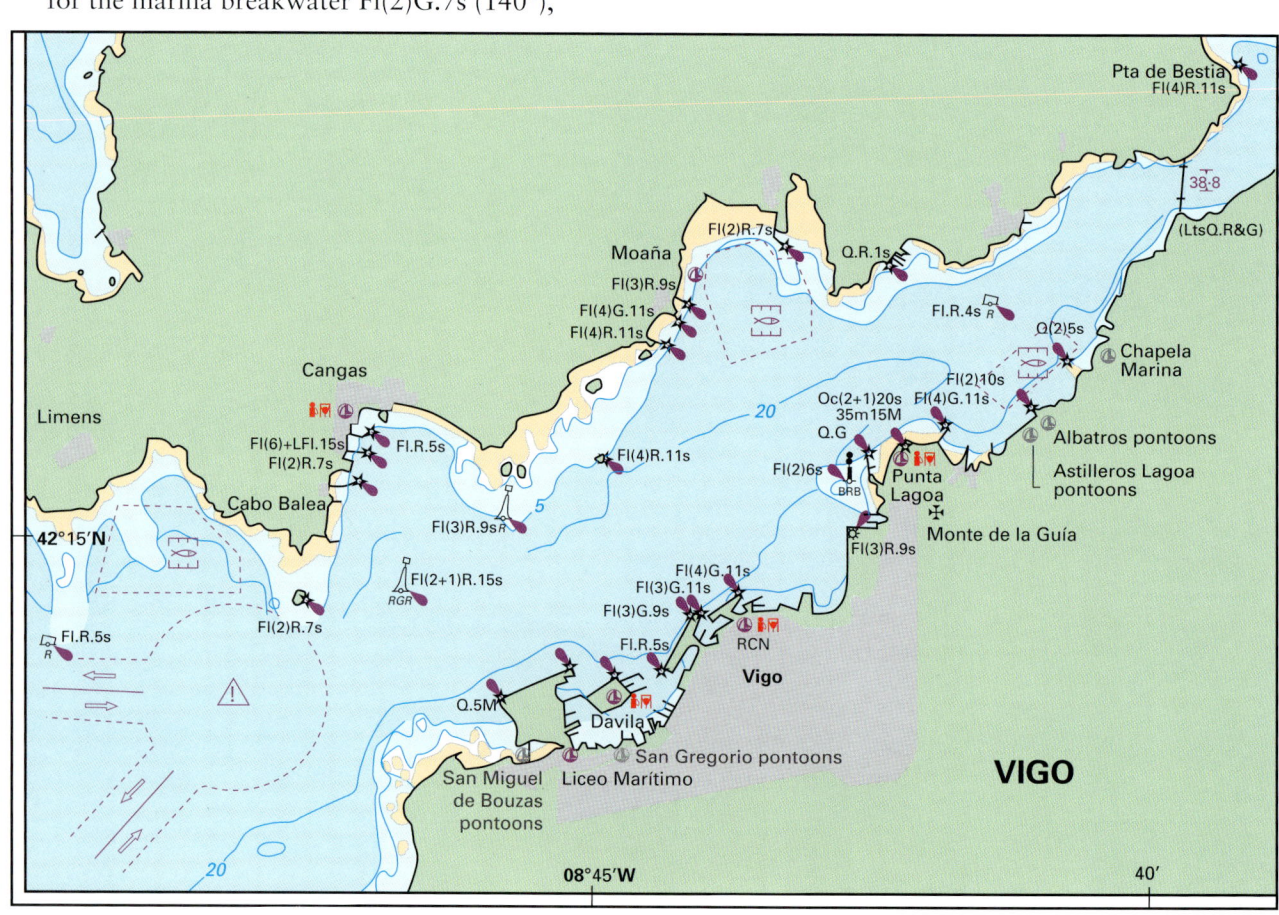

254 CRUISING GALICIA

RÍA DE VIGO

Vigo Bouzas, Liceo Marítimo

Vigo centre from RCN marina

Berthing & facilities

Vigo is a large city and offers several options for berthing in a Marina. With the exception of Punta Lago all are located in busy commercial port areas, close to the city but among heavy equipment, buildings and shipping.

To the south of the city, in the Bouzas harbour area, the old established Liceo Marítimo is a basic marina in close proximity to the town area. Davila Sport is much better equipped but it is quite a walk to get to the city's facilities.

Right in the centre of Vigo, Real Club Náutico de Vigo is the illustrious nautical club of the city. The location of RCN is perfect for the best of the sights in Vigo as well as being close to the railway station.

In the north of Vigo, Puerto Punta Lagoa is very new (2006) and located in a very industrial neighbourhood but next to the pleasant Monte de la Guía with its commanding views over the ría. The disadvantage is distance with the City being 2 miles away.

See the individual sections that follow for details of local marinas and facilities.

Repairs & Chandleries

Vigo is one of the best locations in Galicia for solving problems with a boat. The city's main industries are fishing and shipbuilding, so there are numerous locations for obtaining spares and many mechanics, electricians and riggers that can be called upon. The best way to find expertise is through the marinas, who will have good knowledge of the best people around.

For spares, Vigo has big *Efectos Navales* stores (marine supplies) which are among the best in Galica. These counter-served shops are veritable pandora boxes of bits. Although some more specialised equipment may still need to be ordered, you are very unlikely to walk away without what you need. Some of the more extensive are Betanzos, Enriel and Efectos Navales Fernández Vila in Bouzas (south), Efectos Navales Fernández y Comesaña and Efectos Navales Corona in Vigo centre.

Provisioning & eating

Vigo is a large city with an extensive array of supermarkets and groceries. As always the best can be had at the municipal markets (O Berbés very near the central harbour area), but almost any local supermarket will sell good, fresh produce.

Restaurants and bars are numerous in Vigo. The best areas in the centre are the old town (*Casco Viejo*), just south of the harbour area where Real Club Náutico is located, and the more modern planned streets around Plaza Compostela and the *Alameda*.

Further afield there are good places in the Samil beach area. While the supply of classy restaurants in Bouzas or the northern part of the city is short, there are plenty of bars where tapas will be good.

Interest

Vigo is the largest Galician town, a major economic centre which has grown to almost 800,000 people driven by the expansion of the fishing industry and the port, now an international trans-shipment destination. Its history is complex, although humble in origins and only gaining ascendancy when Spanish King Philip II promoted it. Even then the town barely contained 1,000 people.

The protection offered to the Ría de Vigo by Islas Cíes is the reason why the harbour developed. but it is also the reason why Vigo has been a target for **maritime attacks** over the centuries. Francis Drake raged the port in 1589, a Turkish fleet in 1617, the Portuguese in 1665, an Anglo-Dutch fleet in 1702 culminating in the notorious battle of the Rande strait, the English again in 1709, while in 1809 the Galicians, headed by Don Pablo Morillos, battled here to be the first in Spain to eject the Napoleonic forces. Visit the very interesting **Museo del Mar** in Alcabre (sited in an old cannery) to gain more insight into this tumultuous past.

The history of development of Vigo as an industrial centre and a major port is intertwined with the salting, canning and later freezing of **fish**. There is evidence of salting along the shore of the ría by small enterprise that supplied ships. These industries, centred on fishing, grew and led the world from the 18th century, when Catalan families established pioneering practices. In latter times the Pescanova phenomenon revolutionised treatment

CRUISING GALICIA

RÍA DE VIGO

Vigo

- A Coruña 150km, Santiago 90km, Ourense 110km, Pontevedra 35km
- ✈ Aeropuerto de Vigo: frequent domestic flights to major Spanish cities (Madrid, Barcelona best for onward connections)
- 🚌 Bus station: Av. de Madrid, 57 ☏986 373411
- ⇌ Train station: Plaza de la Estación (along Rúa Urzáiz)

- Ferries to Islas Cíes from Estación Marítima in the centre

- 🛒 Markets:
  - Mercado de O Berbés, Rúa Teófilo Llorente (centre, west of Tourist Office)
  - Fish at Rúa Pescadores (centre, old town, level Real Club Náutico)
  - Mercado Municipal, La Sierra 5 (just east of Plaza de América)
  - Mercado as Pradesas, Rúa Espedregada (between Castelao and Florida near Plaza de América)
  - Mercado at Bouzas, Rúa Pescadores

- 🛒 Supermarkets:
  - El Corte Inglés, Avda Gran Vía 25 (between Plaza España and railway station)
  - Mercadona, Mercado as Pradesas, Rúa Espedregada
  - Gadis, Rúa Rosalía de Castro 58 (centre, north of railway station)
  - Froiz, Torrecedeira 13 (centre, near Puerto Berdés)
  - Froiz, Bouzas, at Mercado building

- 🛒 Hypermarkets:
  - Alcampo, Avda de Madrid (near Plaza España)
  - Carrefour, Travesia de Vigo 202

- ℹ Tourist office: Cánovas de Castillo 22 ☏986 430577

- ✕ Restaurants - very many all over the city, for best areas:
  - *Casco Viejo*: the old town area in the centre immediately below Real Club Náutico
  - Plaza Compostela, Alameda, Areal: the planned streets going east from the old town area
  - Bouzas: limited, smaller establishments
  - Samil: the beach area to the west of the city, below Bouzas

- ⚓ **Bouzas** Chandlers - Efectos Navales (marine supplies):
  - Efectos Navales Fernández Vila, Eduardo Cabello 49 ☏ 986 231 049 (behind church)
  - Efectos Navales Jesús Betanzos, Eduardo Cabello 51
  - Enriel, Avda. Beiramar 217-219, ☏ 986 21 35 35 / 986 21 45 46
  - Marina Davila Sport ☏ 986 244612

- ⚓ **Centre** Chandlers - Efectos Navales (marine supplies):- Fernández y Comesaña, S.A. (puerto Berbés), Avda. Orillamar, 47, ☏ 986 204012
  - Efectos Navales Corona, Avda Beiramar 25, ☏ 986 233142 / 986 233622, info@coronavigo.com

- Banks, chemists, other shops: numerous in all areas

- ✚ Hospitals and medical centres (all near Plaza España)
  - Centro Médico el Castro Vigo, Rúa Manuel Olivie 11 ☏ 986 411466
  - Hospital Xeral (General Hospital), Rúa Pizarro 22 ☏ 986 816000
  - Policlínico de Vigo, Rúa Salamanca 5 ☏ 986 413566

of fish at sea using freezing techniques. The best insight into this world is given at the lovely museum in Bueu (Ría de Pontevedra) but you will sense it in Vigo, indeed you cannot escape from it.

Vigo became a town in the 12th century, before it was a scatter of uncoordinated villages. Noble charters and adventures passed, Vigo became one of the fastest growing cities in Europe during the 20th century, multiplying its population by 15 on the back of intense **industrialisation**. In this town of superlatives the port was a major point for emigration for Galicians escaping the poverty of their region in search of better luck in the Americas. You can see how this related to the city by the sheer amount of streets whose names are dedicated to countries of Latin America.

Vigo acquired its own university and developed its own dynamic impetus, much of it channelled through the combative Celta de Vigo football club. Its increasing importance has not, however, allowed Vigo to rest the seat of power from Pontevedra, the provincial capital, an issue that occasionally encourages a bit of city to city friendly verbal sparring.

Vigo has many **art and cultural centres** that are worth visiting. For maritime history and context visit Museo del Mar. Modern art is celebrated at the Centro de Arte Contemporáneo, and the foundations of Caixagalicia (old Fraga cinema at Rúa Uruguay) and Caixanova put on different collections of themed or individual artist works.

Rúa das Cesterías

Tortilla de patatas

One of the universal Spanish pinchos or tapas, served all over the country. Galicia may claim it as the first European region where potatoes were introduced from the Americas. Simple to cook but skill is required half way through the process to turn the omelette over.

Ingredients

One onion, cut into small pieces
Olive oil
6 medium size potatoes, cut into thin slices
5 eggs, beaten
Optional chorizo, small chunks
Large plate/wooden platter to turn omelette over

Preparation

Fry the onion and potato together in olive oil. Cook with lid on to almost steam the potatoes.

Remove the potatoes and onion from the pan and drain oil. Mix with the egg (and chorizo if using it).

Add the egg and potato mixture into the pan, perhaps adding a drizzle of oil, turning up the heat for a short period to achieve a quick base to the omelette, which should slide freely in the pan. Reduce the heat and cook for 5 minutes.

Now place the large plate or wooden platter over the pan and turn over. You need to be determined and quick, otherwise the uncooked egg (and hot oil) will spill, possibly over your exposed forearm.

Cook for another five minutes and remove, repeating the turning over procedure which you have now mastered. Lista!

Serve hot or cold, in portions, small pieces or with any other food that catches your fancy. Best with a beer and lot of friends.

RÍA DE VIGO

Casco Viejo, centre

Museo Municipal de Quiñones de León holds an extensive collection of Celtic and Roman art as well as some more modern Galician works.

Museo de La Palabra in Samil is a striking slate and glass building that affords good views of the ría, holding an intriguing introduction into the science of language.

For **atmosphere** head to the old town (*Casco Viejo*) right in the centre, an area of narrow streets with traditional Galician granite and galleried balconies. See the fish stalls at Rúa de Pescadeiros, where the *Ostreras* sell oysters brought from Arcade in Esenada de San Simón. Also see the basket making shops at Rúa Cesterías (Praza da Constitución), a good place to buy one of the traditional Vigo crafts.

To the east of the old town, Praza Compostela is the perfect place to join in with the local promenading, everybody dressed to impress while strolling slowly along. If you tire plenty of cafeterías will let you sit for hours without missing a bit of the action.

Further south, the old historic part of **Bouzas** near the harbour area around the park (*Alameda*) retains the character it had as a local harbour before it was absorbed into Vigo. Restoration is underway to bring back some of the old buildings from a state of disrepair.

The beach area of **Samil** is where *Vigueses* get away from it all in the summer, but it has atmosphere all year round.

In the city itself go to **Parque do Castro** for the views. **Monte del Castro** within it displays anchors from the galleons that were sank at the Battle of Rande. To the north, **Monte de la Guía** is worth journeying to for good views and to stand at the location that is used by most boats to guide themselves towards Vigo.

For shopping, the streets with the boutiques and large stores are Calle del Príncipe and Gran Vía, where the ubiquitous Corté Inglés is located. If you need giant shopping malls go no further than Praza Elíptica or As Camelias (Praza de América).

As to popular events, there is no shortage as anywhere in Spain. Carnival involves a ceremonial burial of the sardine, Procesión del Cristo de la Victoria is a massive religious procession the first Sunday of August, Bouzas sports a major fireworks competition in July and the celebrations of San Roque take place on 15 July. The best approach is to visit the Tourist Office to find out what is happening the week you are in Vigo.

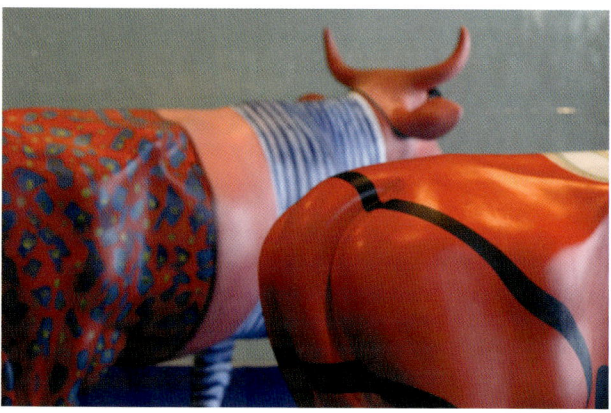

Fun decoration, Museo de la Palabra

Pulpo a feira

One of the classic Galician dishes, served as a *tapa* in every bar and restaurant, is Pulpo a feira, the delicious plate of octopus, potatoes and pimentón.

Ingredients

For six people you need:

1 octopus 2kg, fully thawed if previously frozen
Olive oil
0.5kg potatoes, boiled or steamed in the water from the octopus
Pimentón, both sweet and spicy (paprika can be used as a substitute)
Salt to taste

Preparation

Octopus meat is very tough, and was traditionally softened by whipping the dead animal against the harbour wall. This could be the right spectacle to perform if you have managed to catch one, by dangling a string and some bait down into the water. For a more discrete approach bash the meat with a kitchen mallet or, better still, freeze it, a process that stretches and breaks the meat fibres.

Turgalicia

'Scaring' the octopus

Place sufficient water in a large pan. When boiling, dip the octopus whole in the water for a minute and take it out for another minute. Repeat this process 3 or 4 times until the octopus has fully curled its tentacles ('scaring the octopus' or *espantar o pulpo* in Galician). Then boil for 30 minutes.

Take out the octopus and cut the tentacles into bite site pieces using scissors.

Mix with the boiled potatoes, drizzle with olive oil and pimentón and serve hot with *pan gallego*.

RÍA DE VIGO

Vigo: North

⚓ Puerto Punta Lagoa

Puerto Punta Lagoa is a new (2006) marina, equipped to a high standard. It is located some distance away from the centre of Vigo but it provides a quieter base for a visiting yacht. Shore access to the marina is poor (road is planned for upgrade) and there is little local interest.

Approach & entrance

To reach **Puerto Punta Lagoa**:

- Use Monte de la Guía Oc(2+1)20s as a guide up the Ría. Continue north after leaving the isolated danger mark for Bajos Lagos Fl(2)6s to starboard
- The entrance to Puerto Lagoa is marked by Q.G.1s, at the start of a channel marked by closely spaced Port hand beacons that bound the northeast side
- Beware rocky shallow bank to port on entrance.

Berthing & facilities

Puerto Punta Lagoa is modern, spacious and well equipped for service of yachts. The facilities are excellent and can accommodate any size boat, with good workshops for maintenance and space ashore for wintering.

There is very little ashore and transport from the marina is either a long walk into town (through a

Vigo - Punta Lagoa   42°16'N 08°42'W

Puerto Punto Lagoa
- Entrance night and day
- Shelter all directions
- Depth minimum 4m
- Berthing: pontoon mooring, up to 24m
- Visitors' berths 25 (from a total of 350)

- ☏ 986 411 711 Fax: 986 410 096
- VHF Channel 09
- pablo.yatesport@telefonica.net

- Water, electricity at the pontoons
- ⛽ Fuel at pontoon by travel lift (cul de sac)
- ⚓ Chandlery: some supplies at Yatesport
- 🔧 Repairs: local workshop and extensive services
- 🏗 70-ton travel lift

- Showers, toilets good
- Excellent restaurant

Punta Lagoa marina entrance

Fuel and travel lift

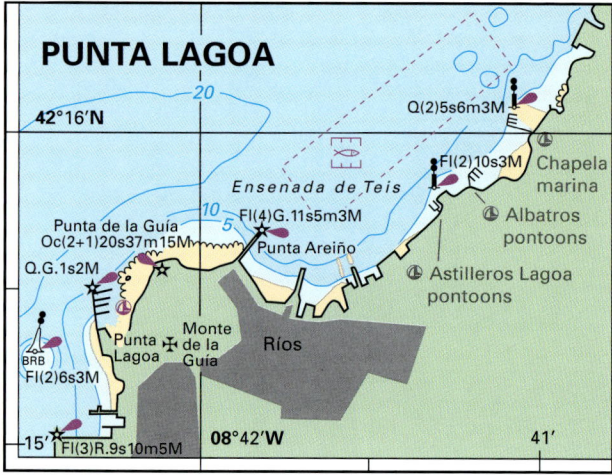

very industrial neighbourhood) or taxi arranged through the helpful staff at Yatesport. The marina is close to the pleasant Monte de la Guía with its commanding views over the ría.

There are a number of potential pontoons along the coast north of Puerto Punta Lagoa, which may accommodate a visiting yacht in an emergency, but they are all private, have locked gates to the shore and are not geared to receive visitors. The area is very shallow and it is accessed through the channel between the *batea* grid and the shore so good care is needed with navigation. It is likely that only the outer pontoons offer sufficient depth and they will be exposed to north winds.

For the pontoons for Astilleros y Construcciones Lagoa at CNO Espineiro (TEIS) make contact on ☏ 986 374305. For the Chapela pontoons contact Círculo Cultural de Chapela Marina.

Provisioning & eating

There is very little near the marina, but there are some shops in the local neighbourhood (ask marina for directions).

The restaurant at the marina is excellent, popular with Vigo society. You may need to dress up.

Monte de la Guía church

View north from Monte de la Guía

RÍA DE VIGO

Vigo: Centre

⌛ Real Club Náutico de Vigo

The Real Club Náutico is located right in the centre of Vigo, close to the old town and associated attractions, so it is a very convenient destination if a berth can be organised. Manoeuvring inside the marina is difficult, with space being very tight.

Access to supermarkets, chandlers and repair specialists is excellent, and the club facilities are very good. Vigo centre is very interesting and well worth exploring.

Approach & entrance

To reach **Real Club Náutico de Vigo** from the west:

- Sail past the Berbés and cruise liner docks (*Transatlánticos*), leaving FL(3)G.9s to starboard
- Turn into RCN Vigo immediately after the north corner of the cruise liner dock marked by Fl(4) G.11s
- Beware shipping or tug movements.

| Vigo - Centre | 42°14'N 08°44'W |

Real Club Náutico de Vigo
- Entrance night and day
- Shelter all directions
- Very tight for manoeuvring inside, use fuel pontoon on entrance if unclear about berth
- Depth minimum 2m inside marina, 12m harbour entrance
- Berthing: bow/stern to mooring, up to 22m
- Visitors' berths 25
- ☎ 986 449694 Fax 986 449695
- VHF Channel 09
- puertoderportivo@rcnauticovigo.com
  puertocnv@yahoo.com
- Water, electricity at the pontoons
- ⛽ Fuel pontoon at entrance
- 🔧 Repairs: engine mechanic and electrician
- 🏗 32-ton travel lift
- Showers, laundry being renovated 2007
- Restaurant in the marina building
- Sailing club
- Large expansion plan by Vigo city will surround RCN with new port complex including 600 berths (2007-09)

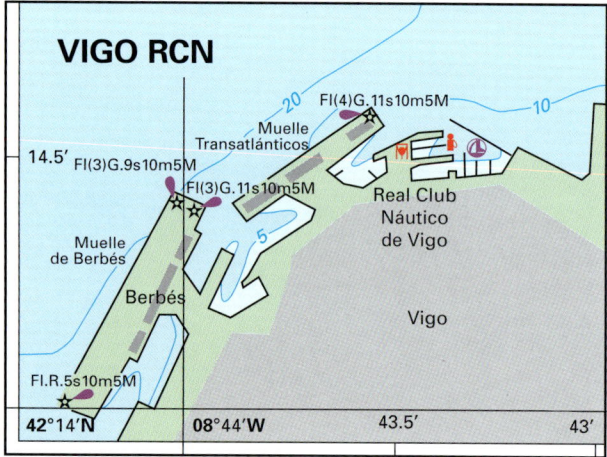

RCN marina, Vigo centre

262 CRUISING GALICIA

RÍA DE VIGO

Berthing & facilities

Real Club Náutico is an established marina, fully equipped and capable of accommodating large yachts. Manoeuvring inside the marina is not easy as space is tight. Unless a clear plan has been described and understood it is best to be accompanied by the *marinero* in his dinghy or tie up at the fuel pontoon on entrance.

Showers, toilets and laundry are in the central area behind the office. An expansion being planned during 2007 is aimed at the renovation of the club as well as growth of activities in other areas, including participating in the large port extension being planned by Vigo city in 2007-09.

There are extensive *Efectos Navales* stores (chandlers) nearby. See the main Vigo introduction listings page for details.

Provisioning & eating

The RCN is right in the centre of Vigo, so access to the old town restaurants and shops is very easy. Mercado de Berbés to the west of the centre is a very good market.

The old town is better for character but the more modern shops are in the area east in the streets that run parallel to Plaza de Compostela.

Local Interest

You are in the centre and very close to the old town, so close to the majority of Vigo's highlights. See the main Vigo introduction listings page for details.

Grand plans for marina expansion

Vigo old town

CRUISING GALICIA 263

RÍA DE VIGO

Vigo: Bouzas

⚓ **Marina Davila Sport**

⚓ **Liceo Marítimo de Bouzas**

The Bouzas area is home to the very new Marina Davila Spot and the more established Liceo Marítimo. They are both quite some distance from the main highlights of Vigo. Marina Davila is situated in the industrial docks and a good 10 minutes walk from Bouzas, but there are plenty of facilities and support for sailors on site. Liceo has more limited facilites but is close to the local area of Bouzas.

Approach & entrance

Refer to the start of the section on Vigo for a night approach to Marina Davila Sport. To approach Marina Davila Sport and Liceo Marítimo in daylight proceed as follows:

- Use Monte de la Guía as a guide up the Ría
- Turn SE past the Freeport area north of Bouzas
- Marina Davila pontoons are east of the port warehouses
- Liceo Marítimo is beyond Davila, right inside Dársena de Bouzas.

Berthing & facilities

Davila Sport is a new marina, attached to one of the main harbour docks, Dársena de Bouzas. The pontoons were laid in 2005 and are very generous in proportion. There is plenty of space for manoeuvring inside and the fuel dock is conveniently located at a pontoon outside and away from obstacles, attached to the south wall. Shower and other facilities are good and there is a convenient chandlery as well as a workshop for repairs on site. These advantages compensate for the remote location of the marina, a good 10 minute walk from the local Bouzas area.

Liceo Marítimo is an old established harbour, situated right inside Dársena de Bouzas. There are some pontoons and buoys but the majority of

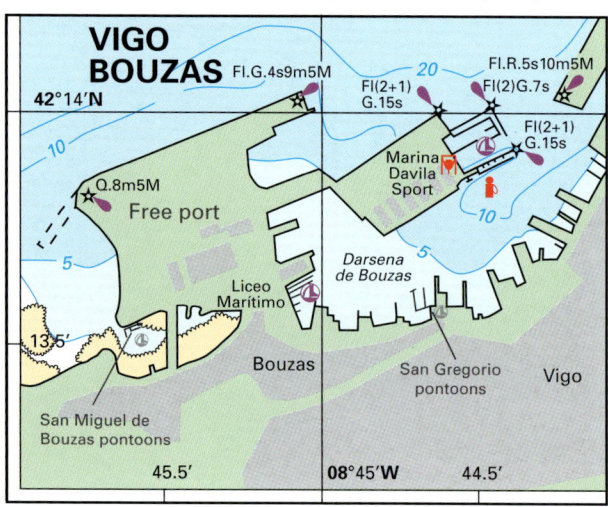

Vigo - Bouzas 42°14'N 8°45'W

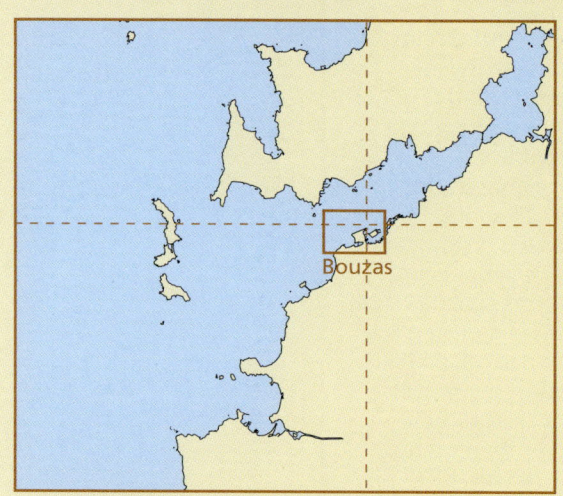

Marina Davila Sport
- Entrance night and day
- Shelter all directions
- Depth minimum 10m inside marina
- Berthing: pontoon mooring, up to 28m
- Visitors' berths 20
- ☎ 986 244612 Fax 986 206809
- VHF Channel 09
- marina@davilasport.es
- www.davilasport.es
- Water, electricity at the pontoons
- ⛽ Fuel at pontoon on south dock wall
- ⚓ Small chandlery
- 🔧 Repairs: mechanic workshop in marina
- 🏗 70-ton travel lift
- Showers. toilets good
- Secure marina for winter storage, space ashore for hard standing

Liceo Marítimo de Bouzas
- Entrance night and day
- Shelter all directions
- Depth minimum 3m inside marina
- Berthing: pontoon and stern-to mooring, up to 10m to length recommended; visitors normally at buoy berths (+ stern line, any length)
- Epansion plan for 2007/08
- ☎ 986 232442 Fax: 986 239955
- VHF Channel 09
- info@liceobouzas.com
- Water, electricity at the pontoons
- Showers, toilets good
- Restaurant and Gym in the Liceo clubhouse
- Sailing and diving club

RÍA DE VIGO

Bouzas market

berths are stern-to or bow-to and space is tight, so a first arrival may be troublesome. Visitors are normally accommodated in the buoys at the entrance, where a stern line is also provided to keep the boats from swinging. An expansion project during 2007/08 will extend the pontoon berths, removing all buoyed mooring. The marina is right next to the Bouzas part of Vigo which has local charm.

Chandlers are in ample supply, head up the main avenue past the church towards the market for several well stocked *Efectos Navales*. See the main Vigo introduction listings page for details.

Provisioning & eating

Bouzas is a local centre with shops and some bars and restaurants in the old streets surrounding the Alameda square. The market building, which includes a supermarket within, is an excellent stop for provisions.

Local Interest

Bouzas has character around the old little area behind the church, but it needs renovation and it is surrounded by industrial buildings from the many local shipbuilding and shipping companies. There is work in progress to lift the character of the many traditional Galician buildings around Alameda.

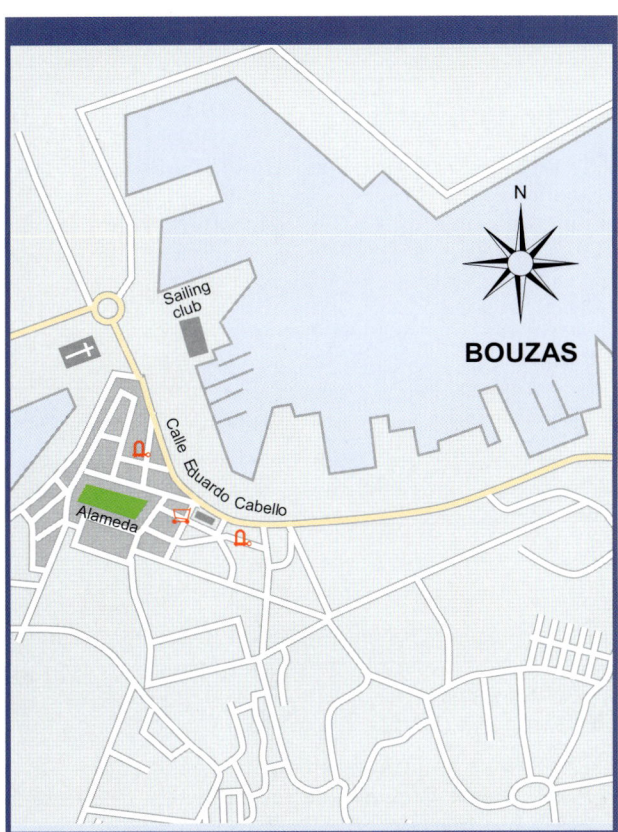

Marina Davila Sport fuelling berth

Marina Davila Sport

CRUISING GALICIA 265

RÍA DE VIGO

Samil, Toralla, Monte Faro

This stretch of coast between Vigo and Baiona is generally unwelcoming for yachts, due to the steep bottom and the numerous rocky patches, but there is an area near the island where anchoring is possible.

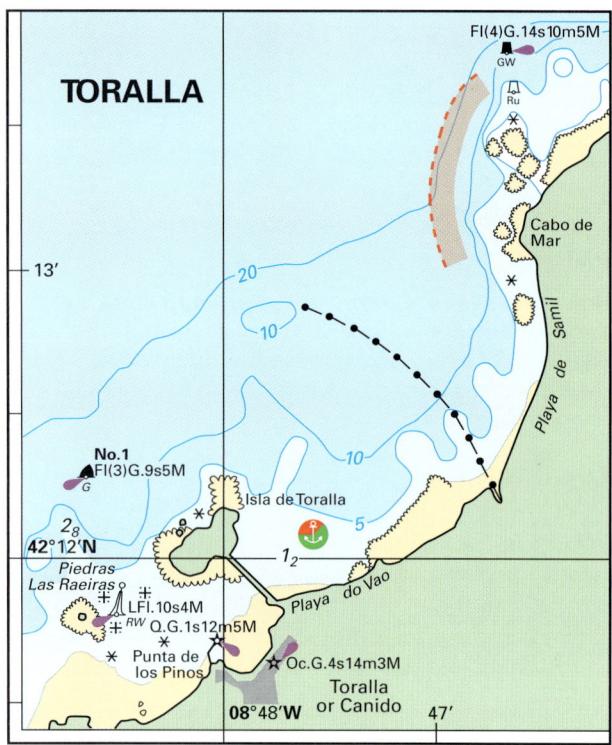

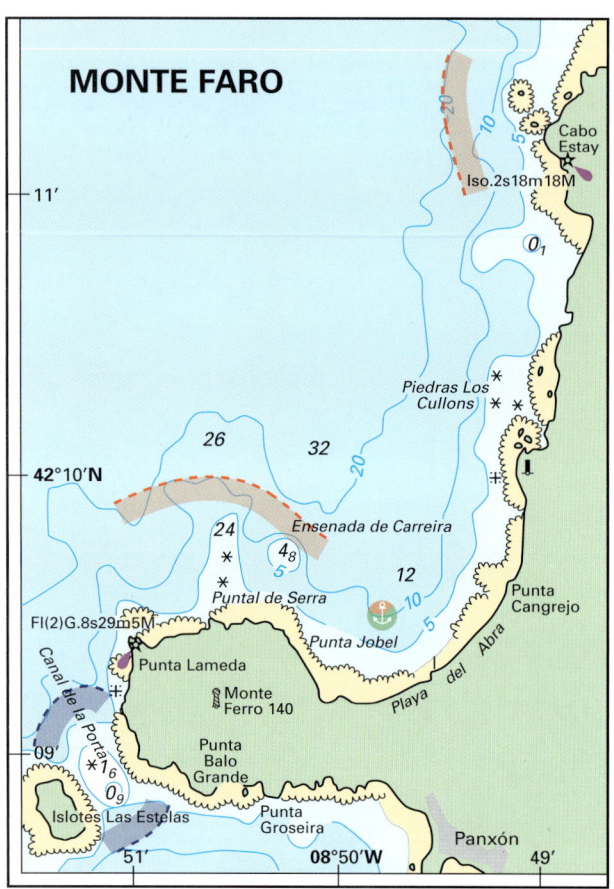

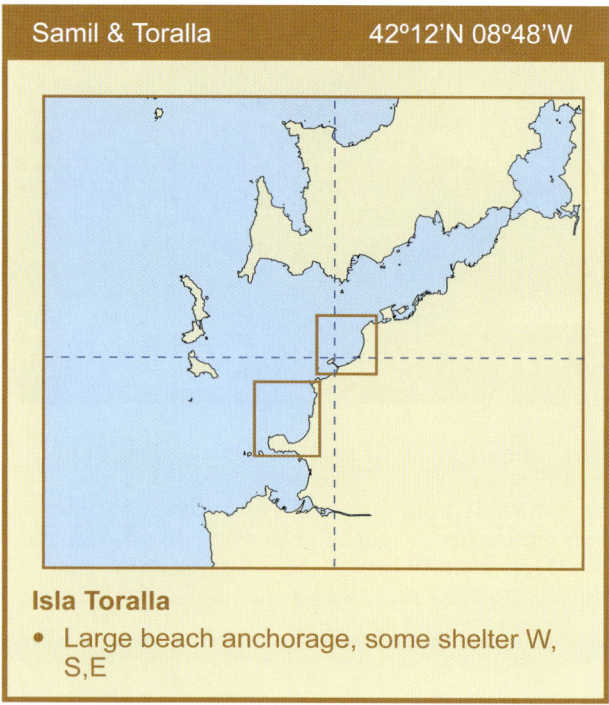

Isla Toralla
- Large beach anchorage, some shelter W, S, E

⚓ Isla de Toralla

The area due east of Isla de Toralla can be a reasonable anchorage if space is available among the many small boats. The spot offers shelter from NE to W winds.

Puerto de Canido is a small fishing harbour, shallow and crowded with small boats, not suitable for yachts.

Interest

The beaches are very popular with surfers because of the swell that easily builds up, particularly at Playa del Abra.

Playa do Samil and Playa Vao are attractive but become crowded in the summer.

Isla de Toralla is a pleasant, quiet location, but it is privately owned and half of it occupied by the unsightly apartment complex tower. The beaches on the island are open to the public.

The Verbum building halfway along the Samil seaside avenue is dedicated to linguistics, a unique focus for a museum. It is very well organised and captures the local keen interest in the regional language, but it may not be easy if you do not have any knowledge of Spanish.

Playa do Vao and Isla Toralla

Columbus, America and Baiona

La Pinta, arriving in Baiona on 1 March 1493, was the first of Columbus' ships to return to Spain after discovering America. Under the command of Martín Alonso Pinzón, the landing place was familiar because the pilot on board, Cristobal García Sarmiento, was a local man, but it is likely that *La Pinta* reached the Ría on the verge of disaster. The boat had suffered damage and was further battered by storms near the Azores, drifting from there for almost two weeks.

La Pinta is credited with the first sighting of land in America, being the faster of Columbus's three ships. Rodrigo de Triana, from Seville, was the man to shout 'land' in the Bahamas on the fateful 12th of October 1492 and was aboard when *La Pinta* returned home.

Among the first of his tasks Pinzón took care to notify the King and Queen of the discovery, an action that prompted immediate decrees forbidding anyone to travel to the new territories without royal authority.

The discovery of America set off a period of enormous expansion for Spain and Portugal. The two countries laid claim to their position as maritime discoverers and were given rights by the Pope in the Treaty of Tordesillas. The treaty divided the undiscovered World in two along a line of longitude passing through Brazil and the Philipines: the west for Spain, the east for Portugal.

For the next two centuries Spanish adventurers were given licence to explore new territories along the Americas and the Pacific, with rights to exploit the lands given by the Spanish Crown. Navigators were required to hand their log books and surveys to the Casa de Contratación in Seville, an organisation set up to co-ordinate passage information into the official chart (the *Padrón Real*) which detailed the geography of the new lands. This period saw huge advances in the theory of navigation, moving charts from the Portolan style of coastal descriptions to a lat/long base, albeit without an accurate method to establish longitude at sea. Among other advances observations of the compass variation became important part of passages.

Spain became the empire of the day, using its new wealth to dominate significant parts of Europe. Carlos I and Philip II controlled the Low Countries and fought wars to keep unruly cities and the German princes under control, ultimately bringing religion to the power struggle - Protestant opposition against Catholic rule.

Columbus made four voyages to the new lands. Initially he was appointed Admiral and ruler of his discoveries, but he was gradually usurped and lost seniority.

The landing of *La Pinta* is celebrated each year in Baiona during the Festa da Arribada, the first weekend in March.

RÍA DE VIGO

⚓ Baiona

Ría de Baiona is one of the classic destinations for yachts, including those crossing the Atlantic as it is one of the last southern fuelling and victualling harbours on the mainland. Located at the southern end of Ría de Vigo, the bay offers good shelter at the marinas and good access to the pretty, traditional town.

Baiona has retained its charm, resisting the high rise development prevalent in other sections of the Galician coast, but it is touristy, particularly in the summer when the better off from Vigo and Spain make it their base for the holidays. Property prices in this stretch of coast are among the highest in Spain.

Approach & entrance

The entrance to Ría de Baiona is dramatic, exposed to swell and with extensive reefs both to port and starboard. The shore marks can be difficult to identify in daylight or poor visibility, but the channel is well marked with lit buoys. It is at least 0.5M wide, which makes entry possible in all conditions. The final approach and berthing is sheltered from the west, has plenty of manoeuvring room and comprehensive facilities when you get in. Puerto Deportivo de Baiona is likely to have spare berths, even in the holiday season.

Approach into Baiona from the south and west:

- Stay in more than 50m of water until past Cabo Silleiro. Note the two yellow buoys SW of this headland (1.8M)

- The transit (84°, Fl.6s front, Dir.Oc.WRG.4s rear) is hard to pick out in daylight. Instead, from the north cardinal Q, off Cabo Silleiro, head for the south cardinal Q(6)LFl.15s (57°), off the reef of Las Serralleiras. This will clear the shallow patch (4.1m) 0.6M E of the north cardinal (Q)

- Alter course to 85° to clear Punta del Buey (north of the Parador/Castle, illuminated at night) when due west of it

- Steer south for the end of Baiona breakwater Q.G.

It is possible to use the channel between Monte Ferro and Islotes Las Estelas, but it should only be done at high water in very settled weather with the largest scale Spanish chart, The channel has two

Baiona 42°07'N 08°52'W

Monte Real Club de Yates
- Entrance night and day
- Shelter all directions
- Depth minimum 4m
- Berthing: bow/stern-to and pontoon, mooring, up to 18m
- Visitors' berths 40
  ☎ 986 385000 Fax: 986 355061 - very busy in summer
- VHF Channel 09
- mrcyb@mrcyb.com
- Water, electricity at the pontoons
- ⛽ Fuel from shore side end of wall from club
- Showers and toilets in club house
- Excellent restaurant

Puerto Deportivo de Baiona
- Entrance night and day
- Shelter all directions
- Depth minimum 3m
- Berthing: pontoon mooring, up to 40m length
- Visitors' berths 32
- ☎ 986 385107 Fax: 986 356489
- VHF Channel 09
- puertobaiona@puertobaiona.com
- Water, electricity at the pontoons
- ⛽ Fuel from from shore quay, end of west pontoon, very tight next to small boats
- 🏗 18-ton travel lift
- 🔧 Repairs: workshop in the marina
- Very basic showers and toilets (shore facilities planned)

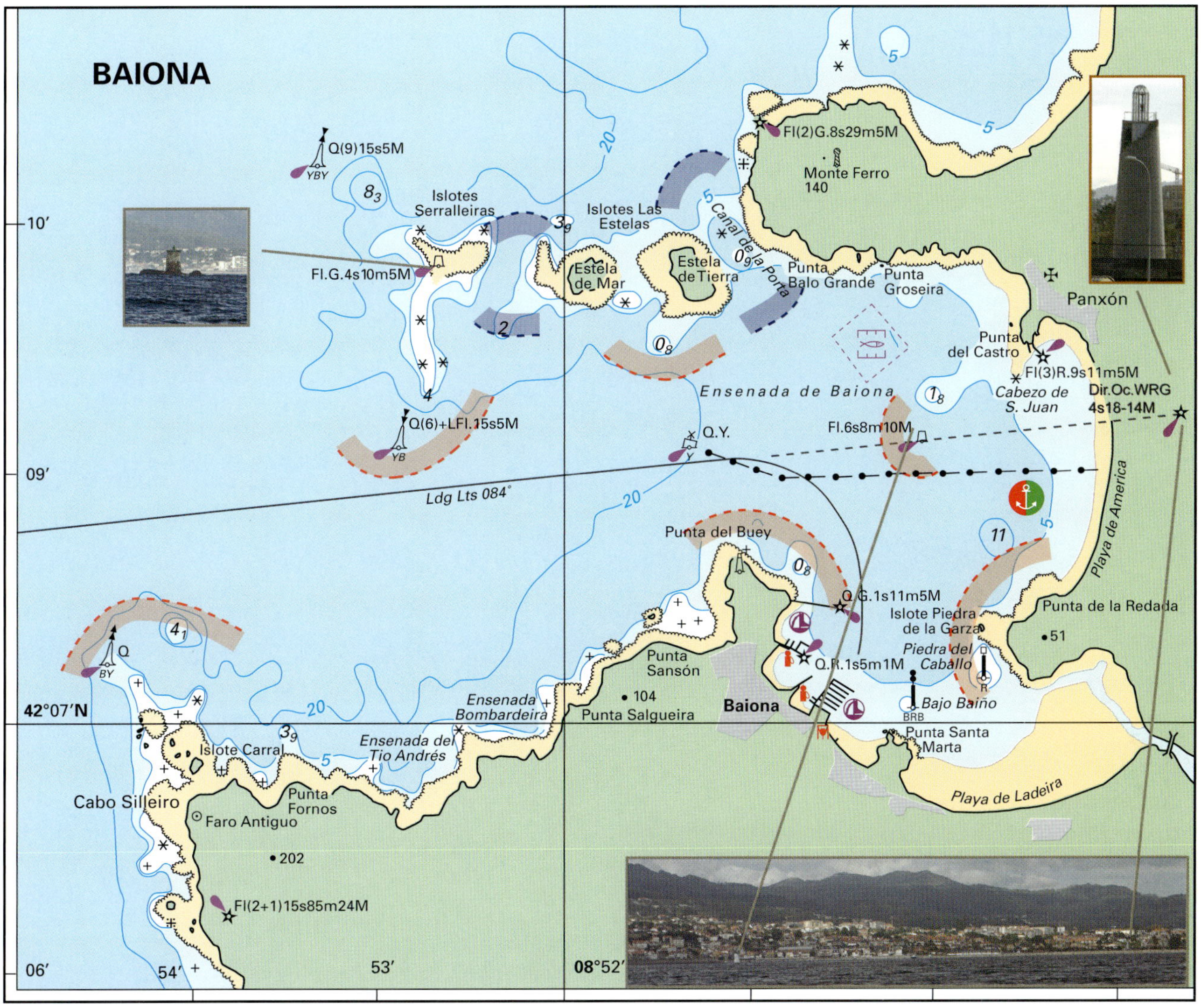

RÍA DE VIGO

Baiona marinas

CRUISING GALICIA 269

RÍA DE VIGO

marked, so the greatest care is required.

Berthing & facilities

Monte Real Club de Yates is the classiest destination in Galicia if you can find space. The marina is extremely welcoming and its facilities and setting are really good, including the restaurant.

Puerto Deportivo de Baiona is relatively new and has a vast set of modern, generous pontoons that will accommodate almost any size. Enter Puerto Deportivo on the east side of the pontoons. Either arrange a berth on VHF 09 or head for the first pontoon bay, generally reserved for visitors. Showers are the downside of the marina, a really poor cousin to the standard of the pontoons. The marina is well equipped for fuelling, with a dedicated pontoon finger, but it is very tight getting in and out close to the small craft area.

⚓ Anchorages

Playa de América is a possible location for anchoring, in sand between 3 and 10m, exposed openly to west wind and swell. There is ample space for a retreat if conditions change, probably towards the marinas.

The picturesque Paxón fishing harbour is not suitable for yachts.

Provisioning & eating

Baiona has a good market, along Calle Carabela La Pinta and further along a couple of supermarkets. These are well stocked and should see to your victualling.

Restaurants and bars are in abundance along the streets of the old town, pricey and set for the tourist season that attracts people in large numbers. The food is good but you will probably feel that the standard is set for mass production.

Transport

The best connections for Baiona are from Vigo. There are buses to the city but the distance of only 20km makes for a quick taxi ride.

Puerto Deportivo fuelling berth

270 CRUISING GALICIA

RÍA DE VIGO

Puerto Deportivo

Interest

Baiona has a long history as a strategic port, guarding the entrance to Ría de Vigo and hence of interest to every nation that has sailed this way or attempted to establish trade. Greeks, Arabs, Romans and Vikings have all been here. Later Drake has his hand at destruction, including the chapel at the Santa Marta peninsula.

The elegant paseo marítimo is a good strolling place, faced by the bay on one side and the old town on the other. It gets busy in the summer but it is a good place to watch the Spanish promenading.

The old town narrow streets have retained the charm of medieval times, albeit now taken over by a myriad of outlets for tourists. The crowning glory of the old buildings is the castle. If you want a truely special occasion, stay a night at the Parador Conde Gondomar, the old fortress for defence of Baiona, now among the best of these type of hotels run by the Spanish government enterprise.

To cap the fame of Baiona, the first of Columbus' boats to arrive back from discovering America, Carabela La Pinta, landed at Baiona on 1 March 1493. In a sorry state but proudly commanded by Martín Alonso Pinzón, the small boat returned from adventure with success, setting the scene for

Baiona old town

Gondomar castle

Monte Real fuel

RÍA DE BAIONA

CRUISING GALICIA 271

RÍA DE VIGO

Baiona

- Vigo 20km, Santiago 95km, Coruña 160km Pontevedra 45km, Ourense 90km
- Ferries to Vigo and Islas Cíes
- Bus stop: Rúa de Elduayen/Rúa Carabela La Pinta, opposite La Pinta pier
- Market: Plaza de Abastos, Rúa Carabela La Pinta
- Supermarket: Glorieta de Colón
- Restaurants: large number in old town, Rúa de Ventura Misa parallel to harbour front
- Tourist office: by the park opposite Castillo de Monterreal, ☏ 986 687067
- Chandlers: basic marine store within Puerto Deportivo and in shoreside street opposite entrance; further hardware stores and electronics along Avenida Monterreal
- Banks, chemists and other shops along harbour front Rúa de Elduayen, Avda Monterreal
- Centro Saude Baiona, Rúa Venezuela ☏ 986 356113 / 356206

the enormous expansion of Spain as the empire of the time. You can see a replica of *La Pinta* moored in the harbour, a slightly touristy affair but worth the visit to learn a bit more about the discoverers and the conditions in which they sailed.

Nearby, Puente de A Ramallosa is a medieval engineering feat over the river. The Albufera to the north is a haven for birds. Playa de América in front is a large beach, very popular in the summer.

Replica of *Carabela La Pinta*

272 CRUISING GALICIA

RÍA DE VIGO

⚓ Islas Cíes

Islas Cíes are part of the Parque Nacional das Illas Atlánticas (Atlantic Island National Park). The islands form a natural barrier that protects Ría de Vigo from ocean swell and climate, and therefore have acted as the key to the development of the Ría as a major harbour. There are a number of anchorages on the east side of the islands.

Approach & entrance

The islands offer temporary shelter from bad weather, providing the opportunity for sail changes and other preparations prior to carrying out a harbour approach.

From Ría Pontevedra to Playa de Rodas, Isla do Faro: there are two lights on the east side of the island. The southernmost Piedra Borrón Fl(2).10s can be used for a night time approach with due care of the Traffic Separation Scheme.

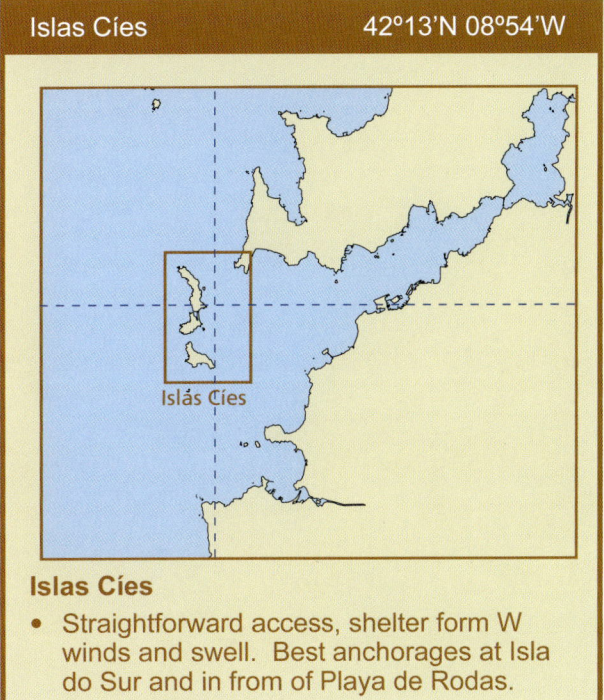

Islas Cíes   42°13'N 08°54'W

Islas Cíes
- Straightforward access, shelter form W winds and swell. Best anchorages at Isla do Sur and in from of Playa de Rodas.

⚓ Anchorages

Playa de Figueiras:

- Anchor in 5-8m sand. Some protection from the south.

Playa de Rodas:

- Anchor south of the Piedra Borrón in 5m sand. Only sheltered from the west.

West of Islote Viños:

- Anchor in 5-10m Sand. Avoid getting too close to the jetty which is often in use. Some protection from the east.

Playa de San Martín:

- Anchor in 3-5m Sand. Some protection from the northwest round to southwest.

Interest

The natural beauty of the islands is indisputable, and they are quiet despite the proximity to the busy mainland. There is no development on the island with an overnight stay ashore only permitted at the well managed campsite on Isla del Norte. The anchorages are among the most picturesque as well as being protected from the majority of wind directions. Because of this they have in the past been a haven for attacking fleets or pirates, from Francis Drake (who attacked Monterreal in Baiona at the end of the 16th century) to Turkish corsairs to various European maritime aggressors.

It is well worth exploring Isla del Norte ashore along the various well maintained paths. Towards the north the path leads to the edge of the bird sanctuary protected area. While it is not possible

CRUISING GALICIA 273

RÍA DE VIGO

to enter this area, there are various places from which it is possible to observe the numerous seabird species that nest on the island.

The path from Playa de Rodas to the south leads to the ruins of a castro (ancient Galcian settlement) and, after a climb, to spectacular views from the top of hill where the lighthouse is located.

Isla do Sur has a wilder feel to it. The path from the beach takes you through a forest from the tranquility of the protected anchorage shelter to the furious beat of the sea against the rock on the other side of the hill.

Islas Cíes looking north

A GUARDA

⚓ A Guarda

Most southern harbour of Galicia before Portugal, suitable only for calm conditions as the entrance may be impassable if the swell builds up. The town is a pretty destination, popular as an out of the way destination in the summer. Nearby, the historical town of Tuy and the prehistoric remains at Monte Tegra are among the best tourist destinations of Galicia.

Approach & entrance

Day only, settled weather, leave if swell is forecast to build up.

From the north:

- Apart from the monastery at Arrabel, there is little of interest close in to the coast on a trip from Baiona so it is best to stand off. Once the dangers off Cabo Silleiro (at the entrance to Ría Vigo) have been rounded, staying in 50m would be a good plan in any sort of sea

- Monte Santa Tecla just to the south of the harbour stand out prominently. A clean broad approach from the west can be made with the

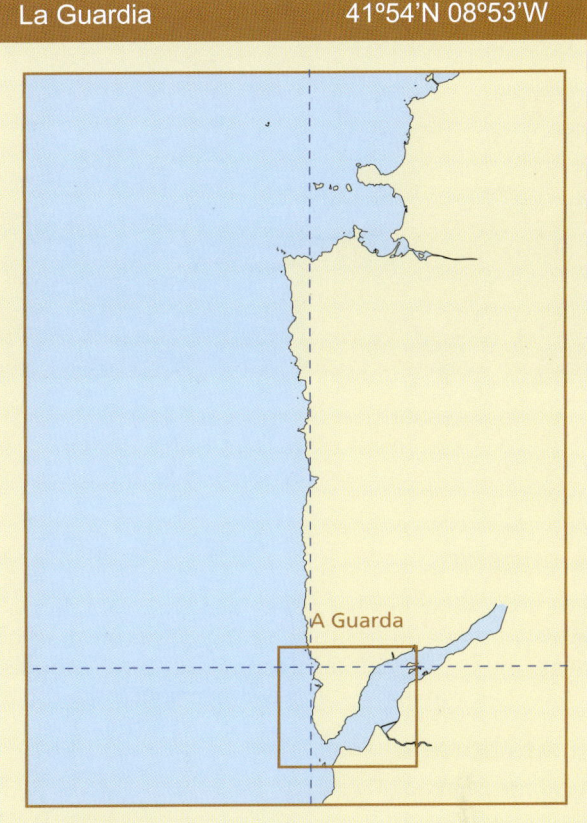

La Guardia 41°54'N 08°53'W

La Guardia
- Entrance calm conditions only
- Shelter inside but swell may block exit
- Depth minimum 2m
- Anchor only between fishing boats and south wall
- Inner mole end suitable for short stay, depth minimum 2m

Camposancos
- Entrance thorough transit south of Isla Insua
- Anchorage by harbour (several spots)
- Shelter W to NE.

A Guarda harbour

A Guarda harbour

CRUISING GALICIA 275

A GUARDA

Río Miño, view towards West

north and south breakwaters lit (Fl(2)R.7s and Fl(2)G.7s). Inside there is an isolated rock (Piedra Barguiña) on the south side that must be avoided.

Alongside

The inner mole has been extended with enough depth to moor alongside the end. It was clean in early 2007, although the depth in any swell would have to be watched. It has a convenient ladder.

⚓ Anchorage

Anchor in 4-5m in the harbour clear of moorings (use a tripping line).

⚓ Camposancos/El Pasaje and Río Miño

Pretty river with possible quiet anchorages and sail up river (tidal heights permitting).

Portugal is a short ferry away across the river. Daylight, calm weather, approach which must also be made towards highwater to the South of Isla Insua with the latest and most detailed information. Few marks are available for navigation once in the river and the banks move.

Anchorages at El Pasaje and Camposancos on the Spanish side with ferries to Portugal.

Approach & Entrance

From the North, and particularly if exiting from La Guarda, then stay outside the 30m contour line until close to the Moledo transit (front and rear Occ.R.5s). Do not use the transit North of Isua Novaz. The next transit (unlit 11°) takes you close to the Bandeira rock. If this is covered and unseen then a small Easterly detour is advised until North of Isua Nova. Note that on highwater neaps there will be less than 2.5m in the channel. If proceeding to Camposancos then wait for the depth to increase to over 5m before turning onto 45°.

Tuy

A Guarda

Camposancos area Portugal across the river

Anchorages

Anchorages at El Pasaje and Camposancos on the Spanish side, as well as in the entrance, and inside Ponto do Cabedelo on the Portuguese side. All anchorages are in sand and could be subject to significant tidal flows on the ebb.

Provisioning & eating

A Guarda has many restaurants and bars along the front by the harbour, rather geared to tourists but offering good fish and Galician food. There are plenty of shops for provisioning up the hill past the San Benito church/hotel.

Supplies are very limited at Camposancos.

Transport

Buses link A Guarda to Baiona, Tuy and Portugal. Check at the Tourist Office at the Town Hall, Plaza del Reloj (℡ 986 614546).

Interest

This area is remote and wild, well worth exploring even if you are based in the larger towns further north. The road from Baiona to Guarda is very dramatic, the open ocean on one side and undeveloped rugged coast on the other. Inland along Rio Mino are some of the prettiest scenes in Galicia, green, mountainous and still pristine.

Guarda was settled as a defensive point and was attacked by the Portuguese on several occasions. Castillo the Santa Cruz in the harbour now stands behind the tall sea defence wall but it played a role in its day. This wall is there to defend the town from the anger of the ocean which used to crash against the town harbour road.

The colourful houses which face the harbour are called Casas de Indias because they were erected by emigrants returned from Latin America, from where they brought a taste for bright decoration.

San Benito was a convent of strict order until 1990 when the nuns sold it, unable to fund ongoing restoration. It is now a delightful hotel, full of antiques from the middle ages.

At Camposancos an impressive building by the ferry dock was the Jesuit School, used by Franco as a prison during the civil war. It now lies empty, awaiting restoration.

Up the river, Tuy is one of the seven historic cities of the old kingdom of Galicia. Set on a hill, it dominates the river below. The old streets are full of character and atmosphere.

At the top of Monte Tecla, the remains of a *castro* are one of the best examples you will see of this type of pre-historic Galician settlement. It is rather over restored but it is impressive for its network of round houses and the spectacular setting. Further up the hill visit the monastery for even better views. A popular *romería* takes place on 23 September.

ABOUT GALICIA

From a 16C chart by monk Fernando de Ojea, dedicated to Don Pedro de Castro y Andrade, principal Noble of Galicia under King Philip II of Spain. Incorporated into an Atlas by Ioannes Vrint.

About Galicia:

'This Kingdom possesses abundant cattle and all kinds of hunt, much and very good fish, from sea and rivers, from which the majority of Spain is supplied. It has an abundance of waters cold and hot that they call baths, much wine among the best that is found in all of Europe, particularly that of Orense and Rivadavia, which is supplied to many provinces of the Kingdom and other lands. It has very many good fruits, limes and oranges of all kinds, silk and linen, many minerals of Gold and silver, iron etc. and some marble quarries. Its temperament is neither cold nor hot.'

Background to Galicia

Introduction

This book covers a section of European coastline that has been shaped geographically, economically and socially by the sea. Sandwiched between a coast exposed to the open ocean and massive mountain ranges on the mainland, the prospects for early human inhabitants would seem to be limited to the use of the land. Galicia, however, is uniquely positioned on the maritime trading route between the English Channel, the door to northern Europe, and the Straits of Gibraltar, entrance to the Mediterranean. No modern sailor can be unaware of the significance of the Bay of Biscay or the long stretch along the Atlantic coast of Portugal and neither were sailors from the past. Galicia, both then and now, provides shelter before or after a long passage. The sanctuary offered takes the form of a multitude of Rías, the drowned river courses that provide a wealth of anchorages and ideal cruising grounds.

The Atlantic connection

Galicia is the northwestern section of the Iberian peninsula. Its position between the Atlantic ocean and the mountainous interior of Spain and north Portugal has for a long time encouraged a culture defined by its independence but also connected to the sea facing coasts of Europe, united by similar environmental conditions and traditions popularly known as Celtic.

During **prehistoric** times Galician tribal groups had more in common with their counterparts along Atlantic facing coasts of Europe than with the inhabitants of Iberia. It was easier to travel by water,, however, perilous, than on foot across densely forested and difficult mountain terrain. Archeological research shows that objects were traded between the peoples of Galicia, Brittany (Armorica), Ireland and Britain. Architecture, including dolmens and burial sites, show that there were also religious and cultural links amongst these early people.

Dolmen de Axeitos, near Ribeira

In the Bronze Age settlements became larger and more organised, built as fortified villages called *castros*. Many of these early villages are well preserved, with their round family dwellings, defensive ditches and walls, and some can be seen at spectacular locations commanding approaches from the sea and land. Visit Castros de Baroña, Santa Tecla and Viladonga for some of the best examples of this prehistoric architecture.

Castro de Baroña, near Posto de Son, Ría de Muros

As the gateway between north and south Atlantic facing coasts, and endowed with rich mineral resources such as iron, gold and tin, Galicia attracted trading nations who established bases there. The **Phoenicians** were the first to brave the long journey north, establishing contact between the sophisticated Mediterranean and rugged Atlantic societies. Wine, oil and objects of luxury would have been acquired by tribal groups, many as status and hierarchy symbols, in exchange for metals needed by Greece and the advanced Middle East. Apart from other routes of contact via the great rivers of France and Germany, the Mediterranean and the north of Europe were linked by Galicia which became a key staging post for products brought from trading centres at Gadir (modern day Cádiz).

The **Romans** reached the region in the first century BC, the last part of Iberia to be brought under Roman rule. They called the province Gallaecia, the origin of the modern name. The administrative system and logistics introduced by the Romans settled side by side with a Castro culture that maintained its own traditions, even of architectural construction. The Empire provided roads and urban development that served the purpose of management and tax for Rome but also facilitated wealth creation. The mineral mines were appropriated by the State but a system was installed whereby local entrepreneurs could acquire licences and keep half of the profits.

ABOUT GALICIA

Roman murals near Lugo

During and following the collapse of the Roman Empire, waves of *barbarians* arrived in Iberia. Sueve people settled in Galicia, later to be ruled by Visigoths who established the early foundations of Christian medieval Spain. This temporary order was wiped aside by the arrival of the **Moors** from north Africa, invaders from the more culturally advanced and better organised muslim world. The conquest was completed in 718 and only resisted by a small Christian force in the Asturian Picos de Europa. As with other invaders Galicia proved a land and people difficult fro the Moors to control, hence Galicia does not have a strong legacy of the Arab culture or buildings that are spectacularly displayed in many of more southern towns.

Santiago

The **Reconquest** of Iberia by Christians of the north found its most powerful icon in Galicia, through the legend surrounding the remains of apostle Santiago (St James), brought to Galicia by his disciples in an epic voyage from Palestine. From the landing at Ría de Arousa to the star signs that revealed his presence to Bishop Gelmírez, Santiago de Compostela developed as a centre of pilgrimage for European Christianity. The Spanish kingdoms emerging in the north, including Galicia, used Santiago as a moral and financial buttress in their ongoing war against the Moors.

Santiago de Compostela is unique, and today the town is classed as a World Heritage Site.

Wealth from pilgrims and the singular position of authority it has occupied for centuries has led to an extensive array of churches, aristocratic buildings and the magnificent Cathedral within an extraordinary urban layout, built almost entirely in granite. The style is Galician, with its *soportales* (covered walkways) and glazed balconies. The lively character inspired by one of the oldest Universities in Europe make it a destination for everyone.

Pórtico de la Gloria in Santiago

Maritime intruders

The wealth of Santiago also attracted the interest of naval raiders. The **Vikings** and Normans made repeated forays into Galicia, the advanced design of their boats enabling a journey so far from home. Ría de Arousa developed defences against such attacks, re-enacted every summer in the town of Catoira.

More modern fleets, French, Dutch and British, have also attacked Galicia, sometimes in search of loot, some for strategic reasons in the constant tussles for supremacy between the states of Europe. A Coruña holds a key place in the relationship between **Britain and Galicia**. The town heroine María Pita repelled an attack by a large British force headed by Francis Drake in 1598. Later in the 19th century British soldiers were in Galicia helping Spain defeat Napoleon. A small force, protecting the retreat of the British from A Coruña, was over-run by the French and British General Sir John Moore lost his life. General Moore is celebrated in the gardens of the old town by the illustrious Galician poet Rosalía de Castro.

Dorna Viking boats

ABOUT GALICIA

Modern history

Galicia's recent history is inextricably linked with its diminished status in the declining Spanish empire and, more recently, years of isolation of Spain during the dictatorship of Franco. All around the world there are *Centros Gallegos*, meeting places for **Galicians** that **emigrated** during the early part of 20th century. Seeking work and wealth they were leaving an impoverished land where industry and agriculture was in decline. In some South American countries the word *Gallego* means 'from Spain'.

Despite the conservative character of Galicia that might have given it pre-eminence during the dictatorship, and the fact that Franco was from Ferrol, Galicia only started to develop after his death in 1975. European funds and the economic success of new Spain have created the roads and modern infrastructure whose absence kept Galicia poor.

Galician bagpipe

Culture

The **culture** of Galicia is strongly regional, like all other parts of Spain steeped in its own traditions, including a distinct music and a separate language. There is much in common with the rest of Atlantic Europe, as you will appreciate listening to music for the bagpipes. Galician is a Roman based **language**, similar to Spanish and Portuguese. Road and street signs often mix Galician and Spanish as do people when they speak. The same location may well have similar but not completely identical names, inconsistent between charts, maps and other publications. This is not difficult to get used to.

The Galician character is more accommodating than that of other Spanish regions, never challenging authority, unlike their coal mining Asturian neighbours or the fiercely independentist Basques. Nevertheless, regional sentiment is strong. The **politics** of Galicia reached a heyday in the turmoil of 1936, the Spanish Parliament on the point of approving a Statute of regional government when the Civil War began. Today Galicia has a large share of devolved government, like the other *Comunidades* in Spain which operate in a system that is quasi federal. Local direction has propelled

Fishing

beneficial development, but the system is far from perfect, witness some of the chaos around forest fire control which becomes a battle of headlines between local and central politicians rather a united exercise to control the flames.

The rugged Galician coastline has enabled a long standing habit of smuggling, cigarettes and alcohol during the times of Franco and narcotics more recently. The Coastguard is well equipped and the problem is given serious attention but high speed boats do operate, however, much surveillance is undertaken.

Superstition is more evident in Galician culture than you might expect in the 21st century, probably due to the fact that only 40 years ago the region was still very isolated and almost entirely rural. Of course today the stories and symbols have become folklore, but there is a rich vocabulary associated with *meigas*, the gentle Galician witches, and much inspiration drawn from sayings and actions of the past. Join a party to ward off evil spirits, drink *queimada* to fend off 'bad eye' and you will soon see the fun side of local tradition.

There is no shortage of **fiestas** in Galicia, all linked with traditions honouring a saint, celebrating an event, a product or a fish, or marking the passage of the seasons. During the summer especially no village worthy of its name will go without some celebration or other. Many are well worth being involved in for the music and costumes alone. See the table later in this guide for a list of the main events throughout the year.

Fresh fruit and veg

CRUISING GALICIA 281

ABOUT GALICIA

Galicia has a wealth of famous writers, all of whom have drawn from aspects of Galician culture as sources of inspiration. Rosalía de Castro is the Gallego writer *par excellence*, the first to dedicate herself, and succeed in, the promotion of the language during the late 19th century. Eccentric Valle Inclán is not well know outside Spain but you will come across his deeds in Ría de Arousa. Camilo J Cela received the Nobel Price for Literature in 1989 and is best known for *The Hive* and *The Family of Pascual Duarte*.

Fiesta

Fish food paradise

Food

Galicia is home to a very large fishing fleet, engaged in coastal, offshore and farmed fishing, supported by a sizeable shoreside industry. Wherever you sail in the Rías you will negotiate grids of *bateas*, 20x20m floating platforms that are used for the cultivation of mussels and other types of shellfish. Areas marked as *viveros* are also used for production of turbot and monkfish. The industry is encouraged by the enormous appetite for fish in Spain, a country that consumes as much fish as the rest of Europe put together.

Ashore you will have access to some the freshest sea produce you will ever find, at fishmongers or better still at *plazas* and *mercados* (markets). If you like **fish** you will be in heaven, but other protein is good too as cattle are raised on lush pastures. Fruit and vegetables produced locally reach the markets without needing to ripen later as is common in urban Europe.

Bars and restaurants are abundant and competitive, serving all the way from simple *tapas* or *raciones* to sit-down sophisticated dishes served by waiters. You will be hard put to find bad food anywhere as the local expectations are of fresh food of a high standard. Generally, however, the more touristy the venue the more expensive and the worse quality, so go wherever the Spanish can be seen. Try sardines, *pulpo a la gallega* (octopus), *mejillones* (mussels), *rodaballo* (turbot), *merluza* (cod), *atún* (tuna), *empanada* (Galician savoury pie), *caldo a la gallega* (a sturdy stew like soup that draws its flavour from turnip tops), any type of beef (which will be very tender), *Pimientos de Padrón* (sweet small pepper with the occasional hot surprise) and douse it all with crisp Albariño or Ribeiro white wine. Take an interest in some of the preserved foods, the offer is vast and some of it very good. *Ventresca de atún* has a reputation for being the best preserved tuna. Food quality in Galicia is in a class of its own.

What to do in Galicia

Galicia combines natural scenery with history and a vibrant local culture, enough to fascinate any visitor. At the same time, its geographical isolation and more inclement weather have kept it from mass tourism. There are exceptions: Santiago becomes crowded in the summer with pilgrims and tourists (but still worth it) and new resorts like Sanxenxo are places to avoid if you are not into Mediterranean style beach holiday culture. 'The rain in Spain falls mainly in ... Galicia' is what has saved it from mass tourism so far.

There are no shortage of destinations along the coast but it is worth making the effort of mooring the boat and going inland for some of the more intriguing and beautiful destinations. Without a doubt you should try to get to **Santiago**, even if you are short of time.

Along the **Rías Altas** use Ribadeo or Viveiro as bases and visit the San Andrés de Teixido sanctuary, the hillside village of O Barqueiro, the village of Bares situated at the prominent Estaca de Bares headland, the cultural centre of Sargadelos and step on the sands among rock towers at Playa das Catedrais.

The province of Lugo is the least developed in Galicia and offers the best walking routes. The mountains to the east are more difficult but offer

Hórreos, grain stores

ABOUT GALICIA

breathtaking scenery, while the northern parks feel remote and unexploited. The old fashioned *aldeas* (small villages) are good landmarks in the wilderness, and O Cebreiro, the mountain village/museum of Seceda, and the forest Devesa de A Rogueira are destinations in their own right.

Lugo (World Heritage Site) and Ourense are both provincial capitals and combine Galician style with their Roman background, still showing much of the fortification and residential building erected by the Empire. Mondoñedo, one of the capital cities of the old Galician kingdom, is a beautiful noble town.

At **A Coruña** wander in the streets of the old town, visit the Roman Hercules lighthouse, the aquarium and travel into the quiet corners of Ría de Betanzos by boat or to Pontedeume inland.

Along the **Costa da Morte** anchor at Sisargas, if weather permits, to get a breathtaking view of the coast at Cabo Vilano (although you will need to ignore the windfarms). Enjoy the quiet setting and shelter from the ocean at Rías de Corme and Camariñas, visit the grand Monasterio de San Xoán

Pretty anchoorages

de Moraime, the legendary Pedras de Abalare os Cadrís at Muxía and feel proud to conquer Cabo Finisterre.

In the **Rías Baixas** the towns of Muros and Noia at **Ría de Muros** are good places to admire local architecture and to relax with the locals promenading the streets and parks. The nearby Castro de Baroña is one of the best examples of pre-roman settlement with a spectacular location commanding views of the sea below. The Dunas de Corrubedo natural park provides a wild setting for sand dunes, vegetation and wildlife at the entrance to **Ría de Arousa**, also home to stone age remains (Dolmen de Axeitos), hill walks with viewpoints (Mirador de Lobeira and others) and medieval towns like Cambados or Pobra do Caramiñal. A large part of the Gailician fishing industry is found within the Ría whose coast is famous for seaborne contact, from the Vikings to the vessel bringing the remains of apostle Santiago from Palestine. Isla Sálvora at the entrance is the first in the Atlantic Island National Park, an attractive spot to anchor together with many others further into Ría de Arousa.

Ría de Pontevedra offers Combarro and Pontevedra as two of the most charismatic Galician towns, the first is full of *hórreos*, the distinct Galician grain stores. Ría de Aldán at the entrance to Pontevedra is one of the prettiest spots to find a quiet anchorage, matched by Isla Ons at the entrance to the main ría, in complete contrast to Sanxenxo on the northern side which attracts mass summer tourism. In and around **Ría de Vigo** the Castillo de Sotomaior at Arcade is worth a day trip, while in Vigo Pazo-Museo Quiñones de León and the Museo do Mar are also interesting. Baiona is another medieval town commanded by the imposing Gondomar castle (now a Parador hotel) and the Islas Cíes complete the Island National Park, a great anchorage.

Inland the *Camino Francés* way to Santiago is an attractive route to follow, through wild mountain scenery and towns that have grown in the centuries of pilgrimage, many with imposing monasteries and medieval buildings (Villafranca del Bierzo, Cebreiro Monasterio Santa María La Real, Monasterio de Samos, Castillo de Pambre). It would be best equipped hiring a car for such a trip but there are often organised tours that you can join from the larger seaside towns.

Towards the border with Portugal in the south, Castro de Santa Tecla near A Guarda is another wonderful example of a prehistoric settlement. The towns of Tui and Ribadavia would complement a round trip there, smaller than the province capitals but bursting with history and character.

As for folklore and celebration the list would be too long to enter into, some of the highlights are given in the more detailed sections. The major event of the year is on the 25th of July. Known throughout the region as Día de Galicia, in Santiago is the celebration of the apostle. This is a holiday worth participating in wherever you are. For uniqueness the street flower carpets constructed during Corpus Christi are unforgettable. The most extensive are Puenteareas but many others as impressive. In the summer there are numerous *fiestas*. Whenever your visit you are likely to find some celebration somewhere.

ABOUT GALICIA

Events, Celebrations, Fiestas in Galicia

Events, Celebrations, Fiestas in Galicia - Key Dates

	2007	2008	2009	2010	2011	2012	2013	2014	2015
Carnival start	15 Feb	31-Jan	19 Feb	15 Feb	3 Mar	16 Feb	7 Feb	27 Feb	12 Feb
Carnival Sunday	18 Feb	3 Feb	22 Feb	18 Feb	6 Mar	19 Feb	10 Feb	2 Mar	15 Feb
Carnival Tuesday	20 Feb	5 Feb	24 Feb	20 Feb	8 Mar	21 Feb	12 Feb	4 Mar	17 Feb
Carnival end	25 Feb	10 Feb	1 Mar	25 Feb	13 Mar	26 Feb	17 Feb	9 Mar	22 Feb
Ash Wednesday	21 Feb	6 Feb	25 Feb	21 Feb	9 Mar	22 Feb	13 Feb	5 Mar	18 Feb
Palm Sunday	1 Apr	16 Mar	5 Apr	1 Apr	17 Apr	1 Apr	24 Mar	13 Apr	29 Mar
Easter Sunday	8 Apr	23 Mar	12 Apr	8 Apr	24 Apr	8 Apr	31 Mar	20 Apr	5 Apr
Whit Sunday	27 May	11 May	31 May	27 May	12 Jun	27 May	19 May	8 Jun	24 May
Corpus Christi	7 Jun	22 May	11 Jun	7 Jun	23 Jun	7 Jun	30 May	19 Jun	4 Jun

ABOUT GALICIA

Event	Date	Location	Province, Ría
Feria del Cocido	Sunday before Carnival	Lalín	Pontevedra. Extensive celebration of hearty stews.
Carnival at Xinzo	Carnival week	Xinzo de Limia	Ourense. The most renowned of the Carnival celebrations, Pantalla masks.
Carnival at Cobres	Carnival week	Cobres. Vilaboa	Pontevedra, Vigo. Carnival in this village of Morrazo Peninsula, numerous events and very colourful.
Fiesta de La Androlla and Carnival	Carnival week	Viana do Bolo	Ourense. Mask processions, Androlla (stew), very colourful mountain celebration.
Carnival at Laza	Carnival week	Laza	Ourense. Peliqueiros (wooden masks with semicircular top), battle of the flour, burial of the sardine.
Carnival at Verín	Carnival week	Verín	Ourense. Cigarrón masks, 'retranca' procession, extensive food celebrations.
Fiesta de la Carabela Pinta	1st weekend March	Baiona	Pontevedra, Baiona. Celebration of the arrival of the first of Columbus' carabelas, La Pinta.
Cheese Festival	1st Sunday March	Arzúa	A Coruña. Cheese from Galicia, mild and creamy.
Amandi Wine Festival	Palm weekend	Sober	Lugo. ine from this stretch of the Sil river valley (Ribeira Sacra).
Romería do Santo Cristo	Easter	Finisterre	A Coruña, Finisterre. Easter Sunday celebration at Santa María da Area church, related to old Sun cult.
Easter at Viveiro	Easter	Viveiro	Lugo, Viveiro. Extensive re-enactments and processions in the old town of Viveiro.
Easter at Ferrol	Easter	Ferrol	Coruña, Ferrol. Sombre Easter processions in streets of strategic naval port.
Muestra de Encaje de Bolillos	Easter	Camariñas	A Coruña. Lace exibition from the renowned palilleira of Caramiñas.
Easter at Cangas	Easter	Cangas	Pontevedra, Vigo. Traditional processions at this town raided so often for its strategic position.
Festival de San Telmo	1st weekend after Easter	Tui	Pontevedra. Fiesta of the patron saint in one of the historical centres of Galicia.
Fiesta de la Ostra	1st weekend in April	Arcade de Soutomaior	Pontevedra, Vigo. Oyster festival near Ensenada de San Simón.
Fiesta de la trucha	1st of May	A Pontenova	Lugo. rout festival celebrating the fish form the rivers of the area.
Os Maios	1st Sunday of May	Ourense	Ourense. Parade of floats made with flowers and fruits woven into creative shapes.
O Ribeiro Wine Festival	Early May	Ribadavia	Ourense. Extensive fair centred on Ribeiro wine in the historic town of Ribadavia.
Fiesta de la trucha	Last weekend in May	Ponte Caldelas	Pontevedra. Trout festival celebrating the fish form the rivers of the area.
Romería da Virxe da Franqueria	Whitsun Monday	A Cañiza	Pontevedra. Procession of the Virgin and auction of offers. Also on 8 September.
Corpus Christi at Ponteareas	Weekend following Corpus	Ponteareas	Pontevedra. Street flower carpets layed in the streets the night before Sunday processions.
Corpus Christi at Redondela	Day of Corpus Christi	Redondela	Pontevedra, Vigo. Processions and dances of Espadas and Penlas.

ABOUT GALICIA

Event	Date	Location	Province, Ría
Offering of the Kingdom of Galicia	Sunday following Corpus	Lugo	Lugo. Solemn ritual at Lugo Cathedral, alternating offering by each of the old 7 cities of the Kingdom of Galicia (Tui, Mondoñedo, Betanzos, Coruña, Lugo, Ourense, Santiago).
Hogueras de San Juan	Night of 23 June	A Coruña	A Coruña. Large number of bonfires in the beach of Riazor, a night of magic and legend.
A Rapa das Bestas of A Estrada	1st weekend of July	A Estrada	Pontevedra. Round up and taming of wild horses. Event also in other parts of Galicia.
A Rapa das Bestas of Candaoso	1st weekend of July	Santo André de Boimente	Lugo, Viveiro. Round up and taming of wild horses in the hills looking over Viveiro Ría.
San Benitiño de Lérez	11th July	Pontevedra	Pontevedra. Popular fair and celebration of the 'most miraculous saint'.
Festival Internacional Celta	3rd weekend of July	Ortigueira	A Coruña, Ortigueira. International celebration of the 'Celtic' world, extensive music events.
Gran Premio de Carrilanas	3rd weekend of July	Esteiro	A Coruña, Muros. Fun race of hand made karts, the only requirement 'without motor'.
Romería da Fraga	24, 25th of July	As Pontes de García	A Coruña. Popular fair. Food, crafts and music in the woodland (fraga).
Santiago Apóstol	25th of July	Santiago de Compostela	A Coruña. Celebration of Apostle Santiago culminating in giant fireworks display at Plaza de Obradoiro in front the Cathedral.
Medieval market at Coruña	Around 25th July	A Coruña	A Coruña. Street stalls and large number of events with medieval flavour.
Fiesta del Carneiro ao Espeto	Last Sunday of July	Moraña	Pontevedra. Meat fair, churrasco, parrillada and many other forms of cooking meat cuts.
Feria del Bonito	1st Saturday of August	Burela	Lugo. Tuna fair, about one of the staples fish catches of Galicia.
Fiesta del Pimiento de Herbón	1st Saturday of August	Padrón	A Coruña. Ultimate feast of the celebrated little sweet green pepper.
Fiesta del Pimiento	1st weekend of August	A Arnoia	Ourense. Another opportunity to try the small pepper and escape the occasional firy one.
Romería Vikinga	1st Sunday of August	Catoira	Pontevedra, Arousa. Fun re-enactment of Viking invasions by the Catoira towers.
Fiesta de la Santa Cruz	1st Sunday of August	Ribadeo	Lugo, Ribadeo. Popular fair in the hill behind Ribadeo.

Turgalicia

ABOUT GALICIA

Event	Date	Location	Province, Ría
Fiesta del Vino Albariño	1st Sunday of August	Cambados	Pontevedra, Arousa. Celebration of Albariño wine, numerous displays and wine tasting.
Fiestas de San Lourenzo	10th of August	Foz	Lugo, Foz. Street processions, displays and music.
Festa da Maruxaina	2nd Saturday of August	San Cibrao. Cervo	Lugo. Parade of the Siren (Maruxaina) that sometimes helps, sometimes deceives the fishermen of this community.
Fiesta del Pulpo	2nd Sunday of August	O Carballiño	Ourense. The ultimate feast for one of Galicia's traditional dishes, octopus.
Buño Pottery Festival	12 -20 August	Malpica de Bergantiños	A Coruña, Costa de Morte. Fair centre on the traditional Buño pottery style.
Festival de San Roque	14 - 25 August	Betanzos	A Coruña. Celebration of the town patron, launch of giant paper balloon.
Festival de San Roque	16th August	Sada	A Coruña. Celebration of the town patron, along the beach front and the modernist glass building.
Festival de San Roque	16th August	Vilagarcía de Arousa	Pontevedra, Arousa. Celebration of the town patron, giant street water party.
Queimada popular	Saturday after 16th August	Cervo	Lugo. Popular fair about the traditional Galicia alcoholic drink.
Folión de Carros	Saturday before 1st Sunday after 21st	Chantada	Lugo. Parade of traditional carts adorned with flowers and pulled by oxen.
Fiesta de la Empanada	3rd Saturday of August	Bandeira. Silleda	Pontevedra. Popular fair about the traditional Galician pie.
Romería do Naseiro	4th Sunday of August	San Pedro, Viveiro	Lugo, Viveiro. Fun fiesta along the shores of the Naseiro river.
Festa da Istoria	Last Saturday August	Ribadavia	Ourense. Historic re-enactment and street medieval party.
Romería da Virxe da Franqueira	8th September	A Cañiza	Pontevedra. Fair and procession around the town Virgin.
Festival de a Virxe de Guadalupe	8th September	Rianxo	A Coruña, Arousa. Maritime procession parading the Virgin image. Midnight music finale with the popular song.
Romería de Nosa Señora da Barca	Sunday after 8 September	Muxía	A Coruña, Camariñas. Popular fair centred on the Sanctuary.
Procesión de las Mortajas	3rd Sunday of September	A Pobra do Caramiñal	A Coruña, Arousa. Street procession of symbolic coffin in memory of 15C offering by the town leader.
Romería de A Saínza	24th of September	Rairiz de Veiga	Ourense. Commemoration of fight between Christians and Moors, ending up in cheerful dance, good and dring party.
Festa da Faba	1st Sunday of October	Vilanova de Lourenzá	Lugo. Celebration of the hearty Galician bean stew.
Festival of San Froilán	1st two weeks of October	Lugo	Lugo. Stalls, crafts and parades, traditionally as the preparation for winter.
Shellfish Festival	Second Sunday in October - Pilar	O Grove	Pontevedra, Arousa. The ultimate shellfish feast.
Feria de As San Lucas	Around 19th October	Mondoñedo	Lugo. Large horse market.

ABOUT GALICIA

Santiago de Compostela

Santiago de Compostela has special status within Galicia as for more than a thousand years it has been a very important destination for pilgrims. Today it is a World Heritage Site (UNESCO) in which tourists and pilgrims alike pay their respects at the cathedral and wander its ancient streets creating a vibrant atmosphere that is not to be missed.

The town was founded after the miraculous events of year 813, when lights were seen above the hills in the field of Compostela (field of stars). Bishop Teodomiro decreed that the remains of apostle Santiago (St James) and his disciples had been found, and this triggered the beginning of an institution. King Alfonso II ordered the construction of a church, perhaps grasping the importance of a such a symbol as a useful tool in the ongoing *reconquista* against the moors.

The magnificent cathedral stands proudly as the final step in a pilgrim's voyage. Originally just a small church, the romanesque building was started in the 11th century, completed and embellished over the next hundred years but added to substantially during the baroque period in the 18th century. The interior of the cathedral is full of elaborate craftsmanship. An external baroque doorway, entered from Plaza do Obradoiro, protects the west door, the Pórtico de la Gloria, an outstanding sculptural panel. Pilgrims queue to place their hand in the space above the figure of Mateo, the 12th century sculptor whose workshop produced this masterpiece.

The Cathedral's Botafumeiro spectacle is famous. The large silver incense holder, large, heavy and exuding smoke, is swung over the nave by a team of men, reaching almost to the height of the ceiling, in a well orchestrated, proud display at the end of Pilgrim's Mass (in summer on Saturdays at 12pm) or at special ceremonies. The event is extremely popular and the cathedral gets completely full. Credit to Armando Raposo, the head of the team or *tiraboleiro mayor*, for over 40 years during which he has managed the occasion.

Outside of the Cathedral Plaza do Obradoiro is one of Santiago's monumental showpieces. The night before the 25th of July (the Apostle's day) it becomes the venue for a huge firework display. When the 25th of July falls on a Sunday the year is called Xacobeo, considered to be special and the only year in which Pilgrims are allowed to enter the cathedral via the Puerta Santa (Holy Door) off Plaza da Quintana. The Xacobeo years are religiously auspicious and the number of pilgrims arriving increase considerably. July 25 is celebrated throughout Galicia but away from Santiago is referred to as Galicia Day.

The momentum of Santiago as a pilgrim destination continued to grow from its humble beginning ten

Plaza de las Platerías

Casino at Rúa del Villar

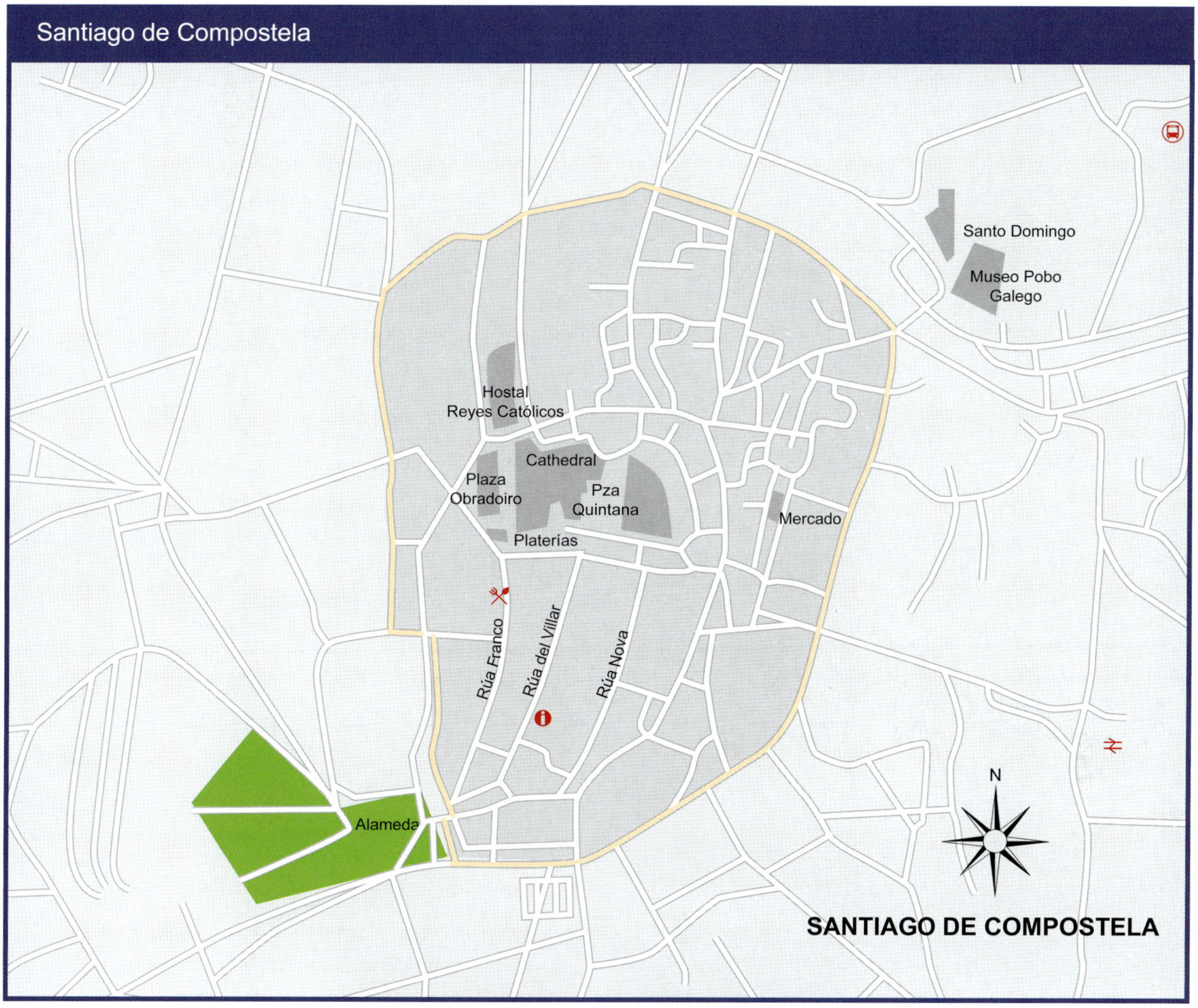

ABOUT GALICIA

Santiago de Compostela

[Map of Santiago de Compostela showing Santo Domingo, Museo Pobo Galego, Hostal Reyes Católicos, Cathedral, Plaza Obradoiro, Pza Quintana, Platerías, Mercado, Rúa Franco, Rúa del Villar, Rúa Nova, and Alameda]

centuries ago. Though many who now make the trip do so for non-religious reasons it continues to attract enormous numbers of European Christians. The impact of the pilgrimage is evident throughout Galicia, with several major routes attracting settlement, religious centres and wealth. These routes continue to be used today and are a great achievement for anyone to complete, whether with pilgrim intent or simply as a long walking or cycling holiday. Even if you have not made the journey yourself, you will notice the many that have and the excitement with which they walk towards the centre of Santiago, the cathedral and the pilgrim welcome offices at the top of Rúa del Villar.

Botafumeiro in action

From Plaza das Platerías, Rúa del Villar and the parallel Rúa Nova is where classic Santiago reveals itself: granite flagstones, solid buildings, galleried balconies and *soportales* (covered walkways), at their best when it is raining heavily. These streets are now sadly loosing many of their permanent residents as more and more old houses are dedicated to meet the needs of tourists but there still is a strong sense of community, not just of a tourist destination. If you walk with a friend or relation from Santiago you will not go far along these streets before meeting someone you know.

Santiago has plenty to keep you occupied for a few days. Besides ambling around soaking up the atmosphere there are many churches

CRUISING GALICIA 289

ABOUT GALICIA

Soportales

full of interesting details including, slightly away from the centre, Colegiata del Sar, a beautiful romanesque church of leaning columns. Convento de Santo Domingo has a superb spiral staircase, and if you have had enough of religious connections Museo do Pobo Galego has a good display of rural and marine life from Galicia. The Alameda is a pretty park with good views across the city and the *plaza/mercado* on the southern side of the old town has a fantastic atmosphere being full of fresh produce sold directly by village women from permanent stalls or on the side of the street.

For eating and drinking you are spoilt for choice as there are numerous places to chose from. Rúa do Franco is especially full of bars that are geared to students from the University, but wherever you go the food will be excellent. Try O Gato or Obispo for example. As there are so many to chose from we recommend a series of hops ordering *tapas* and a saucer of albariño wine in each.

Santiago

Convento de Santo Domingo

Tarta de Santiago

Tarta de Santiago is one of the traditional Galician sweet cakes, delicious for its almond taste.

Ingredients

For the pastry:
1 egg
²⁄₃ cup sugar
Generous 1 cup flour

For the filling:

4 eggs
1 ¼ cups sugar
1 unwaxed lemon, peel grated
2 cups ground almonds
Pinch ground cinnamon
Flour, for rolling out
Butter, for greasing
Confectioners' sugar, for sprinkling

Preparation

Pastry: beat together the egg, sugar and 1 to 2 tablespoons of warm water until light and creamy. Gradually fold in the flour until the mixture leaves the sides of the bowl clean.

For the filling, beat together the eggs and sugar until creamy. Fold in the lemon rind, ground almonds and cinnamon.

Roll out the pastry to ⅛ inch thick on a floured work surface. Line a greased, loose-bottomed 10-inch tart pan with the pastry. Prick it all over with a fork and spoon the filling on top. Bake in a preheated oven at 190°C for about 30 minutes, until golden brown. Leave the almond tart to cool in the pan. Once cool, transfer it to a serving plate and sprinkle with confectioners' sugar before serving. A St. James' cross template can be used to create a pattern.

Serve with a large café con leche.

APPENDIX

Appendix

Weather – sources & times

All transmissions in English unless specified. Dictaphone or other recording device recommended for all languages.

English Channel, west of Isle of Wight

All times are UT except shaded areas that are British Local Time.

Time	Source	Frequency	What
0000	Navtex, Corsen, Ushant	518 kHz	Shipping Forecast
0040	Navtex, Niton, Isle of Wight	518 kHz	Extended , 5 day, outlook
0040	Solent Coastguard	Working Channel but announced on VHF Channel 16, MF 2182 kHz	Inshore Forecast for local area
0048	BBC Radio 4	198 kHz	Shipping & Inshore Forecast
0050	Brixham Coastguard	Working Channel but announced on VHF Channel 16, MF 2182 kHz	Inshore Forecast for local area
0140	Falmouth Coastguard	Working Channel but announced on VHF Channel 16, MF 2182 kHz	Inshore Forecast for local area
0220	Portland Coastguard	Working Channel but announced on VHF Channel 16, MF 2182 kHz	Inshore Forecast for local area
0440	Solent Coastguard	Working Channel but announced on VHF Channel 16, MF 2182 kHz	Inshore Forecast for local area
0450	Brixham Coastguard	Working Channel but announced on VHF Channel 16, MF 2182 kHz	Inshore Forecast for local area
0520	BBC Radio 4	198 kHz	Shipping & Inshore Forecast
0520	Navtex, Niton, Isle of Wight	490 kHz	Inshore & 3 day outlook
0540	Falmouth Coastguard	Working Channel but announced on VHF Channel 16, MF 2182 kHz	Inshore Forecast for local area
0620	Portland Coastguard	Working Channel but announced on VHF Channel 16, MF 2182 kHz	Inshore Forecast for local area
0840	Navtex, Niton, Isle of Wight	518 kHz	Shipping Forecast
0840	Solent Coastguard	Working Channel but announced on VHF Channel 16, MF 2182 kHz	Shipping Forecast for local area
0850	Brixham Coastguard	Working Channel but announced on VHF Channel 16, MF 2182 kHz	Shipping Forecast for local area
0940	Falmouth Coastguard	Working Channel but announced on VHF Channel 16, MF 2182 kHz	Shipping Forecast for local area
1020	Portland Coastguard	Working Channel but announced on VHF Channel 16, MF 2182 kHz	Shipping Forecast for local area
1200	Navtex, Corsen, Ushant	518 kHz	Shipping Forecast
1201	BBC Radio 4	198 kHz	Shipping & Inshore Forecast
1240	Solent Coastguard	Working Channel but announced on VHF Channel 16, MF 2182 kHz	Inshore Forecast for local area
1250	Brixham Coastguard	Working Channel but announced on VHF Channel 16, MF 2182 kHz	Inshore Forecast for local area

1340	Falmouth Coastguard	Working Channel but announced on VHF Channel 16, MF 2182 kHz	Inshore Forecast for local area
1420	Portland Coastguard	Working Channel but announced on VHF Channel 16, MF 2182 kHz	Inshore Forecast for local area
1640	Solent Coastguard	Working Channel but announced on VHF Channel 16, MF 2182 kHz	Inshore Forecast for local area
1650	Brixham Coastguard	Working Channel but announced on VHF Channel 16, MF 2182 kHz	Inshore Forecast for local area
1720	Navtex, Niton, Isle of Wight	490 kHz	Inshore & 3 day outlook
1740	Falmouth Coastguard	Working Channel but announced on VHF Channel 16, MF 2182 kHz	Inshore Forecast for local area
1754	BBC Radio 4	198 kHz	Shipping & Inshore Forecast
1820	Portland Coastguard	Working Channel but announced on VHF Channel 16, MF 2182 kHz	Inshore Forecast for local area
2040	Navtex, Niton, Isle of Wight	518 kHz	Shipping Forecast
2040	Solent Coastguard	Working Channel but announced on VHF Channel 16, MF 2182 kHz	Shipping Forecast for local area
2050	Brixham Coastguard	Working Channel but announced on VHF Channel 16, MF 2182 kHz	Shipping Forecast for local area
2140	Falmouth Coastguard	Working Channel but announced on VHF Channel 16, MF 2182 kHz	Shipping Forecast for local area
2220	Portland Coastguard	Working Channel but announced on VHF Channel 16, MF 2182 kHz	Shipping Forecast for local area

Bay of Biscay

All times are UT except shaded areas that are British Local Time.

Time	Source	Frequency	What
0000	Navtex, Corsen, Ushant	518 kHz	Shipping Forecast, for following 18-36 hrs up to 450M offshore
0048	BBC Radio 4	198 kHz	Shipping & Inshore Forecast
0520	BBC Radio 4	198 kHz	Shipping & Inshore Forecast
0830	Navtex, Coruña	518 kHz	Shipping Forecast, for following 18-36 hrs up to 450M offshore
1200	Navtex, Corsen, Ushant	518 kHz	Shipping Forecast
1201	BBC Radio 4	198 kHz	Shipping & Inshore Forecast
1754	BBC Radio 4	198 kHz	Shipping & Inshore Forecast
2030	Navtex, Coruña	518 kHz	Shipping Forecast

APPENDIX

Spain

All times UT.

Note, Spanish forecasts usually include and estimate of swell as well as sea conditions.

Time	Source	Frequency	What
0005	Coastguard - La Coruña MRSC	VHF Ch 10	Coastal forecast
0015	Coastguard - Vigo MRSC	VHF Ch 10	Coastal forecast
0233	Coastguard – Finisterre MRCC	VHF Ch 11	Coastal forecast
0405	Coastguard - La Coruña MRSC	VHF Ch 10	Coastal forecast
0415	Coastguard - Vigo MRSC	VHF Ch 10	Coastal forecast
0633	Coastguard – Finisterre MRCC	VHF Ch 11	Coastal forecast
07:03	Coast Radio Station: Cabo Peñas A Coruña Finisterre	MF: 1677Khz 1698Khz 1764Khz	Synopsis, 24/48 hr forecasts for Atlantic areas
08:05	Coastguard - La Coruña MRSC	VHF Ch 10	Coastal forecast
0815	Coastguard - Vigo MRSC	VHF Ch 10	Coastal forecast
0830	Navtex, Coruña	518 kHz	Shipping Forecast, for following 18-36 hrs up to 450M offshore
0840	Coast Radio Station: Navisa Cabo Ortegal A Coruña Finisterre Vigo	VHF Ch: 60 02 26 22 65	48 hr coastal forecast in Spanish
1033	Coastguard – Finisterre MRCC	VHF Ch 11	Coastal forecast
1205	Coastguard - La Coruña MRSC	VHF Ch 10	Coastal forecast
1215	Coastguard - Vigo MRSC	VHF Ch 10	Coastal forecast
1240	Coast Radio Station: Navisa Cabo Ortegal A Coruña Finisterre Vigo	VHF Ch: 60 02 26 22 65	48 hr coastal forecast in Spanish
1303	Coast Radio Station: Cabo Peñas A Coruña Finisterre	MF: 1677Khz 1698Khz 1764Khz	Synopsis, 24/48 hr forecasts for Atlantic areas
1433	Coastguard – Finisterre MRCC	VHF Ch 11	Coastal forecast
1615	Coastguard - Vigo MRSC	VHF Ch 10	Coastal forecast
1833	Coastguard – Finisterre MRCC	VHF Ch 11	Coastal forecast
19:03	Coast Radio Station: Cabo Peñas A Coruña Finisterre	MF: 1677Khz 1698Khz 1764Khz	Synopsis, 24/48 hr forecasts for Atlantic areas
2010	Coast Radio Station: Navisa Cabo Ortegal A Coruña Finisterre Vigo	VHF Ch: 60 02 26 22 65	48 hr coastal forecast in Spanish

APPENDIX

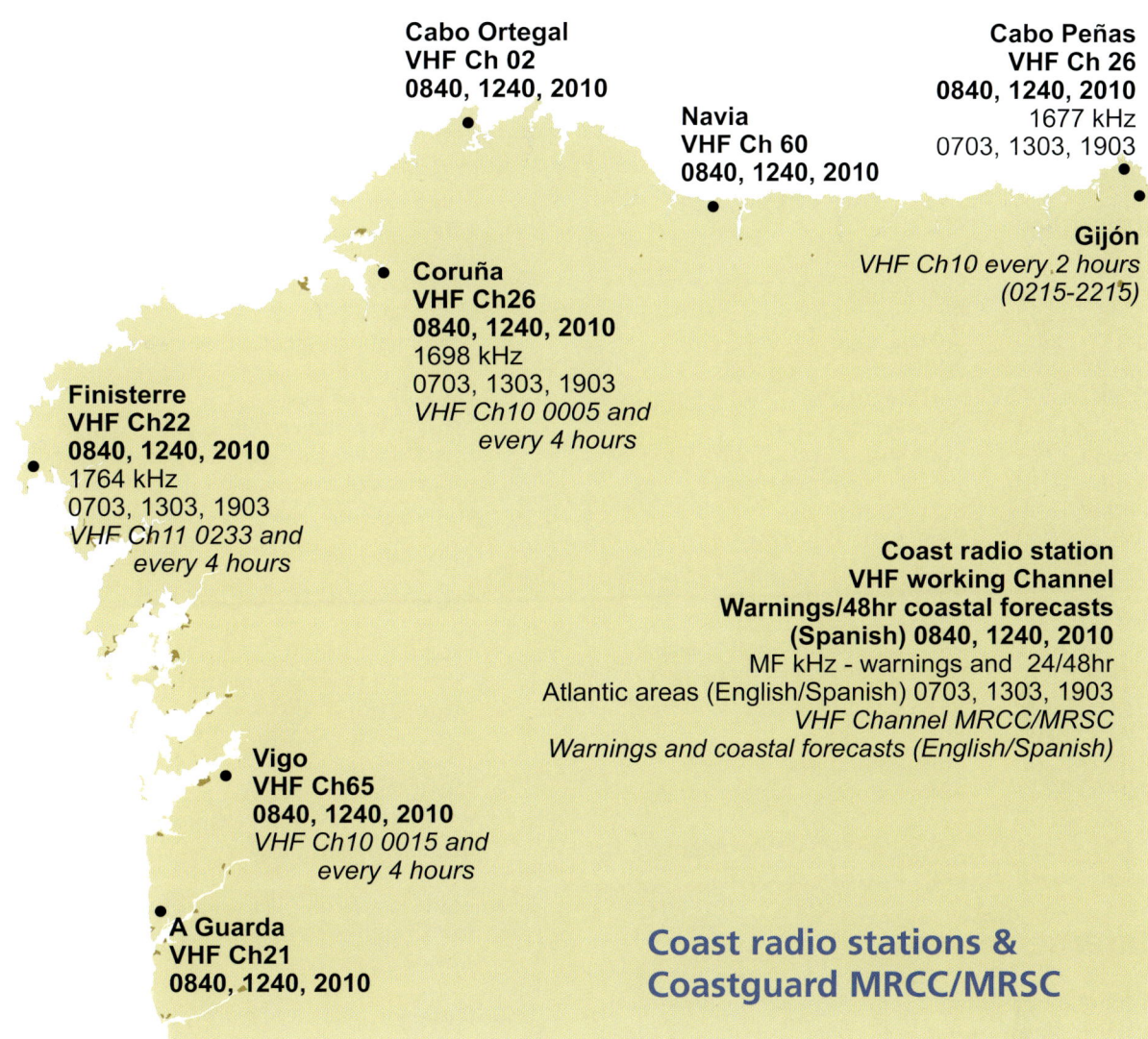

2015	Coastguard - Vigo MRSC	VHF Ch 10	Coastal forecast
1605	Coastguard - La Coruña MRSC	VHF Ch 10	Coastal forecast
2005	Coastguard - La Coruña MRSC	VHF Ch 10	Coastal forecast
2030	Navtex, Coruña	518 kHz	Shipping Forecast, for following 18-36 hrs up to 450M offshore
2233	Coastguard – Finisterre MRCC	VHF Ch 11	Coastal forecast

Radio Nacional de España broadcasts (MW639 kHz 1100, 1400, 1800, 2200) are rather difficult and of poor service to the sailor. The information provided is very superficial and the precise timing random, mixed with the general chatter of Spanish news.

APPENDIX

HF Radio Facsimile Broadcasts

With a suitable receiver and equipment (usually a PC and some software) these useful broadcasts can be received at sea. Northwood transmits the following on 2618.5, 4610, 8040, 11086.5 kHz. All times are UT.

0000 / 1200	Surface analysis
0012 / 1212	24hr surface prognosis
0100 / 1300	Schedule
0300 / 1500	Surface analysis
0336 / 1536	Sea surface temperature
0348 / 1548	Gale warning summary
0400 / 1600	Surface analysis
0412 / 1612	24hr surface prognosis
0500 / 1700	Surface analysis
0512 / 1712	24hr surface prognosis
0524 / 1724	48hr surface prognosis
0548 / 1748	96hr surface prognosis
0600 / 1800	Surface analysis
0612 / 1812	24hr surface prognosis
0724 / 1924	48hr surface prognosis
0748 / 1948	96hr surface prognosis
0800 / 2000	120hr surface prognosis
0824 / 2024	48hr significant wind contour
0836 / 2036	72hr significant wind contour
0848 / 2048	96hr significant wind contour
0900 / 2100	Surface analysis
1000 / 2200	Surface analysis
1024 / 2224	24hr reduced visibility prognosis
1100 / 2300	Surface analysis
1124 / 2324	24hr sea and swell prognosis
1148 / 2348	Gale warning summary

Internet weather

If you have Internet access (see section What you need to know as a tourist) the following are useful links:

- UK Met Office:
  http://www.met-office.gov.uk/
  http://www.met-office.gov.uk/weather/charts/index.html - synoptic charts (3.5 days)

- Wetter Zentrale: the Bracknell black and white fax synoptic charts (5.5 days).
  http://www.wetterzentrale.de/topkarten/fsfaxbra.html - Index
  http://www.wetterzentrale.de/pics/bracka.html - midnight
  Change letter 'a' to get other times: 0 24hr, 0a 36hr, 1 48hr, 2 96hr, 4 120hr, 4a 132hr

- Instituto Nacional de Meteorología - IHM
  http://www.inm.es/web/infmet/predi/metmar/bolmet.html - 24 hour coastal forecast map
  http://www.inm.es/cgi-bin/mariti.cgi.2001?PRODUCTO=p23t&ZONA=gal1 - 24 hour coastal Galicia
  http://www.inm.es/web/infmet/predi/mapgen.html - general weather forecast Spain map
  http://www.inm.es/cgi-bin/p06hesp1.sh.2001 - 3 day general weather forecast Spain (text Spanish)
  http://www.inm.es/wwb/puert/PUERTFIN.html - wind and swell forecast Finisterre 2.5day

- Windiberia: coastal wind and waves, for windsurfers
  http://www.windiberia.com/index.php

- Windguru, the Czech forecasts for windsurfers and flyers
  http://www.windguru.cz - general index
  http://www.windguru.cz/int/index.php?sc=48738 - La Lanzada beach

- Meteogalicia - general weather forecast from Galicia government, includes coastal area wind strength and swell
  http://www.meteogalicia.es/
  http://www.meteogalicia.es/galego/prediccion/maritima/maritima.asp - 3 day coastal and tide chart Coruña, Vilagarcía and Vigo

- Meteo France
  http://www.meteofrance.com/FR/index.jsp

- Frank Singleton's extensive web site for everything you may want to know about weather information sources and connections
  http://www.franksingleton.clara.net/home.html

- GRIB US - free NOAA grib files (7 day pressure, wind) and Windows display software
  http://www.grib.us/

- www.macsailing.net - a useful forum online for all things to do with using Apple MACs for sailing.

Software

There are several pieces of software that will display GRIB files. Here are the authors' familiar tools:

Windows:
- MaxSea: almost the standard, pricey but good display and can do routing.
- GRIB US: free downloadable software, simple but good looking.

MAC:
- GPSNavx: displays GRIB files. Not pretty but it works.
- MacWX: tool for selecting and downloading GRIB files (chargeable) from Ocens. No email involved.
- MultiModeOSX: simple but can create images from the HF radio broadcast weatherfax.

Connection using Bluetooth to mobile phones is straightforward using MACs.

Language cross-reference

General terms

English	Spanish	Galician
address	dirección	dirección
anchor	ancla	áncora
anchor, to	fondear	fondear
basin	dársena	dársena
bay	ensenada	enseada
beach	playa	praia
beacon	baliza	baliza
beam	manga	manga
berth	atracadero	atracadoiro
berth, to	atracar	atracar
black	negro	negro
blue	azul	azul
bottled gas	botella de gas	botella de gas
breakwater	rompeolas	batente
buoy	boya	boia
cape	cabo	cabo
chandlery	efectos navales	efectos navales
channel	canal	canal
chart	carta náutica	carta náutica
church	iglesia	igrexa
coastguard	guardacosta	guardacosta
crane	grúa	gindastre, grúa
Customs	Aduana	Aduana
deep	profundo	profundo
depth	profundidad	profundidad
diesel	gasoil (A leisure, B fishing boats)	gasoil
dinghy	lancha	lancha
diver	submarinista	submarinista
draught	calado	calado
dredged	dragado	dragado
dryer	secadora	secadoira
east	este	leste
eastern	levante, del Este	levante, do Leste
emergency	emergencia	emergencia
entrance	boca, entrada	boca, entrada
factory	fábrica	fábrica
firemen	bombero	bombero
fish farm area	vivero	viveiro
foul	sucio	sucio
gravel	cascajo	cascallo
green	verde	verde
harbour fee (berth)	tarifa de atraque	tarifa de atraque
harbour office	capitanía	capitanía
harbourmaster	director del puerto	director do porto
health centre	centro de salud	centro de saúde
height	altura	altura
high tide	pleamar	preama
inlet	ensenada	ensenada
ironmonger	ferretería	ferretería
island	isla	illa
islet	islote	illote
isthmus	istmo	istmo
jetty, pier	malecón	malecón
knots	nudos	nudos
lake	lago	lago
laundry	lavandería	lavandería
laundry token	ficha de lavadora	fixa de lavadora
leeward	sotavento	sotavento
length overall	eslora	eslora
life boat	salvamento marino	salvamento marino
lighthouse	faro	faro
lock	esclusa	esclusa
low tide	bajamar	baixamar
marina	puerto deportivo	porto deportivo
marina pontoon master	marinero	marinero
market	mercado	mercado
market (food)	plaza	praza
mechanic	mecánico	mecánico
medical services	servicios médicos	servicios médicos
motor boat (leisure)	yate, motora	yate, motora
mud	fango, barro	fango, barro
mussel bed	batea	batea
narrow	estrecho	estreito
Navy	Marina	Marina
neaps	mareas muertas	mareas mortas
north	Norte	Norte
northerly	septentrional, del norte	septentrional, del norte
orange	naranja	laranxa
owner	propietario	propietario
petrol	gasolina	gasolina

APPENDIX

English	Spanish	Galician
petrol station	gasolinera	gasolinera
pier	dique	dique
pier, quay, dock	muelle, dique	muelle, dique
point	punta	punta
police	policía	policía
pontoon	pantalán	pantalán
port	babor	babor
Port of Registry	Puerto de Matrícula	Porto de Registro
post	correo	correo
propane	propano	propano
quay	muelle	muelle
ramp	rampa	rampa
range	repunte, amplitud, rango	repunte, amplitud, rango
red	rojo	rojo
reef	arrecife	arrecife
reef spit	restinga	restinga
registration number	matrícula	matrícula
repair	reparación	reparación
rock, stone	roca, piedra	roca, piedra
sailing boat	velero	veleiro
sailing club	club de vela	club de vela
sailing yacht	velero	veleiro
sailmaker	reparación de velas	reparación de velas
saltpan	salina	salina
sand	arena	area
sea	mar	mar
shipyard	astilleiro	estaleiro
shoal	bajo	baixo
shop	tienda	tienda
shore	orilla	orilla
shower	ducha	ducha
slipway	varadero	varadeiro
small	pequeño	pequeno
southern	meridional, del sur	meridional, del sur
springs	mareas vivas	mareas vivas
starboard	estribor	estribor
strait	estrecho	estrecho
supermarket	supermercado	supermercado
tower	torre	torre
transit	enfilación	enfilación
travel lift	travel lift	travel lift
water	agua	agua
weather forecast	previsión	previsión
weather forecast	boletín meteorológico	boletín meteorológico
weather forecast	'el tiempo'	'el tiempo'
weed	alga	alga
weight	peso	peso
west	oeste	oeste
westerly	occidental, poniente, del oeste	occidental, poniente, del oeste
white	blanco	branco
yacht club	club náutico	club náutico
yellow	amarillo	amarillo

Meteorology and sea state

English	Spanish	Galician
Wind		
calm	calma	calma
light	flojo	flojo
moderate	moderado	moderado
strong	fuerte	fuerte
gale	viento duro	viento duro
warning	aviso	aviso
gust	racha	racha
storm	temporal	temporal
Ssa state		
swell	oleaje	oleaje
smooth	plano, rizado	plano, rizado
slight	marejadilla	marejadilla
moderate	marejada	marejada
rough	fuerte marejada	fuerte marejada
very rough	mar gruesa	mar gruesa
breakers	rompiente	rompiente
overfalls, tide race	escarceos	escarceos
short, steep sea	mar corto	mar corto
ocean swell	mar de fondo	mar de fondo
Forecast terms		
today	hoy	hoy
tomorrow	mañana	mañana
imminent	inminent	inminent
now	ahora	ahora
soon	pronto	pronto
later	más tarde	más tarde

APPENDIX

Visibility and weather		
fog	niebla	niebla
poor	pobre	pobre
good	buena	buena
visibility	visibilidad	visibilidad
north	norte	norte
south	sur	sur
east	este	leste
west	oeste	oeste
mist	neblina	neblina
rain	lluvia	lluvia
squall	chaparrón	chaparrón
thunderstorm	tormenta	tormenta
thunder	truenos	truenos
lightning	relámpagos	relámpagos
hail	granizo	granizo

Wind speed conversions

Beaufort	Knots	m/s	km/h
0	<1	0- 0.2	0-1.8
1	1-3	0.3- 1.5	1.9-5.5
2	4-6	1.6- 3.3	5.6-11.1
3	7-10	3.4- 5.4	11.2-18.5
4	10-16	5.5- 7.9	18.6-29.6
5	17-21	8.0-10.7	29.7-38.9
6	22-27	10.8-13.8	39.0-50.0
7	28-33	13.9-17.1	50.1-61.0
8	34-40	17.2-20.7	61.1-74.0
9	41-47	20.8-24.4	74.1-86.9
10	48-55	24.5-28.4	87.0-101.8
11	56-63	28.5-32.6	101.9-116.6

Galicia place names

There are many town and harbour names that are similar in Spanish and Galician. The list below provides a cross reference between those that are commonly in the path of sailors or tourists.

Galician	Spanish
A Coruña	La Coruña
A Guarda	La Guardia
A Toxa	La Toja
Arousa	Arosa
Baiona	Bayona
Costa da Morte	Costa de la Muerte
Fisterra	Finisterre
Laxe	Lage
Muxía	Mugía
Noia	Noya
Os Farallóns	Los Farallones
Porto do Son	Puerto del Son
Rías Baixas	Rías Bajas
San Cibrao	San Ciprián
Santa Uxía de Riveira	Santa Eugenia de Ribeira
Sanxenxo	Sangenjo
Vilagarcía	Villagarcía
Viveiro	Vivero

Useful Internet sites

- Turgalicia: a vast amount of reference informaton about anywhere in Galicia (tourist offices,transport, health, sites, markets, marinas) Spanish/English/French/German http://www.turgalicia.es

- Google Earth - informative aerial photos of the coast but often out of date

- Google maps Spain - http://maps.google.es

- www.marinas.com – useful photos of most marinas anywhere in the world including Galicia.

- www.feve.es - website of the FEVE train service.

APPENDIX

Charts

Sources in Spain:

- Robinson Náutica, Bárbara de Braganza 10,
  MADRID 28004
  ☎ +34 91 3084 872 *Fax* +34 91 3 199 255
  email: robinson@nauticarobinson.com
  http://www.nauticarobinson.com
  Good Internet site, couriers charts and books

- Librería Náutica Cartamar, Paseo de Ronda 39,
  A Coruña ☎ / *Fax* +34 981 255228
  http://www.cartamar.com/

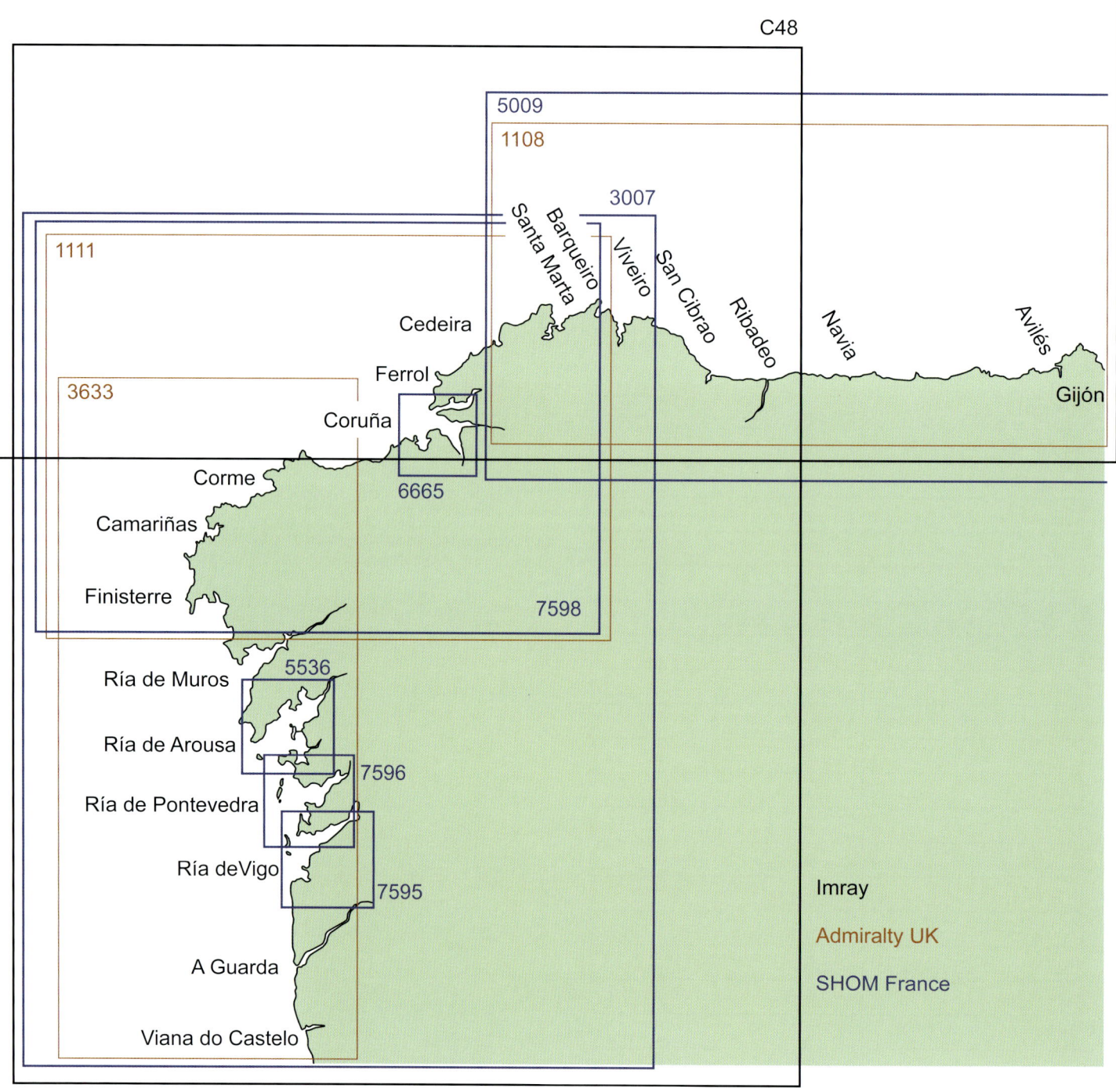

APPENDIX

Sources in Britain:

- Imray, Laurie, Norie & Wilson Ltd
  Wych House
  The Broadway
  St Ives
  Cambs PE27 5BT
  ☎ 01480 462114 *Fax* 01480 496109
  www.imray.com

- UK Hydrographic Office
  Admiralty Way
  Taunton
  Somerset TA21 2DN
  ☎ 01823 337900 *Fax* 01823 284077
  www.ukho.gov.uk

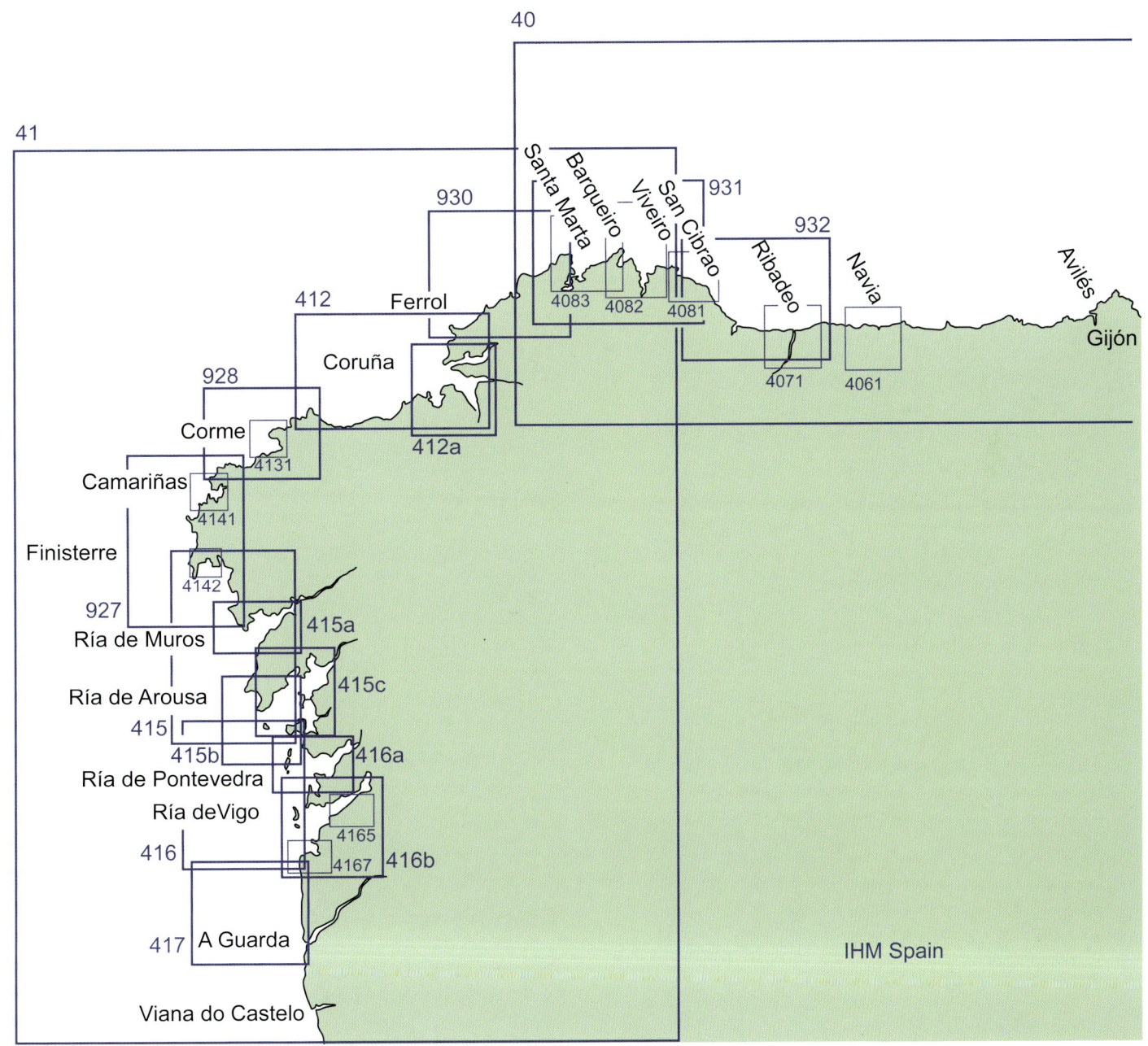

APPENDIX

Useful addresses

British Consulate-General
Paseo de Recoletos, 7/9
28004 Madrid
☎ 91 524 9700
Fax 91 524 9730
E-mail: madridconsulate@ukinspain.com
Email: madridconsulate@fco.gov.uk

US Embassy
Serrano 75
28006 Madrid
☎ 91 587 2200

French Consulate
Marqués de la Ensenada 10
28004 Madrid
☎ 91 700 78 00
Fax 91 700 78 01

German Embassy
Calle Fortuny 8
28010 Madrid
☎ 91 557 90 00
Fax 91 310 21 04

Irish Embassy
Paseo de la Castellana, 46, 4a
28046 Madrid
☎ 91 436 4093
Fax 91 4351677

Recommended Books

Facing the Ocean, Barry Cunliffe, Oxford University Press. A fascinating study of the historic links between the Atlantic facing communities of Europe.

Galicia Guía Total, Antón Pombo, Anaya Touring Club. A comprehensive detailed tourist guide to Galicia, a good reference for sites, hotels and restaurants. In Spanish.

Rough Guide to Spain. Good quality as always but very thin on Galicia, concentrating on the main tourist destinations.

Turgalicia brochures, from any large tourist office or downloaded from www.turgalicia.es as PDF files. Many in Galician, Portugues, Spanish, English, French and German, some Italian. Extensive coverage of Galicia tourist interests (Camino de Santiago, Ribeira Sacra etc) and one of marinas.

Aeroguías, El Litoral de Galicia (Rías Altas and Rías Baixas volumes), Geoplaneta. Mile by mile coverage of the entire Galician coast with aerial photographs. Text extensively researched but in Spanish. Wonderful books for the sailor.

Atlantic Spain and Portugal, RCC, Imray. The pilot book that covers from Coruña to Gibraltar.

South Biscay, RCC, Imray. The pilot book by the late John Lawson that covers from Brittany to Coruña.

Reeds Almanac, the reference manual for any sailor. Thin on Galicia but always up to date with general material.

Camilo José Cela, *'The Hive'* and *'The Family of Pascual Duarte'*. The most famous books by the Nobel price winner Galician writer.

Poems by Rosalía de Castro translated by Michael Smith into English. The easiest way into understanding Galicia's poet laureate in the English language.

Lights of Bohemia (Luces de Bohemia), play by Ramón del Valle-Inclán, the eccentric Galician writer whose deeds you will come across in Arousa. Also *Divine Words* (Palabras Divinas) and *The Grotesque Farce of Mr. Punch the Cuckold* (Esperpento de los cuernos de Don Friolera).

Galicia, the concise history, Sharif Gemie, Histories of Europe. A paperback giving you background on Galicia.

Comrades, Paul Preston. About the Spanish Civil War, viewed through small biographies of the key leaders from both sides. Not about Galicia but a useful insight into some of the background of regionalism.

La Cartografía Náutica Española en los siglos XIV, XV y XVI, Ricardo Cerezo Martínez, Consejo Superior de Investigaciones Científicas. In Spanish, an extensive study of Spanish charts in the age of discovery, beautifully illustrated.

Music

For an introduction to Galician music listen to Carlos Núñez or the group Milladoira. The style is modern but the themes and instruments are traditional. The album *Santiago* by the Chieftains is a good compilation of different Galician themes, played with the endearing Irish group.

Comments on Cruising Galicia

Comments on this guide are welcome. Please forward any view or correction suggestion to:

cruising.galicia@mac.com

Index

A
A Coruña 88
Addresses 302
Aguete 226
Aguiño 170
Anchoring 15
Ares 84

B
Barizo 101
Barqueiro 54
Barra 242
Beluso 228
Betanzos 87
Biscay 8
Bornalle 145
Bueu 228
Burela 44

C
Cabo Prior 66
Cabo Santa Cruz 184
Camariñas 108
Cambados 198
Cangas 244
Cariño 60
Carnota 123
Carril 192
Castropol 33
Castro settlements
    Baroña 158
Catoira 188
Cée 120
Cegoñas 40
Centolo 117
Chandleries 13
Charts 300
Club Marítimo de Oza 89
Combarro 220
Cooking Fuel 16
Corcubión 120
Corme 104
Corsairs, privateers, pirates 217
Costa da Morte 3, 96
Cruising Galicia
    Comments on Cruising Galicia 302
    How to use this book 6
    Symbols 6
Currents 13

D
Dársena Curuxeiras - Ferrol 82
Dársena de la Marina Coruña 88
Domaio 250
Dorna boats 172

E
Electricity 16
Ensenada de Corrubedo 168
Ensenada de Moaña 248
Ensenada de Palmeira 175
Ensenada de San Francisco 142
Ensenada de San Simón 251
Ensenada de San Xulián 196
Ensenada do Baño 82
Espasante 60
Esteiro 148
Ézaro 121

F
Finisterre 116
Firing Range 14
Fishing 14
Food 282
    Albariño wine 201
    Recipes
        Chipirones en su tinta 153
        Cocido 57
        Empanada 95
        Mejillones a la marinera 203
        Pimientos de Padrón 143
        Tarta de Santiago 291
Formalities 17
Foz 42
Freixo 149
Fuel 15

G
Galicia
    Background to Galicia 279
    Culture 281
        Meigas 247
        Music 302
        Recommended Books 302
    Environment 21
    Fiestas 284
    History 281
    What to do in Galicia 282
    Wining and dining 21
Golfo Ártabro 3, 74
Granite 102

H
Health 19
    Chemists 19
    Emergencies 19
Hórreos 221, 222

I
Internet 22
Internet sites 299
Isla Creba 145
Isla de Arousa 196
Isla de Cortegada 192
Isla Ons 233
Islas Sisargas 101

L
Language 21
    Cross-reference
        Galicia place names 299
        General terms 297
        Meteorology 298
Lanzada 204
La Toxa 200
Laxe 104
Laying up 16
Limens 242
Los Farallones 47
Lugo 38

M
Malpica 100
Map
    Costa da Morte 98
    Ría altas 30
    Ría de Arousa 167
    Ría de Muros 141
    Ría de Vigo 241
    Rías Baixas 129
Marina Coruña 89
Marinas 16
Marina Seca (Oza) 89
Meloxo 200
Mondoñedo 37
Money 21
Monte Louro 142
Muros 144
Mussels 177, 182, 183
    Mussel trading 177
Muxía 112

N
Newspapers 20
Noia 150, 152

O
O Grove 200
Ortigueira 58
O Xofre 197

P
Passages
    Sailing in Golfo Ártabro and Costa da Morte 70
    Sailing in the Rías Altas 26
    Sailing in the Rías Baixas 130
Passages to Galicia 8
    Coming from northern Spain 12
    Coming from Portugal 12
    Crossing the Bay of Biscay 8
Passports 21
Percebes 173
    Percebeiros 157
Place names 18
Playa Corosa 175
Playa da Frouxeira 66
Playa de Louro 142
Playa de San Felipe 82
Playa de San Miguel 41
Playa de San Xurxo 66
Playa de Silgar 218
Playa de Vilarrube 63
Playa do Mogor 227
Playa Rueta 47
Pobra do Caramiñal 178
Pontedeume 87
Pontevedra 224
Portocelo 48
Porto do Son 156
Portonovo 214
Portosín 154
Post 22
Provisions 16
Puerto Alúmina Española 47
Puerto Cubelo 123
Puerto Deportivo da Graña 83
Punta de Fazouro 43
Punta do Castro 40

R
Radio Services 17
Real Club Náutico Coruña 89
Repairs 13
Ría de Arousa 4, 126, 160
Ría de Cedeira 62
Ría de Ferrol 82
Ría de Muros 4, 126, 134
Ría de Pontevedra 4, 126, 207, 213
Ría de Vigo 4, 126, 234
Ría de Viveiro 50
Ría do Barqueiro 54
Rianxo 186
Rías Altas 3, 24
Rías Baixas 3, 125
Rías de Betanzos & Ares 84
Ribadeo 32
Ribeira 174
Rinlo 40
Río Ouro 43

S
Sada 84
San Cibrao 46
Santa Marta 58
Santiago de Compostela 4, 185, 288
San Vicente de Mar 205
Sanxenxo 218
Sardiñeiro 116
Security 21
Seno de Corcubión 114
Shipping 15
Submarine Exercise Area 14
Swell 14
Symbols 6

T
Telephone 22
The Serpent 110
Tidal heights 13
Tides 13
Traffic Separation Schemes 14
Transport
    Airports 19
    Bus 19
    Car hire 19
    Train 19
        FEVE 27

V
Vicedo 54
Vilagarcía de Arousa 190
Vilanova de Arousa 194
Vilaxoán 193

W
Water 16
Weather 14
    Bay of Biscay 293
    English Channel 292
    HF Radio Facsimile Broadcasts 296
    Internet weather 296
    Sources & times 292
    Spain 294
Wind speed conversions 299

RÍAS ALTAS
Ribadeo
Viveiro
Ortigueira
Cedeira

GOLFO ÁRTABRO
Ferrol
Ares
Sada
A Coruña

COSTA DA MORTE
Corme
Camariñas
Finisterre

RÍA DE MUROS
Muros
Noia
Portosín

RÍA DE AROUSA
Ribeira
Pobra do Caramiñal
Rianxo
Vilagarcía
Cambados

RÍA DE PONTEVEDRA
Portonovo
Sanxenxo
Combarro
Aguete
Isla Ons

RÍA DE VIGO
Cangas
San Simón
Vigo
Baiona
Islas Cíes

PASSAGE AREAS
Rías Altas

Ártabro /
Costa da Morte

Rías Baixas